The Seventy Great Mysteries of Ancient Egypt

The Seventy Great Mysteries of Ancient Egypt

EDITED BY BILL MANLEY

with 424 illustrations, 344 in color

Thames & Hudson

Contents

56 Did Egypt rule Palestine? translated from the German by David H. Wilson

First published in hardcover in the United States of America in 2003 by Thames & Hudson Inc., 500 Fifth Avenue, New York, New York 10110

thamesandhudsonusa.com

Library of Congress Catalog Card Number 2003100123
ISBN 0-500-28455-5

Printed and bound in Hong Kong by Toppan

Half-title *Detail of Tutankhamun's gold throne*

Title-page *The Temple of Luxor*

ON THE COVER Front *top* view of the pyramids of Giza, photo Heidi Grassley, © Thames & Hudson Ltd, London; *center* the stars of Orion's Belt, Photo © Celestial Image Co./Science Photo Library; *lower left* Ramesses II, Abu Simbel, photo Heidi Grassley, © Thames & Hudson Ltd, London; *lower right* the Qurneh burial, photo © The Trustees of the National Museums of Scotland; *bottom* amulet in the shape of Bes, photo Jürgen Liepe. **Spine** canopic coffinette of Tutankhamun, photo © Justin Kerr. **Back** faience tiles depicting Libyan, Nubian and Semitic captives, from Medinet Habu, photo Jürgen Liepe.

Stela of King Djet

The Earliest Egyptians

Pyramids & Tombs

Interior of the Red Pyramid of Snofru

Sphinx of Hatshepsut, the female pharaoh

Pharaohs & Queens

People & Places

The journey to Punt

Anubis preparing the mummy of the artist, Sennedjem

Ancient Wisdom & Belief

Historical Mysteries

The 'Israel Stela' of King Merenptah

Egypt & the Bible

The Battle of Qadesh

Contributors

Bill Manley is Tutor in Archaeology at the University of Glasgow, Research Associate of the National Museums of Scotland and an Honorary Research Fellow of the University of Liverpool. He has previously been a Lecturer in Egyptology at the universities of London and Liverpool, and has been involved in archaeological surveys in Egypt and Gaza, Palestine. He is a specialist in royal monuments of the Egyptian 18th Dynasty, and has collaborated on the definitive publication of the coffins of the kings of Egypt. His publications include two best-selling books, *The Penguin Historical Atlas of Ancient Egypt* (1996) and, with Mark Collier, *How to Read Egyptian Hieroglyphs* (1998). **19, 22, 44, 45, 48, 51, 57, 58, 68, 69**

Manfred Bietak is Chairman of the Department of Egyptology, University of Vienna, Director of the Austrian Archaeological Institute in Cairo and First Speaker of the International Research Programme on Chronology of the Second Millennium BC, *SCIEM 2000*, at the Austrian Academy. Since 1964 he has directed annual excavation campaigns at Sayala/Nubia, Luxor and at Tell el-Dab'a (Avaris). His publications include 14 books and an exhibition catalogue. He is the editor of the journal *Egypt and the Levant*, and of three monograph series at the Austrian Academy, of which he is a member. **38** with **Nannó Marinatos**, Professor of Classics at the University of Illinois, Chicago, and Research Associate of the Austrian Institute in Cairo. She participated in the evaluation of the Minoan wall-paintings found at Tell el-Dab'a (Avaris). Among her books are *Minoan Religion* (1993), *The Warrior and the Goddess* (2000), *Greek Sanctuaries* (with Robin Hägg, 1993) and, with M. Bietak and C. Palyvou, *The Taureador Scenes at Avaris and Knossos* (forthcoming).

John J. Bimson is lecturer in Biblical Studies at Trinity College, Bristol. He specializes in the historical and archaeological background to the Old Testament. His publications include *Redating the Exodus and Conquest* (1978) and several articles on the origins of ancient Israel. He is also the author, with J. P. Kane, of *The New Bible Atlas* (1985) and editor of *The Illustrated Encyclopedia of Bible Places* (1995). **65, 67, 70**

Mark Collier is Lecturer in Egyptology at the University of Liverpool, Fellow of All Souls College, Oxford, and a recognized authority on the ancient Egyptian language. He is the Director of the project for the archaeological and epigraphic recording of the tomb of Ankhtify near Moalla. His publications include the best-selling book *How to Read Egyptian Hieroglyphs* (1998), with Bill Manley, and *The UCL Lahun Papyri: Letters* (2002), with Stephen Quirke. **23, 36, 46, 47**

Aidan Dodson is a Teaching Fellow in the Department of Archaeology, University of Bristol, where he is Unit Director for Egyptology. His major areas of research are funerary archaeology and aspects of Egyptian dynastic history. He is the author or co-author of over 100 books, articles and reviews; his most recent books include: *The Mummy in Ancient Egypt*, with Salima Ikram (1998), *After the Pyramids* (2000) and *The Hieroglyphs of Ancient Egypt* (2001). **10, 16, 18, 20, 21, 24, 28, 31, 59**

Elizabeth Goring is a Senior Curator at the National Museums of Scotland in Edinburgh, where she is responsible for the collections of Mediterranean Archaeology, including Egypt. She initiated the multidisciplinary NMS Mummy Project in 1996. Her research interests include ancient jewelry and figurines. **14**

Dominic Montserrat is Senior Lecturer in Classical Studies at the Open University and is a Fellow of the Institute of Archaeology, University College London, and of the Royal Asiatic Society. He has a particular research interest in the cultural appropriation of the ancient world, on which he has written extensively. Among his books are *Sex and Society in Graeco-Roman Egypt* (1996), *Akhenaten: History, Fantasy and Ancient Egypt* (2000) and the exhibition catalogue *Ancient Egypt: Digging for Dreams* (2001). **27, 34, 60**

Ludwig D. Morenz is Privatdozent of Egyptology at the University of Leipzig. His main research interests are Egyptian literature, the origins of writing and Egyptian high culture, visual poetry, and cultural contacts between ancient Egypt and the ancient Near East. He is the author of *Beiträge zur Schriftlichkeitskultur im Mittleren Reich und der Zweiten Zwischenzeit* (1996) and *Herrscherpräsentation und Kulturkontakte: Ägypten – Levante – Mesopotamien. Acht Fallstudien*, with Erich Bosshard-Nepustil (in press). He is currently finishing a book on the origins of Egyptian writing. **49, 53, 56, 66; 56** and **66** with Erich Bosshard-Nepustil.

Robert G. Morkot is a Lecturer in Egyptology at the University of Exeter. His publications include *The Black Pharaohs, Egypt's Nubian Rulers* (2000). **29, 32, 33, 40**

Paul Nicholson is Senior Lecturer in Archaeology at Cardiff University. He is the author of *Egyptian Faience and Glass* (1993), co-author, with Ian Shaw, of the *British Museum Dictionary of Ancient Egypt* (1995) and co-editor, with Ian Shaw, of *Ancient Egyptian Materials and Technology* (2000). He has excavated in Egypt since 1983. **62**

David O'Connor is Lila Acheson Wallace Professor of Egyptian Art at the Institute of Fine Arts, New York University; formerly he was a curator at the University Museum of the University of Pennsylvania. He co-directs major excavations at Abydos, southern Egypt. His books (some co-authored or co-edited) include *Ancient Egypt. A Social History* (1983), *Ancient Nubia: Egypt's Rival in Africa* (1993), *Ancient Egyptian Kingship* (1995), *Amenhotep III: Perspectives on his Reign* (1998) and *Abydos* (forthcoming). **6, 7, 12, 15, 35, 50; 6** with Matthew Adams.

José-Ramón Pérez-Accino lectures in Egyptology at Birkbeck College, University of London, where he specializes in ancient Egyptian literature and language. He is the co-founder and co-editor of the journal *Trabajos de Egiptologia–Papers on Ancient Egypt*. **9, 11, 17, 25, 30, 42, 55, 64**

Ian Shaw is Lecturer in Egyptian Archaeology at the University of Liverpool. He is the author of *Egyptian Warfare and Weapons* (1991) and *Exploring Ancient Egypt* (2003), co-author, with Paul Nicholson, of the *British Museum Dictionary of Ancient Egypt* (1995), editor of the *Oxford History of Ancient Egypt* (2000) and co-editor, with Paul Nicholson, of *Ancient Egyptian Materials and Technology* (2000) and, with Robert Jameson, *A Dictionary of Archaeology* (1999). **52, 54, 61, 63**

Steven Snape is Senior Lecturer in Egyptian Archaeology at the University of Liverpool. An experienced director of fieldwork in Egypt, he now leads the major archaeological project centred on the site of Zawiyet Umm el-Rakham, and also has a research interest in Egyptian religious architecture. **43**

Kate Spence holds a Post-Doctoral Research Fellowship in the McDonald Institute for Archaeological Research, Cambridge University. She specializes in the architecture of ancient Egypt. **8, 13, 26**

Louise Steel lectures on Aegean and Near Eastern prehistory at the University of Wales, Lampeter. She has worked on many archaeological projects in Cyprus, and recently co-directed excavations at el-Moghraqa, Gaza, in an Anglo-Palestinian project. She is the author of *Cyprus Before History: From the Earliest Settlers to the End of the Bronze Age* (in press). **37, 39, 41**

Toby Wilkinson is a Fellow of Christ's College, Cambridge, and an Honorary Research Associate of Durham University's Department of Archaeology. He specializes in the early periods of ancient Egyptian civilization, and is the author of *Early Dynastic Egypt* (1999), *Royal Annals of Ancient Egypt* (2000) and *Genesis of the Pharaohs* (2003). **1, 2, 3, 4, 5**

King-list & chronology

The dates of ancient Egypt are generally assumed to be among the most secure in the ancient world – accurate to within two centuries *c.* 3000 BC; accurate to within two decades *c.* 1300 BC; and precise from 664 BC. But this still means that there are no precise dates for most of the period covered by this book. Different books give different dates for the same event, with the result that, for example, Narmer might have become king in 3100, 3050 or 2950 BC and the Battle of Qadesh might have taken place in 1297, 1286 or 1275 BC. Nevertheless, although there is not complete agreement among experts, there are options which are widely favoured. The dates used in this book are listed below, alongside the names of the kings of ancient Egypt.

Egyptologists normally employ a method of dividing the kings of ancient Egypt into 31 *dynasties*, following the practice of the Egyptian priest, Manetho, who wrote a history of his nation shortly after 300 BC. In general these dynasties correspond to particular ruling families, although in the more obscure eras of history some dynasties appear to be little more than convenient groupings of kings, some of whom were contemporary rulers in different parts of Egypt. In fact, Manetho is quite clear about this last point – that often there was more than one line of kings in Egypt.

Modern Egyptologists have grouped the dynasties into broader periods known as 'Kingdoms', when, normally, there was only one king throughout Egypt. The *Old Kingdom* (*c.* 2650–2175 BC) is the age of the Great Pyramid and the Great Sphinx. The *Middle Kingdom* (*c.* 2000–1700 BC) was an age of renewed national unity, and of a great flowering of art and literature. The *New Kingdom* (*c.* 1539–1075 BC) is often described as the imperial, or golden, age of ancient Egypt – the time of Amenhotep III, Akhenaten and Ramesses II, when Egypt was the richest and most powerful nation in the world. The *Late Period* (664–332 BC) became the final assertion of ancient Egyptian independence in the wider world, after which the country was conquered by Alexander the Great and later was absorbed by the Roman Empire.

EARLY DYNASTIC PERIOD

'DYNASTY 0' *c.* 3100 BC
Existence uncertain
Iryhor (?)
Ro (?)
Ka (?)
Scorpion (?)

1ST DYNASTY *c.* 2950–*c.* 2775
Narmer
Aha
Djer
Djet
Den
Anedjib
Semerkhet
Qaa

2ND DYNASTY *c.* 2750–*c.* 2650
Hotepsekhemwy
Reneb
Nynetjer
Weneg (?)
Sened (?)
Peribsen
Khasekhemwy

OLD KINGDOM

3RD DYNASTY *c.* 2650–*c.* 2575
Netjerykhet (Djoser)
Sekhemkhet
Zanakht
Khaba
Huni

4TH DYNASTY *c.* 2575–*c.* 2450
Snofru
Khufu
Redjedef
Khafre
Menkaure
Shepseskaf

5TH DYNASTY *c.* 2450–*c.* 2325
Userkaf
Sahure
Neferirkare Kakai
Shepseskare Izi
Reneferef
Nyuserre Ini
Menkauhor
Djedkare Izezi
Unas

6TH DYNASTY *c.* 2325–*c.* 2175
Teti
Userkare (?)
Pepy I
Merenre Nemtyemzaf
Pepy II

FIRST INTERMEDIATE PERIOD

7TH/8TH DYNASTY *c.* 2175–*c.* 2125
Numerous ephemeral kings

9TH/10TH DYNASTY *c.* 2125–*c.* 1975
Several kings, including:
Khety I
Khety II
Merykare
Ity

MIDDLE KINGDOM

11TH DYNASTY *c.* 2080–*c.* 1940
Inyotef I
Inyotef II
Inyotef III
Montuhotep II *c.* 2010–*c.* 1960
Montuhotep III *c.* 1960–*c.* 1948
Montuhotep IV *c.* 1948–*c.* 1938

12TH DYNASTY *c.* 1938–*c.* 1755
Amenemhat I *c.* 1938–*c.* 1908
Senwosret I *c.* 1918–*c.* 1875
Amenemhat II *c.* 1876–*c.* 1842
Senwosret II *c.* 1842–*c.* 1837
Senwosret III *c.* 1836–*c.* 1818
Amenemhat III *c.* 1818–*c.* 1770
Amenemhat IV *c.* 1770–*c.* 1760
Nefrusobk *c.* 1760–*c.* 1755

SECOND INTERMEDIATE PERIOD

13TH DYNASTY c. 1755–c. 1630
Seventy kings, including (order uncertain):
Sobkhotep I
Amenemhat V
Qemau
Sihornedjheryotef
Sobkhotep II
Hor
Amenemhat VII
Wegaf
Khendjer
Sobkhotep III
Neferhotep I
Sahathor
Sobkhotep IV
Sobkhotep V
Ay (I)
Montuemsaf
Dedumose
Neferhotep II

14TH DYNASTY
Numerous ephemeral kings

15TH DYNASTY c. 1630–c. 1520
Six kings, including:
Salitis
Sheshi
Khyan
Apophis c. 1570–c. 1530
Khamudy c. 1530–c. 1520

16TH DYNASTY
Numerous ephemeral kings

17TH DYNASTY c. 1630–c. 1539
Numerous kings, probably ending:
Inyotef V
Inyotef VI
Inyotef VII
Sobkemsaf II
Senakhtenre (Taa?)
Seqenenre Taa
Kamose c. 1541–c. 1539

NEW KINGDOM

18TH DYNASTY c. 1539–c. 1292
Ahmose c. 1539–c. 1514
Amenhotep I c. 1514–c. 1493
Thutmose I c. 1493–c. 1481
Thutmose II c. 1481–c. 1479
Thutmose III c. 1479–c. 1425 and Hatshepsut c. 1473–c. 1458
Amenhotep II c. 1426–c. 1400
Thutmose IV c. 1400–c. 1390
Amenhotep III c. 1390–c. 1353
Amenhotep IV (Akhenaten) c. 1353–c. 1336
Smenkhkare c. 1336–c. 1332
Tutankhamun c. 1332–c. 1322
Ay (II) c. 1322–c. 1319
Horemheb c. 1319–c. 1292

19TH DYNASTY c. 1292–c. 1190
Ramesses I c. 1292–c. 1290
Sety I c. 1290–c. 1279
Ramesses II c. 1279–c. 1213
Merenptah c. 1213–c. 1204
Sety II c. 1204–c. 1198
Amenmesse c. 1202–c. 1200
Siptah c. 1198–c. 1193
Twosret c. 1198–c. 1190

20TH DYNASTY c. 1190–c. 1069
Sethnakhte c. 1190–c. 1187
Ramesses III c. 1187–c. 1156
Ramesses IV c. 1156–c. 1150
Ramesses V c. 1150–c. 1145
Ramesses VI c. 1145–c. 1137
Ramesses VII c. 1137–c. 1129
Ramesses VIII c. 1129–c. 1126
Ramesses IX c. 1126–c. 1108
Ramesses X c. 1108–c. 1099
Ramesses XI c. 1099–c. 1069

THIRD INTERMEDIATE PERIOD

21ST DYNASTY c. 1069–c. 945
Smendes c. 1069–c. 1045
Amenemnesu c. 1045–c. 1040
Psusennes I c. 1040–c. 985
Amenemope c. 985–c. 975
Osochor (Osorkon 'the elder') c. 975–c. 970
Siamun c. 970–c. 950
Psusennes II c. 950–c. 945

22ND DYNASTY c. 945–c. 715
Shoshenq I c. 945–c. 925
Osorkon I c. 925–c. 890 and Shoshenq II c. 890
Takelot I c. 890–c. 875
Osorkon II c. 875–c. 835
Shoshenq III c. 835–c. 795
Shoshenq IV c. 795–c. 785
Pimay c. 785–c. 775
Shoshenq V c. 775–c. 735
Osorkon IV c. 735–c. 715

23RD DYNASTY c. 830–c. 715
Takelot II c. 840–c. 815
Pedubast I c. 825–c. 800 and Iuput I c. 800
Shoshenq VI c. 800–c. 780
Osorkon III c. 780–c. 750
Takelot III c. 750–c. 735
Rudamun c. 755–c. 735
Peftjauawybast c. 735–c. 725
Shoshenq VII c. 725–c. 715

24TH DYNASTY c. 730–c. 715
Tefnakhte c. 730–c. 720
Bocchoris c. 720–c. 715

25TH DYNASTY c. 800–657
Alara c. 800–c. 770
Kashta c. 770–c. 747
Piye c. 747–c. 715
Shabaka c. 715–c. 702
Shebitku c. 702–690
Taharqa 690–664
Tantamani 664–657

LATE PERIOD

26TH DYNASTY 664–525
Necho I 672–664
Psamtek I 664–610
Necho II 610–595
Psamtek II 595–589
Apries 589–570
Amasis 570–526
Psamtek III 526–525

27TH DYNASTY (PERSIAN) 525–404
Cambyses 525–522
Darius I 521–486
Xerxes 486–466
Artaxerxes I 465–424
Darius II 424–404

28TH DYNASTY 404–399
Amyrtaeus 404–399

29TH DYNASTY 399–380
Nepherites I 399–393
Psammuthis 393
Hakoris 393–380
Nepherites II 380

30TH DYNASTY 380–343
Nectanebo I 380–362
Teos 365–360
Nectanebo II 360–343

31ST DYNASTY (PERSIAN) 343–332
Artaxerxes III 343–338
Arses 338–336
Darius III 335–332

PTOLEMAIC PERIOD 332–30
Alexander III (the Great) 332–323
Philip Arrhidaios 323–317
Alexander IV 317–309
Ptolemy I 305–282
Ptolemy II 285–246
Ptolemy III 246–221
Ptolemy IV 221–205
Ptolemy V 205–180
Ptolemy VI 180–145
Ptolemy VIII and Cleopatra II 170–116
Ptolemy IX 116–107 and Cleopatra III 116–101
Ptolemy X 107–88
Ptolemy IX (restored) 88–80
Ptolemy XI and Berenice III 80
Ptolemy XII 80–58
Cleopatra VI 58–57 and Berenice IV 58–55
Ptolemy XII (restored) 55–51
Cleopatra VII and Ptolemy XIII 51–47
Cleopatra VII and Ptolemy XIV 47–44
Cleopatra VII and Ptolemy XV 44–30

Background: The king-list at Abydos.

Ancient mysteries

What mysteries do lie beyond thy dust,
Could man outlook that mark!
HENRY VAUGHAN, *SILEX SCINTILLANS*, 1650

The modern study of ancient Egypt is now two centuries old. In that time our interest has been transformed from a race to collect curiosities to a professional scientific discipline. And yet many questions remain unresolved and ancient Egypt continues to grip the popular imagination. How can it be that we know so much about this great nation and yet so much remains mysterious? *The Seventy Great Mysteries of Ancient Egypt* celebrates the enigmatic face of the best-known ancient civilization. In some cases, the answers seem to be straightforward; in others, the shroud of mystery still hangs heavy.

A painting of the tombs at Beni Hasan (1845) by Karl Richard Lepsius, one of the great early Egyptologists. Much of our evidence for ancient Egypt comes from tombs.

Survival of the evidence

Of course, although museums around the world contain impressive collections of Egyptian objects, a great deal of the evidence has not survived: most of the palaces and houses, the tools and texts, and the other artifacts of the ancient Egyptians have been lost over the centuries. In Egypt this loss tends to follow a specific pattern. The ancient cemeteries lie on the edges of the deserts which stretch beyond the fertile Nile Valley to east and west, and often survive well in the dry and inhospitable environment. On the other hand, towns and villages by and large lay along the banks of the river, beside the oasis of Faiyum or on the fringes and high grounds of the marshy river delta. Generally, these ancient communities now lie buried beneath modern towns and cities, or have been turned over by farmers and robbed for stone by builders. Material remains therefore tend to emphasize the funerary aspects of ancient Egyptian culture, producing the impression that the ancients spent their lives obsessed with death.

Nevertheless, our understanding of ancient Egypt is improving all the time as we utilize more sophisticated techniques for discovering and analysing material remains, and develop better informed and more astute interpretations of the results. For example, we have begun to recognize

Ancient Thebes, the great religious centre of New Kingdom Egypt. In the foreground are the remains of the massive temples at Karnak, on the east bank of the Nile. In the recent past these temples were treated as isolated monuments, but we now appreciate that they were linked to each other, and also to temples on the far bank and to the Valley of the Kings in the desert beyond, by the routes of the festival processions of the god, Amun-Re.

that the tombs and temples at the great southern city of Thebes are not isolated monuments, but are often related to each other in meaningful patterns. The Theban Mapping Project, headed by Kent Weeks of the American University in Cairo, is plotting the archaeological sites of Thebes in such detail that we can better appreciate these patterns, and also identify new sites, even as they are being destroyed by urban development.

Ancient voices

Unlike archaeologists in many areas of the world who have only material remains to work with and make sense of, those working in Egypt have the benefit of a huge legacy of written texts left by the ancient Egyptians themselves. These take the form of documents or carved and painted monuments, and we can glean from them a surprising amount of detail about people's lives, values and beliefs, and their communities. For example, we know more about the men who built the tombs in the Valley of the Kings than about any other community in the ancient world: not just their names and the names of their families, but also their shift patterns at work, their absences through sickness and the arguments they had with each other. Nevertheless, this wealth of written information keeps its own secrets.

The most typical type of text to have survived is the funerary inscription on a tomb wall, coffin or stela. These inscriptions are invariably linked to a cult, in which the life and character of the deceased is celebrated in the hope that his or her spirit will continue to live beyond death. These inscriptions therefore conform to a standard format of worthy phrases, which mean that such personal details as where and when a person was born, or how old he or she was at death are rarely mentioned. So it is when we are dealing with individuals that we most clearly come up against the selective character of ancient evidence.

Fragment of a wall-painting with a leopard, from the royal palaces at Avaris, in a style showing influence from Crete. Ancient Egypt did not exist in isolation, and its relationships with other nations raise many questions.

Occasionally we get more substantial information, such as in the funerary inscription of Harkhuf, but this may simply generate further questions: Harkhuf tells us that he gained royal approval by making three journeys to trade with the rulers of Yam – but where was Yam? On the other hand, there are once great but now almost forgotten individuals: Smendes and Khababash were once so powerful that they ruled parts of Egypt, but they are mentioned only in the margins of texts about other people, and so now walk in the shadows of history.

Even monumental royal inscriptions are not all they may seem. These were not intended to record the achievements of a king for posterity, or to proclaim his power to the people of Egypt. Most were erected in the dark, inaccessible chambers and passages of temples, where they would remain unread by anyone except the gods themselves. In fact, what they recorded was the relationship between the king and the gods, which was generally focused on building temples, performing rituals and obtaining exotic goods to offer on the altars. As a result, royal monuments often leave out 'the stuff of history' – wars and treaties, births, marriages and deaths. We rarely hear about kings before they actually come to the throne so we do not even know how old they were on their accession, or their age at death.

Others come into view and then disappear from the written record, as their careers or influence wax and wane. For example, Senenmut is a central figure on many of the monuments of the female king Hatshepsut, but why, and what became of him? Nefertiti – famed throughout the world for the beauty of the bust in the Berlin Museum – was the principal wife of Akhenaten, but she suddenly disappears from our sources in about the 12th year of his reign. Did she die, was she disgraced – or did she, as some have argued, re-emerge in a different guise as the king of Egypt herself?

Exploring the mysteries

The Seventy Great Mysteries of Ancient Egypt is divided into seven sections. We begin with the origins of pharaonic Egyptian culture in 'The Earliest Egyptians'. Do we know where the people of Egypt originally came from? This is a subject that has been debated since the earliest days of Egyptology, when great scholars such as Flinders Petrie naïvely argued that the earliest rulers of Egypt came from Mesopotamia. More recently, the debate has been taken in a new direction by Afrocentric scholarship: if the ancient Egyptians were African, were they not also black? And what about writing? Did the Egyptians invent their beautiful and distinctive hieroglyphic script or did they simply borrow the idea from someone else?

In 'Pyramids & Tombs' we look at what the pyramids were for, how they developed and who actually built them. We know that kings were buried in them, but that does not explain everything about these complex structures. Were they aligned with the stars, for instance? And why did King Snofru build at least three pyramids for himself. Apart from the pyramids, the most famous tombs in Egypt are found in the Valley of the Kings at Thebes. This has been explored by Europeans for centuries, and yet even today we cannot be sure we know all that there is in the Valley. For example, the workmen who built the royal tombs venerated King Amenhotep I after his death as their patron deity, and yet his own tomb has never been found. Perhaps the most tantalizing mystery of all is whether there are still more royal tombs waiting to be found in Egypt. Could a tomb to rival that of Tutankhamun's ever be discovered again?

'Pharaohs & Queens' looks at the men and women who ruled Egypt for 3000 years, including those few women who became kings in their own right as well as the men who seized power – and their mysterious, possibly violent fates. Here we come across famous names, such as Hatshepsut, Nefertiti and Cleopatra, around whom great myths have built up.

'People & Places' revisits other names that were important to the ancient Egyptians, but whose significance has been lost to us. The Hyksos kings were vilified in the traditions of the Egyptians as godless and bloodthirsty conquerors, but their archaeological remains now suggest a somewhat different story. The kingdoms of Yam and Punt in Africa, and Alashiya in Europe, were significant trading partners of Egypt, but we cannot even be sure where they were. Sinuhe and Wenamun were great heroes in Egyptian literature: but were they real people?

In 'Ancient Wisdom & Belief' we turn our attention to ancient beliefs and values that seem inexplicable to us today, even absurd. We may find it strange, primitive perhaps, that the ancient Egyptians believed their king was a god: but if he was not divine, what justifiable reason could there have been to execute his courtiers to accompany him into the afterlife? It may seem charming that they worshipped so many peculiar-looking gods: but did they really believe magic spells could change their lives? Mummies are perhaps one of the most familiar aspects of Egyptian culture, but how did the practice of mummification evolve, and why would a man write to his wife three years after her death asking for a divorce?

In the modern world we are often surprised by what the ancients could achieve with apparently limited technology. Many 'Historical Mysteries' arise simply because the ancients did not write down all their knowledge and secrets. Granite is an extremely hard stone used for the doorways of temples and colossal statues of kings: but how did the Egyptians work it without the use of iron tools? In fact, why did the Egyptians choose to make do without iron for more than 1000 years after they first became aware of it? There are also the mysteries of why complex societies come to an end – such as the Old Kingdom, which created the Great Pyramid, or Egypt's vast New Kingdom empire of gold, once the richest nation on earth.

Opposite *Nefertiti, the principal wife of Akhenaten. Although she was a central figure in Egyptian society, she simply disappears from the historical record for reasons which are much disputed.*

Below *The mighty King Ramesses II represented as the helpless child of the sun god. What sense can we make of the religious beliefs of the ancient Egyptians?*

Amenemhat, seated beside his wife, Ay, and embracing his brother(?), Inyotef. All three are dead, whereas Amenemhat's surviving sister, Hapy, is shown bringing food-offerings for their spirits. Why did ancient Egyptians put such emphasis on ongoing relations between the living and the dead?

Doubtless, for many readers, the most intriguing mysteries in this volume will be those concerning 'Egypt & the Bible'. Not a single scrap of evidence has survived in Egypt that directly supports the Bible narratives – not even David's Kingdom of Israel nor the mighty King Solomon himself merit a mention. Nevertheless, there is plenty of circumstantial evidence that seems to confirm the historical background to many of these stories. So do ancient Egyptian sources offer any evidence that the stories of the Old Testament are historically true, or can they only be true for the faithful?

The pace of discovery in Egypt has not slowed. What we have learned about the ancients has often lead us to develop extravagant theories, which are not necessarily well founded on facts. *The Seventy Great Mysteries of Ancient Egypt* is a unique, well-informed and up-to-date exploration of this most romantic and inspiring of all ancient civilizations.

Right *Ramesses III slaughtering his enemies, including the enigmatic 'Sea Peoples', whose identity has been much disputed.*

Opposite *Map of Egypt showing the major sites and places mentioned in the text.*

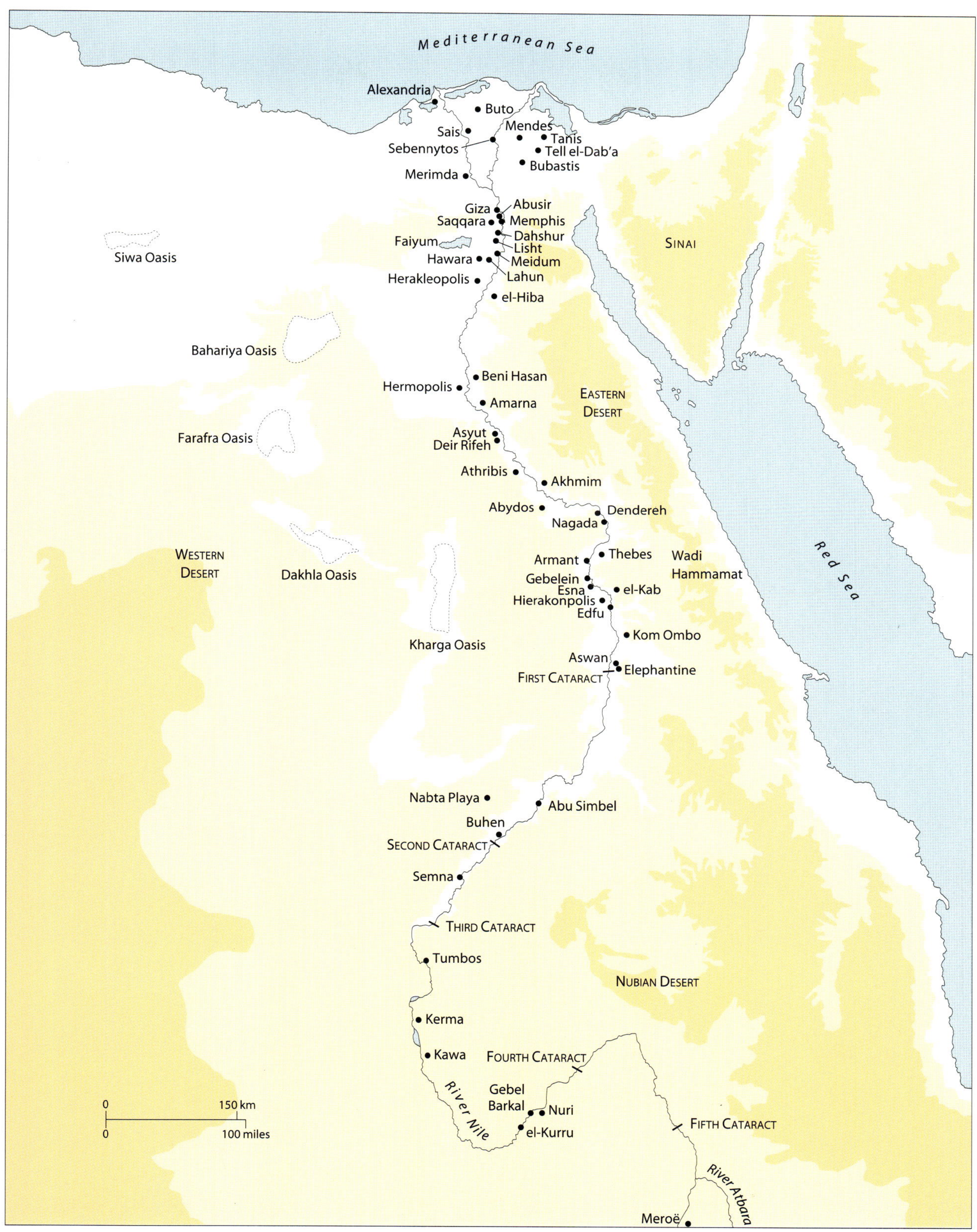

Mediterranean Sea
Alexandria
Buto
Sais
Mendes
Tanis
Sebennytos
Tell el-Dab'a
Bubastis
Merimda
Giza
Abusir
Saqqara
Memphis
Dahshur
Faiyum
Lisht
Siwa Oasis
Hawara
Meidum
Lahun
Herakleopolis
el-Hiba
Sinai
Bahariya Oasis
Beni Hasan
Hermopolis
Amarna
Eastern Desert
Farafra Oasis
Asyut
Deir Rifeh
Athribis
Akhmim
Abydos
Dendereh
Nagada
Western Desert
Armant
Thebes
Wadi Hammamat
Dakhla Oasis
Gebelein
Esna
el-Kab
Hierakonpolis
Edfu
Red Sea
Kom Ombo
Kharga Oasis
Aswan
Elephantine
First Cataract
Nabta Playa
Abu Simbel
Buhen
Second Cataract
Semna
Third Cataract
Tumbos
Nubian Desert
Kerma
Kawa
Fourth Cataract
River Nile
Gebel Barkal
Nuri
el-Kurru
Fifth Cataract
River Atbara
Meroë
0
150 km
0
100 miles

The Earliest Egyptians

In 1939, Sir Flinders Petrie sat down to summarize what he had learned about Egypt during his 70 years in archaeology: 'The uniform result', he concluded, 'is that Egypt never originated any new civilization, but was a fertile ground for implanting the products of other lands. Each new movement entered Egypt at its best, and deteriorated gradually under the easy conditions of life in Egypt.'

Nowadays, few scholars would be inclined to draw such an extreme conclusion, partly because we demand less simplistic explanations of history, and partly because we have more evidence at our disposal. Therefore, in 'The Earliest Egyptians' we look at the origins of pharaonic culture to see what new explanations we can offer for the making of Egypt.

Questions about origins are often the most hotly disputed. Petrie naïvely supposed that all civilizing influences in the ancient world emanated from Mesopotamia. For him and his disciples it was unthinkable that the magnificence of Egypt under the pharaohs could have had its origins in Africa, which they assumed was essentially a primitive continent.

In the 20th century, many still argued that the Egyptians were an immigrant population because they accepted the diffusionist view, which assumes that every major advance in history – such as farming and writing – must have begun in a single place and then spread elsewhere. Nobody argued that this place could have

Rock art, from Wadi Barramiya, showing an enigmatic figure in a boat surrounded by herdsmen and animals. Boats depicted in what is today a desert suggest that in the centuries before the pharaohs many Egyptians were nomads, as familiar with the Nile as with the grasslands which once lay beyond its banks.

The painted walls of this prehistoric tomb may be our oldest encounter with the world of the pharaohs. Decorated with images familiar from later periods, such as hunting, warfare and religious shrines on boats, the tomb was built for a powerful ruler at Hierakonpolis, later the largest and most important religious centre for the earliest kings of Egypt.

been Africa. More recently archaeologists and historians have stressed continuity in the artistic and religious culture of prehistoric Egypt, while others have emphasized changes in the landscape of Egypt since prehistoric times. This has led to a radical new theory that Egypt's first settlers included pastoral nomads from the fringes of the Nile, which in prehistoric times were seasonal grasslands rather than today's deserts. If so, these nomads would have relied on nearby settlements for trade and seasonal work, and it seems probable that archaeologists are beginning to identify these early towns at places such as Merimda and Buto. Today, a local origin for the earliest Egyptians does not seem fanciful.

Nevertheless, there are practices which distinguish Egypt from the countries which surrounded it. One such is writing: in ancient Africa this was essentially an Egyptian phenomenon. So did the Egyptians invent writing or simply adopt the idea from Mesopotamia? Both arguments have their advocates, but both create nagging doubts. Undoubtedly there were close contacts between Egypt and Mesopotamia in prehistoric times, and writing seems to have appeared almost fully developed in Egypt. On the other hand, Egyptian hieroglyphs are beautifully adapted to writing the ancient Egyptian language, and have nothing significant in common – in form or in use – with the scripts of Mesopotamia. If the Egyptians were creative enough to devise a whole new writing system, were they not also capable of inventing the idea of writing itself? Crucial new discoveries at Abydos – Egypt's earliest royal cemetery – may be the key to solving this mystery.

The same discoveries have intensified another debate: who were the earliest kings of Egypt? Until recently, it was widely accepted that the first king was Narmer, and that he became king only after the land had become a unified nation with a common set of beliefs and institutions. However, some scholars have speculated that there could have been earlier kings, whose names we can recognize in tombs at Abydos. Do these obscure hieroglyphs really give the names of a shadowy 'Dynasty 0', which ruled before Narmer? Intriguingly, many ancient accounts agree in listing the name of the first king as Menes, but unequivocal evidence of the existence of Menes has not yet come to light. Is he, as some would argue, a myth? Or is he already known to us by another name? Was he, in fact, Narmer?

Our final pair of mysteries takes us back once more to the graves of the earliest kings of Egypt. First is the gruesome spectre of human sacrifice. The royal cemetery at Abydos seems to suggest that these kings demanded the slaughter – or suicide – of key members of the palace. Like the issue of slavery in Egypt (discussed in Section II), such barbarity does not sit easily with the apparent sophistication of ancient Egypt. So have we simply misunderstood the evidence? Finally, we look at the boat burials, for which the archaeological evidence is unequivocal: complete boats were buried in the Western Desert near the funerary enclosures of Egypt's early kings. The mystery, of course, is why?

Where did the Egyptians come from?

1

The Dynastic people came in the form of a horde invasion ... from the east.
W. B. Emery, 1961

Until the 1890s, the pyramids of the 4th Dynasty were the oldest known surviving monuments from ancient Egypt. Then pioneering excavations by Flinders Petrie brought to light evidence of a much older cultural tradition – earlier even than the historic 1st Dynasty known from records. Initially, this new material was so unfamiliar that Petrie thought it must have belonged to a 'New Race', culturally distinct from the Egyptians of Dynastic times. After further study, however, Petrie realized that he had, in fact, discovered remains from a prehistoric – 'Predynastic' – period. He and his colleagues were particularly struck by the marked differences between this new, Predynastic culture, and the much better-known material from the Old Kingdom and later periods.

Egyptologists working in the early decades of the 20th century came up with a simple explanation for this difference: they argued that classic ancient Egyptian civilization had been brought to the Nile Valley by a 'dynastic race' of invaders. According to this view, the invaders were culturally and politically superior to the native Predynastic Egyptians, and swiftly established themselves as rulers of the country. The then-fashionable but dubious science of cranial metrology – using skull measurements to try to determine racial characteristics – was deployed in support of this theory.

Prehistoric petroglyphs of boats at el-Hosh, around 100 km (60 miles) south of Thebes. Images like these have been cited as evidence that the first Egyptians were invaders from other lands.

Stone handaxes from the Palaeolithic period show that people have lived in the Nile Valley for hundreds of thousands of years.

The 'dynastic race' was believed to have come from a land to the east of Egypt, a reflection of the widespread view that the Orient was a primary source of cultural inspiration. The Mesopotamian-style architecture and Mesopotamian motifs seen in Egyptian royal art of the early 1st Dynasty were thought to be signs that its kings came from present-day Iraq. This view was given a further boost in the 1930s, when the German explorer Hans Winkler found an abundance of ancient rock art in the Eastern Desert, between the Nile Valley and the Red Sea. Particularly striking were numerous images of boats that resembled similarly shaped craft in early Mesopotamian art. The chronology of the ancient world was still poorly understood at the time, and Winkler was not to know that the Egyptian boats pre-dated their Mesopotamian counterparts by many centuries. So, instead, he argued that Mesopotamians had invaded Egypt via the Red Sea, leaving traces on the rocks as they journeyed to the River Nile.

This dynastic race theory was very much a product of its time. Not only was the study of Egyptian prehistory still in its infancy, but diffusionist theories involving superior racial groups bringing civilization to indigenous peoples were also popular among the colonialist powers of western Europe. So, too, was the view that the continent of Africa – labelled 'the heart of darkness' – was incapable of producing an advanced culture without outside influence. Following the defeat of Nazism, and the granting of independence to most of the former European colonies in Africa, theories based upon notions of racial supremacy went out of fashion. The dynastic race theory lingered on among a very few Egyptologists, even to be resuscitated in popular works as late as the 1990s; but in general, scholars abandoned their search for the foreign origins of Egyptian civilization. Instead, they stressed indigenous development, and began to look for the roots of ancient Egypt within the Nile Valley itself.

A more complex picture

After three decades of intensive archaeological research, our understanding of early Egypt has been transformed. Egyptian civilization can now be traced, in a long sequence of development, back to 5000 BC, two millennia before the 1st Dynasty. Evidence has come to light for even earlier communities of hunter-gatherer people in the Nile Valley and on the shores of Lake Faiyum, as well as for a Palaeolithic population dating back some 300,000 years. A better knowledge of the culture of early dynastic Egypt has also changed our view of how classic Egyptian civilization emerged. Sixty years ago, the hallmarks of ancient Egypt seemed to have appeared as if from nowhere at the beginning of the 1st Dynasty: that civilization had apparently been suddenly 'switched on like a lightbulb'. Today, we can appreciate the long gestation of Egyptian culture, and the fact that its roots lie firmly within Egypt itself.

Yet, despite recognizing the essentially indigenous genius of Egyptian civilization, scholars are increasingly aware that Predynastic culture was receptive to ideas from neighbouring lands, at least in its later stages. Foreign architectural and artistic motifs, perhaps even the idea of writing (p. 24), were adopted by the Egyptians at the dawn of history; but all such borrowings were quickly adapted to an Egyptian context. There is certainly no evidence whatsoever for an invasion of dynastic conquerors. Rather, in ancient times as today, Egypt was a cultural melting-pot, where Africa, Asia and the Mediterranean met; the emerging civilization in the Nile Valley absorbed influences from all these areas.

In an unexpected twist, new evidence has recently come to light, once again from the deserts of Egypt. It suggests that the impetus behind the development of civilization may not have been the adoption of a settled, agricultural way of life in the Nile Valley, as archaeologists used to think, but, rather, the stresses of a more precarious existence in the hostile environment of the dry savannahs to the east and west, before these turned into desert. The gradual migration of semi-nomadic cattle-herders into the Nile Valley, as their grassland pastures began to dry out, may have been an important stimulus to the rapid development of Egyptian civilization.

A final phenomenon connected with the mystery of ancient Egyptian origins is the extraordinary popularity, from the 1960s onwards, of 'fantasy archaeology'. Writers have found an eager audience for a variety of theories that attribute Egyptian civilization to extraterrestrials or to refugees from Atlantis. Even though such theories are scientifically flawed – being based on the distortion or highly selective use of evidence – they remain peculiarly attractive.

In summary, despite attempts to prove otherwise, all the evidence indicates that the Egyptians came from Egypt itself: from the Nile Valley and the drier regions on either side. Over several thousand years, environmental changes and foreign influences moulded the gradual development of a civilization that was, in the final analysis, distinctively and uniquely Egyptian.

Above *Petroglyphs of domesticated animals (cow and goat) in the Wadi Umm Salam, Eastern Desert, record the semi-nomadic way of life that helped to forge Egyptian civilization.*

Opposite above *The stone circle at Nabta Playa, in Egypt's Western Desert, was constructed c. 7000 BC as a calendar to herald the arrival of the summer rains. Its prehistoric builders were clearly a sophisticated people.*

Right *Buried in its own tomb, a huge sculpted monolith at Nabta Playa foreshadows the ancient Egyptians' mastery of stone architecture and their fascination for monumental buildings.*

2

Did the Egyptians invent writing?

The written language must have had a considerable period of development behind it, of which no trace has as yet been found in Egypt.
W. B. EMERY, 1961

Hieroglyphic writing – the sacred script of ancient Egypt – is one of the hallmarks of pharaonic civilization. Carved in stone on monuments, painted on the walls of tombs, inscribed in ink on papyrus, writing is peculiarly pervasive in Egyptian culture. It characterized the world of the pharaohs until the last gasp of their great civilization: the final hieroglyphic inscription was carved as late as AD 394, in the reign of the Roman Emperor Hadrian (who still portrayed himself on Egyptian monuments as a traditional pharaoh). As for the beginnings of Egyptian writing, these remain more mysterious, shrouded in the mists of antiquity.

A detail from the Narmer Palette, dating from the beginning of the 3rd millennium BC, shows the early use of hieroglyphs to label the main figures.

The uses of early writing

The discovery in 1900 of the famous Narmer Palette at Hierakonpolis not only brought to light one of the great icons of early Egypt, it also pushed back the origins of hieroglyphic writing to the dawn of Egyptian history. In the reign of the first king of the 1st Dynasty, signs were already being used to label and identify the key players in royal commemorative art. Even if the precise meaning of some signs remains problematic, there can be no doubt about the importance of writing in the palette's overall composition. The characteristic integration of text and image was to remain a feature of Egyptian art for the next 3000 years. To the archaeologists who found the Narmer Palette, as for their successors for much of the 20th century, it seemed clear that Egyptian writing had been invented by the early state to glorify the ruler and record his achievements. Writing was seen as one of the mechanisms devised by Egypt's first monarchs to promote and underpin their authority.

That view began to change after a spectacular discovery in 1987. German archaeologists excavating in the early royal cemetery at Umm el-Qa'ab, Abydos, uncovered the tomb of a ruler pre-dating the 1st Dynasty by over a century. They labelled it tomb U-j, and among its remarkable contents were several hundred bone labels, each measuring not more than 2–3 cm (0.8–1 in) square and inscribed with combinations of a few hieroglyphic signs. Each label has a small hole in one corner, so that it could be attached by means of a cord to a jar or box.

These dockets had clearly been used to label the various commodities destined for the tomb. They are the earliest examples of Egyptian writing found to date, yet their primary purpose was not to glorify the king but to record more prosaic, economic information, such as the provenance, quantity and ownership of goods. This is not, perhaps, so surprising: control of the economy must have been a major concern of Egypt's early rulers, just as it is for governments today. So the discovery of tomb U-j has forced Egyptologists to rethink not only the date for the earliest Egyptian writing, but also the reasons behind its invention.

Bone labels from a prehistoric tomb at Abydos constitute the earliest body of writing yet discovered in Egypt.

The process of invention

Curiously, the writing on the labels from tomb U-j is not a primitive version of hieroglyphs, but appears fully formed. It already shows the distinctive combination of meaning-signs and sound-signs that characterizes Egyptian writing throughout the pharaonic period. For such early written documents, the script and the writing system seem remarkably developed. Do the origins of hieroglyphics, therefore, lie still further back in time?

While conducting his pioneering excavations at Predynastic sites in the late 19th century, the great archaeologist Flinders Petrie noticed that many pots were incised with curious signs, either singly or in pairs. So numerous and diverse were these pot-marks that they seemed to constitute a recording system. Because they pre-dated the earliest hieroglyphic inscription then known (the Narmer Palette), it was tempting to see the pot-marks as the embryonic stages of writing. However, subsequent study has conclusively demonstrated that pot-marks and hieroglyphs

Above *Pot-marks include a wide range of signs and symbols, but comprise a distinct system of communication, separate from hieroglyphic writing.*

Right *Gravestone of the 1st Dynasty, which bears the earliest known example of the hieroglyphic scribal kit sign, used to write the words for 'writing' and 'scribe'.*

are, in fact, two separate systems for recording information. Predynastic pot-marks, rather like the hallmarks used on silver, convey information about the pot, its maker and perhaps its intended use. They did not evolve into Egyptian writing, but remained a distinct system, even after the introduction of hieroglyphs.

Where, then, should we look for the origins of writing? Although we tend to think of hieroglyphs in their monumental, carved form, the most common type of writing in ancient Egypt would have been in ink on papyrus. Indeed, the hieroglyphic sign for 'write' – the oldest known example of which occurs on a gravestone from the 1st Dynasty – shows the scribal kit of inkwells, water bag and stylus.

Papyrus is fragile and does not survive particularly well in the archaeological record. Moreover, the government offices where most documents were generated would have been situated in settlements close to the River Nile. Not only are conditions here not particularly favourable for the preservation of organic materials, but as they now lie beneath fields or modern settlements, most ancient Egyptian towns have not even been located, let alone excavated. So it is not surprising that our evidence for early Egyptian writing is confined to objects from graves. The earliest roll of papyrus found so far, in the tomb of a 1st Dynasty government official, is uninscribed; but it nevertheless shows that papyrus was being used from the very beginning of Egyptian history. If we ever find the palace complexes of Egypt's early rulers, we may be able to trace the origins of Egyptian writing more fully than at present.

Of course, there is another possibility: that Egyptian writing did not evolve gradually, over several generations, but was invented and introduced more or less overnight by the royal court. There are parallels from other cultures in history for such a process. If writing in Egypt was invented primarily for accounting purposes, as the labels from tomb U-j suggest, it is likely to have been an innovation of the court: an effective means of stamping royal ownership on commodities, of keeping track of everything that

entered and left the palace store-rooms, and of controlling the economy on a national scale.

Mesopotamia or Egypt?

This begs the final, tantalizing question: were the Egyptians the first to invent writing? Before the discovery of tomb U-j, it was generally accepted that the earliest system of written records was invented not in ancient Egypt but in Mesopotamia. Clay tablets from the temple at Uruk, dated to 3200 BC, preserve inscriptions – once again recording economic information – that are true writing, unlike the Egyptian pot-marks from the same period. However, in recent years, the archaeologist who found tomb U-j has argued that its labels pre-date the Mesopotamian tablets by as much as a century. He bases his claim on a radiocarbon date from the tomb, even though, for remains of this age, radiocarbon dates usually carry a margin of error of around 100 years.

The earliest known roll of papyrus, from the tomb of a 1st Dynasty high official at Memphis.

There is a degree of professional rivalry here between Egyptologists and their colleagues who work in Mesopotamia, with each keen to claim primacy for their particular culture. Such arguments aside, the evidence still tends to support Mesopotamia as the cradle of writing, although we cannot rule out the possibility that the two systems developed at about the same time. However, it is also distinctly possible that the concept of writing, like other foreign innovations, was borrowed by Egypt's early rulers. In the case of writing, it was an ideal solution to the problems of maintaining economic control over a geographically extensive territory. There was clearly much cultural exchange between Mesopotamia and Egypt during the latter stages of state formation in the Nile Valley. Aspects of Mesopotamian art and architecture were borrowed by the nascent Egyptian court to promote and reinforce its authority, and writing may have come as part of the same package.

Even if the idea of writing originated in Mesopotamia, the system of hieroglyphs devised for Egypt was quintessentially Egyptian. Signs were drawn from the Egyptian environment, and the structure of the script was perfectly suited to the Egyptian language. As a result, hieroglyphic writing quickly embedded itself in Egyptian culture, and became indispensable. Over succeeding generations, the Egyptians realized the potential of their writing system. No longer confined to recording economic data, it could be applied to the whole variety of human communication: everything from royal epics to love poetry.

Hieroglyphs were an integral part of ancient Egyptian civilization, remaining central to government and religion until the very end of the pharaonic era. Yet, unless and until excavations turn up examples of Egyptian documents even earlier than the labels from tomb U-j, a final answer to the mystery of who invented writing is likely to remain elusive.

Clay tablet with impressed signs, from Sumer (present-day Iraq). The Egyptians may have borrowed the idea of writing from their Mesopotamian neighbours.

3 Who were the first kings of Egypt?

Who was the first ruler of a united Egypt? ... analysis of the sources ... leaves us with little doubt that there were several generations of kings before the 1st Dynasty.
BÉATRIX MIDANT-REYNES, 2000

The ancient Egyptians had a clear view of their own history. As set out in the Turin Royal Canon, a king-list inscribed on papyrus in the New Kingdom 19th Dynasty and reiterated by the Egyptian priest Manetho writing in the 3rd century BC, Egypt had been created by the gods at the dawn of time and then ruled by them for many centuries. Next followed a succession of demi-gods, also known as the 'Followers of Horus'. After these came the kings of Egypt, beginning with Menes and stretching in an unbroken line down through the generations. So in the Turin Royal Canon, as in other king-lists of the same, Ramesside, period, Menes appears as the first traditional king of Egypt.

Manetho also devised the system of dynasties that is still used to this day, and Menes was accordingly the first king of the 1st Dynasty, coming to the throne after the last of the demi-gods. Menes is often equated with the king known as Narmer on contemporary, 1st Dynasty inscriptions (p. 33). Hence, in most modern accounts of ancient Egyptian history, Narmer is given first place in the long list of royal rulers.

However, identifying the first kings of Egypt is not quite as straightforward as that. The ancient Egyptians themselves were somewhat ambiguous about the origins of kingship. Although the traditional New Kingdom king-lists began with Menes, the royal annals (a year-by-year account of important events) compiled a thousand years earlier, in the Old Kingdom, gave precedence to a yet more ancient line of rulers. On the largest surviving fragment of the annals, known as the Palermo Stone (p. 227), these first kings occupy the uppermost row. By the time the annals were written, little was known about these early kings, so the Palermo Stone merely records their names. Were these pre-1st Dynasty rulers an invented tradition, akin to Manetho's demi-gods, or do they preserve a faint memory of a real line of kings who ruled Egypt before the beginning of recorded history?

The Narmer Palette, icon of early Egypt, depicts the king of that name who is traditionally credited with unifying the country and founding the 1st Dynasty.

Archaeological evidence

Recent excavations have brought about huge advances in our understanding of ancient Egyptian origins. Although Narmer was certainly a pivotal figure in Egyptian history, and was regarded by later generations as the founder of the 1st Dynasty royal line, it is now clear that he was not the first king of Egypt. Archaeological work in the early royal cemetery at Abydos has uncovered tombs that pre-date Narmer's, yet whose architecture and contents mark them out as royal. Egyptologists have therefore come up with the term 'Dynasty 0' to refer to the group of kings before the 1st Dynasty.

Unfortunately, early hieroglyphic inscriptions are notoriously difficult to decipher, leading to disputes over the identification of Narmer's predecessors. For example, two of the royal tombs at Abydos – pairs of chambers known as B1/2 and B7/9 respectively – produced fragmentary inscriptions which seemed at first sight to give the names of their royal occupants. However, the name read as King Ro may in fact refer to commodities destined for the mouth (*ro*) of the king;

King Scorpion carrying out an irrigation rite, on his ceremonial mace-head found at Hierakonpolis. The king's precise identity remains in doubt.

while the inscriptions attributed to a King Ka may refer instead to the spirit (*ka*) of the king. In other words, it is possible that both 'tombs' are in fact subsidiary chambers belonging to another nearby royal burial, perhaps Narmer's. As fast as new kings come to light, they vanish again!

The Narmer Palette is probably the most striking visual expression of early Egyptian kingship, but it is not the only royal monument from the dawn of Egyptian history. A decorated stone mace-head, found at the same time and at the same site – Hierakonpolis – as the palette, illustrates a different aspect of royal ritual: the opening of an irrigation canal. The king who is shown performing this act is identified by two hieroglyphic signs in front of his face: a scorpion and a rosette. Since the rosette was used at this early period to signify 'ruler', the king is usually identified as a King Scorpion. However, some Egyptologists prefer to interpret the scorpion as a title rather than a name. A few even argue that the king in question is in fact Narmer, based upon the close stylistic similarities between the mace-head and the Narmer Palette.

If King Scorpion was indeed a separate king, he must have reigned at about the same time as Narmer, yet no tomb has been found in the early royal cemetery at Abydos that can be attributed to him with any certainty. Since Hierakonpolis is in the far south of Egypt, it has been suggested that Scorpion may have been a local king, ruling the southernmost part of the Nile Valley, while Narmer ruled further north. Certainly, Hierakonpolis had been an important centre during the centuries preceding the 1st Dynasty, and seems to have lost out to its more northern rival

Abydos in the final stages of Egyptian unification. At present, Scorpion remains on most people's list of early kings, but his position is tenuous.

A whole host of other, enigmatic royal names from the beginning of Egyptian history have been found in diverse contexts. Some are written in ink on pots, some incised as pot-marks, others scratched on rocks in the Western and Eastern Deserts. Our understanding of early hieroglyphic writing is not yet good enough to decipher these names with certainty. What is clear is that the period immediately preceding the reign of Narmer was characterized, in both Egypt and Nubia, by a plethora of rulers claiming royal authority.

The archaeological record suggests that three sites in southern Egypt were politically prominent at this time: Abydos, Hierakonpolis and Nagada. Even outside these main centres, various other local or regional chieftains probably exercised power over limited geographical areas. All such rulers adopted the trappings of kingship, to a greater or lesser extent.

Map of Upper Egypt in the Predynastic period, showing the three competing kingdoms whose rulers were vying for political domination.

New discoveries

In the last 15 years, the whole debate about Egypt's earliest kings has been thrown open once again by two dramatic discoveries in the royal burial-ground at Abydos. The first is a large, eight-chambered tomb, modelled to resemble a royal palace in miniature, and containing objects fit for a king, most notably an ivory sceptre. What is remarkable about this burial, labelled by its excavators tomb U-j, is its date: over a century before the 1st Dynasty. It is the largest tomb of its date anywhere in Egypt, and its owner must certainly have exercised power over the whole of the northern Nile Valley and Delta – since commodities from various Delta towns were included among the grave-goods. His identity is unknown; for although many of the pots bore the sign of a scorpion, this need not be the tomb-owner's name. Anonymous or not, the ruler buried in U-j was clearly a king in every respect.

A second discovery at Abydos pushes the origins of Egyptian kingship even further back into prehistory. In a tomb labelled U-239, archaeologists found a painted pottery vessel dating to about 3800 BC. The decoration includes a motif

Below *Various royal names are known from the years before the 1st Dynasty, but their reading and significance are disputed.*

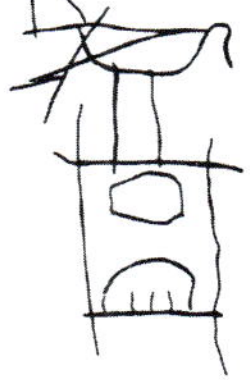

Right *Pot-marks on storage vessels may give the name of an early King Ro, or may simply indicate provisions destined for the king's use.*

Left *Pottery vessel from Abydos with painted decoration showing a ruler figure smiting a group of bound captives.*

Below *Tomb U-j at Abydos is the largest burial from Predynastic Egypt. Its royal owner must already have ruled a large part of the country.*

familiar from every subsequent period of Egyptian civilization: the king with a mace, smiting his enemies. This was to become the quintessential icon of Egyptian royal power. Yet this Abydos example, the earliest found to date, pre-dates the Narmer Palette by as much as 800 years. Evidently, the concepts and images which were associated with Egypt's kings in historic times had much more ancient roots. Kingship, at least in ideological terms, seems to have begun many centuries before the 1st Dynasty.

One answer to the mystery of Egypt's first kings really lies in what is meant by the word 'king'. The concept of a ruler with semi-divine powers was already established in distant prehistoric times, even before civilization put down roots in the Nile Valley, building towns and cities. By the time Egypt was beginning to emerge as a unified nation-state, rulers who had adopted the trappings of royalty were increasingly common. Some were probably no more than glorified provincial governors, but others may already have controlled most of Egypt. It was in the reign of Narmer that political unification and royal power were consolidated, and expressed through powerful art. From then onwards, the ruling elite ruthlessly promoted kingship as the binding force of ancient Egyptian civilization – which it was to remain for the next 3000 years.

King Menes: myth or reality?

4

The priests told me that Menes was the first king of Egypt.
HERODOTUS, *c.* 430 BC

According to the Greek historian Herodotus, writing in the 5th century BC, the beginning of pharaonic civilization could be traced to a single, decisive act: the diversion of the course of the River Nile by King Menes to provide land for the foundation of a new capital city, Memphis. In this very Greek view of ancient Egyptian history, a heroic deed by a legendary figure paved the way for a glorious future. While some aspects of Herodotus' account are clearly fictitious (p. 264), there is no doubting the importance of the central figure, Menes. Indeed, many centuries before Herodotus, the Egyptians revered Menes – Meni in Egyptian – as their first historic ruler (p. 28). Did such a king, therefore, really exist at the dawn of Egyptian history, or was the Menes story nothing more than a myth?

A founder-king called Meni heads the king-lists drawn up in the Ramesside period, nearly 2000 years after the unification of the country. The most famous is that inscribed on the walls of the temple of King Sety I at Abydos. Two long lines of royal names, each of them written within the characteristic cartouche, or name-ring, list the rulers of Egypt since the beginning of recorded history. Another king-list from the same period is the Turin Royal Canon, written on papyrus; it also begins with Meni. In trying to establish whether such a king ever really existed, a major difficulty arises from the different types of royal name used in Egyptian inscriptions.

Right *The Abydos king-list, compiled during the 19th Dynasty, begins the roll of Egyptian rulers with a king called Meni.*

Matching names with kings

The Abydos king-list and the Turin Canon refer to kings by their cartouche-name, whereas inscriptions from the earliest dynasties generally record the Horus-name, written inside a rectangular panel rather than a name-ring. So the cartouche-name Meni which appears in the king-lists, even if

Left *Fragments of a sealing with the name of Narmer next to the hieroglyphic sign* men(i). *This may indicate that Narmer and Menes are the same person.*

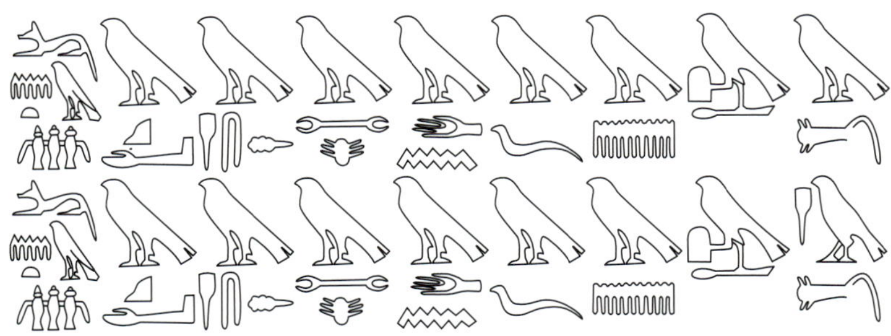

A recently discovered sealing from the royal cemetery at Abydos lists the first eight kings of the 1st Dynasty in chronological order.

it refers to a real king, is unlikely to occur on monuments from his own reign. A further problem lies in the fact that the king-lists contain errors and omissions: not surprising given the huge time-lag between the events they record and the time they were written. Ironically, the Egyptian word *meni* meant 'so-and-so' – it could have been used to indicate a gap in the ancient records from which the king-lists were compiled, rather than the name of a real king.

However, the first eight kings in the Abydos king-list do correspond closely, in name and number, to the rulers known from archaeology as the 1st Dynasty. A recently discovered sealing from the 1st Dynasty royal cemetery known as Umm el-Qa'ab, also at Abydos, lists all eight kings in chronological order. In first place, as founder of the royal line, is a king whose Horus-name was Narmer (p. 28). This agrees closely with modern perceptions, since Narmer is famous for his carved ceremonial palette. This was probably commissioned as an expression of political unification; today it is recognized as an icon of early Egypt, symbolizing the birth of pharaonic civilization. The reign of Narmer also saw the inception of the annals tradition, whereby each year was named after one or more salient events involving the king. So, in a very real sense, Narmer stands at the beginning of Egyptian history; and he is therefore the leading candidate for Menes.

But it is not that simple. In Herodotus' account, Menes' main achievement was the foundation of a new capital at Memphis, while the first king to leave his mark in the vicinity of that city – in the form of a huge tomb, probably built for a close royal relative – was not Narmer, but his successor whose Horus-name was Aha. As a result, many Egyptologists favour the identification of Menes with Aha. Advocates of both points of view can cite 1st Dynasty inscriptions to support their case. A sealing of Narmer shows the king's Horus-name alternating with the sign *men(i)*. This may indicate that Meni was the king's secondary name; but it might equally refer to the king's son. An ivory label from the reign of Aha shows a shrine whose name also incorporates the sign *men(i)*. Depending on one's point of view, it could refer to Aha, to his predecessor, or to neither. Our understanding of these early inscriptions is still too rudimentary to be certain of their meaning.

On balance, the archaeological and inscriptional evidence suggests that the Menes of Herodotus – the Meni of the Egyptian king-lists – was a real historical figure who ruled at the very beginning of the Egyptian state. Whether he is to be equated with the king known to archaeology as Narmer, or with his successor Aha, is still debatable – but Narmer is the more likely identification.

Ivory label of King Aha from Nagada: the name of the shrine at the top right includes the name men(i), *perhaps referring to King Menes.*

Human sacrifice in the royal tombs

The discovery of . . . hundreds of subsidiary burials immediately raised the question of ritual human sacrifice.
Michael Hoffman, 1984

When Flinders Petrie excavated the royal tombs dating to the 1st Dynasty at Abydos, in 1900–01, he was struck by the large numbers of smaller graves that surrounded each king's burial chamber. In the case of King Djer, the royal burial was encircled by no fewer than 317 'subsidiary burials', arranged in massive blocks. This strange phenomenon was repeated elsewhere at Abydos. And in addition to their tombs, the 1st Dynasty kings also built huge 'funerary palaces' nearer to the cultivation lining the River Nile, in full view of the local town. Each of these rectangular enclosures was similarly outlined by rows of numerous small graves. An appalling thought occurred to Petrie: were his discoveries evidence of human sacrifice on a large scale?

Few subjects in archaeology are as emotive or horrific to contemplate as human sacrifice. As far as ancient Egypt is concerned, there are clear indications that this grisly practice was carried out in a ritual context during the 1st Dynasty. Some of the best evidence for early Egyptian culture is provided by small inscribed labels that depict important royal and religious events. Two such labels include a scene of a man plunging a dagger into the breast of a live captive; a bowl is placed between the two figures to catch the blood. The precise significance of this act is not clear, but even in later periods, human sacrifice (of criminals or prisoners-of-war) could occasionally play a part in religious rites.

Royal favour

There is, however, no evidence to suggest that people were routinely killed to accompany the king into the afterlife. Those nearest the king – his family and high officials – might be buried close to their royal master, but only at the time of their own death. Hence the pyramids of the Old Kingdom are surrounded by large court cemeteries; those at Giza comprise row upon row of neatly ordered tombs that were granted to government employees as a sign of royal favour. This practice of 'dependent burial' remained a feature of Egyptian mortuary tradition throughout the pharaonic period.

The subsidiary burials surrounding the royal tombs of the 1st Dynasty differ in one significant respect from their later counterparts. Many of the graves at Abydos were marked on the

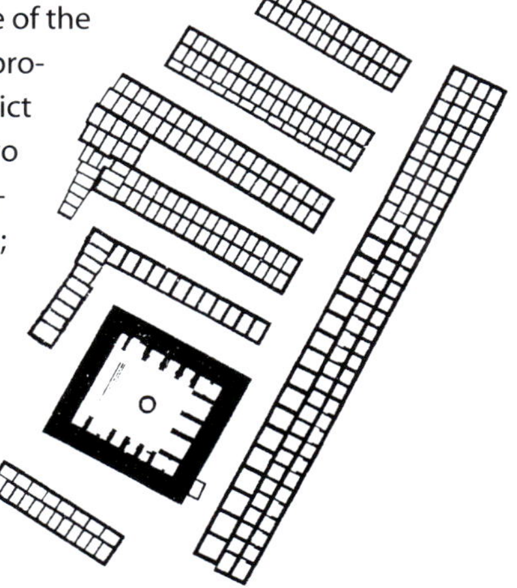

Below left *Plan of King Djer's tomb, with hundreds of subsidiary graves surrounding the royal burial chamber.*

Below *Scenes on 1st Dynasty labels show that human sacrifice was carried out in ritual contexts.*

The graves prepared for King Aha's servants next to his own tomb. The average age at death suggests they did not die of natural causes.

surface by a crude stone slab or 'stela', incised with the name and title of the deceased. To judge from the surviving inscriptions, these gravestones were carved not for members of the royal family or high officials, but for more lowly retainers of the king's household, such as concubines and dwarves (and also for the king's pets). This makes it more likely that the individuals concerned had little or no say in whether they accompanied the king into the afterlife to continue to serve him after death.

Below *Gravestone of a dwarf, one of the many royal retainers buried alongside the 1st Dynasty kings at Abydos.*

To answer the question decisively, the exact circumstances of their death must be established. Unfortunately, before Petrie's excavations at Abydos, centuries of grave-robbing and desecration had destroyed much of the evidence, including most of the human skeletal material. In the rare cases where the occupants of subsidiary burials have survived intact, there is no evidence for them having been buried alive – they do not show the contorted postures found in other cases of human sacrifice, such as in ancient Nubia, Mesopotamia and China. Nor were they interred in mass pits, but rather in individual graves, suggesting they were accorded some degree of respect in death. And no other forensic evidence has come to light for ritual sacrifice, such as decapitation. In fact, the skeletons that have been examined would seem to suggest death by natural causes, were it not for one factor: their age at death. The retainers buried next to the tomb of King Aha were unusually young when they died: none was older than 25. This age profile would not be expected in a normal sample, and does indeed suggest that royal functionaries met their death shortly after their king's.

Murder or suicide?

The most compelling evidence for human sacrifice is provided by two royal tombs from the end of the 1st Dynasty. In the burials of two kings, Semerkhet and Qaa, the subsidiary graves, though few in number, were originally covered by the same superstructure as each king's own burial chamber. This clearly indicates that their occupants must have been interred at the same time as the king, and that their deaths must have coincided with his.

Yet this need not mean that retainers were deliberately murdered. It is also possible that they willingly took their own lives. A startlingly recent parallel illustrates the point: in 1989 when Emperor Hirohito of Japan died, at least one of his faithful old servants committed suicide in order to accompany his master into the next world. In the 1st Dynasty, at the very beginning of Egyptian history, there was little chance of a blessed afterlife for ordinary folk. So for people whose status during life had derived from royal service, the best option for securing some sort of immortality might well have been to accompany the king into his afterlife. In other words, the irresistible force of religious belief and custom could account for subsidiary burials.

Whether or not the retainers buried with the kings of the 1st Dynasty were in fact sacrificed or took their own lives, the practice of subsidiary burial on such a scale did not survive very long. The evidence from the early 2nd Dynasty is unclear, but by the time we reach the end of the 2nd Dynasty, the royal tombs and funerary enclosures at Abydos stand in splendid isolation. The king was now buried surrounded by grave goods rather than human attendants. Retainer sacrifice, or suicide, was an experiment in absolute power, a way of demonstrating the king's authority over life and death. In Egypt, as in other great civilizations, it characterized a newly emerged state whose rulers were seeking ways to extend and consolidate their authority. Yet it was doomed to extinction: the Egyptians were simply too practical a people to continue with a custom that wiped out experienced and valued members of the royal household on a regular basis.

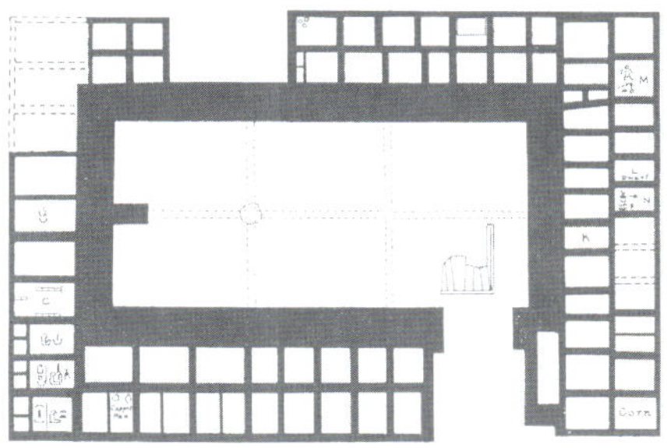

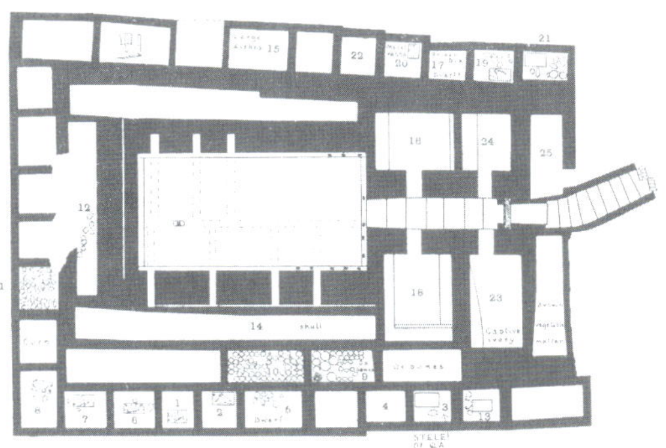

Left *Plans of the tombs of two late 1st Dynasty kings, Semerkhet (above) and Qaa (below), show how the subsidiary graves formed part of the same building plan as the royal burial chamber.*

Below *The tomb of King Qaa at Abydos marks the end of the tradition of retainer sacrifice accompanying royal tombs.*

The royal boat burials at Abydos

Ferried is this [king] Unas to the eastern edge of the horizon.
PYRAMID TEXTS, SPELL 263, *c.* 2325 BC

In 1991 an extraordinary discovery was made at Abydos, in southern Egypt. Twelve enormous, boat-shaped graves, built of mud-brick and each containing an actual boat, lay buried in the desert some 10 km (6.2 miles) due west of the Nile. Why was an entombed fleet 'moored' at this desolate spot? While their archaeological context sheds some light on this puzzle, much about the Abydos boat graves remains mysterious.

Laid out in a neat row (and now known to number 14 in all) the boat graves average 26.25 m (86 ft) in length, with the wooden boats within measuring up to 23 m (75.5 ft). To construct each grave, the wooden hull or shell of the boat was supported in a shallow trench and the brick grave was then constructed around it. The vessel was filled with bricks and the grave's exterior thickly plastered and whitewashed. Each grave rose about 50 cm (20 in) above the then ground level. Long and cigar-like in outline, each grave had a 'prow' and 'stern' boldly modelled in brick. That the entire grave was conceived of as a boat is indicated by the small boulder provided as an anchor or mooring stone in some.

In 1991 and 2000 one boat grave was partially excavated (full excavation will follow). The boat within, although not completely preserved, was built of planks lashed or 'sewn' together by cordage, a technique otherwise unknown for Egyptian vessels. Dating to the 1st Dynasty, the Abydos boats are in fact the earliest built (as distinct from dugout) vessels to survive anywhere in the world. So far, no decking or implements such as oars have been identified. The boats are large enough, and sufficiently well constructed, to be considered functional, rather than models. Rapidly moving craft (not cargo vessels or barges), they could have accommodated up to 30 oarsmen.

Map of Early Dynastic Abydos.

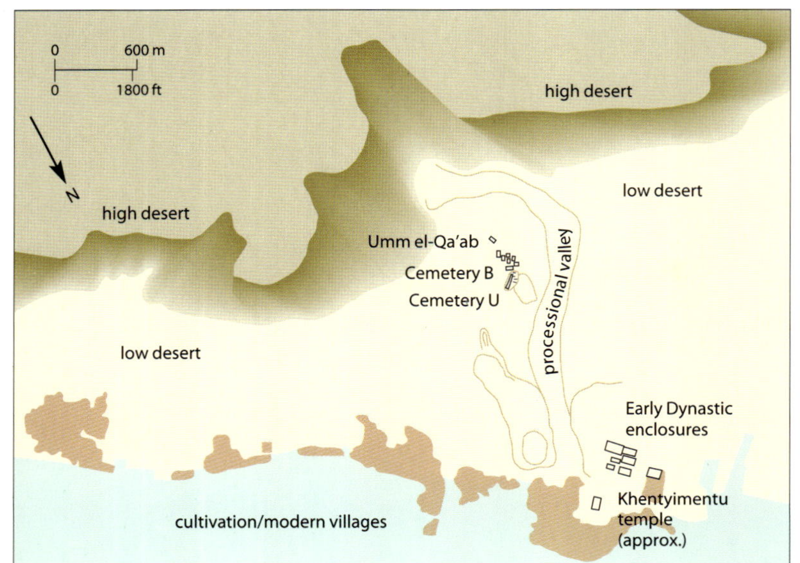

Gifts for a dead king

One function of these boat graves is indicated by their context: in their vicinity are several mud-brick enclosures, each housing a chapel dedicated to the mortuary cult of a deceased king (and a queen-mother) of the 1st Dynasty. These enclosures stood in the desert close to the flood plain, but their royal owners were buried separately from them, at Umm el-Qa'ab, deep in the desert 1.7 km (1 mile) due south. This had been a royal burial ground in earlier times, and continued to be so throughout the 1st Dynasty.

Right *Plan of the Abydos boat graves, showing their relation to mud-brick funerary enclosures dedicated to the funerary cult of Early Dynastic rulers.*

Below *Excavated boat graves at Abydos; in the background is the Early Dynastic enclosure known as the Shunet el-Zebib.*

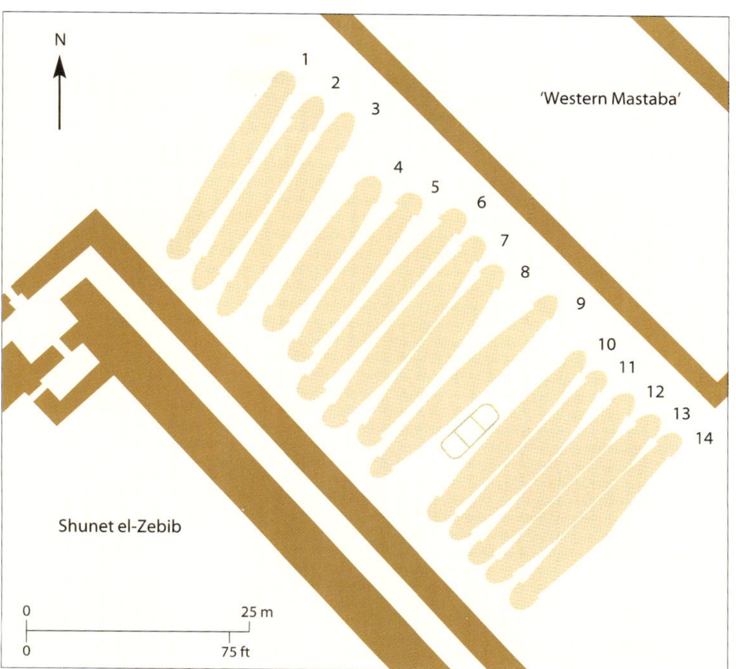

Impressive in overall scale, the enclosures vary in size; the smallest known occupies just 0.07 ha (0.17 acre), while two average 0.18 ha (0.44 acre) and two 0.43 ha (1 acre). Their walls were usually thick, and perhaps rose 9–10 m (29.5–33 ft) high. Yet each enclosure seems to have been deliberately razed soon after the burial of its royal owner. Some enclosures were surrounded by subsidiary graves (as were all the royal tombs) belonging to courtiers and retainers who were perhaps sacrificed so as to be of service to the dead king in the afterlife (p. 36). Even the razing of each enclosure was a form of 'burial', so it too fully entered the

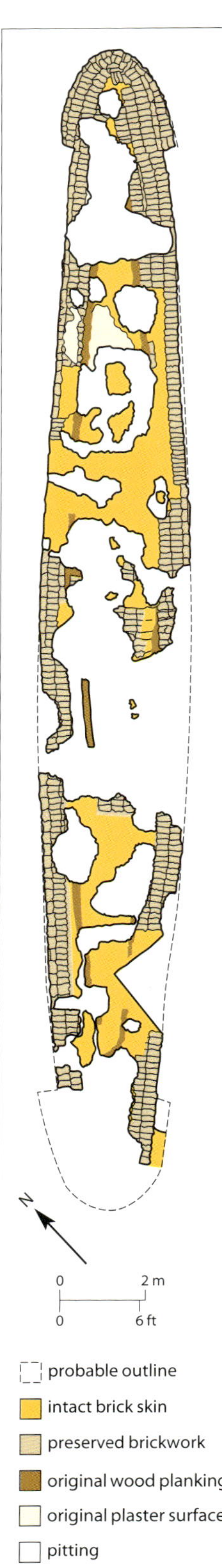

afterlife for the king's benefit. Clearly, the buried boats were believed to do the same, and in fact contemporary elite tombs at Saqqara and Helwan were also sometimes supplied with buried boats. The elite, however, had only one boat per tomb, and the boat graves were smaller and less elaborate than the Abydos examples. Moreover, none actually survived.

Although the mortuary character of the associated enclosures thus helps us to understand something of the nature of the boats and boat graves, many other questions remain unanswered. Which king owned them? Pottery deposited as an offering near the boat graves was associated with mud jar seals impressed with hieroglyphic texts, but as yet no royal name has been found. The boat graves also line up neatly, perhaps purposely, with one of the enclosures, but the owner of the latter is also unknown.

Above *Two of the Abydos boat graves; note the small boulder (an anchor or mooring stone) visible in the centre of the left-hand example.*

Left *Plan of a boat grave; the pitting is due to later graves and intrusions.*

Further, what is the precise relationship between boat and grave? To some degree, the latter reflects the shape of the boat around which it was built, yet the grave, while boat-shaped, is more elaborate in form. Perhaps the actual boat and the boat grave form a single entity, a 'conceptual' boat modelled in wood *and* brick.

Sailing through eternity

What kinds of boats were thus symbolized, and what use was the deceased king believed to have made of them? Did they represent the funerary fleet that conveyed and escorted his body from Memphis (where the kings actually lived) to Abydos, 430 km (269 miles) to the south? Perhaps the boats, like the clothing, furniture, food and drink placed in the royal tombs, were considered items the king would need for practical purposes in the afterlife. They might represent supply ships guaranteed magically to deliver endless amounts of grain. Indeed, a buried boat near an elite tomb at Saqqara was associated with model buildings that might represent granaries.

Could the Abydos boats be more transcendent in purpose? In later mortuary beliefs, as attested in the Pyramid Texts and subsequent sources, dead kings are described as needing boats to traverse the watery wastes of the afterlife, evading danger and reaching safe, protected ground and providing ritual attention and endless sustenance. Moreover, reference is often made to the barques of the sun god – both day and night – which enable him to traverse the world of the living and the realms of the netherworld. This endlessly repeated cycle regenerates both the sun god and the cosmos which depends on him for life and order. Deceased kings and others sought to join the solar cycle, and even assume the sun god's form, to ensure their personal immortality. Two of the Abydos boat graves, set side by side, are subtly different in their proportions from the others: could they represent solar barques? Finally, how do the Abydos royal boat graves relate to the boats, boat graves and boat pits associated with some later royal pyramids of the Old and Middle Kingdoms? The Abydos graves are probably the prototype for the later ones, which sometimes include actual boats, such as Khufu's magnificent vessel, 45.38 m/143 ft long, buried next to his Great Pyramid at Giza, or pits cut in such a way as to embody a boat, much as the boat graves of Abydos do. How we get from the early boat graves to the later examples remains a further mystery, waiting to be solved.

Centre *A wooden boat of King Khufu, which was found disassembled and buried in a large pit next to the king's pyramid at Giza.*

Below *An Abydos boat grave with some of the boat timbers excavated.*

Pyramids & Tombs

'Think of it, soldiers, from the summit of these pyramids, forty centuries look down upon you.' Napoleon Bonaparte, ahead of battle outside Cairo in 1798, encouraged his troops by luring them into Egypt's web of enchantment. Emperors, alchemists, philosophers and archaeologists have all tried to unravel the mysteries of ancient Egypt, not least the secrets of its massive and silent pyramids and tombs.

Of course, there have been other, more cynical views: another Frenchman, Gustave Flaubert, dismissed the pyramids, saying 'jackals piss at the bottom, and the bourgeois climb to the top'. And for some they bear witness to the cruelty and conceit of tyrants. But why were they built in the shape of a pyramid? What do we know about the origins of these extraordinary structures? We certainly know that pyramids were burial places, but we also now recognize that each was the focus for a complex of buildings. So what was a pyramid, in this broader sense, actually for?

Since the 19th century, many writers have argued that the pyramids – especially those at Giza – were built not by Egyptians at all but by a lost civilization, perhaps even extra-terrestrials. One recent claim is that the Great Sphinx is much older than scholars admit when they date it to the reign of Khufu's son, Khafre. Is there any basis to this idea? Another argument is that the pyramids are aligned with stars in the ancient night sky, and that this is the key to their design. Even if such ideas are dismissed, there are innumerable other questions about the Great Pyramid of Khufu. One

A century ago, the Step Pyramid of Djoser (Netjerykhet) at Saqqara seemed to be the oldest monument in the world. Today we know much more about Egypt before his reign, and can start to answer questions about the origins of pyramids.

A corridor within the labyrinthine tomb KV 5, built by Ramesses II as a shared tomb for his many sons in the Valley of the Kings, Western Thebes. It is more complex than any other tomb known in Egypt, and suggests that there may be more surprises in store as we explore the ancient Egyptian way of death.

such is the long-standing claim that a secret repository of knowledge, the 'Hall of Records', waits to be found nearby.

Untold men and women laboured, and no doubt suffered, to build the pyramids. But were they slaves? Khufu was indeed condemned in Egyptian tradition as arrogant and cruel. On the other hand, his father, Snofru, who seems to have built at least three huge pyramids, was remembered as a jovial man. Why would any king, however haughty, need three pyramids? And what of the evidence that those who actually sweated over the stones were willing participants and highly regarded craftsmen?

Napoleon was remarkably accurate in appreciating the age of the pyramids: they do indeed date back 4000 years or more, to the Old and Middle Kingdoms, and served as the traditional royal tomb for 1000 years. Ironically, however, we do not know for sure who was buried in the last major pyramid, built at Abydos around 1530 BC, although here we assess the evidence. Subsequently, during the New Kingdom, the royal cemetery moved to the Valley of the Kings, outside the great southern city of Thebes. The tombs of the Valley have been pored over by Westerners since the last centuries BC, but even today we cannot be confident we know all that is there. For example, the workmen who built the tombs worshipped King Amenhotep I as their patron, and for centuries after his death held festivals in his honour. But his tomb has never been identified, although Howard Carter – who later discovered the tomb of Tutankhamun – claimed he had found it in 1914. Tantalizingly an ancient document has survived describing the exact location of the tomb, albeit in obscure terms. In 1908, near the mouth of the Valley at Qurneh, another celebrated archaeologist, Flinders Petrie, made a discovery which creates the opposite puzzle. He found the intact burial of an exceptionally important woman and child – but who were they?

For 400 years every king of Egypt was buried in the Valley, with the sole exception of Akhenaten. He certainly prepared a tomb at Amarna, but perhaps was never buried in it. So where was the last resting-place of this most controversial king? And how does this relate to the mysterious tomb KV 55? Of course, a key question regarding the Valley of the Kings is why the magnificent grave-goods of the wealthiest rulers of the ancient world are missing. Was this the result of opportunist robbery by desperate peasants? Or was it a systematic policy of the government itself to rob the kings of their treasures in order to bolster the failing economy of a once great nation?

Whatever the Valley's fate, after the New Kingdom the royal cemetery returned north, to Tanis, where, since 1939, several kings' tombs have been excavated – largely intact – by French archaeologists. However, these tombs include only some of the kings of this period. Hence the riddle of the missing tombs of Tanis.

During the last 15 years, the rediscovery and excavation in the Valley of the Kings of a mausoleum built for the sons of Ramesses II has revealed an unparalleled tomb with a breathtaking number of chambers – more than 150 to date with the promise of more to come. Why is it so complex? And does such a discovery allow us one final, haunting question: will the deserts of Egypt ever yield one more golden harvest to rival the discovery of the tomb of Tutankhamun?

Origins of the pyramids

7

Was the Great Pyramid, then erected before the invention of hieroglyphics, and previous to the birth of the false Egyptian religion?
PIAZZI SMYTH, 1864

The pyramid is a classic expression of Egyptian civilization, but its origins are a matter of debate and controversy. Pyramids, and their associated buildings, seem to appear abruptly and on a large scale, as if a radical innovation. The first pyramid complex is King Djoser's (*c.* 2640 BC) at Saqqara; entirely stone built, it comprises a step pyramid 60 m (197 ft) high surrounded by an enclosed complex occupying 13.9 ha (34.4 acres). The previous largest royal monument, a mud-brick enclosure of King Khasekhemwy (Djoser's predecessor) at Abydos, defined a mere 0.81 ha (2 acres) of largely empty space. After Djoser, for a period, pyramid growth

A view of the Step Pyramid of King Djoser at Saqqara; in the foreground are stone chapels – symbolic rather than real, they are largely filled solid with rubble.

Diagram to show a suggested evolution of the pyramid, from the tomb and enclosure of King Djer (1st Dynasty) to the Bent Pyramid complex of King Snofru (4th Dynasty).

1 *enclosure*
2 *surface mound above tomb*
3 *chapel*
4 *dummy tomb or pyramid*
5 *dummy chapel*
6 *step or true pyramid*
7 *mortuary temple*
8 *causeway and valley temple*

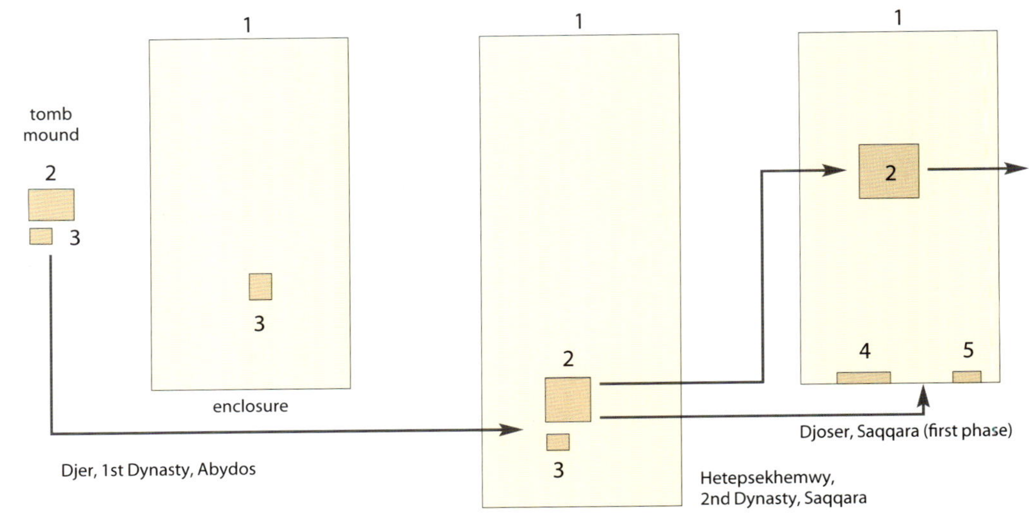

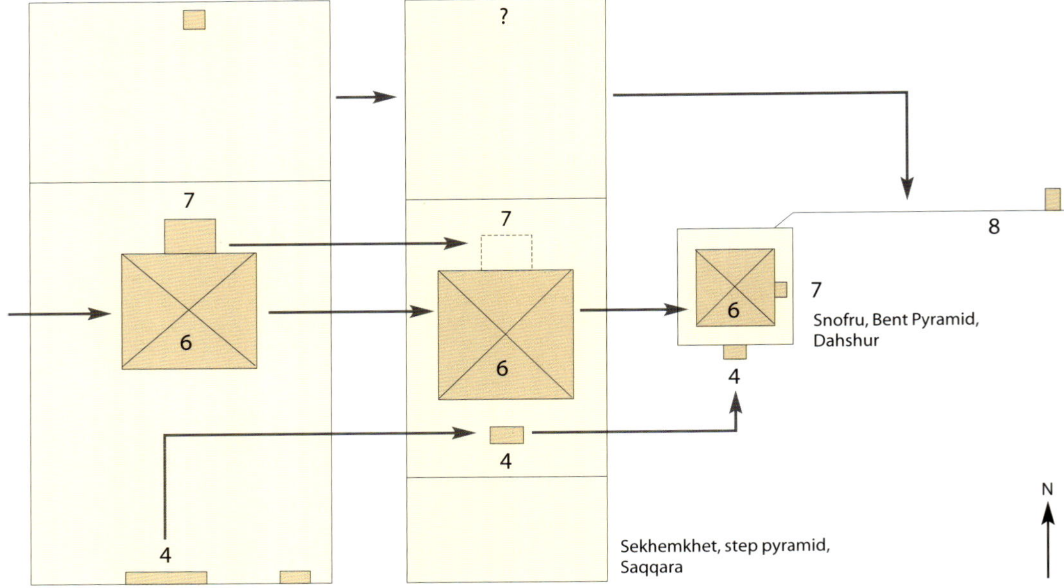

and development was exponential: Djoser's successors throughout the 3rd Dynasty built step pyramids, but in less than a century the true pyramid appeared, and by Khufu's reign (*c.* 2540 BC) had reached staggering proportions – 146.6 m (480.8 ft) high and occupying 5.3 ha (13 acres).

Yet the pyramid complex was not as innovative as it at first seems. Recent discoveries have confirmed earlier impressions that the essentials of the complex were present in the earliest royal mortuary monuments, built through the Early Dynastic period – the 1st and 2nd Dynasties. However, these are modest in both scale and materials, often now severely damaged or denuded, and incompletely known. Consequently, scholars still disagree about the actual evolutionary process.

The proto-pyramid of the 1st Dynasty

Egypt's earliest kings, of the 1st Dynasty, were all buried at Abydos (p. 28). Some scholars suggest that contemporary sepulchres at Saqqara were the real royal tombs and the Abydos ones were cenotaphs (dummy tombs) of more conservative type. But most recognize that the large mortuary enclosures (p. 38) which complement the Abydos tombs establish their unique royal status.

The 1st Dynasty royal tombs always incorporated a large brick structure, built in a pit and capped by a subterranean mound, and were surrounded by subsidiary graves for courtiers and retainers who accompanied their royal master into the afterlife (p. 35). Any surface features of these early royal tombs are debatable, for no actual traces survive. A large amount of sand and gravel would have been removed when the pit was excavated, and this may then have been used to cap the royal tomb with a relatively large surface mound, held in place by brick walls. Given its relationship to the royal tomb, this feature can reasonably be called a proto-pyramid, though we have as yet no indication it was ever stepped.

One tomb (that of King Den) had an anomalous feature – a substantial but subterranean statue chapel outside its south corner. Similar chapels may have stood at surface level outside each tomb, probably south of the surface mound. The inspiration for this feature perhaps came from pre-existing installations for deities – an earlier temple at Hierakonpolis consisted of a large mound with a cult structure to its approximate south.

The 1st Dynasty royal tombs at Abydos were set deep in the desert, at the site of earlier and presumably still significant royal burials, and are so crowded together that none could have had a large enclosed space around it. However, a mortuary enclosure was provided for each king about 1.7 km (1 mile) due north of the tombs, closer to the inhabited flood plain.

Of the eight 1st Dynasty enclosures that are likely to have existed, six definite or probable examples have been located. Clustered together, they vary in size but, judging from available evidence, were similar in plan and layout. Each enclosure was rectangular, and oriented (approximately) north–south. Walls were relatively massive and rose perhaps as high as 9–10 m (29.5–33 ft). Within each enclosure was a chapel, at or close to the centre of its southern half; the remaining space may have been largely empty and the theory that a surface mound stood in the north half has proved untenable. The enclosures are mortuary in function; some are provided with subsidiary graves and one with boat burials (p. 38), like contemporary elite tombs at Saqqara. Moreover, each enclosure seems to have been razed, that is metaphorically buried, soon after the burial of its royal owner. Thus, in some way the enclosure and its chapel serviced the mortuary cult of the deceased king, even if only for a limited period.

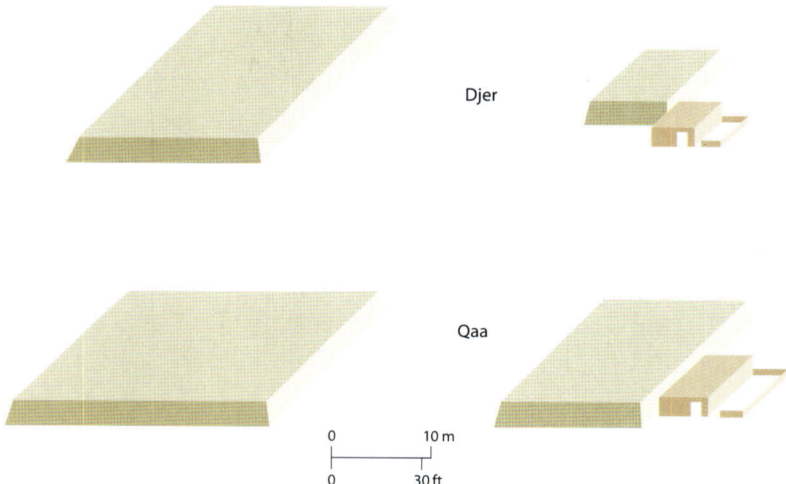

Above *Two versions, suggested by Günter Dreyer (left) and David O'Connor (right), of the surface features above the Early Dynastic royal tombs at Abydos, exemplified by those of Djer and Qaa. Dreyer suggests a large if simple surface mound, O'Connor a smaller surface mound with adjacent chapel near the southwest corner.*

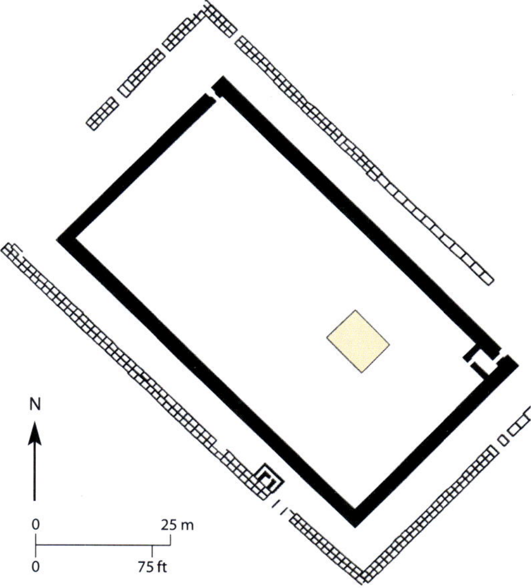

Left *Enclosure of the 1st Dynasty King Djer, with interior chapel and surrounding subsidiary graves.*

Origins of Djoser's Step Pyramid complex

The last kings of the 2nd Dynasty were also buried at Abydos, and they too had separate tombs and enclosures. However, the earlier 2nd Dynasty kings moved their tombs to Saqqara. These kings were buried in deep, rock-cut tombs of much greater size and complexity than the earlier royal tombs at Abydos. Some think that these Saqqara tombs also had physically separate enclosures, but the evidence cited may refer to incomplete step pyramid complexes of the 3rd Dynasty. Instead, as both tomb and enclosure were now close to the flood plain, it is probable that, for the first time, they were combined. An extensive area of subterranean magazines always lay to the north of the tomb complex, and thus in these conjectural Saqqara enclosures the tomb would have been located in the southern half, presumably capped, as at Abydos, by a surface mound and perhaps with a chapel, again on the south.

An aerial view of Djoser's Step Pyramid complex, at Saqqara, with its various features visible.

In its first phase, Djoser's 3rd Dynasty funerary monument consisted of a rectangular enclosure with a stone-built mound (not a pyramid) over the tomb, following the archaic model provided at Abydos and, presumably, Saqqara. Tomb and mound moved to the north half of the enclosure, but in the south half stood the mysterious, non-functional south tomb and a nearby chapel, also non-functional. These may be archaeological fossils – memorials to the tomb and chapel which had literally stood here in the preceding 2nd Dynasty enclosures.

From the step to the true pyramid

Even the transition to what became the standard, true pyramid complex during the 4th Dynasty is problematical, yet a plausible continuity can be made out. Step pyramids of the 3rd Dynasty, insofar as they are documented, had a mortuary temple immediately to the north, and were set within large rectangular enclosures oriented

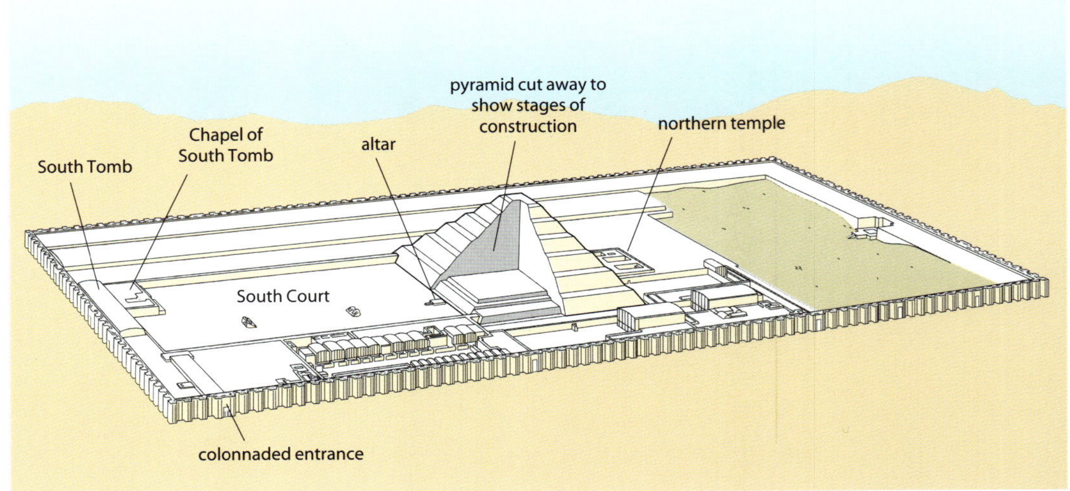

Reconstruction of Djoser's Step Pyramid complex in its final form.

The three classic pyramids of Giza, from right to left: Khufu's, Khafre's and Menkaure's.

approximately north–south. The enclosed area north of each pyramid was especially spacious, and could include an open-air altar, while south of each pyramid was a non-functional tomb in addition to the tomb proper under the pyramid itself. The typical 4th Dynasty complex lacked the extensive rectangular enclosure, its mortuary temple was east, not north of the pyramid, while a small satellite pyramid lay to the south. A long causeway led down to a valley temple, close to the flood plain.

Yet the later developments can be traced back to the earlier. Already under Sekhemkhet, Djoser's successor, the enclosed space around the pyramid shrank and architectural complexity simplified, even if the overall rectangular shape was maintained by added enclosures to the north and south. The 'south tomb' of the 3rd Dynasty is the prototype for the southern satellite pyramid (itself a non-functional tomb) of the later complexes. The movement of the mortuary temple from north to east is more momentous, but not necessarily a shift from a stellar orientation to one following the east–west trajectory of the sun, the regenerative deity of the cosmos. The solar cycle also has a north–south axis (reflecting its annual progression along the horizons) so the 3rd Dynasty mortuary temple could have had solar significance also. Causeway and valley temple are innovative, but may relate to the poorly known features located north of the 3rd Dynasty mortuary temple, now swung around to the east and changed in form, but not necessarily in basic meaning.

Surprisingly perhaps, the transition from step to true pyramid, with the first example built by King Snofru at Dahshur in *c.* 2565 BC (p. 57), may be the least problematical. Some speculate it represents a changed concept, from a stairway to heaven and the stars to a representation of radiating sun rays, but the supporting evidence is weak. Basically, both forms are variations of a gigantically scaled mound, which structurally had to take on pyramidal form to accommodate the stresses and strains created by the great increase in size.

If the origins of the pyramid are therefore becoming clearer, there are still areas of debate and hypothesis which may be confirmed or replaced by future excavations.

What is a pyramid for?

O Atum [creator god], set your protection over this king, over this pyramid of his ...
prevent anything from happening evilly against it ever.
PYRAMID TEXTS, SPELL 600, *c.* 2325 BC

The pyramids are the most famous of all the spectacular constructions of the ancient Egyptians. Despite a 6th-century AD suggestion that they were the granaries of Joseph, and numerous and varied more recent theories as to their purpose, Egyptologists are united in interpreting pyramids as tombs, although the significance of the pyramidal shape remains a matter of debate. Pyramids should not be interpreted as objects in isolation: each major pyramid forms the focus of a larger complex which includes temples or chapels for the mortuary cult, often with a causeway and other ancillary structures, and surrounded by an enclosure wall.

Pyramid Texts inscribed on the walls of a chamber inside the pyramid of Teti at Saqqara.

The majority of pyramids had an entrance in their north face (although this changed in the Middle Kingdom) leading to one or more chambers towards the centre of the structure when looked at in plan. In section, the chambers are located at or below the base of the pyramid, although the Great Pyramid, which has a particularly complex and unusual internal arrangement, has chambers set high up within the built structure (p. 61). In the pyramids of the later Old Kingdom, chambers were decorated with a series of spells known as the Pyramid Texts which were designed to ensure that the king was reanimated after death and would enjoy a continued existence in the afterlife. Vivian Davies and Renée Friedman have described the pyramid as a 'resurrection machine', and there is no doubt that the design of the pyramid was intended to aid the transfiguration of the king. It is clear from the Pyramid Texts that the pyramid was also intended to last for eternity, protecting the king's body and providing a focus for his mortuary cult.

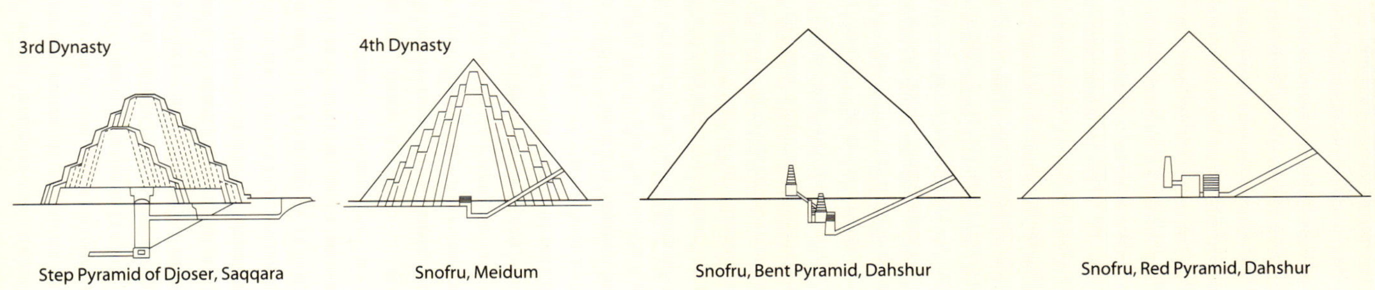

Step Pyramid of Djoser, Saqqara — Snofru, Meidum — Snofru, Bent Pyramid, Dahshur — Snofru, Red Pyramid, Dahshur

The south face of the Step Pyramid at Saqqara. Part of the lowest step has fallen away, revealing the original design of the king's burial place in the form of a mastaba.

Pyramids as tombs

No pyramid has been found with an intact burial in modern times. This is hardly surprising since pyramids are rather obvious places to search for hidden treasure and the majority were ransacked in antiquity. Fragments of mummies have often been recovered, but as they derive from disturbed contexts it is rarely possible to be certain that these body parts belonged to an original occupant of the pyramid and not a later intrusive burial. However, many pyramids contain stone sarcophagi dating to the time of their construction and these clearly demonstrate the intention to bury someone within. In the case of the Great Pyramid, the granite sarcophagus is too large to fit through the door of the burial chamber and can only have been placed there during construction.

The function of pyramids as tombs is also clear when their development is studied. Antecedents for the pyramids can be traced to the tombs of the kings and elite of the Early Dynastic Period (p. 45), many of which were found to contain corpses and burial goods when they were excavated. These tombs are often referred to as mastaba or 'bench-shaped', and the change from the mastaba to the stepped pyramid can be seen in Djoser's pyramid at Saqqara. The outer casing of this pyramid has fallen away on the south face to reveal the constructional phases through which a mastaba tomb was first enlarged and then transformed to a four-stepped and later a six-stepped pyramid enveloping the original tomb.

The change from stepped to true pyramids occurred at the beginning of the 4th Dynasty in the reign of Snofru, who constructed first a stepped pyramid (Meidum) and then a true pyramid which turned out to be unstable and had to be finished off at a shallower angle (the Bent

The development of the pyramid in the Old Kingdom: north–south sections, to the same scale. The sequence is not complete but illustrates trends in the evolution of the pyramidal form to the end of the 5th Dynasty.

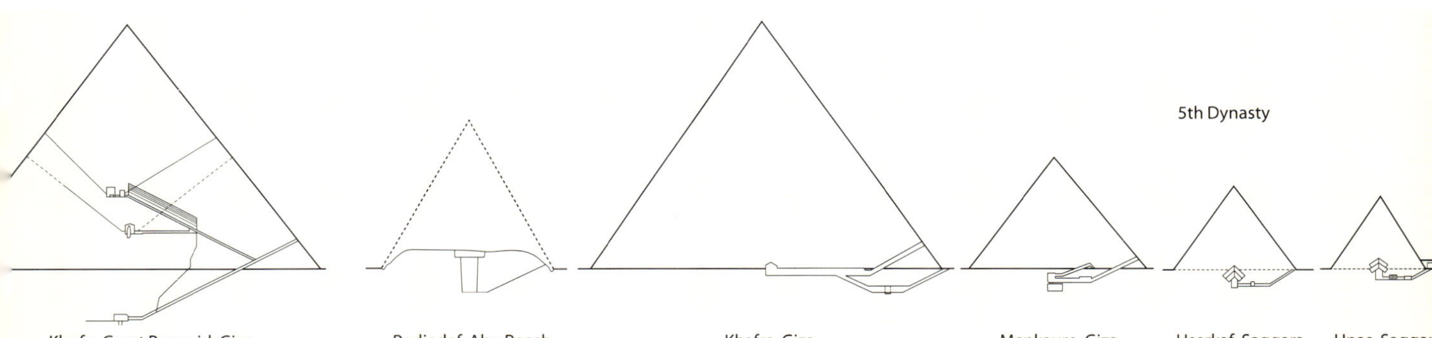

A small stepped pyramid at Zawiyet Sultan in Middle Egypt. One of a series of small, non-funerary pyramids built in the 3rd or 4th Dynasty, these pyramids may be markers of royal authority in provincial capitals around the country.

Pyramid). Finally he constructed a shallow true pyramid (the Red Pyramid) and returned to Meidum to case his original stepped pyramid so that this too was a true pyramid (p. 57). Today the pyramids of the 4th Dynasty are the best preserved because they were the most carefully constructed. Later pyramids were not as large and since they therefore did not need to be so well-built they are now poorly preserved.

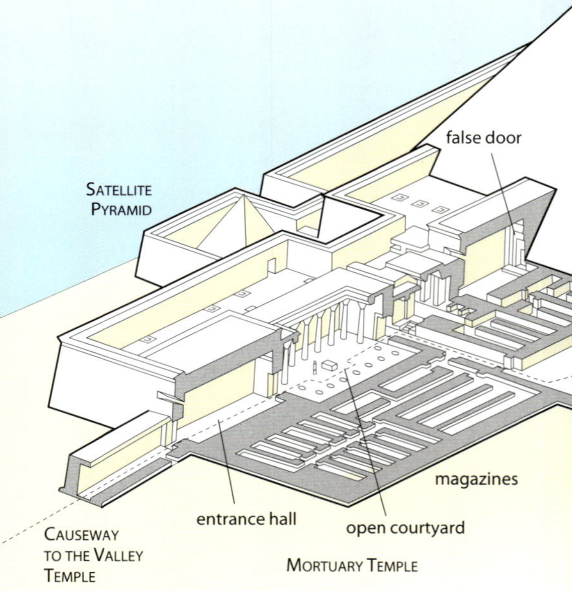

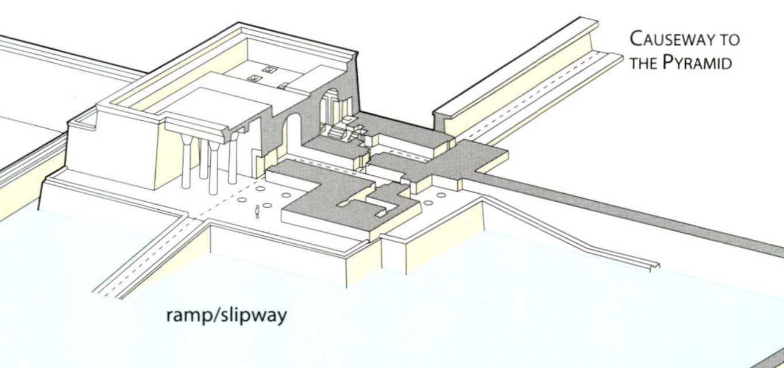

Reconstruction of Unas' pyramid complex showing the many elements which, together with the pyramid itself, provided suitable mortuary provision for a king.

Other pyramids

The first pyramids were built for kings but, before long, the pyramidal shape was employed also for the tombs of important wives and daughters of the king. These ancillary pyramids are usually built just outside the enclosure wall of the main pyramid complex. The pyramid continued to be the preferred form of royal burial until the beginning of the New Kingdom when royal burials began to be carved into the cliffs of the Valley of the Kings at Thebes. At about the same period, the custom of incorporating small pyramids into the design of private tombs was initiated.

There are exceptions to most rules and there are indeed two groups of Egyptian pyramids which were never intended to contain burials. First, there are 'satellite pyramids' which are small pyramids found adjacent to the majority of royal pyramids. While these were not for burials they are unquestionably part of the mortuary provision of the main pyramid's owner. Each has a small internal chamber which is possibly a symbolic burial place for the *ka* (the 'double' or 'life force') of the king. Secondly, there is a group of small stepped pyramids which do not contain burial chambers and which date to the 3rd or early 4th Dynasty. These are found along the Nile in places which were once provincial capitals. Their design derives from the larger step pyramids built as tombs, and one suggestion is that they were intended to be markers of royal authority in the provinces.

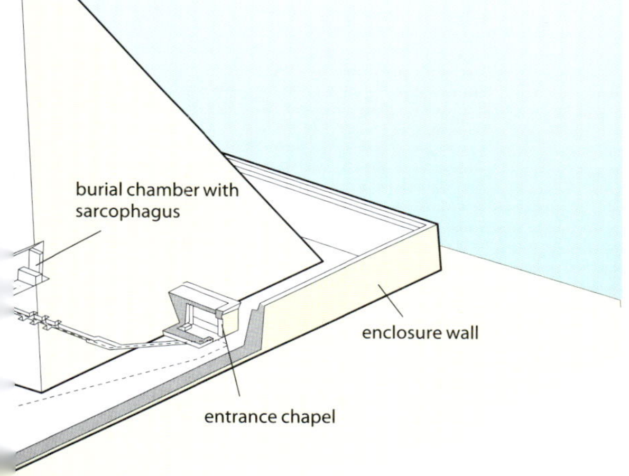

The 'Black Pyramid' of Amenemhat III at Dahshur. The core of this pyramid was made of mud-brick, hence its distinctive dark colour. Pyramids built after the 4th Dynasty were often built with mud or rubble cores, and as a result preservation is generally poor.

Function and form

While the function of pyramids as tombs is well established, the reason why tombs were constructed in a pyramidal shape is much less certain. At one level, the pyramidal shape unquestionably served to differentiate the burial of the king from those of his retainers and subjects, thus reinforcing the difference between his semi-divine nature and that of ordinary mortals. Because of their scale and unusual shape, pyramids were visible from great distances – a constant reminder of the presence and power of the divine king. The Pyramid Texts associate the pyramid with the primeval mound and the shape could be interpreted as a stylized mountain. The stepped form of the early pyramids is often interpreted as a staircase to the sky and the early true pyramids, which are massive, may have been an extension of the intention to build the tallest structure possible, thus allowing the deceased king to mount to the sky. In purely practical terms, a pyramid is a good shape to use when building such a huge structure to counter all the stresses created by the weight of material. Other theories associate the pyramidal shape with the sun's rays as they break through the clouds or with the *benben* stone, a sacred stone in the temple at Heliopolis which some have suggested was a meteorite.

Were the pyramids built by slaves?

[Khufu] brought the country into all sorts of misery. He closed all the temples, then, not content with excluding his subjects from the practice of their religion, compelled them without exception to labour as slaves for his own advantage.

HERODOTUS, *c.* 430 BC

Although admired by ancient and modern people alike, a grave question mark hangs over the building of Egypt's pyramids: how do we reconcile our minds to the paradox that one of the greatest achievements of humanity may have been the result of the suffering and exploitation of human beings at the hands of their fellow men? This accusation has been made since ancient times, including by great historians such as Herodotus, and the image of the pyramids being built by oppressed Hebrews during their captivity in Egypt still holds some sway today in the popular imagination.

A fanciful 19th-century image of the pyramids being built by hundreds of slaves, labouring under oppressive conditions.

Written records and social status

But practical considerations alone pose some problems for the proponents of slave labour. For example, the physical control of the masses of people coerced in this way – whether Egyptian or foreign – would have demanded a security apparatus of extraordinary magnitude: would this have exceeded the abilities of Egypt in the Old

Kingdom? And even if not, the enforced conscription of slaves on a vast scale would surely have merited a prominent mention in the written records of such a literate society. Yet there are no references to slaves or slavery in texts from the Old Kingdom period.

Of course, written records are not the only form of evidence available to Egyptology. For over a century, the villages of the workers who built and decorated the royal tombs of the New Kingdom have been known at Deir el-Medina and Amarna. In both places the study of the archaeological evidence points to the fact that these villagers were far from being enslaved. On the contrary, the workmen led pleasant lives as members of a social elite, exempt from producing their own food and clothes, and were employed as skilled and trusted craftsmen manufacturing all the things which conferred on the deceased king an eternal life among the gods. Earlier still, texts and remains from the Middle Kingdom town of Kahun, which serviced the funerary cult of the pyramid of Senwosret II, reveal a population whose social status is above that of their neighbouring communities. Could Egyptian society have changed so much that tasks performed in later periods (Middle and New Kingdoms) by a privileged elite were consigned to slaves in an earlier period (Old Kingdom)? No comparable inversion of social values is known for any other aspect of ancient Egyptian culture.

Tombs and homes of the pyramid builders

Nevertheless, for many years the evidence provided by the later workers' villages at Deir el-Medina, Amarna and Kahun was not matched by any evidence from the Old Kingdom that corroborated what common sense and archaeology suggested. But now the Giza plateau has yielded a number of structures related to the pyramid builders themselves. In the late 1980s, Zahi Hawass unearthed a series of mud-brick buildings to the east of Khufu's pyramid. Inside were thousands of fragments of everyday pottery, bread moulds and kitchenware. These buildings probably form the town known from contemporary documents as *Gerget Khufu* ('settlement of Khufu'), and it is likely that its inhabitants were engaged in building and maintaining the Great Pyramid of that pharaoh. And since 1992 Hawass has also excavated a number of tombs belonging to the people of the town, some with reliefs and inscriptions. Owning a tomb is hardly typical for a slave in ancient Egypt, and so it is clear that some at least of these people were among the elite of the population.

Other recent work on the plateau has revealed the importance of a town, first discovered in 1906 by George Reisner, in the shadow of the pyramid of Menkaure. This town continued in existence after the death of the king in order to maintain his funerary cult in return for tax exemptions. The specific relationship between such funerary towns and the

Above *Casing and core blocks at the base of Khafre's pyramid, in which the characteristic shape of the hieroglyph meaning 'order' can be perceived.*

Below *A modern reconstruction of pyramid building tested various possible methods by which the huge blocks could be moved.*

Above *A mud-brick tomb of one of the pyramid builders found at Giza. Such tombs are evidence that the builders of the pyramids were of high status.*

workers' villages themselves is far from certain. However, in the case of Giza, the answer might have been provided by excavations currently going on southeast of the 'Wall of the Crow', a stone wall apparently bordering the whole sacred precinct. Structures in this area have been identified as refectories and dormitories, and Mark Lehner has located the remains of what seems to be a bakery and a place for preparing and preserving fish. Here we are probably among the facilities that provided food and shelter for the 20,000 or more people engaged in building the pyramids. All these discoveries seem to confirm that the workers on the royal pyramid enjoyed a special status, often more elevated than that of their fellow citizens.

So there is nothing in the written or archaeological record to suggest that the pyramid builders were slaves. On the contrary, their work was probably perceived as an essential contribution to an important task. The communities of Egypt in the Old Kingdom – literate, well administered, cohesive and economically interdependent – were able to co-ordinate their efforts in an organized manner to proclaim the presence of the divine monarch on earth. Without doubt the workers came from within Egyptian society as conscript levies drawn from different parts of the country. The technical achievement of these gigantic structures reflects a massive social accomplishment, which drew thousands of human beings away from their homes, then housed, fed and clothed them during their time at Giza.

As a final and everlasting testament to subsequent generations, this administration dedicated the pyramids to the power and beneficence of the king whose reign made such an achievement possible. So the pyramids are the result of developments both in funerary and religious ideas, and in the Egyptian social body itself. Block by block, the construction of a pyramid was a celebration of the order established by the Egyptian state, with the king at its summit.

A reconstruction, based on excavated evidence, of a bakery in the shadow of the Giza pyramids. Bread and beer would have been the principal food rations that sustained the workforce building the pyramids.

The multiple pyramids of Snofru

10

May heaven rain with fresh myrrh, may it drip with incense upon the roof of the temple of King Snofru.
GRAFFITO OF AAKHEPERKARESONB, *c.* 1475 BC

Only one of the pyramids of the 3rd Dynasty has survived entire until today – the Step Pyramid of Djoser. However, from the reign of the founder of the 4th Dynasty, Snofru, we have something of an embarrassment of riches, with no fewer than four pyramids associated with his name, and yet more potentially built by him.

The smallest of the four was built at Seila, on the margin of the Faiyum. Only 30 m (98 ft) square, it has no internal chambers, but a stela naming Snofru was recovered from a chapel on the eastern side. Six similar monuments are known, stretching from Zawiyet Sultan in Middle Egypt to Elephantine in Upper Egypt; none have revealed royal names, although architecturally they clearly belong around the end of the 3rd or the beginning of the 4th Dynasty. It has been suggested that their builder was Huni, the last king of the 3rd Dynasty, but their close similarity with the Seila structure suggests that they may have also been built by Snofru for the same, unknown, purpose.

The remaining three pyramids associated with Snofru are in some ways more problematic, as all were 'proper' pyramids, of considerable size and with a full set of interior passages and chambers. Clearly, only one can have been the king's actual tomb: were the remaining two structures really Snofru's at all, and, if so, why did he build them?

The Dahshur pyramids

We do in fact know that Snofru did have at least two pyramids, since two are mentioned in an

Stela of Snofru from the chapel of the subsidiary pyramid of the Bent Pyramid at Dahshur.

inscription of Pepy I from Dahshur. Indeed, two pyramids at this site, the Bent Pyramid and the Red Pyramid, have contemporary inscriptions which leave no doubt that Snofru was their builder. Architecturally, the Bent Pyramid is the earlier of the pair; it is also unique in changing its angle half way up and having two separate substructures, one approached from the north and the other from the west. Both feature high, corbel-vaulted chambers and vestibules, distinctive of the reigns of Snofru and his successor, Khufu. (In corbel-vaulting the roof is spanned by successive courses of blocks, each set slightly further out than the one below until they meet at the apex.)

The Bent Pyramid's peculiarities seem to be the result of structural problems experienced during the early stages of construction. As a result, the northern substructure may have been regarded as potentially dangerous, with a wholly new set of chambers provided on the west, and the overall weight of the pyramid reduced by lowering the angle of the upper section. These expedients were apparently judged insufficient to guarantee the eternal safety of the king's mummy, however, since another pyramid was

The Red Pyramid of Snofru at Dahshur is the earliest geometrically 'true' pyramid and the third largest in Egypt.

begun 2 km (1.25 miles) to the north, which seems to have been used as the king's tomb and final resting place.

Snofru's Red Pyramid, the earliest geometrically 'true' pyramid, is built uniformly at the lower angle of elevation adopted for the upper part of the Bent Pyramid. Quarry-marks indicate that it was built towards the end of the king's reign, while the design of the whole complex is considerably more developed than that of the Bent Pyramid. The interior contains three spectacular corbelled chambers, the innermost of which probably once had a sarcophagus built into its now-destroyed floor. Fragments of what may have been the king's mummy were found in the pyramid in the 1950s.

The Meidum mystery

The Dahshur pyramids thus neatly fill the role of the 'Two Pyramids of Snofru' spoken of in Pepy I's inscription. However, there is a third full-scale pyramid that has every appearance of also belonging to the same king, which provides the greatest of the problems concerning the king's building programme. This lies not far from Seila, at Meidum, and in its current ruined form is one of the most singular buildings in Egypt, having the appearance of a tower perched atop a low hill.

This strange form is the result of the structure having been begun as a seven-stepped pyramid, enlarged as an eight-stepped one, and then converted to a true (straight-sided) monument. When stone-robbers began to remove blocks in later times, these discontinuities in its structure seem to have conspired to cause a partial collapse, with elements of all three phases of

Above *The Bent Pyramid changes its angle half way up; the lower part of the structure had its masonry laid in inward-sloping courses, a feature otherwise found in 3rd Dynasty pyramids. In the foreground to the right is the monument's subsidiary pyramid and to the left in the distance is the Red Pyramid.*

Left *All three chambers of the Red Pyramid have magnificent corbelled roofs. Such ceilings are a particular feature of Snofru's reign, and are found in all three of his large pyramids.*

The Meidum pyramid is one of the most spectacular in Egypt. The stepped phases employ inwardly sloping masonry in 3rd Dynasty style, but the outer mantle has horizontal courses, suggesting that it post-dates the lower part of the 4th Dynasty Bent Pyramid.

construction now visible. Architecturally, the outer mantle post-dates the lower section of the Bent Pyramid.

Internally, the Meidum pyramid shares the corbelled roofing of the Dahshur pyramids, although it is not entirely finished. Also unfinished is the mortuary temple, of a design intermediate between those of the Bent and Red Pyramids; its stelae were never inscribed with the name of the king. However, quarry marks which must relate to the reign of Snofru appear in the outer mantle of the pyramid, and his name is found in the contemporary private cemetery north of the pyramid. In addition, 18th Dynasty tourist graffiti call the temple that of Snofru.

Nevertheless, many have doubted whether Snofru could have built three major pyramids, totalling over three and a half million cubic metres of stone, preferring to attribute the Meidum pyramid to his predecessor, Huni, explaining away the graffiti and other evidence by arguing that Snofru may have finished and converted Huni's monument. This suggestion has been further buttressed by pointing to the apparent lack of an alternative pyramid for Huni.

Against this is the fact that there are no parallels for such major work by one king on completing a predecessor's monument: numerous unfinished pyramids and tombs are ample indication of this. In addition, a likely pyramid for Huni has now been identified – the Brick Pyramid at Abu Roash. While nothing has been found there to prove the connection, the form of the substructure of this monument makes it difficult to date it to any other period than around the 3rd/4th Dynasty transition.

Thus we are left with the surprising likelihood that Snofru did indeed build three major pyramids, in addition to up to seven small ones. Although an explanation might be sought in three-fold symbolism, it is perhaps more likely that they represent successive reactions to, first, the uncertain theological imperative that possibly lay behind the switch from the step to the true pyramid and, second, the structural problems encountered at the Bent Pyramid. The final conversion of the Meidum pyramid is rather more obscure, but may reflect an availability of surplus resources as construction of the Red Pyramid drew to a close.

Whatever the explanations, Snofru stands out as by far the greatest of the pyramid builders. Curiously, while the building of the Great Pyramid at Giza left its author, Khufu, condemned as a megalomaniac tyrant in later folklore, his father Snofru, who piled up 40 per cent more hewn stone than his son, was more highly regarded by posterity than almost any other Old Kingdom pharaoh.

The Great Pyramid

11

The sheer antiquity of its manufacture suspended me. I felt it was older than men, older than the earth....
'This palace is made by gods', I thought at first. I explored the uninhabited precincts and corrected:
'the gods who built it are dead'. I realized its peculiarities and said: 'the gods who built it were mad'.
Jorge L. Borges, 1949

For visitors since antiquity, the Great Pyramid at Giza has demanded an explanation beyond its mere practical use as a tomb for the 4th Dynasty pharaoh Khufu, who died around 2550 BC. This vast monument, a veritable mountain of stone, is eternal and incorruptible, defying time and the elements. Rising from the Egyptian desert to a summit which seems to touch the heavens, it embodies the distance between our own earthly form of existence and another – unknown and unreachable except by the dead king.

For centuries people have been searching for a meaning in the Great Pyramid beyond its use as a royal tomb.

The mysterious inner chambers

The internal layout of the Great Pyramid has no obvious parallel in any other royal monument, with three distinct chambers set at different levels within the masonry and linked by passages. It was once thought that the separate chambers were the result of changes in plan as the pyramid was built, but it is now generally believed that they were all part of one, original, unified scheme. The deepest element, the Subterranean Chamber, was cut 30 m (98 ft) below ground level from solid bedrock but was never finished. One suggestion is that it was intentionally left incomplete in order to symbolize the dark and formless underworld.

The uppermost chamber, known as the King's Chamber, is the highest ever built within a pyramid. Entirely lined with red granite, it still contains the king's undecorated granite sarcophagus. Two small shafts, often mistakenly referred to as 'air shafts', lead from this chamber upwards at an angle through the pyramid and point towards particular stars (p. 71), perhaps representing the ultimate destination of the dead king's spirit among 'the imperishable stars'. If so,

Above *The King's Chamber, with Khufu's red granite sarcophagus. The chamber was robbed in antiquity, probably even before the end of the Old Kingdom.*

Right *This corbelled niche in the so-called Queen's Chamber may have been intended to house a statue of the king.*

it may be that the purpose of the three chambers was to represent the process by which the king ascended to the heavens. From the 5th Dynasty the same process would be expressed through Pyramid Texts inscribed in and around the king's burial chamber. An intermediate stage of this journey would then be symbolized by the middle chamber, the Queen's Chamber (a modern name in no way connected with the real use of the room), where a corbelled niche in the east wall probably housed an over life-size statue of the king. There are two shafts here too, though they originally did not penetrate through the chamber's walls.

Such a scheme would also explain perhaps the most remarkable feature of the Great Pyramid, the Grand Gallery. This soaring passage is beautifully constructed with a fine corbelled roof. Its sectional plan reproduces those of the inner chambers of the pyramids built by Snofru, father and predecessor of Khufu. The plan is also similar in a stylized way to the exterior profile of the Step Pyramid of Djoser, which probably served as a model for the kings of the 4th Dynasty – and indeed as an achievement to be surpassed. Since this shape is also that of the hieroglyphic sign which indicates 'ascension', the Grand Gallery can be seen as another aspect of the symbolic journey by which the king ascended to the stars.

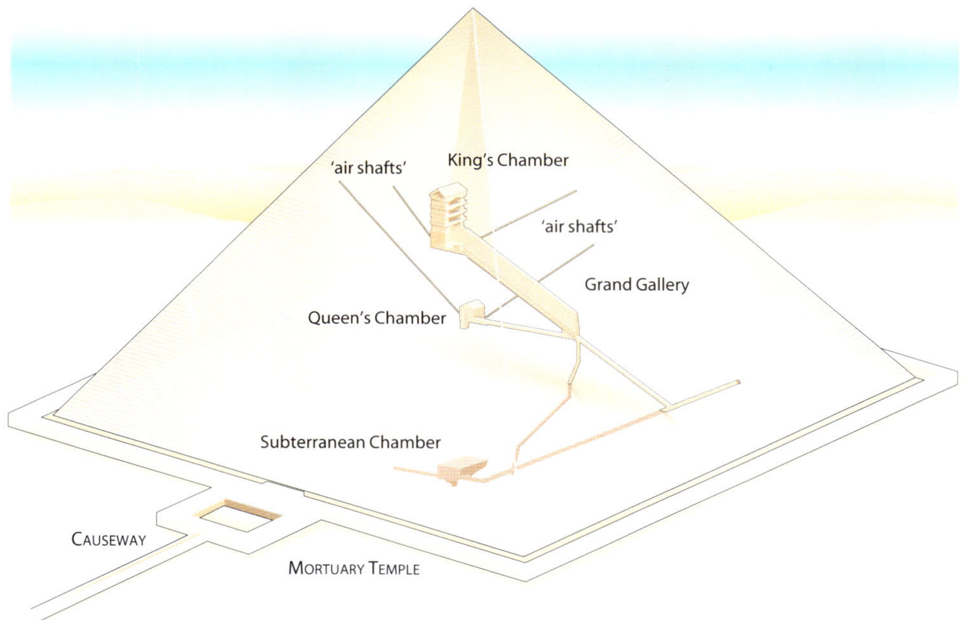

Above *The Grand Gallery is a magnificent architectural achievement, but also served a practical function as the place where the blocks used to seal the pyramid entrance were stored before the tomb was sealed.*

Left *The complex arrangement of passages and chambers within Khufu's pyramid is without parallel in other royal monuments.*

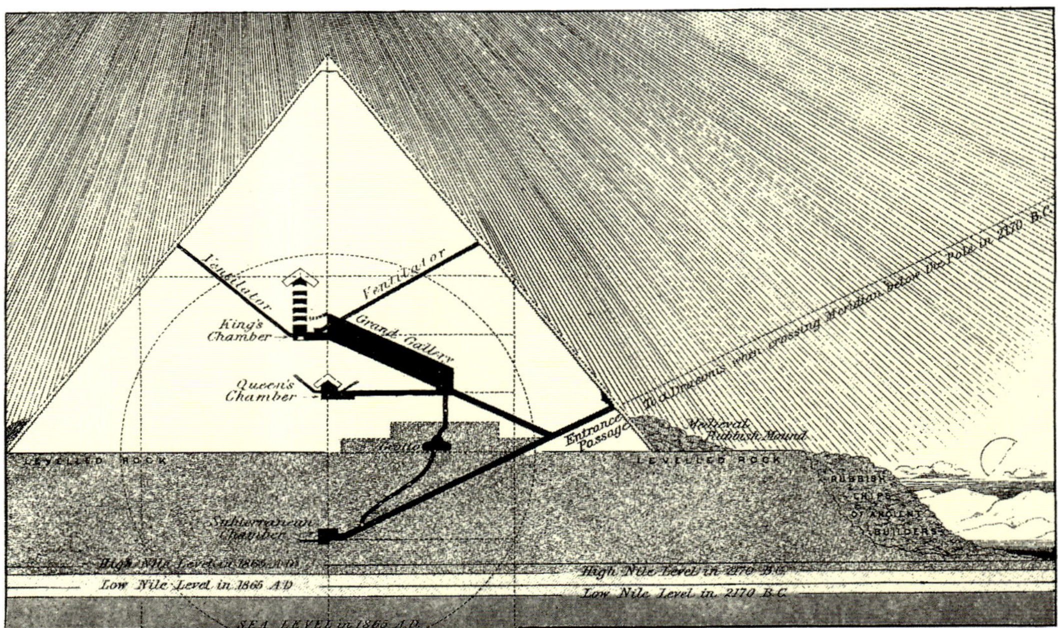

A drawing of the Great Pyramid by Piazzi Smyth. He was Astronomer Royal of Scotland from 1845 to 1888 and one of those who attempted to find a hidden significance in the measurements and proportions of the pyramid.

The mystery of the masons

The ambiguities of the awe-inspiring Great Pyramid have found a fertile ground in the imagination of observers and visitors. According to one commonly recurring view, as the Pyramid points to the heavens its authors may be from other planets. The need to find a meaning in the Pyramid beyond its use as a tomb often resolves itself into a quest to seek revelations in its dimensions. The most extreme examples of this see its measurements as a mathematical code, which, upon decipherment, would reveal the past, explain the present and enlighten the future of the human race.

It is indisputable that the calculations carried out by the Egyptians in order to design and build the pyramid were complex, but only because of the sheer magnitude of the work. An example often cited is that some measurements within the pyramid show a knowledge of π (the ratio between a circle and its radius): the fact that spherical drums were probably used to measure long distances during construction would be sufficient to explain this. Other mathematical ratios have been highlighted which seemingly relate the Pyramid's measurements to the distance from the earth to the sun, to the Fibonacci series or the Golden Section. In other words, according to such theories, the Great Pyramid could have been a huge theodolite, an astronomical observatory, a perpetual calendar or simply one of a series of geodesic landmarks.

A desire to understand the measurements of the Great Pyramid motivated a detailed study in 1864 by Piazzi Smyth, Astronomer Royal of Scotland. He concluded that its perfect dimensions could only have been the work of the Israelites, under divine command, during their captivity in Egypt. These conclusions, together with interests in surveying and the Bible, inspired one young archaeologist, without any formal education or training, to produce a highly accurate survey of Giza. His name was Flinders Petrie, and his survey, even by modern standards, is an excellent piece of work. His meticulous study demonstrated the fallacy of Smyth's arguments because it revealed imperfections in the Pyramid – there are irregularities in the alignment of stones, in the orientation of the monument as a whole, and areas where the workmanship is careless. Petrie went on to introduce scientific methods such as stratigraphy and pottery typology to fieldwork in Egypt, and today is regarded as the first and greatest archaeologist in Egyptology.

The Hall of Records

Perhaps the most tantalizing mystery associated with the Great Pyramid is the supposed secret Hall of Records, which, according to proponents, must be within the Pyramid or beneath the Great Sphinx. Followers of the American medium Edgar Cayce believe that Giza hides documents from the legendary Atlantis, hidden when the Pyramid was built – in 10,500 BC according to Cayce's adherents. Other theories are taken as support of this notion, such as the supposed alignment of the Giza pyramids with the three stars of Orion's belt as they would have appeared at that date (p. 71). Furthermore, a geological analysis carried out on the Sphinx by Robert Schoch concluded that damage on its surface was due to water erosion which must have occurred when the region had a wet and rainy climate – in other words towards the end of the glacial melts of the last Ice Age (p. 67).

All this is considered relevant by believers, despite the fact that such a timescale does not fit with our available knowledge about Egyptian prehistory. To accept the existence of a prehistoric culture in Egypt capable of creating the Great Pyramid and the Sphinx, but about which all direct information has disappeared, not only questions our knowledge of Egypt, but makes a wasteland of centuries of scientific understanding of human activity on our planet.

In fact, the date of the Great Pyramid is beyond doubt, since graffiti with the name of Khufu were found inscribed on walls in the relieving chambers above the King's Chamber. These were sealed at the time of the construction of the Pyramid and not re-opened until 1837 by Howard Vyse – with the aid of dynamite.

However, there are ancient Egyptian texts – already known and translated at the time of the hypnotic readings of Cayce – that seem to provide some background for those seeking the Hall of Records. The main source is a literary tale in which Khufu is portrayed as a king obsessed with the desire to discover 'the secret number of the chambers of the sanctuary of Thoth', presumably with the intention of copying them in his own tomb.

Edgar Cayce

The dream of eternal knowledge

Edgar Cayce (1877–1945) was an American medium whose hypnotically induced teachings began the search for the Hall of Records. He became famous during the 1930s when he was able to diagnose and treat diseases mis-diagnosed by conventional doctors. While in a state of trance, Cayce also developed mystical religious ideas, centred on the existence of a race of technologically advanced giants from Atlantis.

The most complete picture of any culture in Cayce's readings is that relating to Egypt dating to around 10,500 BC. The central character in this account is Ra Ta, a priest from the Caucasus, who advised his king, Arart, that their tribe would invade Egypt and make it the most powerful region on earth. This duly happened, and Ra Ta became High Priest of Egypt.

Ra Ta then planned the construction of the Great Pyramid which was constructed by means of the occult levitation of stones. Finally, he encoded a prediction of the future for mankind until 1998, to be preserved in a hall – the Hall of Records – between the Sphinx and the Great Pyramid.

Ivory statuette of Khufu, the only verified image of the king, from Abydos. Ironically for the builder of Egypt's greatest pyramid, it is just 7.5 cm (3 in) high.

The tale says that this information is to be found in the temple of the god Thoth at Hermopolis, inside a box made of flint and named *sipty* – a word which can be translated as 'inventory' or 'record'. Also, Spell 30 in the much later Egyptian *Book of the Dead* is headed by a formula which claims the spell was written by Thoth himself, and then found by a son of Khufu named Hordedef.

These references then passed into popular Egyptian tales, and so later we find an Arab legend that the pyramid is the tomb of the god Hermes (Hermes having been identified with Thoth by Greeks in Egypt). According to this legend, Hermes built the pyramids to preserve literature and science from the Flood. Such tales were probably the justification for the forced but futile opening of the Great Pyramid by the Caliph Al-Mamun (*c.* AD 820) in search of fantastic treasures – it had been plundered many times already in antiquity.

Ultimately, nothing is more human than the desire to transcend the limitations of the human condition itself. The quest for esoteric knowledge hidden within the Great Pyramid has paradoxically helped to advance our understanding of the ancient world – not by ever solving any of these so-called mysteries, but by inspiring the search for a more detailed knowledge of this most fascinating of monuments.

The desire to understand a numerical perfection reflecting a divine will led Flinders Petrie to the Great Pyramid, and from there to become one of the greatest archaeologists of all time. More recently, the quest for the Hall of Records has motivated a modern archaeologist, Mark Lehner, to explore the Giza plateau and so to become one of the most respected scholars in his field. Both figures eventually departed from their initial positions and found themselves instead immersed in the field of scientific research that also flourishes in the shadow of the Great Pyramid.

The Vizier Hemiunu: probably a grandson of Snofru, he was in charge of the actual construction of Khufu's pyramid and therefore ultimately responsible for one of the most extraordinary monuments in history.

Riddles of the Great Sphinx

12

It is a riddle wrapped in a mystery inside an enigma.
WINSTON CHURCHILL, 1939

The Great Sphinx of Giza is among the most impressive sculptures ever produced by the ancient Egyptians. It represents a gigantic, recumbent lion – alert and poised to spring into action – with the head of an Egyptian king wearing the standard *nemes* headdress (the striped and pleated head cloth with two front lappets falling over the wearer's chest). In total the Sphinx measures about 73 m (240 ft) in length and is 20 m (66 ft) high; it lies within a deep pit-like excavation, adjacent to the eastern end of the causeway leading up to the pyramid of King Khafre of the 4th Dynasty. Largely sculpted from living rock, parts of the Sphinx may have been built up with stone masonry.

The limestone of the Giza plateau is layered, with harder strata alternating with softer ones. The Sphinx's head is carved from a harder layer (otherwise almost completely quarried away) and is well preserved, despite weathering and some intentional damage – its most noticeable disfigurement is the loss of its nose. The body of the Sphinx (except for its lowest portions) is carved from much softer limestone and is severely eroded.

Several times throughout its history the Sphinx has been partially or completely covered by stone masonry laid and carved to replicate the original contours of its body. Beginning in the 18th Dynasty, these masonry skins protected the body from further erosion. At other times, the

The Great Sphinx, usually dated to the reign of Khafre, and in front of it a stela of Thutmose IV from over 1000 years later. This alluring monument was as inspiring to later ancient Egyptian kings as it is to modern audiences.

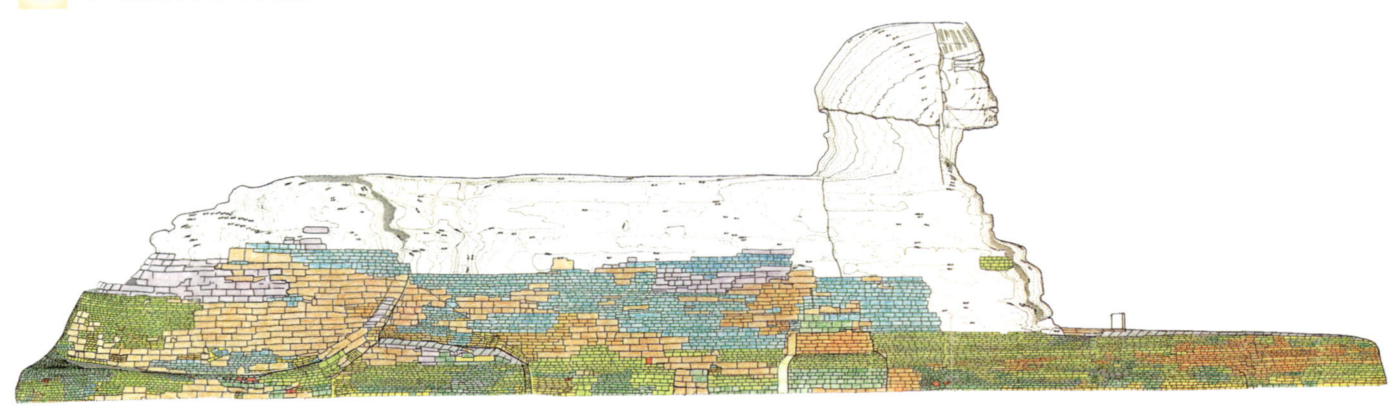

Above *Detailed side view of the Great Sphinx illustrating some of the later restorations and masonry coatings.*

Sphinx was largely buried in wind-blown sand, another, more natural, form of protection. For long periods of time, however, the Sphinx would have been fully exposed. Perhaps from as early as the Old Kingdom, it was probably painted in bright colours: the face and body were likely red, while the stripes of the *nemes* headdress were of alternating yellow and blue. Today, this tremendously impressive visual effect is replaced by another – the romantic charm of the Sphinx's time-ravaged body and its well-preserved head.

Two mysteries adhere to the Great Sphinx. The first concerns its age. Exciting much popular interest, this is the less significant question but it deflects attention from a more fundamental one: what was the purpose of the Great Sphinx?

The Sphinx: primeval or historic?

First, the age issue. The Sphinx is a component in an ensemble of great monuments distributed over the Giza landscape, in particular the stone-built pyramids of kings Khufu (the Great Pyramid), Khafre (Khufu's son) and Menkaure (Khufu's grandson). Yet some argue the Sphinx's relationship to this ensemble is fortuitous and that it was actually carved long before, between 7000 and 5000 BC – that is some 4500 to 2500 years before construction of the Great Pyramid was begun.

Below *Modern scaffolding on the Great Sphinx during restoration emphasizes how it has been changed and adapted by Egyptians over the millennia.*

This proposal rests on the observation, by geologist Robert Schoch in particular, that the severe erosion of the Sphinx's body is due to persistent and heavy rainfall, not to strong winds carrying scouring desert sands. Sufficient rainfall could only have occurred many centuries before the semi-arid climate that already prevailed in Egypt by the time of the Old Kingdom. Only a minority of geologists, however, accept this argument. Most find the Sphinx's appearance compatible with severe and sustained wind erosion, especially affecting the soft limestone of the greater part of the Sphinx.

Archaeologists point to the other data supporting a 4th Dynasty date for the Sphinx. For example, the archaeological remains of Egyptian culture of 7000–5000 BC reveal a level of technology and social organization not likely to be capable of producing such an enormous sculpture, or the artistic sophistication it displays. Even more importantly, the adjacent Khafre valley temple and the so-called 'sphinx temple' next to it are largely constructed of massive limestone blocks quarried from the same pit as the Sphinx – a pit in which the distinctive patterning of layers and compositional variation of the stone are clearly visible. Some argue the limestone structures were built earlier (like the Sphinx) and then sheathed in granite during the 4th Dynasty, but in fact the two processes took place at the same time, and are archaeologically dated to the 4th Dynasty. Moreover, on art historical grounds – supported by computerized matchings and restorations – comparison between the Sphinx's head and dated statues of King Khafre strongly indicate they are contemporary.

The 'mystery' of the Sphinx's age is therefore an irrelevancy. More fundamental, and still highly debatable, is the issue of the Sphinx's purpose, and its relationship to the other Giza monuments of King Khafre.

Guardian of the pyramid

Most of the limestone for Khafre's pyramid probably came from an expansion of a gigantic quarry created for Khufu's pyramid, located due south of the latter and southeast of Khafre's pyramid. However, the stone for Khafre's valley temple and its neighbour the 'sphinx temple' was provided by a separate quarry, conveniently located next to both. The locations, and perhaps placement, of the two temples were fixed by several factors: first was the causeway to Khafre's pyramid, angling away from the pyramid for topographical reasons; second, the quarry itself; and third, the immediate topography and perhaps a pre-existing harbour (dating to Khufu). All these factors circumscribed the amount of ground available on which buildings could be constructed.

Although many scholars believe the Great Sphinx was planned from the outset, it is equally plausible to propose that it was an inspired accident. In the course of quarrying blocks for the two temples, it was perhaps realized that a substantial remnant taking shape between two deeply cutting quarry operations would not be required, and the idea of transforming this into a Sphinx came into being, suggested perhaps both by its shape and by contemporary ideas described below.

The 'sphinx temple', however, was a pre-planned component of Khafre's monuments, and if it and the Sphinx were spatially and culturally linked then the latter might also be pre-planned. According to this view, the Sphinx is so located in relation to the 'sphinx temple' that it represents either the recipient of cult as an embodiment of the creator and sun god Atum, or the king in sphinx form, literally presenting the temple and its cult to the embodiment of the sun god, the solar orb, as it traverses the sky above during the course of the day. However, while the 'sphinx temple' may have solar associations, it is by no means certain that it is connected to the Sphinx.

For example, Sphinx and temple are not in fact on the same central axis, which the supposed

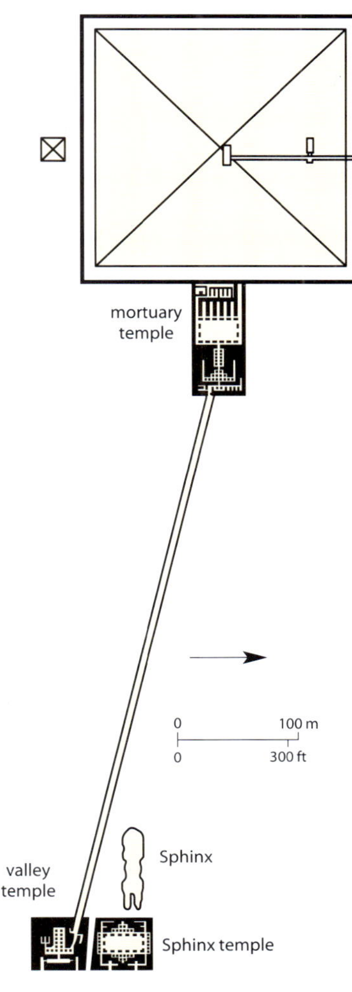

Plan of the pyramid complex of King Khafre, showing the position of the Sphinx in relation to the other elements of the complex.

connection seems to require, and pre-planning could have ensured. Moreover, the 'sphinx temple' does not have a major cult place on the west, oriented to the Sphinx, as might be expected when such a visually powerful image is present. Finally, it is plausible to hypothesize that it is the valley temple that conceptually links to the 'sphinx temple', not the Sphinx. Though not directly connected, the two temples sit side by side and are carefully aligned with each other. Moreover, each is very similar, but not identical, to different parts of Khafre's pyramid temple. Menkaure's later valley temple incorporates a large open court, the principal feature of Khafre's 'sphinx temple'. In Khafre's case, the limited space available may have precluded such a combination.

In these circumstances, the Great Sphinx could be conceived of as an initially unplanned guardian figure, akin to the sphinxes which, in relief, guard the causeway entrances of later Old Kingdom pyramid complexes. Here they trample and rend Egypt's foreign enemies, helpless before this leonine embodiment of royal power. Foreigners equate with the negative chaotic forces which attacked the cosmos as a whole, and hence sphinxes also protected pyramid complexes – representations of the cosmos as well as royal cult places – against penetration by supernatural evil that could threaten the deceased ruler, ritually evoked in his remote offering chamber every day.

The Great Sphinx, appropriately positioned near the end of Khafre's causeway, can be read as another manifestation of this concept, mirrored perhaps in the smaller sphinxes that may have flanked the entrances of Khafre's valley temple. Thus, there would be no specific cult of the Sphinx, and the 'sphinx temple' is actually part of Khafre's mortuary establishment, explaining why only personnel of his cult (and none of the Sphinx's) are referred to in contemporary and later inscriptions.

The Great Sphinx in its role as the guardian of access to Khafre's pyramid complex.

Are the pyramids aligned with the stars? 13

The King will not die . . . for the King is an Imperishable [circumpolar] star.
PYRAMID TEXTS, SPELL 571, *c.* 2325 BC

There is no question that the stars played an important role in ancient Egyptian mortuary religion. References to the night sky and the stars are found in many of the Pyramid Texts which were inscribed in royal pyramids of the late Old Kingdom, while the names of some Early Dynastic Period royal domains, such as that of Khasekhemwy, which was called 'Horus, the Star of Souls', suggest that stars may have been important in mortuary religion even earlier. References to the stars are also found on a pyramidion of Amenemhat III from Dahshur showing that stellar associations of pyramids continued at least until the end of the Middle Kingdom and are therefore applicable to all phases of royal pyramid construction (though there is no evidence that the small pyramids constructed over nobles' tombs from the New Kingdom onwards had stellar associations).

The existence of stellar aspects of mortuary religion is widely accepted in Egyptology, but the extent to which this is reflected in the design of pyramids is disputed. Recently this has become a highly controversial subject and a number of popular books have been published which explore the link between pyramids and the stars.

Theories associating the design of pyramids with stars tend to focus on pyramids of the 4th Dynasty, as these are the best preserved and therefore the best known, and they are usually also the best surveyed and recorded. However, there are many royal pyramids in Egypt and the most convincing theories are those which can be applied to at least a significant group of pyramids of a particular period. Given the absence of textual evidence detailing astronomical practices at this time, any theory becomes extremely difficult to prove: probability depends on how well the theory fits with the evidence and the context. The three most prominent areas of discussion, in order of probability, are: the alignment of the bases of pyramids towards the cardinal points using the stars; the alignment of shafts in the Great Pyramid towards the culmination of particular stars; and the so-called 'Orion correlation theory', which interprets the layout of the three pyramids at Giza as representing in plan the three stars of Orion's Belt.

The alignment of pyramid bases using the stars

The majority of pyramids are aligned to the cardinal points with great precision. The most accurately aligned are those of the 4th Dynasty, the sides of which diverge from the cardinal points by just fractions of a degree, although later pyramids are less precisely oriented. It seems probable that a stellar orientation method was used in the 4th Dynasty at least, because this would have achieved greater precision than a solar method and therefore fits better with the evidence for great accuracy.

The pyramidion of Amenemhat III from his pyramid at Dahshur. Although solar iconography is prominent on the east face, the north face is associated with stellar themes.

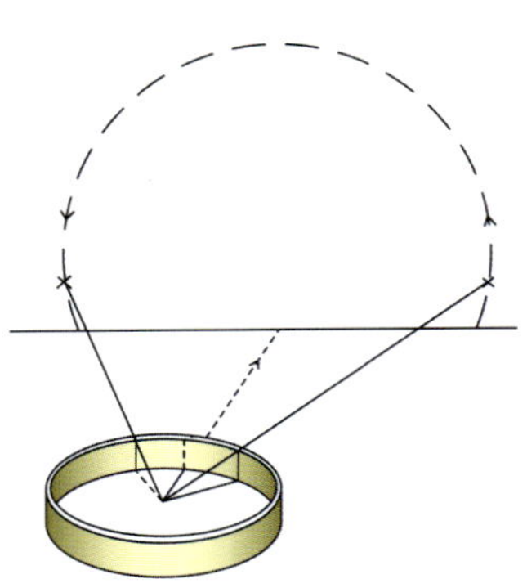

Above *Two of several possible methods of orientation to true north using the stars. I. E. S. Edward's method involves bisecting the angle between points of equal elevation on the trajectory of a northern star; it is one of a number of bisection methods which have been proposed. An alternative method involves sighting towards two stars in vertical alignment.*

A number of different stellar methods have been proposed and opinion is divided over which is most likely to have been used.

Most of the stellar methods proposed for these pyramids use one or more of the circumpolar, or northern, stars. At the time the pyramids were built there was no star accurately marking the position of the north celestial pole, so one sighting towards a single star could not have given precise results. Other possible methods involve bisecting the angle between two points of equal elevation or the most easterly and westerly positions on the trajectory of a single star, both of which are capable of producing great precision. Alternatively, the orientation could have been established using two stars on opposite sides of the pole when they were in vertical alignment. Because the position of the celestial pole drifts slowly over time as a result of precession, this method would result in a corresponding slow drifting of the precision of pyramid orientation. This does in fact appear to be a feature of the alignments of 4th Dynasty pyramids, providing support for this method.

The 'star'-shafts of the Great Pyramid

In the Great Pyramid of Khufu at Giza four small shafts, approximately 20 cm (8 in) square, run upwards at an angle from the north and south walls of the King's Chamber and the so-called 'Queen's Chamber'. Traditionally these have been interpreted as ventilation shafts, but the discovery of a 'door' blocking one shaft and the fact that other pyramids do not contain similar shafts make this unlikely. Speculation that the passages in this pyramid were oriented towards the culminations (highest points on the trajectories) of particular stars goes back to at least the 19th century. Research by Alexander Badawy and Virginia Trimble in the 1960s, updated more recently by Robert Bauval on the basis of new measurements of the shafts by Rudolf Gantenbrink, suggests that these small shafts are aligned towards the culminations of Sirius, Alnitak (δ Orionis), Thuban (α Draconis – the closest star to the celestial pole at the time) and Kochab (β Ursae Minoris). Thuban and Sirius were unquestionably of great importance to the ancient Egyptians, as were the constellations of Orion and Ursa Minor.

Although debate as to the nature of these shafts continues to rage on, and a recent attempt to discover what lies behind the 'door' proved inconclusive, an increasing number of Egyptologists are now accepting that they may be aligned towards star culminations.

The 'Orion Correlation Theory'

In his book *The Orion Mystery* (co-authored with Adrian Gilbert), published in 1994, and a series of related articles, Robert Bauval proposed that the layout of the three pyramids at Giza – Khufu's, Khafre's and Menkaure's – represented the three stars of the 'belt' of the constellation of Orion. Although this idea has caught the imagination of

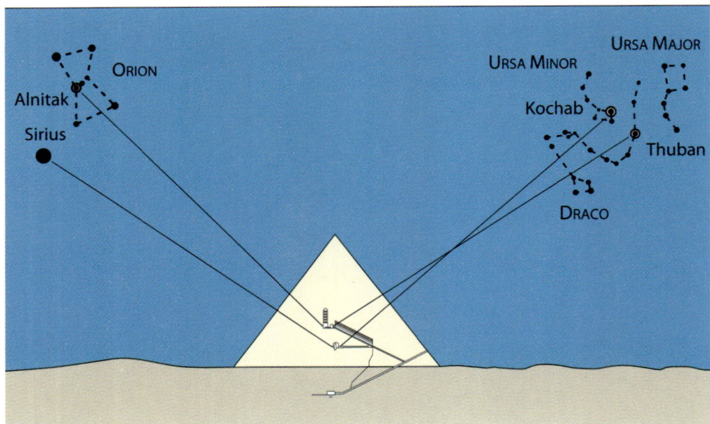

Left *Diagram illustrating Robert Bauval's theory of the star-shafts in the pyramid of Khufu, which he suggests are aligned towards the culmination of particular stars.*

The pyramids at Giza feature in all discussions of aspects of stellar alignment. Their layout (below left) follows the contour of the ridge on which they are built, with each aligned to the cardinal points. Mark Lehner suggests that the southeast corners of the pyramids may have been deliberately aligned.

the public and has sparked much heated debate, it is not accepted by Egyptologists.

There are many reasons why the theory is unlikely to be correct, of which only a few can be mentioned here. Probably the most important is that the apparently significant diagonal layout of the three pyramids can easily be explained by pragmatic considerations. A combination of the site's topography – the pyramids are built along the edge of a ridge which runs northeast to southwest – with the need for each individual pyramid to be oriented towards north with a clear view of the northern stars, explains the positions of the pyramids. Work by the American Egyptologist Mark Lehner suggests that the slight offset of the third pyramid may result from aligning the southeast corners of the pyramids along the edge of the ridge. And despite the fact that several other important groups of pyramids are preserved in Egypt, there is no evidence from these that the precise layout of groups of pyramids or other structures mapped constellations or was otherwise significant. Bauval's theory also does not take account of any of the minor pyramids at Giza.

There is therefore both a more plausible alternative explanation for the layout and a lack of any parallel for this type of significance attached to architectural planning of groups of structures. In addition, each pyramid complex was designed as a complete and fully functioning entity in its own right and from what we know of Old Kingdom kings it is very hard to imagine a ruler considering his own mortuary provision as subordinate to, and therefore reliant on, a broader plan.

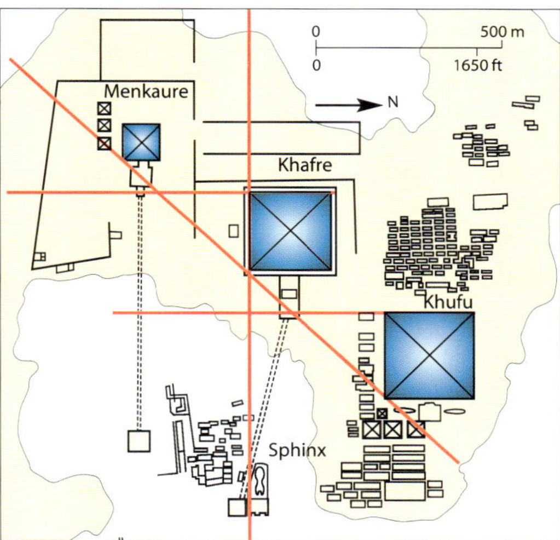

Above *The 'belt stars' of Orion, which Robert Bauval suggests provided the inspiration for the layout of the pyramids at Giza.*

Why were pyramids aligned with stars?

The alignment of the pyramid base using the northern stars ensured that it was oriented to the celestial pole – the invisible point in the sky which appeared to govern the movement of the stars and other celestial bodies. The entrance/exit passages of all pyramids until the Middle Kingdom were also directed towards the northern circumpolar region. The shafts in the Great Pyramid seem to be intended to provide symbolic exit routes for the spirit of the deceased king, directing him towards particular stars or constellations with which he hoped to be associated after death. Aligning the pyramids with stars therefore provided a link between the king's earthly burial place and the celestial realm within which he intended to spend eternity in the company of the sun, stars and gods.

14

The anonymous Qurneh burial

It was the largest group of goldwork that had left Egypt . . . So then, for the first time, a Museum man came to inspect it. He whispered under his breath 'We did not know it was such a fine thing'.

W. M. Flinders Petrie, 1932

Below *Petrie's photograph of the burial-pit as discovered in December, 1908. The coffin of the child can be seen on the feet of the woman's coffin.*

Below right *Sketch drawing of the burial made by the excavators on the day of its discovery.*

On 29 November, 1908, Flinders Petrie arrived in Egypt to start another season of excavation. His plan was to return to Luxor, where he had excavated more than a decade earlier, and to search the northern valleys, following up reports of promising tombs. Eight days later the expedition reached Qurneh.

The first weeks were disappointing and Petrie, who had badly injured his leg, was confined to bed. Then, at the cusp of the New Year, something remarkable turned up. Petrie's diary entry for 30 December records the clearing of an 'untouched XVII burial in valley'. The astonishingly rich contents of this burial have excited Egyptologists for almost a century. Petrie excavated, described and published the entire group within months of its discovery, and most of its artifacts have been on public display in Edinburgh ever since. Surprisingly, the identity of the two people buried in the grave has been largely ignored. Only recently have scholars begun to fit together the clues: and it seems clear that what Petrie had found was something – or someone – quite exceptional.

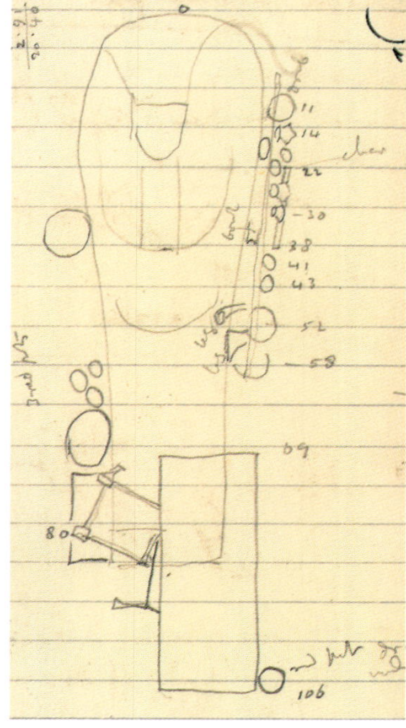

A spectacular discovery

Petrie had discovered the undisturbed burial of a woman and child placed within two coffins laid in a shallow pit covered with rocks. One of the coffins was very striking, being exceptionally tall and gilded with elaborate blue, black and gold feathered decoration in the so-called *rishi* style, which can be dated on stylistic grounds to the 17th Dynasty. At its foot lay a simple unadorned box coffin. Each coffin contained a mummy, which Petrie unwrapped the same evening, finding that the bodies were poorly preserved.

In the large coffin was the body of a slender woman, about 1.52 m (5 ft) tall, who was in her late teens or early twenties at the time of her death. She was left-handed, had enjoyed good health and had taken part in no demanding physical activities. Unusually, her teeth showed signs of decay, which was comparatively rare in ancient Egypt, where there was little sugar in the diet. The small coffin contained the remains of a child aged 2 or 3; the sex of such young infants cannot be determined from the bones. It is not (yet) possible to prove scientifically that the woman and child were related to each other, but the poignant proximity of their coffins strongly suggests this was the case.

The woman and child were buried with an assemblage of grave-goods that indicate exceptional wealth and importance. For example, the woman wore a heavy gold collar, elaborate gold earrings, four gold bracelets and a girdle of fine electrum beads. She also had a scarab tied to the third finger of her left hand. Her collar and bracelets are approximately 87–88 per cent gold, while her earrings are around 95 per cent gold. Such purity is unusual for Egypt and probably indicates gold from Nubia. The collar, earrings and beads each represent the earliest examples of their types known in Egypt, but all went on to become standard jewelry types in the New Kingdom. The child had strings of blue-glaze beads around the waist and ankles, and wore a necklace of tiny electrum beads, two gold earrings, and three ivory bracelets. The ivory probably came from African elephants, found in ancient times in Nubia and other lands south of Egypt.

Other prestige items were vessels of eggshell-thin pottery from Nubia of a type known as Kerma ware, many suspended within mesh-bags from a tamarisk pole. The rich assemblage of burial equipment also included a ceremonial flail of blue-glaze beadwork (a type of object usually carried by the king), alabaster vessels, an obsidian cosmetic pot, a blue stone bowl carved with apes, a Syrian oil-horn inlaid with ivory, *shabtys* (funerary figurines), a wooden headrest inlaid with ebony and ivory, and a wooden box with a sliding lid, as well as a sewing kit. The unusually rich food offerings

Above *A modern reconstruction of the woman's face, shown as a Nubian and an Egyptian, following the skin-colour conventions of New Kingdom art.*

Right *The gilded coffin of the woman, now on display in the National Museums of Scotland together with all the accompanying grave- goods.*

Some of the remarkable grave-goods, including the magnificent gold collar and other jewelry, Kerma ware pots, and alabaster and obsidian vessels.

included loaves of bread, dom-palm nuts, dates and grapes. So exactly who was buried in this modestly built but richly furnished tomb?

Who were they?

At the time the woman and child were buried, Egypt was politically divided and economically weakened. The great kingdom of the 12th Dynasty had been divided between several royal lines for at least a century. At Thebes, the 17th Dynasty held sway over a relatively restricted area, with an economy severely constrained by the Hyksos rulers of Avaris in the eastern delta (p. 162), while to the south a powerful king ruled Nubia from Kush. The rulers of Thebes were therefore denied access to both the trade routes of the Mediterranean and the gold mines of Nubia. As a result, Theban royal tombs of the period were often very simple, and sometimes lacked any grave-goods. So why was this burial at Qurneh so exceptionally wealthy? The tomb offerings included several special objects, many of them imported, such as the oil-horn from Syria and the beautiful Kerma ware from Nubia. Raw materials had been imported too: resins from the Levant, woods from East Africa and Nubian gold. What does this mean?

This egg-shell thin Kerma ware vessel is a high-quality prestige item imported from the kingdom of Kush, perhaps as a gift to the woman at the time of her marriage or burial.

The most likely explanation for the burial is that the woman and child belonged to the Theban royal family. There are also clues suggesting a mix of cultures: the Kerma ware and some of the jewelry hint at cultural links with Kush. Analyses of the woman's diet, from a sample of her skeleton, have also produced striking results: by comparison with published data for ancient African remains, her diet fell somewhere between those typical of Egyptians and Nubians. This suggests that she was either an Egyptian with an unusual taste for Nubian foods, or a Nubian who had moved to Egypt.

There are two well-known arrangements which could explain the woman's links with Nubia: either gift-exchange, whereby some of her grave-goods were gifts from the Kushite king; or dynastic marriage, whereby she was a Nubian princess given as a wife to the king of Thebes. If it was a case of gift-exchange, the woman could be ethnically Egyptian or from many other ethnic backgrounds; if was a dynastic marriage, she would probably be ethnically Nubian.

Although the woman and child still remain anonymous, we now know much more about them. The evidence from their burial certainly suggests that we must reconsider our view of the 17th Dynasty, which is usually assumed to have been a time when Thebes was in conflict with the kingdom of Kush.

Abydos: the last royal pyramid?

15

'My Person has desired that a pyramid and chapel be built for [Tetishery] in the necropolis beside the monuments of my Person.'
KING AHMOSE, FROM A STELA IN THE SHRINE OF TETISHERY AT ABYDOS, *c.* 1520 BC

The remains of a substantial pyramid, consisting of a rubble core with a casing of dressed stone, was discovered at the southern extremity of Abydos in 1899. In 1902 the pyramid was dated to the reign of Ahmose, the first king of the 18th Dynasty, towards the end of the 16th century BC. In addition to the pyramid (with a temple in front), located at the junction between the low desert and the floodplain, the total complex also included a large, unfinished rock-cut tomb far out in the desert, and beyond this, at the foot of the cliffs, a stone- and brick-walled platform intended to support a building which seemingly was never constructed. Roughly half-way between pyramid and tomb was also a brick shrine dedicated to Ahmose's grandmother, Tetishery, where a stela which recorded Ahmose's decision to build a shrine for her was found.

These discoveries were revealing and exciting – Ahmose's is the last royal pyramid known to survive from Egypt – yet much remained mysterious. In 1993, therefore, the Pennsylvania-Yale-Institute of Fine Arts Expedition, under the direction of Stephen Harvey, undertook a new survey of the complex, initiating ongoing excavations at and around the pyramid. Spectacular results so far include the discovery of a hitherto unknown shrine or pyramid for Ahmose's queen,

The rubble core of Ahmose's pyramid stands near the desert edge, beyond the cultivated floodplain. In the distance rise the high cliffs, near which Ahmose's symbolic tomb is cut.

Ahmose-Nefertiry, next to his pyramid, and the remains of the first known scenes depicting Ahmose's campaign against the Hyksos kings (p. 162).

Ahmose's pyramid complex

Ahmose's pyramid can reliably be reconstructed as standing originally about 49.5 m (162 ft) high, and unusually steeply angled (about 65.5 degrees); its base covered an area of around 2750 sq. m (29,600 sq. ft). The badly destroyed temple on its northeast side is harder to reconstruct, though it is known that a high brick pylon fronted a stone-built structure flanked by brick-built wings. Between the temple and the pyramid is a large, unexcavated area (about 1612 sq. m/17,350 sq. ft), which Harvey surmises might contain the remains of further buildings. The simplest reconstruction of the temple consists of a porticoed courtyard (its stone-faced walls once decorated with scenes, including ones depicting the war with the Hyksos) with a small cult building beyond, decorated with offering scenes focused on the deceased Ahmose. It is likely that the latter was built, or at least decorated, by Ahmose's son and successor, Amenhotep I. However, the unexcavated space in front of the pyramid may in fact contain an additional cult building, in which case the temple may have consisted largely of an open court, with a columned portico at its southwest end.

The recently discovered Ahmose-Nefertiry structure is equally intriguing; Harvey suggests it included a small pyramid, but this remains to be proved. As for Queen Tetishery's shrine, its partially preserved remains consist of a mass of brick-walled casemates occupying some 495 sq. m (5328 sq. ft), penetrated by a deep, narrow chapel. A beautiful stela was discovered in the chapel, its text quoting a conversation between King Ahmose and his queen, in the course of which he decides to provide Tetishery with a mortuary monument at Abydos in addition to her tomb (at Thebes) and her cenotaph or memorial chapel (already built at Abydos). The original form of Tetishery's monument remains uncertain, but Harvey plausibly suggests a platform supporting a small, steeply angled brick pyramid, into which the chapel is set. Ahmose's own tomb was almost certainly at Thebes, though it has never been found, and so his tomb at Abydos was probably a symbolic, not an actual one – in fact, its burial chamber was never cut. We also do not know what kind of a structure the terraced platform (measuring about 111 x 24 m/364 x 78 ft) west of the tomb was intended to support.

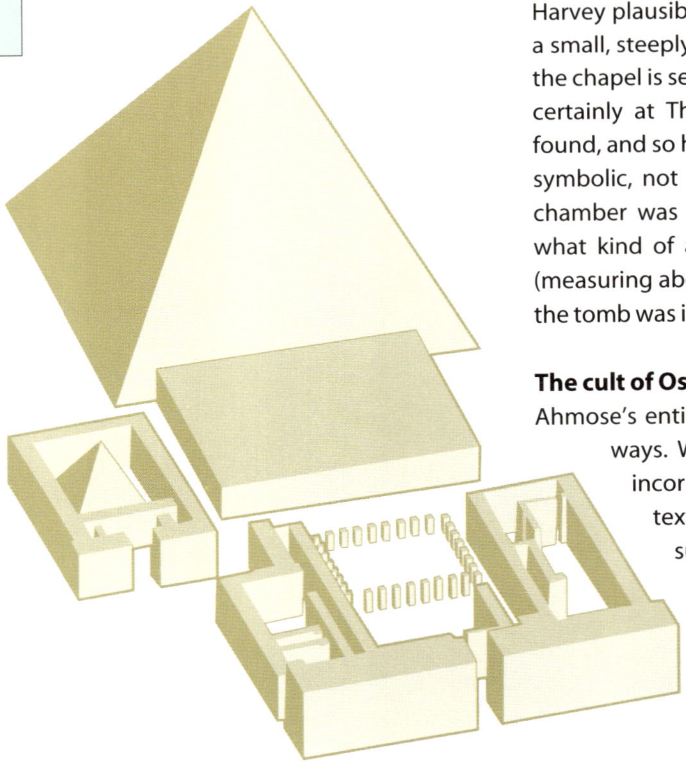

The cult of Osiris

Ahmose's entire complex is mysterious in many ways. Why was it built, and why does it incorporate a pyramid? Although a textual reference indicates his second successor, Thutmose I, may also have had a pyramid at Abydos, Ahmose's stands at the end of the long line of surviving royal pyramids in Egypt. His successors throughout the New

Above *Plan illustrating the chief components of King Ahmose's complex at Abydos.*

Right *Stephen Harvey's reconstruction of one possible configuration (of several) for Ahmose's pyramid and the temple on its northeast. To the left is Queen Ahmose-Nefertiry's newly discovered shrine, reconstructed with a small pyramid of its own.*

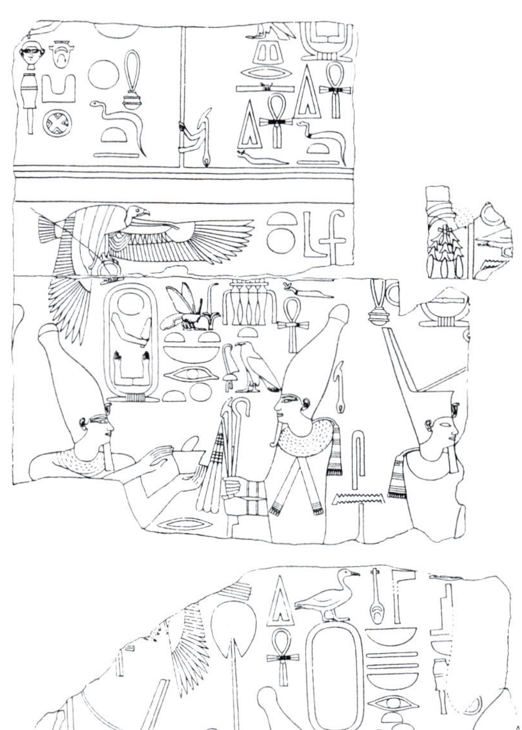

the separation between mortuary temple and tomb seen at New Kingdom Thebes.

Ahmose's predecessors in the 17th Dynasty were buried under similarly steeply angled, if much smaller, pyramids at Thebes, and Ahmose's may be the last, if most grandiose, of this 'family tradition', as is most likely true of Tetishery's pyramid. It is also possible, as Harvey suggests, that Ahmose's pyramid is intended to evoke those of the powerful national rulers of earlier periods, and hence reinforce his legitimacy as their heir. Given the substantial size of Ahmose's pyramid, this is an attractive suggestion. Ahmose's pyramid and complex continue to offer many intriguing challenges, some likely to be resolved by Harvey's excavations.

Far left *Relief fragments from a chapel near the temple of Osiris, far to the north of Ahmose's pyramid, where the cults of both Ahmose and his son, Amenhotep I, were celebrated.*

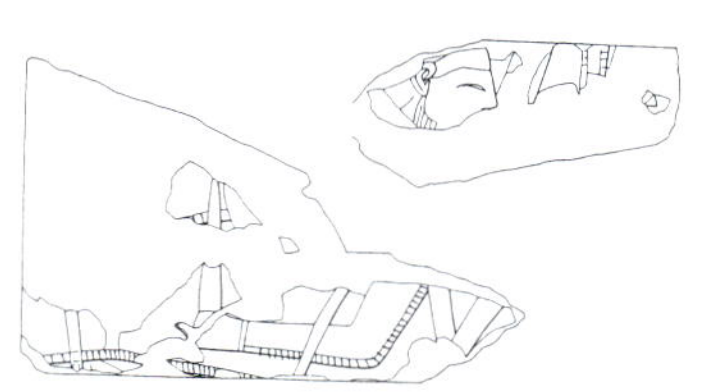

Left *Asiatics or Hyksos are depicted on relief fragments from Ahmose's pyramid temple: the figures are from a scene showing Ahmose overcoming the Hyksos in battle.*

Below *In mirror-image scenes, Ahmose makes offerings to Queen Tetishery on the stela found in her shrine.*

Kingdom (apart from Akhenaten; p. 84) were buried at Thebes in tombs cut deep into the cliffs of a desert valley, while their mortuary temples stood some distance away along the edge of the floodplain. None included a pyramid, the classic form of royal burial in earlier periods.

By building his complex at Abydos, Ahmose intended to associate his mortuary cult with that of Osiris, chief deity of Abydos and also ruler of the dead and guarantor of immortality. The physical separation between pyramid and tomb may have reflected a similar arrangement built for Osiris, with the supposed tomb of the god deep in the desert and a cult-temple at the floodplain edge. Stephen Harvey also suggests that the layout was inspired by the nearby one belonging to the Middle Kingdom ruler Senwosret III, which is similar, and that perhaps it also anticipated

16 The lost tomb of Amenhotep I

The horizon of eternity of King Djeserkare, the son of Re Amenhotep, which makes 120 cubits down from its structure/ridge (?), which is called 'the High One', north of the House of Amenhotep-of-the-Garden.

PAPYRUS ABBOTT, *c.* 1111 BC

Only a handful of tombs of the kings of the New Kingdom have never been positively identified. And of these, the most intriguing is that belonging to Amenhotep I, since the tomb's location is actually described in an ancient papyrus. In Year 16 of the reign of Ramesses IX, a commission examined a number of royal tombs for signs of robbery. The first was that of Amenhotep I, described as being '120 cubits' (*c.* 61 m/200 ft) below a certain visible feature, and north of a temple known as the 'House of Amenhotep-of-the-Garden'.

In the absence of any other information, locating this particular temple could be crucial in finding the king's tomb. Unfortunately, however, no temple of that name is otherwise known, and confusingly a number of temples in western Thebes are associated with persons named Amenhotep. Apart from Amenhotep I, the kings Amenhotep II and III both had their mortuary temples in the Theban necropolis: the scanty remains of the latter are opposite the Sheikh Abd el-Qurneh hill, while the entrance to Amenhotep III's is marked by the Colossi of Memnon at the southern end of the cemetery. In addition,

The coffin in which the mummy of Amenhotep I was found, now in the Cairo Museum. The body had required restoration only 40 years after his tomb had been found 'intact' by Ramesses IX's commissioners, when this new (but second-hand) coffin was provided. Ten years later, in Year 16 of Smendes, another restoration was required. The royal mummy had been removed from its own tomb before Year 10 of Siamun, when it was to be found in the tomb of Queen Inhapy, a wife of Amenhotep I's father, Ahmose, though its location is uncertain. Finally, after Year 11 of Shoshenq I Amenhotep's body was deposited in the tomb of Pinudjem II at Deir el-Bahri (TT 320), where it remained until the 19th century AD.

Amenhotep, son of Hapu, the great official of Amenhotep III, had a large mortuary temple – unique for an official of the period at Thebes – near Medinet Habu.

As for sanctuaries of Amenhotep I himself, one seems to have lain somewhere south of el-Tarif, as the Papyrus Abbott records that the tomb of Inyotef II is 'north of the House of Amenhotep-of-the-Forecourt'. Another lies at the foot of Dra Abu el-Naga, dedicated to both the king and his mother, Ahmose-Nefertiry. It had the formal name 'Men-iset', but the incarnation of Amenhotep I may have had a specific name – such as 'of-the-Garden'. Another structure was built for the king at Deir el-Bahri, where his wife, Merytamun, had her tomb (TT 358); its name is unknown. Deir el-Medina, the workmen's village for those who constructed the tombs in the Valley of the Kings, had Amenhotep I as its patron deity. The village thus housed a number of shrines of the king, which again could have included the elusive 'house' of Papyrus Abbott.

Archaeological investigation

Various Egyptologists have attempted to locate Amenhotep I's tomb on the basis of the Abbott

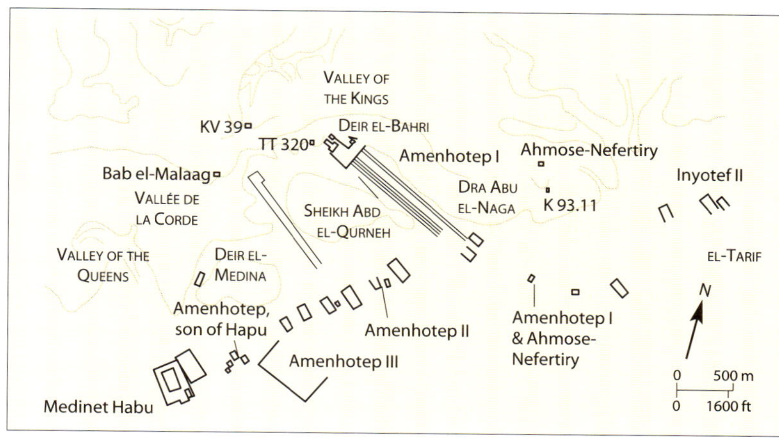

Map of western Thebes showing the monuments mentioned in the text.

description. Arthur Weigall suggested in 1909 that it might be KV 39, a then recently opened tomb at the head of the Valley of the Kings. He estimated that this lay the requisite distance below a group of workmen's huts located on the ridge above the tomb.

South of the site of this tomb is Medinet Habu, and Weigall suggested that the 'House of Amenhotep-of-the-Garden' was actually the 18th Dynasty temple in the main Medinet Habu complex. Unfortunately, there is no evidence for Amenhotep I having any involvement in the

Below *The Valley of the Kings as it begins to open out below tomb KV 39, with the path used by the workmen from Deir el-Medina visible at the right.*

Above *View from tomb KV 39 towards the temple of Medinet Habu, which Arthur Weigall identified as the 'House of Amenhotep-of-the-Garden'. Nearby was the temple of Amenhotep, son of Hapu, a courtier who lived much later than Amenhotep I, but was well known to the Theban community.*

building of this temple. On the other hand, the temple of Amenhotep, son of Hapu was later found some way to the north, and still further north is Deir el-Medina and its chapels of Amenhotep I.

Right *The entrance to KV 39, which has become the focus of the search for the tomb of Amenhotep I.*

The tomb labelled KV 39 has thus appeared an attractive option for the king's tomb, although not fitting in particularly well with the rest of the Abbott itinerary, which otherwise concentrates on the northern part of the necropolis – and actually only lying about 40 cubits vertically below the ridge. However, KV 39's excavation since 1989 has revealed a unique plan and material that suggests that it was a communal tomb, probably for members of the royal family. As to its date, items from foundation deposits bear the name of Amenhotep II, although some fragments do bear Amenhotep I's name.

In 1914 Howard Carter discovered a tomb on the summit of the Dra Abu el-Naga hill, north of the Amenhotep I/Ahmose-Nefertiry temple on the plain below. In contrast with KV 39, this tomb contained ample evidence of an early 18th Dynasty date, with items naming both Amenhotep and his mother. Carter accordingly claimed the sepulchre as the king's. Its position north of a sanctuary of Amenhotep was clear enough; however, the '120 cubit' datum was only achievable by using the interior measurements of the tomb – and even then by double-counting the depth of the 'well' in the tomb ('down and up again'). Since Papyrus Abbott was concerned only with the location of tombs, and there is no indication that Amenhotep I's tomb was entered by the inspectors, such an interpretation is unlikely. The tomb has therefore generally been interpreted as that of Ahmose-Nefertiry. On the other hand, Nicholas Reeves noted in 1990 that a cairn (one, however, of many on the hilltop) lies an appropriate distance above the tomb, which shows signs of having been enlarged, potentially for a (re?)burial of the king with his mother.

Two further possibilities were mooted by Elizabeth Thomas in 1966. These were a pair of tombs lying high up in the Theban cliffs, but far below the cliff-top path from Deir el-Medina to Deir el-Bahri. However, neither of these – the Bab el-Malaag and the tomb in the 'Vallée de la Corde' – have revealed anything attributable to Amenhotep I.

Yet another candidate was proposed by Franz-Jürgen Schmitz in 1978. Amenhotep I's mummy was found in 1881 in the great cache at Deir el-Bahri (TT 320), and Schmitz proposed that this was where the king lay at the time of the Abbott inspection. However, his interpretation of the papyrus' measurement is highly questionable, while it also seems clear that the tomb did not take its final form until 150 years after Ramesses IX's time, and that the royal mummies were interred there even later, during the reign of Shoshenq I.

Amenhotep's tomb discovered?

A fresh candidate was not forthcoming until 1993, when Daniel Polz's excavations high on Dra Abu el-Naga revealed a very large pillared rock-cut tomb chapel (K 93.11), due north of the Amenhotep I/Ahmose-Nefertiry temple. Within, a 10-m (33-ft) shaft opened into a spacious gallery, with a small burial chamber and cutting for a coffin at the end. The chapel had been extended on a number of occasions between the 18th and 20th Dynasties by such worthies as a Mayor of Thebes, a High Priest of Amun, a God's Wife of Amun and a head of the Deir el-Medina community, arguing for a most exalted original owner. In addition, it lies close to the tombs of Amenhotep's 17th Dynasty predecessors, and resembles them in design. While no proof has yet been found, this tomb seems at present the most credible candidate for Amenhotep I's tomb – the last royal tomb of the New Kingdom to be built outside the Valley of the Kings.

Dra Abu el-Naga, the most likely location of Amenhotep I's tomb. The pyramids of the kings of the 17th Dynasty were built here and it is thus a logical site for the tomb of Amenhotep I. His successor, Thutmose I, was certainly not his son and, interestingly, abandoned the ancient cemetery in favour of a new one: the Valley of the Kings.

17 Where is the body of Akhenaten?

Splendid you rise in heaven's lightland, O living Aten, creator of life!
When you have dawned in eastern lightland, you fill every land with your beauty.
You are beauteous, great, radiant, high over every land....
THE GREAT HYMN TO THE ATEN, c. 1348 BC

Akhenaten died around 1336 BC in the 17th year of his controversial reign (p. 120). His last years are cloaked in obscurity, and even the final destination of his body is an ongoing mystery. Presumably, his original intention was to be interred in the Valley of the Kings at Thebes, close to his father and his distinguished ancestors of the 18th Dynasty. Nothing certain is known about any tomb that may have been built for him there, although it has been suggested that the unfinished tomb WV (West Valley) 25 might have been originally planned for his burial.

The Valley of the Kings, Thebes, in a photo taken around 1910. The entrance to the controversial tomb KV 55 is in the foreground.

Nevertheless, following the decision to make Amarna (ancient Akhetaten) the political and religious capital of Egypt, work on Theban royal tombs was halted in favour of a new and bigger project.

The royal tomb at Amarna

A new royal tomb was designed for the new capital, and this tomb was unusual in many ways. Instead of being oriented towards the west and the setting sun, the royal tomb of Amarna was oriented towards the east and the sunrise. And instead of placing the burial chamber sharply to the left of a series of antechambers and corridors, the new tomb was arranged in a straight line so that the sun's rays could penetrate to the place of eternal rest of a king who had dedicated his reign to proclaim the unique truth of the sun god.

This innovative tomb was located far from the centre of the new capital, more than one hour's ride eastwards from the mouth of Wadi Abu Hasa el-Bahri. However, despite its apparent remoteness, Michael Mallinson has suggested that this tomb actually served as the focus for a huge architectural scheme for the construction of the new capital. Placing the tomb in the east reinforced the idea that the king would return every day, eternally united with the body of his father, Re, the sun god. It was probably part of Akhenaten's original plan to provide his new capital with a counterpart to the Valley of the Kings, with his successors being buried in the vicinity of his own tomb in this remote desert.

The Egyptian conception of the tomb, most especially the royal tomb, represents the cosmic mechanism which ensures the continuity of order on earth and the perpetuation of the memory of its owner. It is not a static place to be abandoned after the burial. This is crucial in the case of the Amarna tomb, because the tomb itself seems to have been designed to ensure the continued

Above right *The haunting face of Akhenaten, exhibiting the distinctive style for depicting royalty first developed during the reign of his father, Amenhotep III.*

Right *Akhenaten and Nefertiti worship the Aten in a scene from a wall relief from the Royal Tomb at Amarna.*

Tomb KV 55 in the Valley of the Kings at Thebes may perhaps have been the final resting place of the 'heretic' king.

The smashed sarcophagus found in Tomb KV 55 was prepared for Queen Tiy, mother of Akhenaten, but was adapted and could have contained the body of Akhenaten himself. It has been restored and is now in Cairo Museum.

existence of a universe of which the new capital was merely a scale model. It is not surprising, therefore, that when Amarna was abandoned after the death of Akhenaten, along with the beliefs that had inspired it, this focal tomb was also dismantled. At this moment, quite probably, the bodies of the king and of anyone who was perhaps buried with him were removed. The question then is where to?

It has been assumed that the royal family returned with Tutankhamun, Akhenaten's son and successor, not to Thebes, the city where Amun-Re was worshipped, but to Memphis, the oldest capital of Egypt. Here the boy-king proclaimed his 'Restoration Decree', restoring the cult of Amun-Re. In the Saqqara necropolis, to the west of Memphis, have been found the tombs of some of his most important courtiers, such as the treasurer Maya and the general Horemheb, who later became pharaoh.

However, no trace of the whereabouts of the body of Akhenaten, or of any other king, has been found at Memphis because royal burial returned immediately to the Valley of the Kings. Moreover one mysterious and enigmatic tomb in the Valley has been proposed as the final resting-place of the 'heretic' monarch.

The mysterious Tomb 55

Tomb KV 55 was discovered by the American millionaire, Theodore M. Davis, in 1907. It contained many items of diverse provenances, mostly deliberately broken and in a state of considerable disarray. Most importantly there was a fine but decayed coffin prepared originally for a noble woman but subsequently adapted for use by a king. The name in the royal cartouches, however, had been erased, and its mask had been smashed to obscure the identity of the owner, presumably the decomposed mummified body that lay within. As well as the coffin, parts of a wooden shrine dedicated to Tiy, mother of Akhenaten, were found, and materials belonging to the burial equipment of Kiya, a secondary wife of Akhenaten (and probably the mother of Akhenaten's only known son, Tutankhamun). Finally, there were 'magic bricks' bearing the name of Akhenaten himself.

The diversity of the materials puzzled the experts. Because of an early identification of the body as female, Davis published his find as *The Tomb of Queen Tiyi*, while Arthur Weigall, supervisor of Davis's works on behalf of the Egyptian government, argued from the beginning that the identity of the occupant of the coffin was none other than Akhenaten. However, the anatomist, Grafton Elliot Smith, fixed the age at death of the body in the coffin as around 25 years, which was too young for Akhenaten, with his 17-year reign. Other studies have fixed the age of the body as above 35 years old, and closely related to Tutankhamun, sharing even his blood group, though a recent re-examination by Joyce Filer put the age at 20 to 25; consensus has still not been reached.

In 1967, the Russian Egyptologist Yuri Perepelkin, proposed that KV 55 was, in fact, the tomb to which both Akhenaten and Tiy were moved after the abandonment of Amarna. Nicholas Reeves has since argued that, at a later date – probably during the excavation of the tomb of Ramesses IX (who died *c.* 1108 BC), directly above KV 55 – the tomb-builders stumbled upon the tomb by mistake. At this point they panicked at the discovery of the embarrassing burial of the heretic king, and so removed the body of Tiy (p. 137), erased the names and other identifying features of the coffin, even dropping a stone on its face.

If the body inside the coffin in this mysterious tomb really does belong to Akhenaten – and we still cannot say this for certain – then we would have both the body and the final resting-place of a king who wanted to change the course of human history and religion.

Above right *A portrait of Queen Tiy, mother of Akhenaten, from Berlin Museum. Much of the burial equipment found in KV 55 belonged to her, and it was first thought that the body in the sarcophagus was hers also.*

Left *One of the canopic jars from the royal burial in KV 55 – the traditional heads of the Four Sons of Horus which usually form the lids of such jars have been substituted with female heads, probably the royal princesses.*

Right *A magic brick found in KV 55 bearing the name of Akhenaten.*

18 The mausoleum of the sons of Rameses II

Proceeding along the central branch, we arrive at the Fifth Tomb, *on the left side.... As we proceed, the destruction becomes greater; and at length ... nothing is seen but rubbish and fragments of stone, through which a passage has been made with difficulty and danger.*
EDWARD LANE, 1827

The mode of burial for Egyptian kings and for members of the royal family varied considerably over time. In the New Kingdom, during the 18th Dynasty, the kings were buried in multi-chambered, rock-cut tombs carved deep into the cliffs of the Valley of the Kings. For their wives and children a range of provisions are known, from simple interments in side-rooms of the king's own tomb to individual sepulchres. One particular innovation, however, was the development of the communal tomb, in which a series of people might be laid to rest.

A colossal head of Rameses II in the king's mortuary temple, the Ramesseum, at Thebes.

The most elaborate of these seems to have been KV 39 (in the system of numbering the tombs in the Valley), at the far southern extremity of the Valley of the Kings. Material from the tomb suggests that it was (re-?)founded by Amenhotep II, and then extended at least twice for the burials of nine or more people, whose coffins seem to be datable to the second half of the 18th Dynasty. Although on a much smaller scale, KV 39 would appear to be the precursor of one of the most extraordinary monuments of ancient Egypt – KV 5.

Discovery and rediscovery

The tomb simply labelled KV 5 lies in the outer part of the Valley of the Kings, roughly opposite that belonging to Ramesses II (KV 7). Its location features on a number of early maps of the Valley and the first person to enter it in modern times seems to have been the explorer James Burton (1788–1862), in 1825. With great difficulty, Burton managed to locate a huge, 16-pillared hall, together with a series of subsidiary rooms; he also recorded the cartouche of Ramesses II in the tomb. The last individual known to have penetrated the structure before 1987 was Howard Carter, at the beginning of the 20th century. Subsequently, the entrance became buried and a sewer pipe was laid above it – leakage from which would later do considerable damage to the tomb. There was little discussion of the identity of its owner, although opinions included Ramesses II himself, before he abandoned it in favour of his final resting place, KV 7, and one or more of that king's many sons – the names of some 50 of them are known.

During the 1970s, the Theban Mapping Project was established, first based at the University of California-Berkeley, and later at the American University in Cairo, under the direction of Kent Weeks. Its aim was to prepare detailed maps of the Theban necropolis, with both above- and below-ground features included. Where appropriate, known buried tombs were re-opened to permit their inclusion, and since KV 5's precise position was now lost, excavations began in 1987 to locate it.

Having found the tomb where expected, a programme of excavation was begun that has continued into the 21st century. The outermost two chambers immediately revealed scenes of Amenhirkopshef and Ramesses, two of the elder sons of Ramesses II. At the time, it was assumed that the plan produced by Burton in 1825 represented nearly all of the tomb's layout. However, in 1995, a long gallery was located at the rear of the 16-pillared hall, leading to a cross-passage, all lined with small chambers and decorated in relief. Later, two further chamber-lined passages were found leading from the other side of the 16-pillared hall. The total number of chambers in the tomb thus far amounts to at least 150.

The form of the tomb is without parallel in the Valley – or indeed elsewhere – with its massive central hall, and its ramifications extending in all directions. The oddest parts are two galleries leading back under the Valley, the ends of which have yet to be reached by the excavators. They seem to be heading towards Ramesses II's own tomb (KV 7 – currently under excavation by a French team), diagonally opposite KV 5 on the other side of the Valley path, and it is not impossible that the two sepulchres may have some kind of subterranean connection: only the completion of the clearance of both will tell.

The outermost part of KV 5 seems originally to have been an 18th Dynasty tomb, taken over and massively enlarged during the reign of Ramesses II – a graffito in the tomb states that in 'Year 19 [took place] the continuation of the work'. Although its purpose as a burial place for sons of Ramesses II is made clear by the fragmentary decoration and objects found, the intended functions of specific parts of the tomb are obscure. The large room to the left of the 16-pillared hall (Y) seems to have been a burial chamber, perhaps with two rows of pillars, and

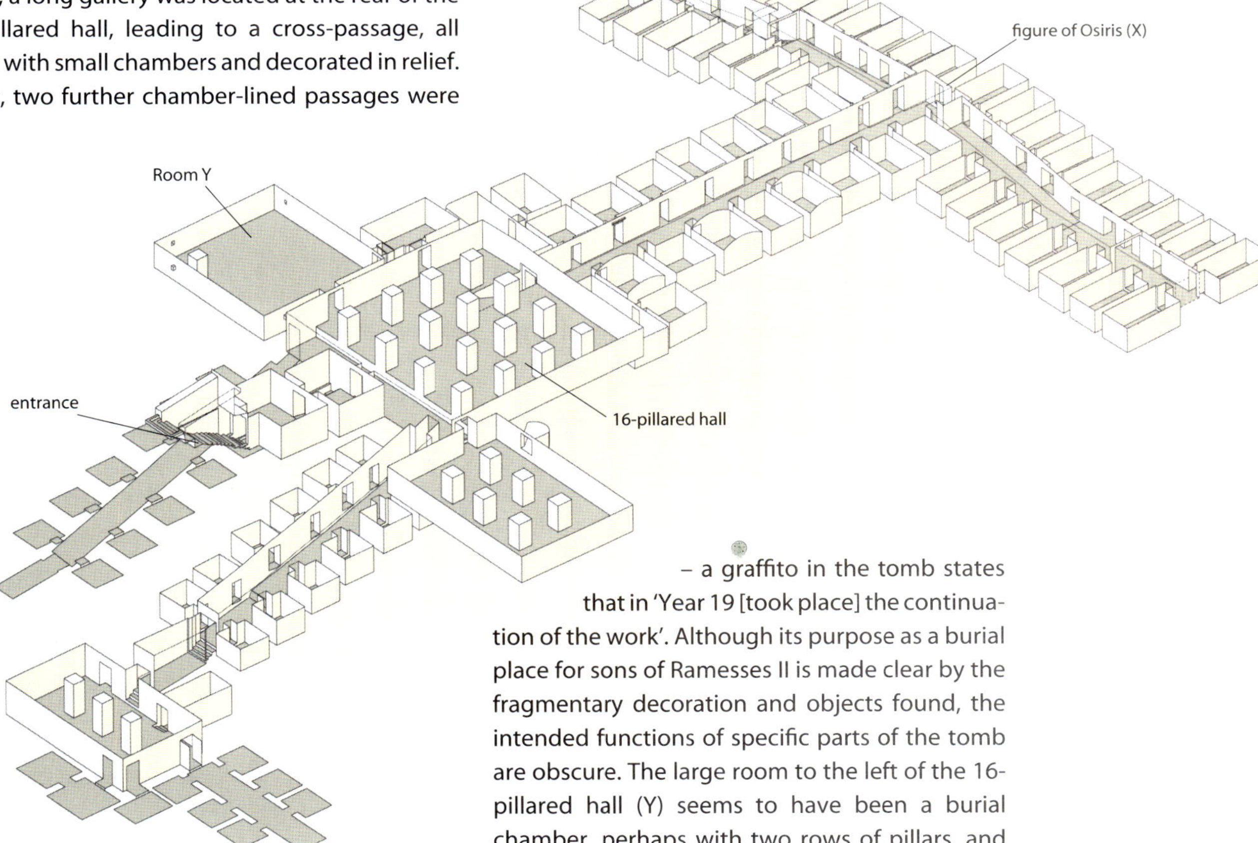

Isometric drawing of the tomb of the sons of Ramesses II as revealed in 2000.

Above *Prince Amenhirkopshef, the eldest son of Ramesses II, stands behind his father as the latter makes offerings. Behind them is the cow of Hathor. This scene is on the west wall of the first chamber of the tomb.*

niches for protective magic bricks in its walls; a side-room contained a considerable number of pottery containers for food and drink offerings, now broken, together with the remains of their contents.

Few other rooms show clear evidence for having been actual burial chambers, although a pit in the second chamber of the tomb contained a body that might represent an original interment. In particular, the purpose of the numerous (70+) small chambers that flank the long galleries is obscure, being seemingly too small to contain burials in coffins and displaying no evidence for other uses.

These mysteries are increased by the scarcity of material bearing princes' names. Only Amenhirkopshef and Ramesses are definitively shown on the walls of the tomb, although there are various depictions of other princes in the tomb whose names are lost. Fragmentary canopic jars have been found belonging to Amenhirkopshef, Meryatum, Sety and (perhaps) Meryamun, confirming that they were interred in KV 5. Clearly, the tomb is far too large for just these five men. It is possible that much more inscribed material will be found at the lowest points of the tomb, where they could have been deposited by the flooding that is responsible for most of the debris found in the tomb: only time (and excavation) will reveal more of the secrets of KV 5.

Right *One of Kent Weeks's team at work in KV 5; the debris in front of him was washed into the tomb by one of the many floods that had choked the tomb with rubble by the beginning of the 19th century* AD.

Opposite *The en-face figure of Osiris that is carved in the wall at the end of the principal gallery of the tomb (marked X on the isometric drawing on p. 89).*

18

Who robbed the Valley of the Kings?

The scribe of the Tomb from the cemetery area, Harsheri, son of Amennakht, and the scribe of the Tomb, Pabes, told me five very grave offences deserving death. Now I will send about them to Pharaoh, my lord, in order to have Pharaoh's men sent to deal with all of you.

PASER, MAYOR OF EAST THEBES, *c.* 1111 BC

Right *Macabre photograph of mummies found in the tomb of Amenhotep II, which the Theban authorities had used for the secret reburial of kings during the 21st Dynasty. Their bodies had been mutilated by modern tomb-robbers. The identities of the dead are not known, though the woman on the left (the 'Elder Lady') has been the subject of much speculation (p. 137).*

Opposite left *Letter to Ramesses XI's general, Piankh, from the security chief, Karu, and other workmen responsible for the Valley of the Kings. Written at a time of political turmoil in Thebes, issues discussed include opening and inspecting an unnamed tomb.*

In 24 BC the Greek geographer Strabo explored the Valley of the Kings and found some 40 tombs belonging to Egypt's ancient kings lying open and empty. The tradition of burying people with valuables dates back many centuries before the pharaohs, and it is not difficult to suppose that Egyptians had looted the tombs of their forebears, despite the terrible punishments laid down for such crimes, such as beating, mutilation and impalement. As early as the 4th Dynasty, Khufu had the exquisite grave-goods of his mother, Hetepheres, reburied beside his pyramid at Giza, presumably because her original burial had been violated. By the New Kingdom,

royal tombs were well known as repositories of finery, and the behaviour of the men who worked in the Valley of the Kings was carefully monitored by the authorities of Thebes.

Even so, allegations of tomb robbery, such as that reported by Paser, were not unheard of. The tomb of Tutankhamun was violated twice within months of his burial around 1322 BC. One century later, a foreman in the Valley, a notorious character called Paneb, was accused of stealing from the burial of Sety II while it was still being prepared. Most importantly, several papyri from the 20th Dynasty detail allegations of tomb robbery in and around the Valley. There were major investigations under Ramesses IX around 1111 BC and then some 25 years later under Ramesses XI.

In each case, investigators uncovered systematic looting of burials by the workmen of West Thebes, who were interested in precious metals, woods and ivory and the highest quality linens and perfumes. Now, it is hard to imagine how ordinary workmen could benefit from these goods. In a non-monetary economy, it would be difficult to exchange such items for anything other than the kinds of goods and favours only at the disposal of the authorities. For this reason, the ancients recognized that tomb robbery called into question the integrity of the community at all levels, and many modern commentators have concluded that it must have taken place with the connivance of officials. It is also noteworthy that the three main periods of tomb robbery, at the ends of the 18th, 19th and 20th Dynasties, were times of significant political tension at Thebes. In periods of political stability, robbery – and corruption – might have been less prevalent.

The royal dimension

In 1881, following some detective work by Émile Brugsch of the Egyptian Antiquities Service, a secret tomb was discovered in the Theban hills above Deir el-Bahri. In it were some 40 bodies, including at least 11 pharaohs of the New Kingdom, such as Ramesses II and his father, Sety I. Seventeen years on, Victor Loret discovered another cache of kings in the Valley itself, in the tomb of Amenhotep II. Notes scribbled on coffins explained that these caches were the work of Theban officials, though apparently for reasons of safety rather than in response to robbery. In the 21st Dynasty the royal cemetery, along with the royal residence, had been transferred to Tanis, and the security infrastructure of the Valley had been dismantled. By the time of the high-priest Pinudjem I (*c.* 1050–1030 BC), most royal burials in Thebes had been secretly gathered together and only the controversial Amarna

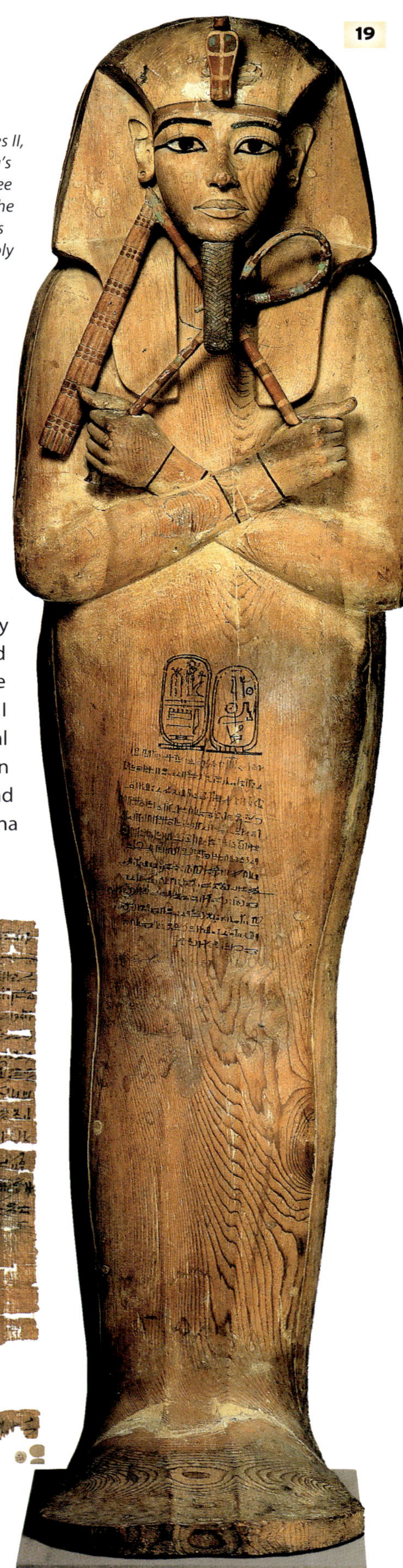

Wooden coffin used to rebury Ramesses II, found at Deir el-Bahri in 1881. The king's body was moved by priests at least three times following the abandonment of the Valley of the Kings, as recorded on texts inked on the lid. This coffin was probably not the king's original one, and his valuable grave-goods were removed, perhaps by the authorities themselves.

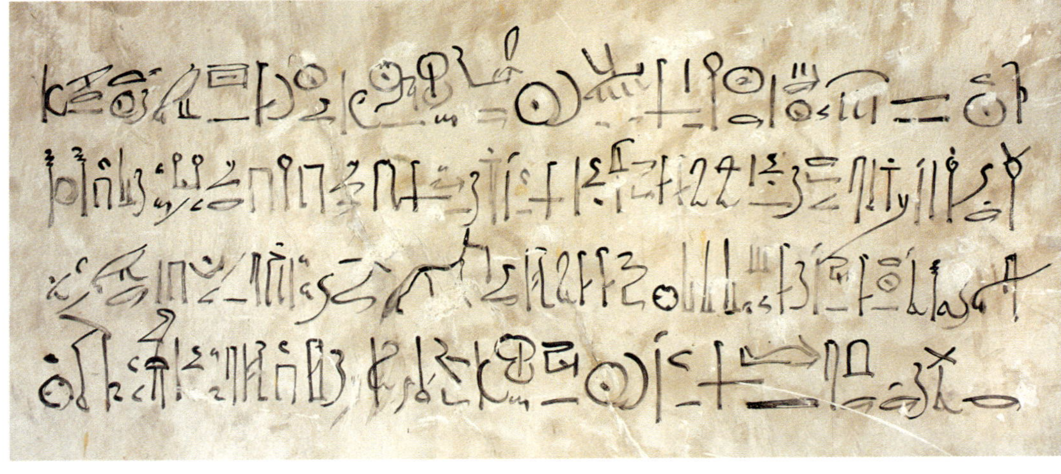

Right *Graffito inside the tomb of Thutmose IV, written around 1312 BC by the authority of Maya, a royal official investigating the desecration of the king's burial.*

Below *Ostracon (limestone flake) with a sketch of a mason at work. The Valley of the Kings was a busy workplace, and the locations of royal tombs were well known to the many people involved in building them.*

Bottom *Ostracon with a plan made during the construction of a royal tomb.*

period pharaohs, such as Tutankhamun and the body in KV 55 (p. 84), were left behind. The coffins and mummies had been stripped of their finery, not by robbers but by the officials themselves.

Confirmation of this emerged when the royal tombs at Tanis were excavated from 1939 (p. 95). Two sarcophagi in the tomb of Psusennes I had originally come from Thebes; one still bore the name of Merenptah, son and successor of Ramesses II, some 200 years earlier. Likewise Psusennes' gold mask (p. 220) bears a strong similarity to the celebrated mask of Tutankhamun, and objects naming rulers such as Ramesses II were also discovered. On the other hand it is also true that the mask of Amenemope and the coffins of Psusennes (p. 249) and Shoshenq II (p. 97) are stylistically distinct from those of the New Kingdom, and so it appears that the kings of the 21st and 22nd Dynasties could still command the best craftsmanship. Nevertheless, the dismantling of the Valley undoubtedly offered a simple opportunity to obtain goods and materials of the highest quality, made venerable by belonging to Egypt's greatest kings.

So who robbed the Valley of the Kings? Over the centuries, many people have had a hand in pilfering items, including even the workmen who built the tombs, and, for that matter, some archaeologists who rediscovered the Valley for the benefit of a modern audience. However, none of these were responsible for the empty sepulchres visited by Strabo. These had long before been cleared by the Theban authorities, and their occupants and grave-goods removed to safe hiding places, or else cannibalized to meet the ongoing imperative of providing for the burial of the reigning king of Egypt.

The missing tombs of Tanis

20

It was evident that water had found access ... to the tomb [of Shoshenq II], as ... the bones of the lower limbs ... were covered in fine rootlets, while the hip bones and sacrum had a deposit of earthy material which was carried into the coffin by water.
DOUGLAS DERRY, 1939

The tombs of a number of the kings of the Third Intermediate Period were built at Tanis (modern San el-Hagar), which at that time was the principal seat of government. In all, seven sepulchres of rulers of the 21st and 22nd Dynasties have been found there since 1939 (see table). However, by no means all the kings of these two dynasties are present in the necropolis at Tanis, the principal absences being Smendes (p. 140) and Amenemnesu of the 21st Dynasty, and Shoshenq I and Osorkon I of the 22nd.

Intriguingly, examination of the architecture of the tombs shows very clearly that NRT-I was constructed before NRT-III – reversing the generally accepted historical order of their occupants – since the outer wall of the former was trimmed to accommodate the latter. In addition, NRT-III's chambers were arranged to avoid the earlier structure.

This apparent chronological anomaly has been used to argue that received wisdom is actually wrong, and that Osorkon II preceded Psusennes I on the throne. The 'gap' in the royal sequence has also been used – along with another 'gap' in the sequence of Apis bulls at Saqqara (p. 251) – to support a radical revision of

TOMB	ULTIMATE PRIMARY OCCUPANT	DYNASTY	OTHER ROYAL OCCUPANTS	DYNASTY
NRT-I	Osorkon II	22nd	Takelot I Shoshenq (V?)	22nd
NRT-II	Pimay	22nd	None	
NRT-III	Psusennes I	21st	Amenemope Siamun Psusennes II Shoshenq II	21st 22nd
NRT-IV	None: built for Amenemope	21st		
NRT-V	Shoshenq III	22nd	Shoshenq IV	22nd
NRT-VI	Not known	21st/22nd		
NRT-VII	Not known	22nd		

Above *Table to show the various occupants of the royal tombs of Tanis.*

Right *View of the royal necropolis of Tanis, with NRT-III on the left, and NRT-I on the right. These stone structures would originally have been deeply buried under the pavement of the temple, and probably surmounted by small chapels.*

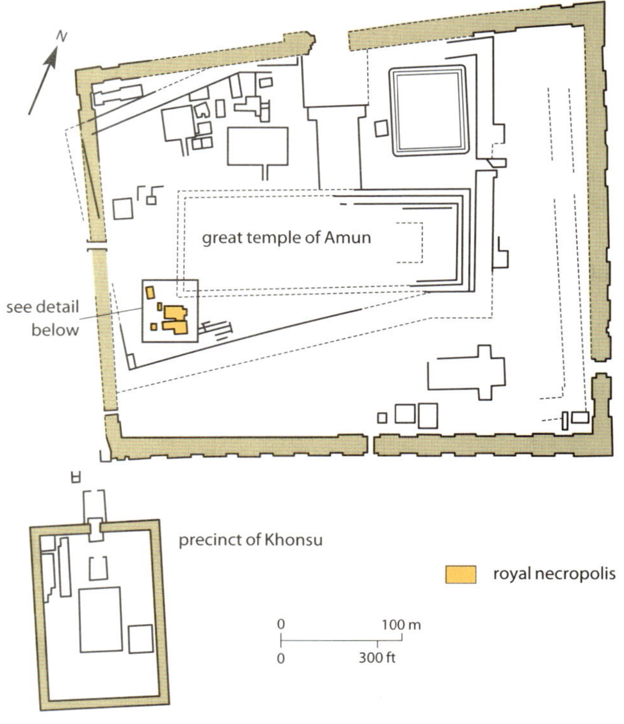

Left *Plan of the temple area of Tanis, showing the location of the royal necropolis.*

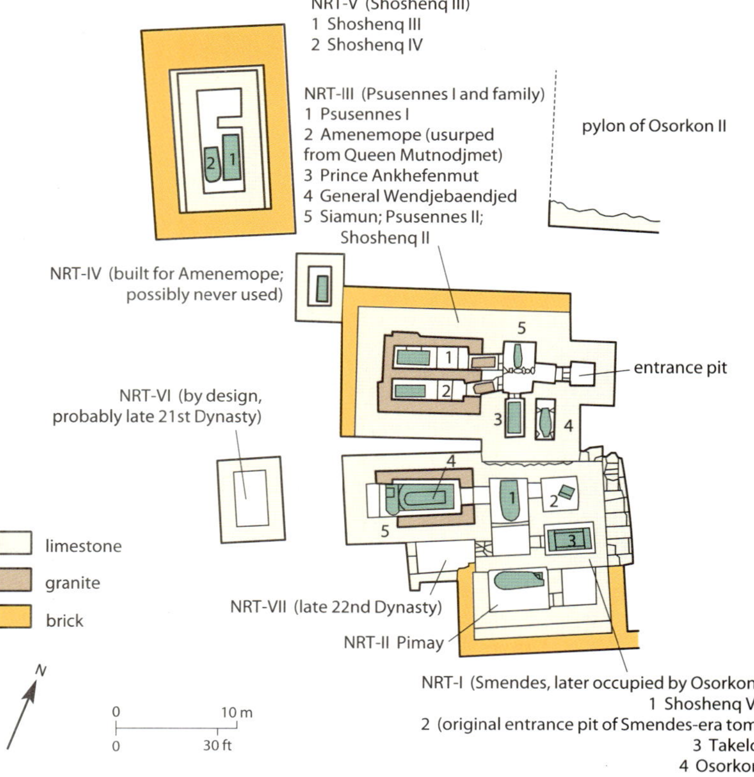

Below left *Plan of the royal necropolis at Tanis; the ultimate occupants of the various chambers are currently assessed as listed.*

the relative placement of kings and dynasties at this time. Therefore, it is important to take a closer look at some of these issues at Tanis.

The Smendes problem and dating NRT-I

The questions surrounding the apparent dating of Osorkon II's tomb, NRT-I, and the lack of a tomb for Smendes are intimately linked, as there is ample structural evidence to show that NRT-I's current form is the result of considerable modifications. Both NRT-I and III are unique at Tanis in having granite burial chambers within a basic limestone structure – all the others are built purely of limestone, and are of much simpler design – and they thus clearly belong together chronologically.

Given the fact that it had certainly been rebuilt, it seems very likely that NRT-I originally belonged to Smendes – his burial at Tanis is suggested by the fact that one of his canopic jars was purchased nearby (p. 140). No trace of any decoration belonging to this hypothetical first phase has been identified, but it is important to note that decoration was never *de rigueur* for royal burial chambers: leaving aside the vast majority of pyramids, at Tanis tombs NRT-II, IV, VI and VII all had their walls left bare.

As with so many ancient monuments in Egypt – and especially at this period – NRT-I had been usurped from a predecessor, in this case perhaps after robbery. Osorkon II's changes to the tomb seem to have comprised the addition of decoration, alterations to the eastern part of the sepulchre – in particular the addition of a sarcophagus for his father, Takelot I – and the introduction of a new sarcophagus into the principal burial chamber for himself. The latter operation probably accounts for the dismantled state of the west wall of the burial chamber, into which was also added a sarcophagus for a son of Osorkon II, Hornakhte.

Allocating NRT-I to Smendes still leaves Amenemnesu without a tomb. He may have been buried in NRT-VI, but the king's status is obscure and it is possible that he may have been based – and perhaps therefore buried – in the south of Egypt, particularly as he bears the epithet within his cartouche of 'Ruler of Thebes'.

The 'gap'

While the next two kings of the 21st Dynasty, Psusennes I and Amenemope, both have tombs at Tanis – although the mummy of the latter was ultimately placed in the sarcophagus of Psusennes I's queen in NRT-III – no dedicated royal tomb is then known until the time of Osorkon II, who, as we have seen, also incorporated a chamber for his father, Takelot I, into his rebuilding of NRT-I. Two completely decayed mummies in the antechamber of NRT-III seem, on the basis of *shabtys* found with them, to be those of Siamun and Psusennes II. These may perhaps have been buried in this modest way as a result of the eclipse of the 21st Dynasty line that accompanied the foundation of the 22nd Dynasty. However, nothing is known of the burials of the first Libyan kings, Osochor, Shoshenq I and Osorkon I, with the exception of the canopic chest of the second, now in Berlin but of unknown provenance. It is possible that one or the other of them might have owned NRT-VI, but its modest size makes it unlikely that it could have belonged to either Shoshenq I or Osorkon I, and would in any case still leave two of three kings lacking a tomb.

A clue to the solution of the problem of the tombs at Tanis lies in a third body that was found in Psusennes I's antechamber. It belonged to Shoshenq II – probably a co-regent of Osorkon I – and was lying in a silver coffin which showed signs of having been moved to this spot from elsewhere. Plant growth found on the mummy is consistent with it having spent some time in standing water – something for which there is no evidence in NRT-III. This implies that the mummy had first been buried in a different tomb which was subject to flooding, presumably well away from Tanis. Shoshenq II's burial in another location would imply similar arrangements for the earlier members of his family – perhaps near Bubastis, which seems to have been the home town of the new dynasty.

Such a scenario would also explain Osorkon II's usurpation of an old tomb rather than the building of a new one, as well as the odd situation of providing a chamber within it for his father. Flooding of the tombs of Shoshenq II and Takelot I, and perhaps his own intended tomb, could have led to an evacuation from this location back to the old necropolis at Tanis, where the tombs of Psusennes I and Smendes were placed at the disposal of the refugees – one simply as lodging for Shoshenq, the other entirely refurbished to accommodate Osorkon and Takelot.

The mummy of Shoshenq II was enclosed in a silver coffin: ***above*** *is a detail of his cartouches incised on the coffin;* ***right*** *is the striking falcon head that is typical of mid-Third Intermediate Period royal coffins.*

21 Are there more royal tombs in Egypt?

I fear that the Valley of the Tombs is now exhausted.
THEODORE M. DAVIS, 1912

Over two centuries of excavation in Egypt have revealed countless sepulchres of the great and the not-so-great. Among them are some 100 tombs that can be attributed with confidence to specific kings. However, from the dawn of Egyptian history around 3000 BC to the end of the country's ancient independence in 30 BC, approximately 300 kings ruled over the land. Where, then, are the 'missing' tombs, and might anything remain of them?

Curiously, the very first royal dynasty of Egypt has the best 'record', with all eight rulers having tombs at Umm el-Qa'ab in the great Abydos cemetery. The tombs of the first and the third kings of the 2nd Dynasty are at Saqqara, which would suggest that the intervening ruler, Reneb, was also buried there – especially as his tomb-stela was purchased nearby. The rest of the dynasty, however, is problematic, as only two definitely assigned tombs exist – both at Abydos. There are also two tombs at Saqqara, overbuilt respectively by Djoser's 3rd Dynasty Step Pyramid enclosure, and another by the 18th Dynasty tomb of Meryneith, High Priest of the Aten, which may include that of Reneb and some of the 'missing' kings. However, as the latter part

The pitiful remains of the 8th Dynasty pyramid of Ibi lie at South Saqqara, next to the causeway of the much mightier monument of Pepy II. It is probable that other kings of the dynasty were interred in this general area.

Behind the Sheikh Abd el-Qurneh hill at Thebes lies the foundation-platform of an early Middle Kingdom royal temple-tomb. It remains uncertain whether it belonged to Montuhotep III, or to Amenemhat I, as no inscriptions survive.

of the 2nd Dynasty is known to have been riven with civil war, the construction, let alone survival, of royal tombs seems rather uncertain.

The Old Kingdom which follows has an almost unbroken string of tombs. This is the Pyramid Age, during which almost every king built such a monument in one of the cemeteries that stretch from Abu Roash, north of modern Cairo, to Meidum, on the edge of the Faiyum. There are a few times during this period when the attribution of a particular pyramid is not definite, being based on design or location only, but until after the death of Pepy II there is only one king to whom no tomb can be allocated. This is the ephemeral Userkare of the early 6th Dynasty, who, at best, seems to have held the throne for a very short period and in irregular circumstances.

Intermediate problems

After Pepy II, however, there is a great gap in the record, covering perhaps a century. During this time – the 7th to the end of the 10th Dynasties – only one kingly sepulchre has been identified, the tiny pyramid of Ibi at South Saqqara. There is also a mention of the pyramid of the 10th Dynasty King Merykare on the stela of one of his mortuary priests. Its findspot implies that the king's monument may have lain close to the 6th Dynasty pyramid of Teti, but the only 'spare' pyramid in this area is, on the basis of its design, most likely to be that of the 5th Dynasty Menkauhor.

Of the remaining kings of this 'gap', most are little more than names in later king-lists. It is probable, therefore, that their tombs were small (witness the pyramid of Ibi, no larger than an Old Kingdom queen's tomb), likely to be unfinished, and with any ruins now well hidden under the sands of Saqqara. Although the area has seen extensive excavations, huge tracts remain untouched, particularly at South Saqqara, where the 6th Dynasty kings were buried, and where Ibi's diminutive pyramid was also found.

In contrast, the 11th and 12th Dynasties present few problems – the only difficulties lie at their respective ends. A number of Middle Kingdom graffiti mention the priesthood of the tomb of Montuhotep III, but the structure itself has never been positively identified. An unfinished temple-tomb of the right type lies behind Sheikh Abd el-Qurneh at Thebes, but is uninscribed, and has also been proposed as an initial tomb of Amenemhat I, abandoned when he built a pyramid at Lisht. A record also exists of quarrying the sarcophagus of Montuhotep IV, but no potential tomb to house it has ever been detected.

All kings of the 12th Dynasty have well-known pyramids, except for the last two, Amenemhat IV and Nefrusobk. Many of their 13th Dynasty successors also lack known burial places, and although a number of anonymous ruined pyramids in the Dahshur area can be dated to the period on grounds of their design, they represent only a fraction of the gap. A clue to the kind of burial that may have been employed for these kings is provided by the tomb of Hor (p. 233). A simple shaft-tomb, located in the pyramid-enclosure of Amenemhat III at Dahshur, formed

Below *Gemeni, who was buried near the pyramid of Teti at Saqqara, was, among other things, a priest of the lost pyramid of Merykare.*

Above *The principal royal necropolis of the later Middle Kingdom was Dahshur, and it is likely that many of the 'missing' kings of the 13th Dynasty were buried here. Hor was certainly interred in the area, at the foot of the 'Black Pyramid' of Amenemhat III.*

the basis of the tomb, and although extensively modified, it is unlikely that archaeologists would have identified it as belonging to a king had its contents not largely escaped the tomb robbers. Perhaps others remain unrecognized.

The short reigns enjoyed by most of the kings of the 13th to the 17th Dynasties, together with the political instabilities of these times, doubtless contributes to the lack of identified tombs. The cemetery of the 17th Dynasty at Dra Abu el-Naga at Thebes is imperfectly known, but in 2001 the tomb of Inyotef VI was rediscovered there (it had been found in the 19th century and then lost again), making it likely that others will also be revealed, some of which (like Inyotef's tomb) are mentioned in ancient records. The same excavator, Daniel Polz, may also have found another lost tomb, that of Amenhotep I (p. 80) in the same area, in which case it may contain the burial place of Ahmose, of which nothing is known. On the other hand, Ahmose may originally have been buried at the pyramid of Abydos (p. 77) that is usually held to be a cenotaph.

Left *The pyramidia of at least two lost pyramids seem to have been carried by the Hyksos to the northeast Delta. This one belongs to Ay of the 13th Dynasty.*

The New Kingdom and beyond

The following New Kingdom pharaohs nearly all have well-known tombs in the Valley of the Kings at Thebes, the main exception being Akhenaten, interred, originally at any rate, at Amarna (p. 84). The only substantive gap in the record is the tomb of Ramesses VIII – but since he reigned for under a year, it is likely to have been insignificant, or completed for another person. It is possible that he may have intended to continue the tomb he had begun as a prince (KV 19), which was ultimately used for Ramesses IX's son, Montuhirkhopshef.

Neither Ramesses X or XI appear to have been buried in their Valley of the Kings tombs. Their actual burial places (and perhaps that of Ramesses VIII) were presumably at their residence-city, Piramesse, near modern Qantir. If this is the case, they may yet come to light there. However, the cities of the Delta, where most of the later kings of Egypt lived and were probably buried, suffer from high water-tables and stone-robbing, making it unlikely that much remains to be found. The main exception is Tanis, where five royal tombs of the 21st and 22nd Dynasties have been discovered, though even here some are missing (p. 95).

The tomb of a queen named Kama was found at Tell Muqdam, where a royal line was based at the time of the invasion of the Nubian 25th Dynasty, around 730 BC. Only a handful of royal tombs of the Third Intermediate and Late Periods have been identified in the Delta. High water-tables and human destruction have made it unlikely that many more will be found.

The 26th Dynasty royal tombs are known to have been at Sais, where two were described by Herodotus; interestingly, at least one queen of the dynasty was buried at Athribis, and another possibly at Sebennytos. The kings of the 29th Dynasty had their tombs at Mendes, where the devastated remains of one, belonging Nepherites I, have been identified, centring on his massive sarcophagus. Sarcophagi are all that is known of the burials of the first and last kings of the 30th Dynasty, both examples being found reused, in Cairo and Alexandria respectively. This fact would indicate that their tombs are likely to have been destroyed; it is generally assumed that they probably lay at the dynastic home city of Sebennytos, although no certain evidence exists.

The final set of ancient royal tombs, those of the Ptolemies at Alexandria, are known from literary sources, but have never been identified. Ptolemy I had begun by building a sepulchre for Alexander the Great, whose body he hijacked on its way from Babylon to its intended burial place in Greece. The location of Alexander's tomb has long been a matter of dispute and theorizing, but seems to have lain within the 'The Palaces', the residence-area of the Ptolemaic Dynasty, part of which is now under the sea. Alternatively, in the modern Terra Sancta Cemetery are the remains of the substructure of a large tumulus-tomb of Macedonian type, conceivably the first of the two tombs built for Alexander by the Ptolemies.

The burial places of the Ptolemaic Dynasty itself seem initially to have been constructed near, but separately from, Alexander's sepulchre. Under Ptolemy IV Philopator a new royal mausoleum was constructed, known as the Sema, in which were buried not only the later Ptolemaic monarchs, but also their predecessors, including Alexander himself. Once again, little is known of this tomb, although a description by the Roman writer Lucan suggests some form of pyramidal superstructure covering subterranean vaults. The Sema tomb-complex was apparently destroyed, together with most of 'The Palaces', as a result of rioting under the Roman emperor, Aurelian, in around AD 273.

So could another royal tomb yet be found to match the dazzling splendours of Tutankhamun's? Unfortunately, many of the 'missing' tombs belong to kings whose reigns were short or in troubled times and so they are unlikely to have been buried in such magnificence; and even these, like so many of Egypt's royal tombs, may have been looted long ago.

The sarcophagus of Nectanebo II, the last native pharaoh, was found in a mosque at Alexandria; the king's intended tomb presumably lay at his native town, Sebennytos.

Pharaohs & Queens

The faces of the kings of ancient Egypt are well known to us in modern times. They have left a vast array of painted and sculpted images of themselves and their consorts, timeless in their eternal youth. Which ancient monuments are more recognizable than the gold coffins of Tutankhamun, or the temple at Abu Simbel, with its colossal statues of Ramesses II enthroned? Even the mummified bodies of many of Egypt's greatest kings have survived, so to this day we can look upon the embalmed face of Ramesses II – an old man seemingly asleep 33 centuries after he led his troops amidst the terrible slaughter of the Battle of Qadesh.

What do we know about the men and women behind these inscrutable faces? In fact, ancient texts tell us very little about their personalities or the personal issues which motivated them. Theirs was a world driven by superhuman forces which inspired or manipulated people as much as their own wishes and desires. In this world, even the will of the king could seem secondary: recalling his overwhelming victory at the Battle of Megiddo in Palestine around 1458 BC, Thutmose III insisted that 'it was my father, [the god] Amun-Re, who did it, it was not the act of men'.

Nevertheless, many of us remain fascinated by the lives – and deaths – of the pharaohs and their queens. There is one famously troublesome aspect to their relationship. Did the pharaohs marry, and have sex with, their own sisters and even daughters? If so, what justification could there be for incest?

The golden inner coffin of Tutankhamun is a defining image of ancient Egypt, combining the divine splendour of a pharaoh with the youthful beauty of a mortal man. Despite decades of speculation, we know few details about the king's life, and darkness surrounds the nature of his death.

Ramesses III depicted in the Great Harris Papyrus, which records endowments of land and workers to his mortuary cult. Ramesses III is the one king for whom we have undeniable documentary evidence about an attempt on his life, although we cannot be sure whether or not it was successful.

We also need to weigh the evidence for assassination in order to establish whether any king was ever killed by his own people. We do have some reason to suppose that such a fate might have befallen Amenemhat I and Ramesses III, although the evidence is not beyond question. Recently several writers have speculated that Tutankhamun too was murdered, but here the evidence is more problematic. There is no suggestion that Akhenaten was murdered, but his name and his memory were condemned after his death. Why? Was he a madman, a revolutionary, a religious zealot, or are these modern fantasies?

While much has been written about such kings, others have almost been erased from the pages of history. For example, what do we know today about Smendes, who founded one – perhaps two – royal dynasties? Or about Khababash, who briefly led his nation against the might of the Persian Empire? Perhaps the most troubling mystery is the 'dark age' of Nubia. After centuries of Egyptian control, Nubia became independent around 1080 BC. Subsequently it was ruled in pharaonic style by kings of the 25th Dynasty from around 800 BC onwards. But what about the 280 years between these dates? Can we really accept claims that Nubia was then a land without rulers or even a population?

The few exceptional women who ruled Egypt have generated mysteries of their own, not least who was the first woman to become king? There is no doubt that Nefrusobk became king, following her father and brother, at the end of the Middle Kingdom, but there are tantalizing suggestions from ancient records of earlier female pharaohs. In the New Kingdom Hatshepsut was so controversial as king that her name and memory were erased from monuments as emphatically as those of Akhenaten. This has led to speculation about how she died, and what finally became of her body.

Three mysteries concern perhaps the most celebrated women of ancient Egypt. Famed in the modern world for her beauty – captured in busts now in Cairo and Berlin – Nefertiti was the principal wife of Akhenaten, but she suddenly disappears from our sources around the 12th year of his reign. Did she die, was she disgraced or did she, in fact, reappear with a different name as king of Egypt herself? A woman from the age of Nefertiti was buried alongside kings but anonymously, so that she is known today simply as 'the Elder Lady'. Who was she? Indeed, was she Nefertiti? The last woman to rule Egypt was Cleopatra VII, whose name has become an enduring byword for female cunning and the seduction, then destruction, of great men. Does she deserve this ambivalent reputation, or is it the work of her enemies?

One final mystery concerns the courtier Senenmut, apparently not royalty himself but a central figure on many of the monuments of Hatshepsut and her daughter. What was the nature of their relationship? Were he and Hatshepsut, as some have speculated, secret lovers? More pointedly, could we ever hope to learn such intimate detail about the lives of pharaohs?

Did the pharaohs marry their sisters?

22

As for me, I have called to mind the mother of my mother and the mother of my father, the King's Great Wife and King's Mother, Tetishery, true of voice.
STELA OF KING AHMOSE, *c.* 1520 BC

At the beginning of the New Kingdom, Queen Ahhotep II married a king who was also her brother, presumably either Taa or Kamose. The pair had a son, Ahmose, who in turn married his sister, Ahmose-Nefertiry; they became parents of Amenhotep I, who probably then married his own sister, Ahmose-Merytamun. The next king, Thutmose I, was not a member of this family, although his wife probably was. Hatshepsut (p. 118) was their daughter, and she married her half-brother, who became Thutmose II. There is no doubt, therefore, that at this time brother-sister marriages were typical and were genuinely incestuous, not simply ritualistic. Later in the New Kingdom, Tutankhamun married his half-sister, Ankhesenamun.

Also attested, though rarer, is father-daughter marriage: we know of daughters married to Amenhotep III and Ramesses II. Indeed Ramesses apparently had a child by a daughter, Bintanat. Apart from vague hints from the Old Kingdom, there are few other suggestions of incest until the reign of Ptolemy II in the 3rd century BC, when brother-sister marriage once again became typical for two centuries. So the first question to consider is not whether incestuous marriages did take place, but why they happened at certain specific times.

Greywacke statue of Menkaure and an unnamed wife (perhaps Khamerernebty II) from his pyramid-complex at Giza, posed as equals united in an affectionate embrace and in an image redolent with religious symbolism. There is no evidence that royal marriages during the Old Kingdom were typically incestuous.

Right *Akhenaten and Nefertiti – Nefertiti was not related to her husband, but was so powerful she may have ascended the throne in her own right (p. 127), emphasizing how close the king/queen relationship was in the New Kingdom.*

Below *A statue of Hatshepsut enthroned. She was the daughter of Thutmose I and the wife of her half-brother, Thutmose II.*

We can be sure that incest was normally unacceptable in society, and no secure case of incestuous marriage is known outside the royal family. Contemporary attitudes to sexual behaviour are revealing. For example, during the New Kingdom, a chief workman on the royal tomb, Nebamun, was accused of activities unbecoming to his office. Among these are accusations of having sex with a mother and daughter, and of sharing a woman with his son. While not illegal, such behaviour does seem nevertheless to be regarded as distasteful. If sex entangling two members of one family with a third party seemed improper, how much more so sex between members of the same family? So the second question is why royalty behaved openly in a way that would have been unacceptable for the rest of society.

Explanations for incest

One popular explanation derives from an early classic of anthropology, Sir James Frazer's *The Golden Bough* (1890). According to his 'heiress theory', inheritance of the throne passed down the female line, but the right to exercise power was given only to men, that is to husbands. Therefore, for a king to secure the succession for his son, he must marry the son to a daughter. The attraction of this theory for many scholars was that it explained incestuous marriage as a survival of a primitive stage of human thinking, and so suggested that the sophisticated pharaohs were bound by tradition and did not consciously endorse incest. Nevertheless, the heiress theory has now been thoroughly debunked: incestuous marriages rarely occurred, so those that did take place represent a break with tradition, rather than a continuation.

Presumably brother-sister marriage could have brought political advantage by ensuring that the heir belonged to a single family. Undoubtedly the family of Ahmose – who came to power at a time when Egypt was politically divided – and the Ptolemies – who were foreign by descent – felt surrounded by rivals and enemies. By the same token, however, they would not have set themselves above public morality, as the Roman emperors sometimes did, because they were seeking to win support among the nobility. So what would have promoted such behaviour at these particular times?

It seems likely that these kings were actually adopting the behaviour of the gods, who were also incestuous. All the earliest gods were children of the Creator, and so they had no option but to reproduce within their own family. Each king was seen as the equal of the gods and a bodily son of the Creator, so incest – astutely presented – could enhance the sacredness of the royal family. This would have benefited the Ahmosids and the Ptolemies, who could portray themselves as rulers by right of inheritance from the gods. Likewise, Amenhotep III and Ramesses II, although secure on the throne, were preoccupied with how best to present themselves as gods. As long-lived pharaohs, they chose new wives from the next generation of their family.

Gilded wooden coffin of Ahhotep II. She was daughter, sister, wife and mother to kings. Accordingly her coffin is decorated with symbols of divinity, such as golden skin, and of authority, such as the royal cobra (although its head was removed in antiquity).

Of course, this practice also enhanced the prestige of the king's principal wife – his divine counterpart. In the case of the family of Ahmose, this culminated in the career of Hatshepsut, who was the daughter, sister and wife of kings, and so, around 1473 BC, took the throne as king in her own right alongside Thutmose III.

This situation created its own dynastic and religious tensions, and accordingly brother-sister marriage was ended after her death (p. 118). Thereafter it was revived as a matter of policy only by the Ptolemies – a foreign dynasty seeking to justify its claim to the throne in specifically Egyptian terms.

23 The assassination of kings

... bear welcome in your eye,
Your hand, your tongue; look like the innocent flower,
But be the serpent under't. He that's coming
Must be provided for ...
SHAKESPEARE, *MACBETH*, ACT I, SCENE 5, 1606/7

Granite statue of Ramesses III greeted by the gods Horus and Seth, who embody order and continuity and turmoil and change, respectively.

Were ancient Egyptian kings ever assassinated? Everything we know about ancient and medieval court and palace life, whether in ancient Rome, medieval England or Egypt, or the courts of the Ottoman Sultans, tells us that royal power is luxurious, desirable and also frequently precarious. The mystery lies in identifying exactly which ancient Egyptian kings were assassinated. The reasons for this are twofold.

First, there are no contemporary chronicle accounts from ancient Egypt detailing the history of its kings. Sadly, we also lack those more salacious and gossipy stories about court and palace life which do so much to enliven Roman history for modern readers. What little we do have comes from very late sources, such as Manetho, who was writing in the Ptolemaic Period in the 3rd century BC and whose account is preserved only as extracts in even later works dating to the early Christian era. Instead, we are left to piece together the stories of individual kings from the scraps of evidence which happen to have survived from antiquity.

Here the second problem complicates matters. The ancient Egyptians regularly projected an ideological view of kingship, in which a seamless succession of kings follow one another

– the King is dead, long live the King. So ascertaining whether a king was in fact assassinated is now something of a detective story, in which those who committed the crime have taken great pains to hide it. There are, however, still some clues, which do suggest that at least two kings of Egypt might have been assassinated by the people closest to them. (The more problematic mystery of the death of Tutankhamun is considered on p. 132.)

Ramesses III

Ramesses III is usually regarded as the last great king of the New Kingdom – vigorous defender of the boundaries of Egypt and prodigious benefactor of the country's great temples; in Egyptian terms, he was the defender and broadener of *maat* (the proper order of the world) and provider of offerings for the gods. None the less, there is evidence that Ramesses III may well have come to an untimely end.

The primary evidence for this event comes from four papyri which deal with the subsequent trial and punishment of the conspirators. From these, it emerges that a widespread conspiracy had been set up against the king to bring to the throne one of his sons by a minor wife (rather than the expected heir, the later Ramesses IV). The size of the conspiracy can be gleaned from the fact that nearly 40 people, men and women, are mentioned in the Turin papyrus, many of whom held high offices connected with the palace and harim.

It has been suggested that the assassination took place at western Thebes, in the palace at the temple of Medinet Habu. Was the assassination successful? The record is not clear unfortunately, although the old king seems to have died soon after. But his eldest surviving son and heir, Ramesses IV, did succeed to the throne, the conspirators were caught and it was they who suffered a grisly death.

In the surviving record, the criminals are all given fictitious names (perhaps based on their original names), damning them. For example, one of the principal conspirators is called Mesudre, 'Hated by Re', presumably modelled on the name Meryre which means 'Loved by Re'. The key man was one Pabakkamen, meaning 'The blind servant', modelled on the usual name Pabakenamun 'The servant of Amun'. The Turin papyrus deals with him as follows:

Scene from the mortuary temple of Ramesses III at Medinet Habu, western Thebes, showing the king in the harim attended by one of his daughters.

> The great enemy Pabakkamen who had been Chief-of-Chamber, he was brought because of his colluding with Teye [the minor wife of Ramesses III] and the women of the Harim and joining up with them and setting about taking their words out [from the harim] to their mothers and their brothers, saying, 'Gather people, incite hostility' to foster rebellion against their lord. So he was brought before the great officials of the Examination-place; they examined his crimes, they found that he had indeed committed them; his crimes seized him, and the officials who had examined him ensured that his punishment was applied to him.

The euphemistic way in which the punishment is phrased should not mislead us. Some of the more fortunate conspirators were allowed to take their own lives, other minor figures simply had their noses and ears cut off. Pabakkamen's death was assuredly a painful one.

Remains of the pyramid complex of Amenemhat I at Lisht. In its original condition it rivalled the monuments of the Old Kingdom, and incorporated blocks from the Great Pyramid at Giza.

Amenemhat I

Dating from almost a millennium earlier, the case of Amenemhat I is rather more shadowy – a mystery tantalizingly at the edge of our reach. Amenemhat I was the first king of the powerful 12th Dynasty which went on to rule Egypt through much of the Middle Kingdom from *c.* 1938 BC. Amenemhat was not related to the preceding 11th Dynasty and is very probably to be recognized as the Vizier Amenemhat of the last king of that dynasty, Montuhotep IV.

Amenemhat I, depicted in his mortuary temple at Lisht. The circumstances of his accession to the throne of Egypt are unclear, but he was a victim of assassination.

The sources are silent on how Montuhotep IV's short reign came to an end and how Amenemhat I then found himself on the throne, but our suspicions are surely aroused. In the *Prophecies of Neferti*, a literary text written later but composed as a set of prophecies delivered in the reign of King Snofru of the 4th Dynasty in the Old Kingdom, Amenemhat is portrayed as a saviour who would come to deliver Egypt from the woes of disorder and who would reimpose *maat*, the proper order of things:

A king will come from the south,
Ameny his name....

The Asiatics will fall to his sword,
and the Libyans will fall to his flame,
the rebels to his wrath,
and the disaffected to awe of him....

Maat [order] will come to its place,
Isfet [disorder] having been cast aside.

Amenemhat I was himself fated to be a victim of assassination and his death is related in another literary text – the *Instructions of Amenemhat* – in which the dead Amenemhat I advises his son and successor – Senwosret I – on good kingship. Much of the text focuses on the loneliness of rule and the need for a calm head. But for us, the key point is where the dead king relates his own end:

It was after supper and night had fallen,
I took an hour of relaxation;
I lay on my bed, because I had become weary,
and my heart began to follow my sleep....
As I came to, I awoke to (the sound of) fighting –
I found that it was an attack of the bodyguard.
If I had taken weapons quickly in my hands,
I would have made the cowards retreat with
a charge.
But there is no one strong at night; there is
no one who can fight alone –
no success can be achieved without a protector.

This account entered into Egyptian tradition. In an extract from Manetho's account, written some 1600 years after the death of the king, he mentions 'Ammanemes, [king] for 38 years: he was murdered by his own eunuchs'.

The first woman to rule Egypt

24

There was a queen Nitokris, the noblest and loveliest woman of her time; she had a fair complexion and is said to have built the Third Pyramid.
MANETHO, *HISTORY OF EGYPT*, c. 300 BC

The mythic background to the Egyptian kingship was very much male. The king was an incarnation of Horus, the offspring of Osiris and Isis, by definition a male. Normal practice was that a king would be succeeded by his senior surviving son: no grounds exist for the frequently repeated assertion that the throne passed through a succession of heiresses, whom a prince had to marry to succeed (even if she was his full sister).

Nevertheless, supreme power was more than once held by a woman during pharaonic times (disregarding the rather unusual arrangements of the Ptolemaic Dynasty). One category of such women were those who acted as regents during a male king's minority: one, Merytneith of the 1st Dynasty, was rewarded with a kingly tomb in the royal cemetery of Umm el-Qa'ab at Abydos.

Possible female kings

The earliest candidate for an actual female king (the English term 'queen' can mean both a female king and the wife of a king, while in Egyptian the terms for the two are wholly distinct) is Khentykaues I, at the end of the 4th Dynasty. On the granite doorway leading into the mortuary chapel of her unusual tomb at Giza is a set of titles that can be read equally well as either 'Mother of Two Kings' or 'King and Mother of a King'; in fact both translations might be implicit, given the 'constructive ambiguity' we see in Egyptian texts.

The second interpretation is backed up by the fact that Khentykaues' image has been altered to show her in kingly pose, along with a false beard. This could mean that she had ruled during the minority of her son – presumably Sahure – perhaps in conjunction with Userkaf, founder of the 5th Dynasty. It should be noted, however, that she did not utilize a royal cartouche, although she was apparently regarded as the ancestress of the 5th Dynasty and was commemorated in the mortuary chapel at Abusir of Khentykaues II, wife of Neferirkare and mother of Reneferef and probably Nyuserre Ini.

There is another, rather more mysterious, candidate for the first female king, described many centuries later in the work of the Egyptian historian, Manetho: 'Nitokris ... said to have built the Third Pyramid'. Writing over a century earlier, Herodotus tells us that Nitokris 'killed hundreds of Egyptians to avenge the king, her brother, whom his subjects had killed, and had forced her to succeed. This she did by constructing a huge underground chamber,

The first woman who seems to have wielded executive power in Egypt was Merytneith, apparently a wife of Djet and regent during the minority of Den (1st Dynasty). This monumental stela comes from her tomb at Abydos. Her career may lie behind a statement by Manetho that under king 'Binothris' it became legal for a woman to occupy the throne.

in which ... she invited to a banquet all those she knew to be chiefly responsible for her brother's death. Then, when the banquet was underway, she let the river in on them, through a concealed pipe.... After this fearful revenge, she flung herself into a room full of embers, to escape her punishment.' Elsewhere, Herodotus also relates that the third pyramid (at Giza) was built by a woman – but in this case a courtesan of the 26th Dynasty, Rhodopis.

Above *The great tomb erected at Giza for Khentykaues I of the 4th Dynasty, with Khafre's pyramid behind. Sometimes dubbed the 'fourth pyramid', it comprises a lower segment cut from the living rock, and incorporates a chapel and burial chamber, together with a masonry-built upper storey.*

Left *At the entrance to the chapel are granite pieces, adorned with Khentykaues' problematic title, which can be read equally well as either 'Mother of Two Kings' or 'King and Mother of a King'.*

In Egyptian 'Nitokris' is 'Neitaqerti', and in the Turin king-list, dating to the 19th Dynasty, the latter name appears on a fragment that seems to belong to the late 6th Dynasty portion of the papyrus, and many have made the apparently obvious link with the legendary queen. However, work on linking the misplaced parts of the papyrus in the mid-1990s has suggested that the 'Nitokris' cartouche is actually part of the titulary of a clearly male king, named Siptah. Furthermore, it has also been suggested that 'Neitaqerti' is the result of a faulty transcription of the prenomen – the first cartouche, assumed by a king on his accession – 'Netjerkare'.

This would fit with the only other list to cover the period, that of Abydos, which places a 'Netjerkare' in exactly the right spot. However, it is clear that by the early 19th Dynasty – when both lists were compiled – there was some confusion in the scribal mind that resulted in a 'Neitaqerti' being inserted in some 'historical' documents concerning the period after Pepy II, but not others. This may give us a clue to Nitokris' pyramidal links: three reigns after Pepy II, the Abydos list has a King Menkare, a name which is very close to Menkaure, the 4th Dynasty builder of the third pyramid at Giza. Given Manetho's attribution of that monument to Nitokris (and Herodotus' story that it was built by a woman), a transformation Menkaure -> Menkare = Neitaqerti -> Nitokris could be used to suggest that the prenomen of Neitaqerti was Menkare. On the other hand, could the Giza pyramid female connection actually be with the tomb of Khentykaues I, the size of which has sometimes led to its being called the 'fourth pyramid'?

However, these links are very weak, and there is no contemporary trace of a King Nitokris. A suggestion that she was none other than Neith, wife of Pepy II, is also very unlikely. So it is not until the Middle Kingdom that we find the first undoubted female king of Egypt: Nefrusobk.

Nefrusobk

The latter years of the 12th Dynasty were ones of prosperity under Senwosret III and Amenemhat III. They were also innovative ones, including hints that Amenemhat III may have been contemplating a female heir. The person in question, Nefruptah, was invested with a cartouche around her name – something never before done for anyone other than a king – and titles often used by a king's wife, though apparently she was never married to a king. Not only this, but after her death, she was first buried in her father's burial chamber and then reburied in her own pyramid, around 2 km (1.25 miles) away – all circumstances without precedent.

Amenemhat III was ultimately succeeded by a man – Amenemhat IV – but after his early death a woman did accede to the throne. This was Nefrusobk, presumably a sister of Nefruptah. She reigned for some four years, and is known from a number of monuments, including five statues, fragments relating to the mortuary temple of Amenemhat III at Hawara, scarabs, seals and beads, and a Nile-inundation record. This last record indicates a poor flood, and dates to Nefrusobk's last year.

Nefrusobk's successor, Sobkhotep I, founder of the 13th Dynasty, seems to have been the son of Amenemhat IV, but what this might mean for the political and personal relationships of the time is unfortunately wholly obscure. Interestingly, however, Nefrusobk is the last ruler prior to the New Kingdom to appear in the offering lists found at Abydos and Saqqara, suggesting some kind of posthumous verdict that separated her from the equally short-reigned kings who followed her.

Nothing is known of Nefrusobk's death or burial – suggestions that hers might be one of the pyramids at Mazghuna are very unlikely. Thus disappeared from history the figure who remains the earliest woman without doubt to have occupied the throne of the pharaohs.

Nefrusobk was the first woman unquestionably to succeed to the throne: this broken statue depicts her wearing kingly garb over conventional woman's dress.

25 Senenmut: a partner for Hatshepsut?

I was the greatest of the great in the whole land. I was the guardian of the secrets of the King in all his places; a close adviser, [...] secure in favour [...] with whose advices the Mistress of the Two Lands was satisfied, and the heart of the God's Wife was entirely filled.

FUNERARY INSCRIPTION OF SENENMUT, *c.* 1458 BC

Opposite *Senenmut and Nefrure, the daughter of Hatshepsut. The courtier and the princess adopt a posture typical of sculpture groups in which the baby king (the heir to the throne) sits on the lap of the goddess Isis, acting as his mythical mother.*

Hatshepsut had impeccable royal connections: she was the daughter of Thutmose I, the wife and half-sister of Thutmose II and the stepmother of Thutmose III, for whom she ruled as regent when he ascended the throne as a boy. One of several women known to have governed Egypt as regents during the pharaonic period, Hatshepsut went one step further – she had herself crowned as king and was represented as a man, in the regalia of kingship, on the monuments she erected throughout Egypt.

One of the more frequently discussed aspects of the reign of Hatshepsut is the possibility of a physical relationship she had as king with the official and courtier, Senenmut. Not related to royalty by blood, Senenmut seems to have played a fundamental role in the development of her reign. It is common to find among orthodox studies of this era the interpretation of Senenmut as the 'necessary' male presence behind the bold decisions of the queen and her accession to the throne. The idea that a woman could not have carried out the recorded actions of Hatshepsut without the connivance of an ambitious male figure, who not only served as a counsellor but also introduced himself into the monarch's bedroom, has tainted the interpretation of the relationship between the two characters.

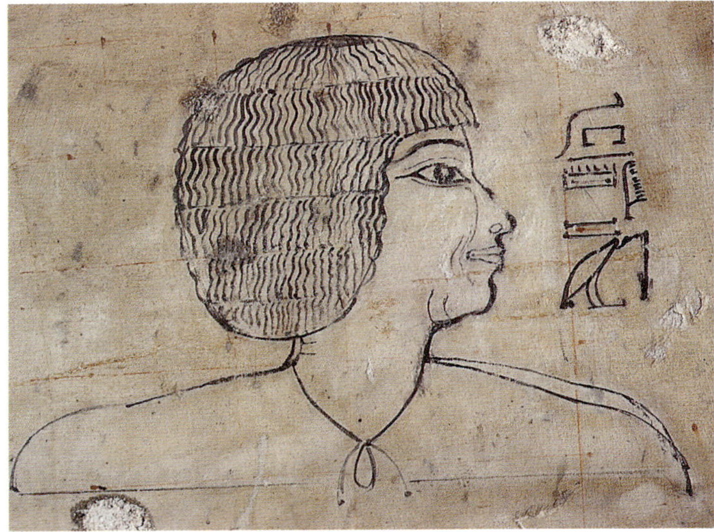

Left *Portrait of Senenmut, bearing his name and title, from his tomb at Deir el-Bahri.*

Royal privilege

Since our own access to the royal bedroom is of course out of the question, the first issue to appreciate is that, once Hatshepsut acceded to the crown, she was monarch, and as such exercised the rights pertaining to all Egyptian monarchs. Among these, and prominently, was the right of kings to enter into sexual relations with whomsoever they wished. This being obvious to any male king, it ought to have been exactly the same in the unusual case of the king being incarnated as a woman. When the legitimacy of a king was beyond doubt because he was the son of a former king, he would have no problem choosing a partner outside the royal family – as we know happened many times. This was equally true for Hatshepsut as the daughter

Right *The name and title of Senenmut, erased in an attempt to eradicate his memory. The names of his parents, Ramose and Hatnefer, are undamaged.*

Below *A watercolour by Howard Carter showing the state of the burial chamber of KV 20, where the sarcophagi of Hatshepsut and her father Thutmose I were found.*

of Thutmose I, which relationship was probably ultimately more relevant to her legitimacy than being the widow of her half-brother Thutmose II.

Hatshepsut's gender as king almost inevitably resulted in a series of incongruities or consequences which had to be skilfully presented in public in a way that conformed with logic, tradition and convention in order to express a 'normal' situation. This was a necessary part of the process of the legitimation of power, which began when Hatshepsut assumed the royal office. Without any doubt, Senenmut played a crucial role.

Representations of Senenmut

If Senenmut had been a woman and Hatshepsut a man, the title *hemet nesu* or 'King's Wife' would have been conferred on Senenemut and the situation would have been clear. However, his gender precluded him from receiving this title and there was no possibility of making him *hy nesu* or 'King's Husband', a title never attested in Egyptian history before or after this time. Accordingly, we have to infer his real position from more indirect indications.

Senenmut's prominent social position was reflected in a number of his representations. Uniquely, in statues depicting him together with Hatshepsut's daughter, Nefrure, courtier and princess are always shown in a very close relationship, often interpreted as a proof of his paternity. Such statues represent the well-established group of a royal mother with a baby king, albeit with the genders of the characters reversed in this case. Nefrure usually sits on the lap of Senenmut, and he supports her in his arms; often he sits in a position normally used for breastfeeding the royal child. In other cases, Senenmut incorporates the child into his own block statue, making her part of his own body.

Senenmut seems to portray himself as Nefrure's 'mother' in the same way that the mythical figure of the goddess Isis (whose name means 'the throne') is represented in a classic Madonna-and-child pose. But this should not be taken as incontrovertible evidence of the biological paternity of Senenmut – for one thing it would have involved sexual relations between the courtier and queen going back to the period when Hatshepsut was still Great King's Wife of the reigning king Thutmose II. While not impossible, presumably such intimate access to her person would have been not only difficult, but also dangerous. The need to establish the royal succession without any ambiguity is paramount in any monarchy. On the other hand, if the king can choose the partner he or she wishes, the chosen individual will be represented according to the accepted iconography. It seems improbable that the ways in which Senenmut represented himself with the royal daughter, Nefrure, could have occurred without the acquiescence and even the indulgence of the reigning monarch.

The 'motherly' aspect of Senenmut is reinforced by the choice of place for his tomb, TT 353 at Deir el-Bahri, where he supervised the building of the magnificent funerary temple of Hatshepsut. Senenmut's tomb seems to reproduce on a smaller scale the structure of tomb KV 20 in the Valley of the Kings, in which the bodies of Hatshepsut and Thutmose I were buried. The plan of KV 20 (p. 121) gives the impression of being designed so that the burial chamber would be positioned under the sacred area of Deir el-Bahri; likewise TT 353 has its burial chamber under the precinct of the queen's temple, although the entrance to the tomb lies outside it. It seems impossible that work on such a tomb in such a sensitive place could have been carried out in secret. Furthermore, the tomb lies in an area traditionally consecrated to the goddess Hathor who is related to concepts of motherhood and the protection of the new-born king.

Deir el-Bahri has provided another representation of the courtier, which is often seen as a token of his unlimited ambition and eventual disgrace. Inside the shrine of Hatshepsut's temple, where the sacred barque of Amun-Re rested on its journey transporting the statue of the god during the Festival of the Valley, Senenmut represented himself in relief in an attitude of adoration. This figure is not prominently displayed inside the chapel and was probably hidden from view behind its doors. From this discreet spot the courtier witnessed the ritual re-enacted there, and in a way also facilitated it as both designer of the queen's funerary temple and supervisor of the Temple of Amun-Re at Karnak, his highest position. Amun-Re's annual visit to this chapel on his journey from Luxor to Karnak had important implications for celebrating fertility and rebirth – both ideas connected with the realm of sexuality in Egyptian thinking. Again, it does not seem credible that this representation of the courtier in such a place could have happened without the knowledge and permission of the monarch, and, unusual as it seems, it is reasonable to assume that it constituted part of the original plan of the complex.

A graffito in a shelter on the rocky cliffs above Deir el-Bahri has been interpreted as a reference by the workers there to the alleged sexual relations between Senenmut and Hatshepsut. Setting aside the difficulties of identifying the protagonists of the scene, some of its elements – such as the royal headdress of the female figure and the erotic pose of the group, with the woman in a sexually humiliating position – might lead us to suppose that what we are looking at here is a satire of a situation which was well known at that time, but in which the interchange of gender roles was as little understood then as it often seems now.

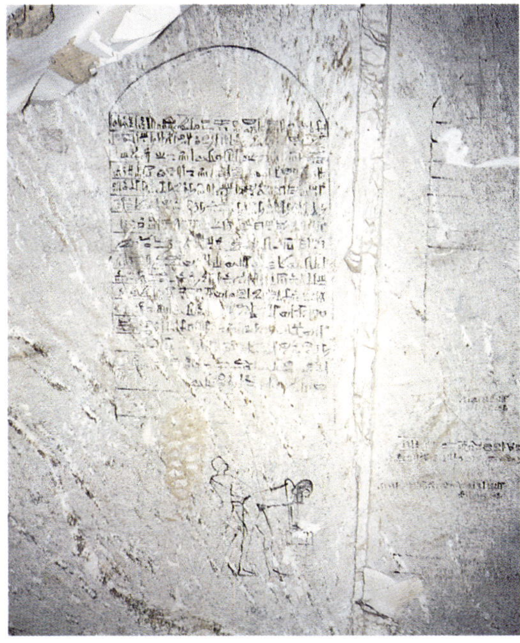

Graffito found in a shelter in the cliffs at Deir el-Bahri showing a crude sexual scene which could be a reference to the relationship of Senenmut and Hatshepsut.

What became of Hatshepsut?

Oh my mother, Nut [sky-goddess] raise me up – I am your daughter.
May you dispel my weariness.
Second sarcophagus of Hatshepsut, *c.* 1458 BC

Although unusual in being female, Hatshepsut was like any other Egyptian king in spending much of her reign preparing for her own death. Even before she became king she had excavated an impressive rock-cut cliff tomb for herself in one of the valleys to the south of the Theban mountain and equipped it with a decorated stone sarcophagus. After she had been crowned king, she set about excavating the first royal tomb in the Valley of the Kings, complete with another stone sarcophagus. She later ordered a third sarcophagus and adapted the second for her father, Thutmose I, whom she reburied in her new tomb.

Throughout her reign she also worked on her funerary temple at Deir el-Bahri, an immensely inventive and influential architectural project which surpassed the mortuary temples of her New Kingdom predecessors in scale and complexity. This monument was largely completed during her reign, although modifications were still in progress when work was abandoned. Hatshepsut clearly intended that on her death she would be buried as king with all the expense, pomp and ceremony which that entailed.

Although Hatshepsut's monuments provide much information on the achievements of her

Left *Osirid statue of Hatshepsut from her funerary temple at Deir el-Bahri, showing her holding the symbols of kingship. The statue has been heavily restored.*

Opposite *The remains of a head of an Osirid figure of Hatshepsut from her mortuary temple, with the traditional false beard of kings.*

reign, the facts about her later years are few and far between, and this has led to speculation about her fate. References dated after Year 17 of her joint reign with her stepson Thutmose III, for whom she acted as regent, are rare, and the last secure date is in Year 20. She may have died in Year 22 as Manetho records a queen ruling for 22 years and 5 months around this period. The suggestion that an erased episode on Thutmose III's Armant stela records the exact date of her death is speculative and, given the context, very unlikely to be correct.

Left *Hatshepsut is purified by the god Thoth in a scene from Karnak temple: the image, names and associated text of Hatshepsut have been systematically erased. The scene was never restored as it was covered by building work of Thutmose III.*

Below *The goddess Isis protects the foot end of Hatshepsut's third sarcophagus in which she was finally buried.*

Death and burial

After her death, Hatshepsut's images and names were systematically removed from her monuments on the orders of Thutmose III. This act has traditionally been interpreted as destruction of her memory in revenge for her 'usurpation' of the throne. As an extension of this, Hatshepsut has been cast in the role of 'evil stepmother', with her disappearance interpreted as the triumph of the true heir. It has been variously suggested in the past that Thutmose III ousted her from power or even had her murdered. Such dramatic interpretations of feuds and personal animosity are no longer followed since they are not supported by the evidence, which is more complex than it might initially appear.

First, there is a considerable amount of evidence that Hatshepsut was indeed buried in the Valley of the Kings. A mummified internal organ in a box bearing her name was found in the royal cache at Deir el-Bahri, and fragments of her coffins and burial goods were found in the tombs of Ramesses IX and Ramesses XI where they were probably placed for safekeeping after the New Kingdom. Presumably, therefore, Thutmose III had honoured her intentions and had her buried in her kingly tomb.

Secondly, researchers such as Charles Nims and Peter Dorman have examined the erasures of Hatshepsut's names and images in their architectural settings. Where it is possible to establish a date, their research has shown that the erasures occurred after Year 42 of Thutmose III's reign. If Thutmose III had been desperate to rid himself of the queen during her lifetime, it seems extraordinary that he should have waited for 20 years after her death before expunging reminders of her from state monuments. Establishing a motive for the erasures with any certainty is impossible, but her position as king could have been seen as superfluous because she never ruled alone. Her reign may well also have been considered problematical in that it prevented the Thutmosid succession conforming to the divine archetype of the throne passing directly from father to son as it had passed from Osiris to Horus. Perhaps, as he approached death and contemplated his place in the historical record, Thutmose also decided that

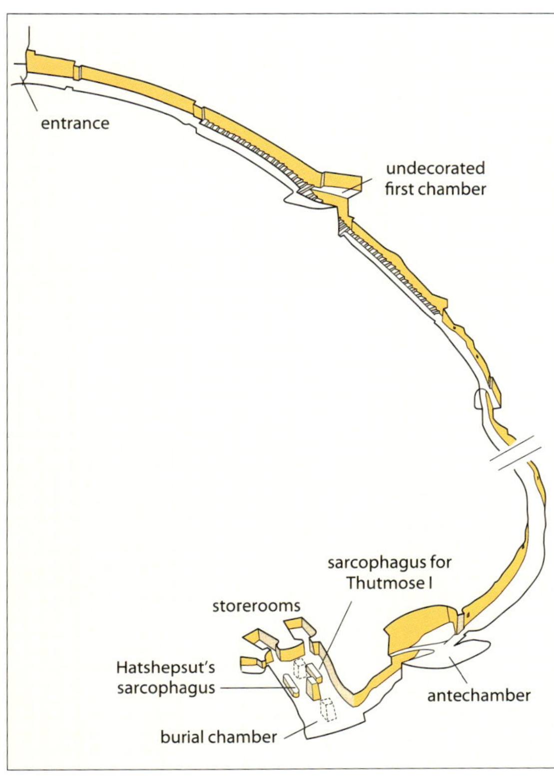

Left *A cross-section showing the extraordinary twisting shape of KV 20, the tomb of Hatshepsut.*

he wished to be remembered for his military prowess rather than for the fact that he had, for a time, shared the throne with his stepmother.

The most plausible interpretation of Hatshepsut's demise is that she simply faded from public prominence as Thutmose III reached maturity. Assuming Thutmose III was aged six at most on his accession (based on the estimated age at death of his mummy), he would have been in his early 20s when he started to take full control of the country around Year 17. If Thutmose was indeed such a young child on coming to the throne, the extent of Hatshepsut's power in the early part of the reign is easier to understand. And she would have been relatively elderly by Year 17, so that the apparent infrequency of references to her after that date may suggest that she occupied a position of semi-retirement until her death.

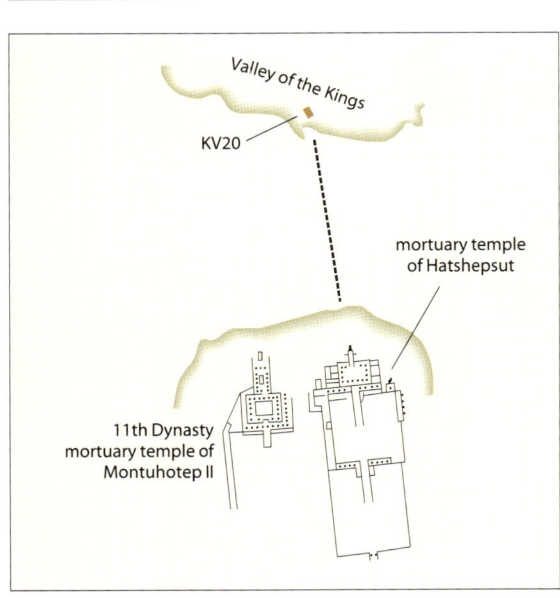

Above *The relationship between Hatshepsut's tomb in the Valley of the Kings, KV 20, and her mortuary temple at Deir el-Bahri. Hatshepsut constructed her temple adjacent to the mortuary temple of Montuhotep II, the founder of the Middle Kingdom.*

Right *Hatshepsut's mortuary temple at Deir el-Bahri. The Valley of the Kings lies behind the lower cliffs.*

27

The enigma of Akhenaten

The Tel el-Amarna period has had more nonsense written about it than any other period in Egyptian history.... In the case of Akhenaten the facts do not bear the construction often put on them.
MARGARET MURRAY, 1949

The pharaoh Akhenaten presided over a time of theological controversy and cultural upheaval unprecedented in Egyptian history. His programme of religious reform marginalized most of Egypt's traditional gods and concentrated worship on the Aten, the divine sun disk, which, unlike other Egyptian gods, had no human or animal form. His reign also saw wide-ranging and radical changes in Egyptian art.

Relief of Akhenaten wearing the blue crown, traditionally associated with the warlike activities of the pharaohs. In some respects Akhenaten held conventional views about the role of the king.

So who was this apparently revolutionary ruler and what were his motives? The second son of Amenhotep III and Tiy (his older brother who would have become king had died), he began his reign under the name Amenhotep IV. He adopted the new name Akhenaten – which means something like 'he who is beneficial to the Aten' or possibly 'intermediary of the Aten' – out of devotion to that god. New religious writings – some of them probably by the pharaoh himself – explored his close relationship with the Aten using poetical vocabulary and imagery from nature.

Struggles between the king and the religious establishment swiftly followed his reforms. As a result, Egypt's capital city was moved from Thebes to the virgin site of Akhet-aten or 'Horizon of the Aten', now usually (though inaccurately) known as Amarna. An extensive city was hurriedly built to house at least 20,000 people, who were resettled here. Amarna was also planned as an elaborate performance space for the rituals of worshipping the Aten, in which Akhenaten himself played the main part, though his principal consort, Nefertiti (p. 127), was almost as prominent. Images of her were all over the city, indicating her political role. In art, the couple were shown in unusually relaxed and intimate poses with their daughters. Akhenaten and

Nefertiti seem to have enjoyed an exceptionally close relationship, but he also had other co-wives, some of whom were important enough to be depicted on official buildings.

Akhenaten's experiment in kingship, religion and art survived less than two decades. The last documents mentioning him are dated to the 17th year of his reign, after which he vanishes. Nefertiti vanishes too – at least under that name. Religious and political orthodoxy, after a fashion, was re-established within a few years.

The capital soon returned to Thebes, and Akhenaten's successors as pharaoh, including Tutankhamun, his son, tried to eliminate all evidence that he had ever existed. This deliberate destruction means that many of the fascinating historical conundrums about Akhenaten will probably stay unsolved. However, it is possible to try to answer some of the puzzling questions about this pharaoh that have encouraged most controversy and so helped to create the enigma of Akhenaten.

Akhenaten's co-wife Kiya, possibly the mother of Tutankhamun. This image of her was later adapted to represent one of Akhenaten's daughters, suggesting that Kiya may have died or been disgraced.

What did Akhenaten look like?

Perhaps the single most extraordinary thing about Akhenaten is how he chose to be shown in art, with elongated features and large, almost feminine, hips and thighs. The art of his reign is often said to be 'realistic' or 'naturalistic', so there is an assumption that images of him must bear some relation to his real-life appearance. As a result, many people have tried to identify medical conditions behind Akhenaten's strange physical depiction. Marfan's Syndrome and Froehlich's

Akhenaten, his wife Nefertiti and their older daughters. This relief almost seems to be a snapshot of domestic life, but sculptures like this were set up in shrines to be venerated and are more like icons than family photographs.

27

Colossal statues of Akhenaten from the temple of the Aten at east Karnak in the course of being excavated. The statues, once part of an elaborate colonnade, were broken up and buried after Akhenaten's death in an effort to erase his memory.

Syndrome have been suggested, both disorders which can lead to the development of some physical traits superficially similar to those in Akhenaten's statues. But such interpretations are over-literal and underestimate the subtlety of Egyptian art as a medium for expressing complex religious ideas.

Throughout Akhenaten's reign, representations of him changed as his ideas about the nature of the Aten became more complex. Put simply, as the Aten is shown with more of the attributes of a pharaoh, such as royal insignia and titles written in cartouches, so Akhenaten is shown with more of the attributes of a god. He appears as a hybrid of human and divine physical elements – a perfect illustration, to Egyptian eyes, of Akhenaten's dual role.

Images of Akhenaten are therefore not intended as realistic representations of how he looked in life, but ideological and theological statements about the relationship between god and king. If Akhenaten was trying to represent himself as something beyond the human, no wonder he looks different from the run of humanity. But what does this suggest about Akhenaten's real beliefs about the Aten and the other gods?

What did Akhenaten really believe?

Speculation about what Akhenaten believed centres on the question of whether or not he was a monotheist – a believer in one sole god. To answer this we need to know what Akhenaten thought about the other Egyptian gods, apart from the Aten. If he thought that they absolutely did not exist in any way, and that the only god was the Aten, then Akhenaten was a sort of monotheist.

But what if Akhenaten did believe that the other gods did exist, but wanted to keep them powerless by ignoring them and by denying them worship? This may in fact be the case. For a supposed monotheist, Akhenaten permitted a

Right *One of the group of colossal statues from Karnak: Akhenaten is shown with royal insignia, but his body has breasts and fatty deposits around the waist and hips, which are attributes of many Egyptian divinities. Perhaps one of the most extraordinary aspects of Akhenaten is the way he chose to be represented in art, but it may have been a medium for expressing his religious ideas.*

surprising number of gods to appear in Atenist theology. He and Nefertiti sometimes identified themselves with the gods Shu and Tefnut, the children of the sun god and original divine couple. Such an identification fitted Akhenaten's self-image as intermediary between the human and divine worlds. Akhenaten also allowed the sacred bull of Heliopolis, who was believed to transmit oracle-messages from the sun god, to be kept at Amarna. All this suggests that Akhenaten was willing to tolerate other gods when they suited his project – which in turn implies that he thought they existed.

So did Akhenaten have a sincere desire for religious change, or was he merely using it as a political tool for his own ends? Akhenaten was once held up by scholars as a pacifist and an idealist, but many are now rather more cynical about his motives. It is argued that the aim of all his reforms was to revert to an earlier form of kingship, more like that of the Old Kingdom when the monarch had greater power through his unique dialogue with the gods.

It is possible that Akhenaten identified with the great pharaohs of old as political role models in some way. A fragmentary bowl inscribed with the name of the 4th Dynasty pharaoh Khafre, builder of the second Giza pyramid, was discovered in the debris of Akhenaten's tomb goods. At any rate, he can certainly now be seen as politically conservative rather than revolutionary – he is often shown engaging in the usual martial or imperialist activities of pharaohs, such as vanquishing enemies, reviewing military personnel and receiving tribute from foreign states.

In some respects, then, Akhenaten was a thoroughly conventional pharaoh, with traditional views about the political role of the king. His religious reforms therefore need to be seen in this context.

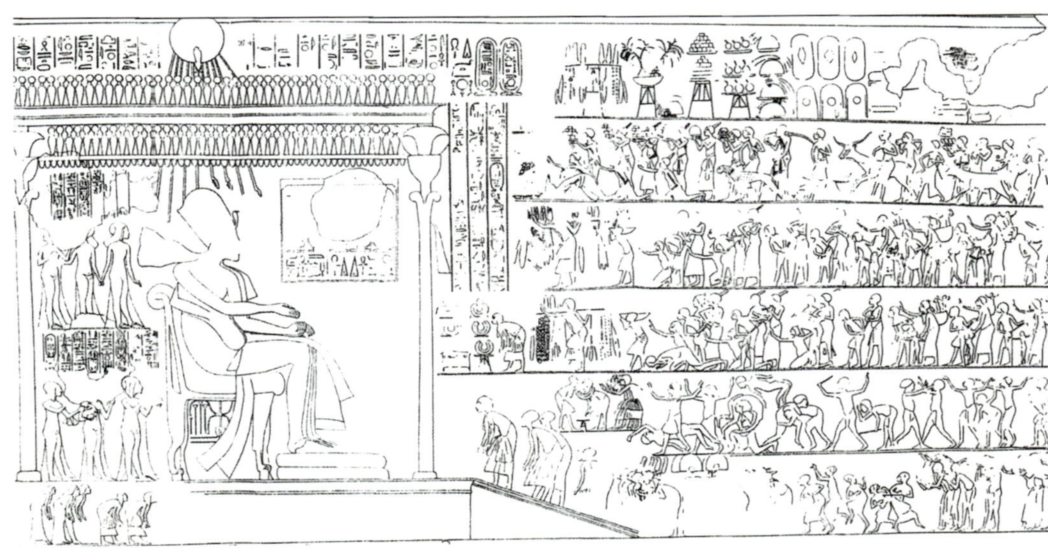

Akhenaten and Nefertiti, so closely united that it is hard to distinguish them, receive the tribute of Egypt's colonies in Year 12 of Akhenaten's reign. Their six daughters are shown behind them. Drawing of a relief in the tomb of Meryre II at Amarna.

What happened to Akhenaten?

Yet more mystery surrounds the fate of Akhenaten. Although there is little hard evidence for the last years of Akhenaten's reign, there are some signs that matters were not under control. Major building works at Amarna ground to a halt – perhaps the king was short of financial resources, or his experiment was becoming unpopular. Abroad, there was trouble in the Egyptian colonies on the eastern Mediterranean coast. Some members of the royal family died, including at least one of Akhenaten's daughters. Finally Akhenaten himself disappears from the written record in Year 17. Presumably he died and was buried outside Amarna in the tomb he had built for himself and his family. Within a few years his burial had been ravaged. What happened next is the subject of much speculation (p. 84).

All this mystery has allowed a romantic story about Akhenaten to be fabricated. Even the bare outlines of Akhenaten's history read like a romance – an idealistic king, a beautiful queen, court intrigue, a mysterious and probably tragic end – so, unsurprisingly, he has become the most controversial and hotly contested figure in ancient Egyptian history. He is all things to all people. At various times Akhenaten has been compared to Moses, Martin Luther, Oliver Cromwell, Hitler, Stalin, Anwar Sadat and Christ, or whoever happens to suit a particular set of cultural and political circumstances that requires a hero or a villain.

The real man hides behind a mask carefully constructed both by himself and by the modern world that attempts to understand him – and that is the true enigma of Akhenaten.

The Central Reading Youth Provision Black History Mural (1991), England, shows a black Akhenaten and Nefertiti as the first in a lineage of great black heroes which goes on to include Martin Luther King and Bob Marley.

Why did Nefertiti disappear?

28

In recent years … [t]he domestic idyll with Nefert-iti … has suffered brutal blows.
Cyril Aldred, 1968

Nefertiti, whose beauty is immortalized in the famous portrait bust now in Berlin, was the King's Great Wife of Akhenaten, who, in the latter part of the 18th Dynasty, promoted the worship of a single sun god, the Aten, above Egypt's traditional pantheon (p. 122). Her origins are obscure, but she may have been related to Ay, the general who was later to succeed Tutankhamun as pharaoh. She first appears with Akhenaten shortly after he became king, and henceforth plays a very prominent role in much of the art of the period. She is constantly shown alongside her husband, and the royal couple are frequently depicted in scenes of domestic intimacy with their daughters, who eventually numbered six.

The elevated political and religious position of Nefertiti is illustrated in a number of ways. In the early part of Akhenaten's reign, there seems to have been an emphasis on the king and queen as incarnations of Shu (god of sunlight) and his sister-wife Tefnut (goddess of atmosphere and moisture) respectively. Akhenaten became king as Amenhotep IV but changed his name as an evocation of his own god; Nefertiti's name was expanded by adding the element 'Nefernefruaten' – 'most perfect of the perfections of the Aten'. This is written rather oddly, with the signs spelling out 'Aten' facing in the opposite direction from those of the rest of her name. Nefertiti's status is further illustrated by her depiction at least once in the classic pose of a pharaoh smiting her enemies.

Seen against the background of this high profile, Nefertiti's apparent complete disappearance from the archaeological record during the last third of Akhenaten's reign has long been remarked upon. Her latest certain depiction is in scenes in the Royal Tomb at Amarna that show the king and queen mourning their second daughter, Meketaten, who apparently died in childbirth. As the princess is shown in scenes dated to Akhenaten's 12th regnal year, her death may have occurred around Year 13.

Akhenaten, Nefertiti and two of their daughters, showing the extreme artistic style of the early years of Akhenaten's reign, and the informality of composition that typifies the period.

The names of Akhenaten's successor(s).

	FIRST NAME (PRENOMEN)	SECOND NAME (NOMEN)
A	Ankhkheperure	Smenkhkare-djeserkheperu
B	Ankhkheperure *beloved of* Waenre* Ankhkheperure *beloved of* Neferkheperure* * All names of Akhenaten	Nefernefruaten *beloved of* Akhenaten*
C	Ankhetkheperure‡ *beloved of* Waenre ‡ Female name	?

Theories and evidence

So what did happen to Nefertiti? The most straightforward explanation, of course, is that she died at this point – the existence of a *shabty*-figure bearing her queenly titles may point in this direction. In this case she may have been buried in the royal tomb built by Akhenaten at Amarna, or another nearby, whose design suggests that it may have been intended for a number of members of the royal family.

One theory that was popular for some time, and is still often quoted by those unfamiliar with modern research, is that Nefertiti was disgraced and forced into retirement. The evidence cited for this was a number of Amarna monuments on which a queen's image and name had been covered over with plaster and re-worked to commemorate Akhenaten together with Nefertiti's eldest daughter, Merytaten. But this has proved to be a classic case of mistaken identity – the 'victim' was actually Kiya, a junior wife of Akhenaten (p. 123).

Nefertiti's status was exceptional for an Egyptian queen, and she was on occasion even shown in the traditional pharaonic pose of smiting an enemy, as here in the cabin of a royal barge.

Another possibility is that Nefertiti did not disappear at all, but simply changed her role. At almost the same moment that the queen vanishes from history, at least one new figure appears on the stage – a co-regent for Akhenaten. And around this time a number of sets of royal names are found, all built around a prenomen (first cartouche name) whose core reads 'Ankhkheperure' (see table above).

Various suggestions have been put forward to account for this situation, which can be grouped under three explanations. First, that all these names belong to a female king who changed her nomen at least once; second, that Nefernefruaten was female, but Smenkhkare was a separate, male king; and third that all names except for Ankhetkheperure belong to one male king. In this case, the feminine 'Ankhetkheperure' is to be regarded only as a tag adopted by a woman in the royal family – perhaps Merytaten – at the end of Akhenaten's reign.

Although other candidates have been proposed – in particular Kiya and Merytaten – adherents of the first two scenarios generally believe that the 'mystery female king' is none other than Nefertiti, particularly because they share with her the name 'Nefernefruaten'. However, it may be significant that the king's cartouche never employs the reversed hieroglyphs that are invariably used by Queen Nefertiti.

If all the names do belong to one, female, king it is assumed that the 'Nefernefruaten' second name, or nomen, is the earlier, with all references relating to Akhenaten then dropped after the latter's death and a fresh nomen, Smenkhkare, adopted to emphasize this break. But if so, why did Nefertiti (if that is who she was) not simply revert to her birth name?

The major problem, however, with the existence of one, female king to whom all these names refer, is that there is fairly definitive evidence that Smenkhkare was a man. On the wall of the tomb of an official named Meryre (II) at Amarna and on a block from Memphis, Smenkhkare's name set is accompanied by that of the 'King's Great Wife, Merytaten'. Unless it is argued that the former Nefertiti had taken her eldest daughter as her nominal 'wife' – something for which there is no parallel among other ruling women, such as Hatshepsut and Twosret – or alternatively that Merytaten was now the wife of Akhenaten, although she is never shown with him as such – it is highly likely that Smenkhkare was a married male.

An important piece of information on the potential chronological order of these various royal names is provided by a graffito in the tomb of an official at Thebes, which is dated to Year 3 of Nefernefruaten. Given the paucity of material relating to him/her, this is likely to date towards the end of the reign, implying that 'Nefernefruaten' is actually the later nomen. Further, the content of the graffito makes it clear that at the time the cult of Amun-Re was current. This is interesting because at a certain point in his reign Akhenaten persecuted Amun-Re, hacking the god's name and image from monuments, and Amun-Re's cult was presumably only restored after Akhenaten's death.

A key piece of evidence in the Nefernefruaten/Smenkhkare question may be the set of miniature gold coffins that ultimately held the internal organs of King Tutankhamun. These had been made for an earlier king, but were reused for

Nefertiti as an older woman. This was once part of a dyad with her husband Akhenaten.

Right *Smenkhkare and the 'King's Great Wife' Merytaten reward the official Meryre II in his tomb-chapel at Amarna.*

Opposite *The canopic coffinettes used in Tutankhamun's burial had originally been made for another person. The latter's names are visible under those of Tutankhamun in the texts on the interior.*

Below *The characteristic profile and headdress of Nefertiti from a sculptor's trial piece.*

Tutankhamun – as had a considerable number of other objects found in his tomb, including the middle of the three coffins that had enclosed the king's mummy. All cartouches on the coffinettes had been usurped, but traces of the originals are visible in a number of places inside the troughs.

Careful analysis of the traces strongly suggests that the cartouches originally read 'Ankhkheperure *beloved of* Waenre Smenkhkare *beloved of* Akhenaten', which had been altered to 'Ankhkheperure *beloved of* Waenre Nefernefruaten *beloved of* Waenre', before ultimately being reinscribed for Tutankhamun. If correctly interpreted, this is a titulary intermediate between those of Smenkhkare and Nefernefruaten. Therefore, it would seem difficult to doubt that Smenkhkare and Nefernefruaten were one and the same person, and that, since the former was almost certainly male, Nefernefruaten cannot have been Nefertiti.

While this leaves ajar the possibility that Nefertiti could have been the mysterious 'Ankhetkheperure', it is perhaps more likely that this was indeed Smenkhkare/Nefernefruaten's widow, Merytaten. She may briefly have replaced her erstwhile husband as Akhenaten's co-ruler, and/or served as regent for her probable younger (half-?) brother, Tutankhamun, during the first months of his reign.

So we are in fact left with no direct evidence as to the fate of Nefertiti. Accordingly, the most straightforward thesis – that she died not long after Meketaten – seems the most attractive of all the various possibilities. While she would certainly have been buried at Amarna, there remain tantalizing hints regarding the ultimate fate of her mummy.

Nefertiti's remains could have been moved a decade later, when at least one royal body was taken from Amarna to tomb 55 in the Valley of the Kings (p. 87). Both tomb 55 and Tutankhamun's tomb (p.84) are in an area later buried deeply in debris. If Nefertiti, and perhaps some of her daughters, were reburied, their tomb will almost certainly have been in this area, untouched until excavations began in 1998. Although other writers have suggested that her corpse may be one or other of two mummies found in the tomb of Amenhotep II (p. 137), the evidence is ambiguous, and possibly those women were wives of Amenhotep II.

It is thus possible that Nefertiti's last resting place may yet await discovery. Only time will tell.

The Tutankhamun conspiracy

Greetings, perfect-of-face, possessor of sun-rays, whom Ptah-Sokar has completed, whom Anubis has exalted, to whom Thoth has given the distinctions of perfection of face.
GOLD FUNERARY MASK OF TUTANKHAMUN, *c.* 1322 BC

The Amarna period never fails to attract speculation, and the rich burial of the 'boy pharaoh' Tutankhamun has exerted an irresistible fascination. Since the discovery of his tomb in 1922, the reason for Tutankhamun's death at an early age has excited the imagination of Egyptologists and the wider public.

All examinations of Tutankhamun's mummy have suggested that he died aged about 18 or 19, but some Egyptologists, basing their arguments on sculptural depictions, have claimed that he was 10 years older, dying in his late 20s. The depictions of the king are supposed by some to show that he was sickly, and the drawn features of a number of his statues that he died of consumption (tuberculosis), but the king's mummy shows no signs of this disease.

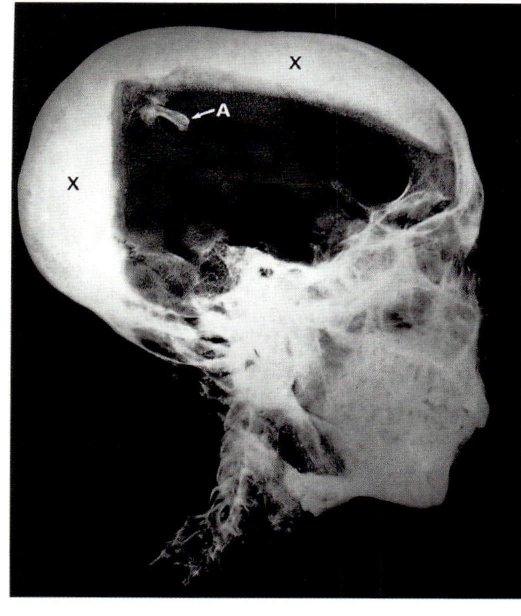

A radiograph of Tutankhamun's skull showing resin (X) from the embalming process, and a sliver of bone (A). An area of damage at the base of the skull shows that the king suffered a blow to the back of the head, but before or after death is unclear.

Opposite *The gold funerary mask that covered the head of the mummy, with the idealized features of the youthful king.*

More speculation was aroused by re-examination of the mummy in 1968 that revealed damage to the skull consistent with a blow to the back of the head. Although various possibilities have been raised, such as damage caused during embalming, a tumour or a fall from a chariot, a number of Egyptologists now suspect that Tutankhamun was murdered. The injury may not have killed the king immediately, but left him lingering for some time. Unfortunately, there is very little good historical evidence from the end of the reign, or from that of Tutankhamun's successor, Ay. Inevitably, there are varying interpretations, and just about every possible – and barely possible – scenario has been offered up.

One crucial document often quoted in this context is a letter from an Egyptian queen which was preserved in the Hittite archives. The queen wrote to the Hittite king 'My husband has died and I have no son...' and sought a Hittite prince in marriage. So shocked was the Hittite king at receiving this unheard of request that he wrote and demanded confirmation that it was not a hoax. Unfortunately, the queen is not named and the letter has therefore been attributed to either Nefertiti or Meritaten following the death of Akhenaten, or to Ankhesenamun on the death of Tutankhamun. We do know that in response to the letters a Hittite prince, Zannanza, was sent to Egypt. One recent reconstruction of events identifies the writer of the letter as Meritaten and equates Zannanza with the obscure ruler

Above *A painting in the burial chamber of Tutankhamun shows (far right) Ay as king performing the funerary rituals for the dead Tutankhamun.*

Below *Ay, as one of Akhenaten's officials, depicted in his first tomb at Amarna.*

Smenkhkare, but most other writers have assumed that Zannanza was murdered on his way to Egypt. Inevitably the finger has been pointed at the two officials who succeeded Tutankhamun as pharaoh, Ay and Horemheb.

Prime suspects

Indeed, the evil hand of the 'God's Father' Ay is always implicated in the Tutankhamun conspiracy. Ay certainly had a very close association with the royal family. He possessed a fine tomb at Akhetaten (Amarna) in which he and his wife, the nurse of Nefertiti, are shown being rewarded by Akhenaten and his family. Another factor which has attracted attention is Ay's use of the title 'God's Father'. This was a relatively lowly priestly title, but in Ay's case clearly has greater significance, as he included it in his cartouche when he became pharaoh. The title has been interpreted as 'King's father-in-law' and has been taken to allude to Ay as father of Nefertiti, and hence grandfather-in-law to Tutankhamun. Although it has been widely accepted, there is no substantial evidence to confirm this relationship.

Nor is there any solid evidence to confirm the equally popular view that Ay was the brother of Queen Tiy, the wife of Amenhotep III and mother of Akhenaten. Earlier Egyptologists assumed that Ay married Ankhesenamun in order to legitimize his rule, but it is Ay's wife Tiy who appears on monuments as his queen. Whether or not he had a blood relationship to the pharaoh, Ay was depicted accompanying Tutankhamun on a number of monuments, clearly attesting to his influential role at court.

The other key protagonist, Horemheb, is not yet known from any monuments of Akhenaten's reign, but his high military office means that he must have served that pharaoh. We know nothing of either his ancestry or connections. Horemheb's vast array of titles (nearly 100, including variants, are known) during Tutankhamun's reign certainly indicate his pre-eminent position among the nobility, and suggest that he was the king's designated heir. This in itself perhaps indicates that Tutankhamun was not expected to live for long or produce an heir.

But it is Ay, not Horemheb, who is depicted in Tutankhamun's tomb officiating at the funeral as his legitimate successor. Some Egyptologists have detected deft political manoeuvring while Horemheb was away in Palestine disposing of the Hittite prince, or engaged in military actions further north around Qadesh. When he later became pharaoh, Horemheb's queen was Mutnodjmet, whom some have identified with the sister of Nefertiti and another daughter of Ay.

Evidence from the tomb

It is possible to interpret the evidence from Tutankhamun's tomb as a sign of a hasty burial. The middle of the three magnificent coffins and canopic equipment for the internal organs were all recycled, as were various religious statues. The use of a relatively small, private tomb, rather than the tomb being prepared in the West Valley which was later used by Ay, might also be taken to show a lack of reverence for the king. The painted decoration in Tutankhamun's burial chamber is also unusual in containing scenes of the royal funeral and the ceremony of 'Opening of the Mouth', which is clearly placed here as an act of legitimation by Ay.

A few objects had been placed in the burial by high officials. Several *shabty* figures carry the name of a military official, Nakhtmin, who was almost certainly the son of Ay. Another image was given by an official named Maya, but there was nothing offered by Horemheb, suggesting to some writers that he played no part in the burial. It could be speculated that Ay took advantage of Horemheb's absence to bury the king, and thereby assume the

Horemheb as pharaoh, seated with the god of kingship, Horus.

throne. There is further evidence to suggest that there was some later conflict between Horemheb and Ay's heir.

Tutankhamun's successors

A splendid head of Nakhtmin, with parts of an inscription, and part of a statue of his wife, show clear signs of official destruction. Lines have been hammered through the eyes and mouth and the nose smashed, all intended to deprive the statues' owners of eternal life. So, it has been claimed that following Ay's death, Nakhtmin was prevented from ascending the throne. However, the inscription on the statue carries the damaged title 'King's Son', suggesting that Nakhtmin had predeceased Ay.

The accession of Horemheb following Ay has been viewed by some Egyptologists as the triumph of the military, although both Ay and Nakhtmin were also military officials. Despite the fantasy of some Egyptologists that Akhenaten was a pacifist who allowed the army to decline, he was constantly surrounded by contingents of soldiers, and evidence for his 'neglect' of the army has probably been overplayed. It is unlikely that the Egyptian army should be regarded as a separate institution in the way that is familiar from more recent times.

The Egyptian elite was very small and its education included both military and scribal skills; most elite families included priestly, scribal and military officials. There were certainly rivalries and factions within the elite, but these may have been family or district based rather than institutional.

Left *One of the five* shabty *figures that were dedicated by Nakhtmin at the burial of Tutankhamun.*

Above right *The head of a statue of Nakhtmin, deliberately mutilated by smashing the nose, mouth and eyes, thus depriving the owner of eternal life.*

What can we say with certainty? In fact, very little. This is one of the episodes of Egyptian history in which the few pieces of evidence are more frequently manipulated to suit a writer's theory than interpreted dispassionately. Although there are some who still wish to identify the queen of the Hittite correspondence with Ankhesenamun, there are more convincing arguments in favour of Nefertiti.

Some architectural fragments from the temple of Karnak carry the titularies of both Tutankhamun and Ay, indicating that the transfer of power was effected before the young king's death. This, it has been suggested, took place while Tutankhamun was in a coma. A peaceful transition is also indicated by the continuity in many of the offices of state, with key officials serving Tutankhamun, Ay and Horemheb. Even if Ay did supplant Horemheb as heir, he did not have him removed. It may also be that Ay, who must have been quite elderly, by this time had no male heir of his own. What actually happened behind the walls of the Egyptian palace still remains unclear, but provides a fine source for speculation.

The 'Elder Lady'

30

The first mummy is a middle-aged woman with long, brown, wavy, lustrous hair, parted in the centre and falling down on both sides of the head on to her shoulders. Its ends are converted into numerous apparently natural curls. Her teeth are well-worn but otherwise healthy.... She has no grey hair.

G. Elliot Smith, 1912

Egyptian archaeology can offer the unusual opportunity of coming face to face with some of the known protagonists of ancient history – monarchs whose deeds are famous through inscriptions and texts. Sometimes the face we see represented in a statue or a relief-scene is present in front of our eyes, perhaps with recognizable features, thanks to the skills of the ancient Egyptian embalmers. Among the royal bodies preserved in this way, some can be identified beyond any doubt, such as Tutankhamun, whose body still lay inside his tomb. Others were found in hidden caches, removed from their original burials and coffins, and often only clues and speculation can lead us to their identity.

Such is the case of the mummy of the woman catalogued in Cairo Museum as CG 61070. She was found in 1898 by Victor Loret, together with many other bodies, inside the tomb of Amenhotep II in the Valley of the Kings (p. 92). This tomb was intended to be the secret and final resting-place for a number of royal mummies, including Amenhotep himself. Scholars were immediately attracted by mummy 61070 because of the excellent state of preservation of her face, with a beauty untarnished by the mummification process and the passage of time. However, the absence of written texts among the bandages meant her identity could not be established. This beautiful and enigmatic woman was named the 'Elder Lady' by the anatomist Grafton Elliot Smith, to distinguish her from another female mummy found beside her. He classified the 'Elder Lady' as a middle-aged woman, an expression so imprecise as to leave any possibility open.

Dating the Elder Lady

One indication of the possible date of mummy 61070 was the fact that her left hand was clenched, as if to hold a cylindrical object, which had been lost. This pose was characteristic of queens of the 18th Dynasty, who held a sceptre. In 1978 James Harris carried out an analysis which apparently narrowed the dating down, as he demonstrated that the hair of mummy 61070 corresponded to a lock of hair found in miniature coffins in the tomb of Tutankhamun. These coffins bear the name of Tiy, the mother of Akhenaten (p. 122), and so the posture of the mummy, her queenly status and the provenance of the lock of hair pointed almost conclusively to Tiy as being the enigmatic 'Elder Lady'.

Nevertheless, some aspects of this identification do not fit with the information from other sources. The age at death of Tiy is crucial. She is mentioned in Year 2 of Amenhotep III, on the occasion of her marriage to the king, whose reign extended to 38 years. She was certainly alive in Year 8 of her son, Akhenaten, because she visited his new capital at Akhetaten, an event which was recorded. She died some time after this, perhaps long after. These and other arguments indicate an age at death for Tiy well above 40 years old.

The mummy of the woman found in the cache in the tomb of Amenhotep II numbered 61070. The position of her left hand suggests she may have held a sceptre.

Right *Steatite head of Queen Tiy from the temple of Hathor, Serabit el-Khadim. Tiy, the mother of Akhenaten, was a strong candidate for mummy 61070, but doubts about the age at death of the mummy have meant this has had to be reconsidered.*

Below *The front view of mummy 61070, the 'Elder Lady'. The remarkable state of preservation of this mummy has attracted much speculation as to her identification.*

Recent analyses of the 'Elder Lady' suggest that her probable age at death was around 30 years old, and so the identity of the mummy as Tiy is put in doubt.

Other candidates

This ambiguity allows two other queens of the period to emerge as possible candidates. On the one hand, we have Ankhesenpaaten, the daughter of Akhenaten, who is present in documents up to her mid-20s (under the name of Ankhesenamun), and who became the wife of Tutankhamun. On the other hand, we have no less than Nefertiti, wife of Akhenaten, and the mother of Ankhesenamun.

Susan James has recently argued that the possibility that mummy 61070 is Ankhesenamun could easily be proven or dismissed because a lock of her hair seems to have been preserved, together with another belonging probably to her husband, in a decorated box found in the antechamber of Tutankhamun's tomb. In the absence so far of a DNA test, James proposes to identify mummy 61070 as Nefertiti. Although the fate of Nefertiti is unknown (p. 127), it is possible that she died around Year 14 of Akhenaten's reign, when she apparently vanishes from monuments and her titles were divided between her elder daughter, Meritaten, and Smenkhkare, the elusive co-regent of Akhenaten.

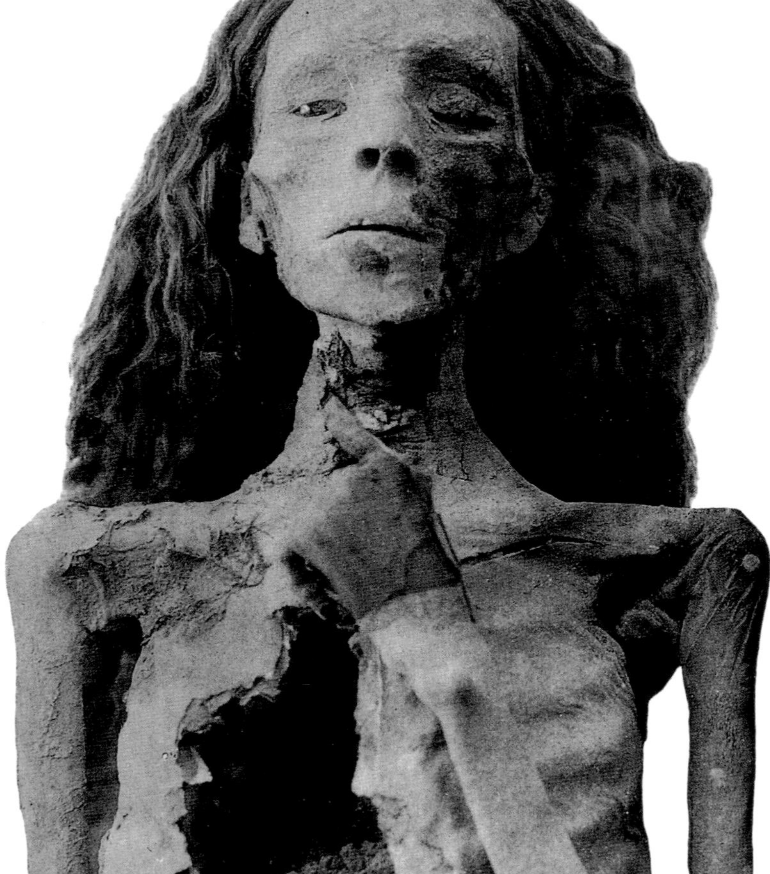

Assuming Nefertiti was close to puberty when she married, she would have been about 30 when she died, which fits well with mummy 61070. Moreover the face of the 'Elder Lady' is eerily reminiscent of famous portraits of Nefertiti now in Berlin and Cairo. Even allowing for artistic conventions, features such as the shape of the upper lip and chin seem similar. However, it has recently been claimed that a body found near mummy 61070 is actually Nefertiti. This 'younger lady' was certainly a contemporary of the 'Elder Lady', but

An unfinished stone head of Nefertiti from the workshop of the sculptor Thutmose at Amarna. The face shows some resemblances to the well-preserved features of mummy 61070.

her remains suggest she was only a teenager at death – too young to be Nefertiti. Perhaps analysis of mitochondrial DNA (which is inherited only through the maternal line) and comparison of the hair of mummy 61070 with the locks from Tutankhamun's tomb can solve this mystery. In the meantime, the beautiful and enigmatic 'Elder Lady' still keeps her secret.

31 Smendes: the alternative king?

On the day of my arrival at Tanis, the place where Smendes and Tentamun are, I gave them the dispatches of Amun-Re, King of the Gods.
THE *REPORT OF WENAMUN*, *c.* 1075 BC

The end of the 20th Dynasty – and with it the end of the New Kingdom also – presents various problems, but one of the more intractable is that of the origins and affiliations of the man who took over the mantle of the great line of Ramesside pharaohs and who founded the 21st Dynasty. According to Manetho and most modern reconstructions, Smendes (Nesbanebdjed) reigned for 26 years, yet only a tiny handful of monuments survive as a memorial to him. Indeed, the most substantive reference to him is from before he even became king.

This occurs in the *Report of Wenamun* (p. 181), dating to Year 5 of the 'Renaissance Era' that occupied the last decade of the reign of Ramesses XI. While en route to Lebanon to obtain wood for renewing the divine barque of Amun-Re, Wenamun arrived at Tanis (modern San el-Hagar, formerly the port-suburb of the royal residence-city Piramesse), 'the place where Smendes and Tentamun are'. The couple then sent Wenamun off in a ship to Syria, where Smendes is cited as one of those who contributed money to the expedition, along with the High-Priest of Amun, Herihor, and others. Smendes is also described as being the one to whom Wenamun gave his letters of credence from Herihor.

One of the canopic jars of Smendes. The formulation of its inscriptions is unique, as are those on a second jar of the king, in the Metropolitan Museum of Art, New York.

Smendes and Tentamun are thus shown to be people of the greatest importance, equals at least of the powerful Herihor. The latter's pretensions are shown by his assumptions of royal titles, apparently while Ramesses XI yet lived, in the temple of Khonsu at Karnak. The implication would seem to be that Smendes was of similar standing in the north. And the fact that Ramesses XI was presumably resident at Piramesse, only 20 km (12 miles) to the southwest of Tanis, makes Smendes' status appear even more remarkable.

King Smendes

Nothing is known of Smendes' origins, although a suggestion has been made that he was a brother of Nodjmet, wife of Herihor. However, Tentamun (presumably Smendes' wife) may have been a member of the Ramesside royal family – an attractive suggestion making her the daughter of a woman also called Tentamun and a king, very probably Ramesses XI. The elder Tentamun was certainly the mother of Henttawy, later the wife of the High-Priest of Amun and king, Pinudjem I. As a royal son-in-law, Smendes' status is more easily explicable, if not his apparent total eclipse of his father-in-law.

Whatever his original status, on Ramesses XI's death, Smendes became king. Only two sources explicitly name him as pharaoh, a stela in a quarry at Dibabia near Gebelein, and a small depiction in the temple of Montu at Karnak, while no unambiguously dated documents are known. However, the contemporary High-Priests of Amun, Pinudjem I, Masaharta and Menkheperre, used year-numbers without a king's name, and it is generally believed that (up to 25) these refer to Smendes' reign.

It seems therefore that during Smendes' reign (and for most of the 21st Dynasty), Egypt was effectively split in two, Lower Egypt being under the direct authority of the king in Tanis, but with the southern area controlled by the High-Priests of Amun based at Thebes. They seem to have held sway over an area stretching from north of el-Hiba to the southern frontier of Egypt, and their aspirations become apparent around Year 16 of Smendes, when the High-Priest Pinudjem I seems to have begun taking steps to take full pharaonic titles, although at all times deferring to Smendes as senior king. Nevertheless, the reality of his kingship is emphasized by the fact that Pinudjem's high-priesthood was passed on to his own sons while he yet lived.

Some troubles seem to have occurred after the death of the first of Pinudjem's high-priestly sons, Masaharta. His third son, Menkheperre, had gone to Thebes in the 25th year of Smendes' reign to 'pacify the land and suppress his enemy', as recorded on a stela in the Louvre. Nevertheless, it was another of Pinudjem's sons, Psusennes I, who was to be Smendes' ultimate successor at Tanis.

Smendes was probably buried at Tanis, as one of his two known canopic jars was bought nearby. However, he apparently did not rest in peace for long. The tomb that was ultimately used for Osorkon II had clearly been taken over and modified for that king's use (p. 95): Smendes is the most probable original owner, although the only decoration visible today derives from the tomb's final occupant. Presumably the tomb had been robbed during the period after the apparent abandonment of the Tanite royal necropolis in the early 22nd Dynasty and then taken over on Osorkon II's return to the old cemetery.

Left *The only surviving contemporary depiction of Smendes, in the gateway of Thutmose I in the precinct of Montu at Karnak.*

Below *The ruins of Tanis (San el-Hagar), city of Smendes and Tentamun. Most of the stone had once formed parts of the temples of Piramesse, and had been removed to its former port-suburb, Tanis, after the latter had replaced it as Egypt's capital.*

32 The Nubian 'Dark Age'

Napata ... is lost to view for the next four centuries in a perplexing historical void.
TIMOTHY KENDALL, 1982

The Nubian 'Dark Age' was once an accepted fact, its appearance in books the inevitable result of Egyptological attitudes to Nubia, and to chronology. But did it ever actually happen?

Nubia lies to the south of Egypt, and the two lands interacted in various ways throughout the pharaonic period. In the late 19th century, before archaeology began in Nubia, our knowledge of the country's history was based entirely on Egyptian monuments and papyrus documents, and the (not always accurate) works of Greek and Roman authors. These sources informed us about two of the major phases of Nubian history: the Egyptian empire of the New Kingdom, when Nubia was ruled by Egypt through a Viceroy and many temples were constructed; and the period when the tables were turned, and the Nubians conquered Egypt. This later period, the 7th and early 6th century BC, was known, following Manetho's chronology, as the 25th Dynasty. The Kushite pharaohs (Kush was the name of the kingdom), Shabaka, Shebitku and Taharqa, were recorded in Greek and Roman authors, and Taharqa was mentioned in the biblical Book of Kings as defender of Hezekiah of Judah against the aggression of the Assyrian emperor, Sennacherib.

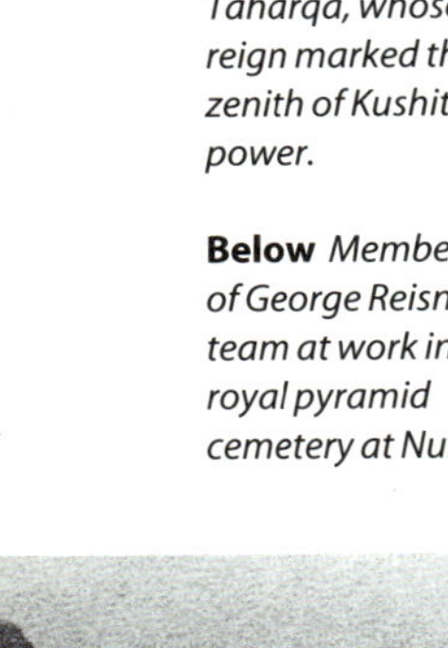

Right *Head of a colossal black granite statue of the pharaoh Taharqa, whose reign marked the zenith of Kushite power.*

Below *Members of George Reisner's team at work in the royal pyramid cemetery at Nuri.*

Excavations in Iraq in the middle of the 19th century brought to light reliefs depicting Sennacherib's campaigns, notably the attack on Lachish in Judah (701 BC), that appeared to confirm the biblical narrative. Assyrian royal inscriptions and numerous clay tablets, first translated in the 1860s and 1870s, added more to our knowledge of the Assyrian conflicts with the Nubian pharaohs. In 1862 several large stelae were discovered at the temple of Gebel Barkal in Sudan, which added Piye and Tantamani to the group of kings listed by Manetho.

This information fitted with our knowledge of Egypt quite well: the New Kingdom empire came to an end, then, during the period when Libyan kings ruled Egypt, it was assumed that a Nubian kingdom slowly developed around Gebel Barkal at the Fourth Cataract. It had to develop slowly because the exact dates BC were established as about 1070 BC for the end of the New Kingdom, and around 800 BC for the beginning of the 25th Dynasty – a gap of almost 300 years. This did not worry Egyptologists as they were dealing with Nubia, and racial attitudes assumed that Nubia would be a slow developer.

Excavations in Nubia

The next major new archaeological evidence came when the American archaeologist George Reisner began excavating, first in the temples of Gebel Barkal (in 1916), then in the pyramid cemetery at Nuri on the opposite side of the river. At Nuri, Reisner found the tomb of Taharqa and those of a number of later Nubian kings, dating from around 650 BC to about 300 BC. Following the excavations at Nuri, Reisner transferred his attention to an apparently much less inspiring archaeological site, el-Kurru, a few kilometres from Gebel Barkal.

The 'miserable little heaps of ruins' that formed the cemetery at el-Kurru proved to be more significant than Reisner had ever expected. Here he excavated the plundered burials of the 25th Dynasty pharaohs Piye, Shabaka, Shebitku and Tantamani. But these were not in the most prominent position in the cemetery. Reisner found that there were 14 tumulus and other burials, which he attributed to the ancestors of the 25th Dynasty kings. Somewhat strangely, Reisner interpreted these burials as family groups, rather than a single line of rulers. His calculation (modified only slightly when the excavations were published by his assistant, Dows Dunham) was that the first burial in the cemetery had been made about 950 BC, over 100 years after the end of the Egyptian New Kingdom empire.

This inexplicable gap did not trouble Reisner, nor, apparently any other historians of Nubia. So the gap remained as a 'fact'. The surveys and excavations that took place in Lower (northern) Nubia as a result of the raising in height of the old Aswan Dam and the construction of the new Dam in the 1960s were generally interpreted as confirming this cultural gap. Archaeologists assumed that the Nubian population had gradually dwindled in the later New Kingdom, due to low Nile floods, and that in the following period there

The extensive ruins of the great temple of Amun-Re stand at the foot of the cliffs of Gebel Barkal.

Nearly 1100 shabty figures were excavated in the pyramid tomb of Taharqa at Nuri, ranging in height from 18 to 60 cm.

were hardly any settled inhabitants of the region. Some archaeologists went so far as to propose that there was no permanently settled population between Aswan and the Fourth Cataract of the Nile for 300 years. Recent surveys and excavations have now shown that this idea is completely wrong.

New interpretations

Since the late 1970s there have been many studies which question older interpretations of the archaeology of Nubia. There is very little evidence to support the theory that there were low Nile floods in the later New Kingdom, and the apparent 'disappearance' of the local Nubian population is now seen as the result of growing Egyptian cultural influence ('acculturation'). Some archaeological material has also been reassessed and ascribed to the period following the New Kingdom. If Lower Nubia was not under the direct rule of Egypt, or of rulers to the south, then there would have been no official monuments set up. It is possible, as we know from earlier and later periods, that Lower Nubia had a small population surviving by subsistence agriculture.

The material from el-Kurru has also been re-examined in recent years, although there is no consensus as to how the evidence should be interpreted. Some archaeologists continue to follow Reisner's interpretation of the cemetery, but others argue that all the burials belonged to rulers and should therefore spread over 14 generations. This would mean that, on the conventionally accepted Egyptian chronology, the first ruler buried in the cemetery of el-Kurru would have reigned about 50 years after the end of the New Kingdom. One cemetery, however, does not fill a 'Dark Age' of three centuries.

Attention has also been focused on a relief and inscription in the temple of Semna at the Second Cataract. Although it had long been known, the very difficult language of the text had been tackled by few scholars. The publication of a new copy of the text, with a partial translation by Ricardo Caminos, has made considerable advances in our understanding of the relief. The style of the figures indicates that it belongs to the period following the New Kingdom, but before the 25th Dynasty. Certain features of the language are also typical of Libyan period Egypt. The inscription names a queen, Karimala or Katimala, and refers to an attempt at usurpation by 'Makaresh'. The defeat of the rebel is attributed to the god Amun. Unfortunately, the king associated with Karimala is not named, nor their power base. Nevertheless, it indicates that the emergence of the Kushite state was not a simple or peaceful process. The inscription also shows that there were power centres in Nubia other than the Gebel Barkal region. The most likely base for rulers is the important site of Kawa, standing in a rich region to the south of the Third Cataract. Kawa was a major centre both in the time of Egyptian rule and during the 25th Dynasty and the later Meroitic period. If evidence for continuity is to be found, it is probably there.

A gold pectoral depicting the goddess Isis, from one of the later royal burials at Nuri.

Challenging chronology

The most radical solution to the mystery of the Nubian 'Dark Age' questions the basis of Egyptian chronology itself. Challenges to Egyptian chronology have been proposed by a number of different writers with different reconstructions (and personal agenda). The most academic challenge was made by Peter James and colleagues in *Centuries of Darkness* (1991). Although the solution they proposed, lowering the date for the end of the Egyptian New Kingdom by some 200 years, was generally dismissed by Egyptologists, it resolves many archaeological problems throughout western Asia, and would have a significant effect on the Nubian 'Dark Age'. In the decade since the publication of *Centuries of Darkness*, a number of Egyptologists have proposed smaller reductions in Egyptian chronology which, if combined, would add up to about 100 years.

What would it mean? Lowering the date for the end of the Egyptian New Kingdom would dispose of the old idea that Nubian development was slow. The Kushite kingdom would be a direct successor to the Egyptian empire, and perhaps played a significant role in bringing Egyptian rule over Nubia to an end. The Nubian 'Dark Age' is a lesson in the dangers of interpreting the archaeology of one country by the history of another, and over-reliance on the material from, and interpretation of, one archaeological site, in this case el-Kurru. In western Asia, the reliance on Egyptian chronology has caused numerous arguments in the interpretation of the archaeology; in Nubia it created a yawning void. It was not until recently that the existence of this void was questioned, as ingrained assumptions about Nubian political and cultural development were still dominated by old racist presumptions.

The temple of Semna at the Second Cataract. The relief and inscription of Queen Karimala is carved to the left of the doorway.

Khababash, the guerrilla king

The sea-land ... was granted by the king ... Khababash, living for ever, to the gods of Pe and Dep, after his Majesty had gone to Pe and Dep to examine all the sea-land in their territory ... to examine every arm of the Nile which goes into the Great Sea, to keep off the fleet of Asia from Egypt.

From the 'Satrap Stela' of Ptolemy, 311 BC

Below *A gold coin of the Persian Great King, Artaxerxes III, who regained control of Egypt, and was vilified in later Egyptian tradition.*

Opposite below *One of the few ancient records to name Khababash is the 'Satrap Stela' set up by Ptolemy I when he was still acting as governor of Egypt for the infant Alexander IV of Macedon.*

Khababash is certainly one of Egypt's mystery pharaohs, associated with the period when Egypt was intermittently part of the Persian Empire in the 4th century BC. The strangeness of his name, which is not Egyptian, has led to a number of suggestions about his origins, but no real agreement. While some have seen him as a Persian rebel satrap, others suggest Arab, Libyan or Nubian ancestry. Khababash's Egyptian royal style associates him particularly with Memphis and its gods, Ptah and Tjenen, so whatever his origins, Khababash was backed by the most powerful priesthood in Egypt.

Even putting a firm date on Khababash's reign is rather difficult. It seems most probable that he assumed power either in the last years of the reign of the Persian king Artaxerxes III, or at the troubled time between the murder of that king (338/337 BC) and the accession of Darius III (336/335 BC). Changes of ruler were always a time of crisis in the Persian court and empire, usually with several rival claimants to the throne and rebellions in the more distant provinces. Egypt had regularly rebelled against the Persians, and the rule of Artaxerxes III was regarded in later priestly traditions as particularly hostile to the Egyptian temples. Rightly, or wrongly, the Egyptian and Greek literary traditions accuse the Persians of various acts of desecration: the removal of divine statues, ritual books and furniture to Persia; and the killing (and eating) of the sacred Apis bull of Memphis. News of the Persian king's murder would have been an ideal moment for an Egyptian rebellion backed by the priesthood.

Some confusion has been caused by the attempt to identify Khababash with a figure named in the lengthy 'historical' inscription of the early king of Meroë, Nastasen. The stela of Nastasen, now in Berlin Museum, is dated to the eighth year of his reign and records the king's military actions, including a campaign in the north of Nubia against a ruler whose name had generally been read 'Kambasweden'. The leading Meroitic scholar, Fritz Hintze, argued that 'Kambasweden' should actually be read as 'Khababash given life'. Hintze's reading has been accepted by some writers on Nubia, but is certainly wrong. Furthermore, Hintze did not adequately explain what Khababash was doing wandering around in Lower Nubia with large herds of cattle. This seems a rather improbable explanation of the text and it is most likely that Kambasweden was a local Lower Nubian ruler and not the pharaoh Khababash.

The reign of Khababash is in fact known from only three ancient records: a demotic papyrus of his first year; the sarcophagus of an Apis bull, buried in his second year; and the 'Satrap Stela' of Ptolemy, now in the Cairo Museum.

Historical reality

The importance of Khababash as a legitimate Egyptian ruler in opposition to the Persians is clear from the one inscription that tells us most about him, the 'Satrap Stela' of Ptolemy (later

The inscription on an Apis bull sarcophagus that was buried in Khababash's second regnal year shows that he had been recognized as pharaoh in the city of Memphis.

Ptolemy I). Following the death of Alexander the Great in Babylon (323 BC), his generals acknowledged his successors Philip Arrhidaios and Alexander IV as kings, but quickly seized portions of the empire for themselves under the Persian-style title of 'satrap' (governor). Ptolemy took Egypt, and ruled there as satrap for nearly 20 years before assuming the style of a king.

The 'Satrap Stela' is dated to Year 7 of Alexander IV (311 BC), but begins with a eulogy of Ptolemy and his restoration of the temples. It then tells us that Ptolemy confirmed a donation of land made by Khababash to the temple of the goddess Wadjyt in the Delta city of Buto – the same temple where the Stela was originally set up. Ptolemy's action is presented as a response to a petition made by the priests, and reputedly records a speech of Khababash. The donation of land by Ptolemy and the prominence of the record clearly show how the new Macedonian ruler (king in all but name) tried to win over the Egyptian priesthood and officials through support of local cults. Whatever its political motivation, Ptolemy's inscription does contain details that suggest it is based on some historical reality.

We are told that Khababash's original donation was made when he visited Buto and was petitioned by the priests. But Khababash's visit was not part of a royal progress, it was a specifically military operation: he had gone there to examine the marshland and every branch of the river that ran into the sea in order 'to keep off the fleet of Asia from Egypt'. Egypt was difficult to attack: the sea was bordered with long sand dunes, and inland there was a dense papyrus marshland. Invasion by ship required sailing along one of the Nile branches, and Persian forces had already come to grief in the Delta on more than one occasion. Khababash's hope of keeping the Persians from regaining control was by patrolling the marshes and dunes. Although he held Memphis and the western Delta, it seems likely that Khababash's rule did not extend over the whole of the Nile Valley and it was perhaps Persian garrisons in the south, rather than the feared Persian fleet, that brought his kingdom to an end.

34 The fatal attraction of Cleopatra

Age cannot wither her, nor custom stale
Her infinite variety: other women cloy
The appetites they feed, but she makes hungry
Where she most satisfies.
Shakespeare, *Antony and Cleopatra*, Act II, Scene 2, 1604

Above *Cleopatra has remained a potent symbol through 2000 years of history and her image has been used in many different ways.*

Cleopatra, the last native-born pharaoh of Egypt, has appeared in numerous different guises through the ages. Even in 1604, when Shakespeare was writing *Antony and Cleopatra*, her image was of 'infinite variety'. Today, she is projected through more lenses than Shakespeare ever imagined possible – Orientalist paintings, Hollywood movies, romantic novels, comic strips and advertisements. Cleopatra has inspired some of the most potent and erotic images of femininity and, 2000 years after her death, she is still famous and glamorous enough to sell soap, hair products, cigarettes or anything associated with sensual pleasure. She personifies the passionate beauty ready to die for love, the ruthless and ambitious woman, and the death-bringing seductress. Many mysteries lie behind these masks of Cleopatra. Was she a Greek, an Egyptian, a black woman, or something of all three? Was she really a great beauty? What were her political ambitions? And how exactly did she kill herself when these ambitions collapsed?

Right *Marble bust identified as Cleopatra, apparently confirming Plutarch's description of her looks as being unexceptional.*

Birth of a legend

Born in 69 BC, Cleopatra was the second daughter of Ptolemy XII and his sister-wife Cleopatra V Tryphaena. The Ptolemaic monarchs were the successors of one of Alexander the Great's generals, Ptolemy, who had seized control of Egypt in the squabbles in the aftermath of Alexander's death. Originally Greek, they had borrowed the Egyptian gods' practices of sibling marriage and joint male-female rule in order to appear more divine to their subjects. Accordingly, Cleopatra and her brother-husband Ptolemy XIII became co-rulers of Egypt on their father's death; she subsequently married another brother, Ptolemy

XIV. Although Cleopatra is usually numbered as the seventh queen of the name, it is uncertain that any Cleopatra VI preceded her.

On her accession, Cleopatra inherited her father's uneasy relationship with Rome, the dominant Mediterranean power at the time, then controlled by Julius Caesar. Egypt was the last of the Hellenistic kingdoms that had not fallen under Roman dominion, but Rome interfered in its affairs – especially since Ptolemy XIII and Cleopatra both wanted sole control of Egypt. Caesar restored Cleopatra to power after Ptolemy XIII expelled her in 48 BC: he arranged Ptolemy's murder and left three legions in Egypt to safeguard Cleopatra's throne. She and Caesar became lovers, and their son, Ptolemy Caesarion ('little Caesar'), was born in 47 BC.

After Caesar's assassination in 44 BC, Cleopatra became a key mover in the power politics of the day by allying herself with Mark Antony. Together they were the principal opponents of Augustus, Caesar's ambitious heir and adopted son. Antony and Cleopatra's political alliance ultimately proved disastrous for them, though history gained its most famous royal romance.

Cleopatra supposedly used her dazzling beauty to lure Mark Antony away from his wife. However, the only near-contemporary description of Cleopatra to survive says that her looks were unexceptional, but her intelligence, vivacity and sparkling conversation were truly outstanding. The same author, Plutarch, also credits her with such a gift for languages that she could speak to any foreign dignitary in his own tongue.

'Lover of her Homeland'

Classical writers like Plutarch record many of the anecdotes about Cleopatra that have helped make her into a romantic legend and a mystery. But if the evidence from Egypt is considered, a different side of Cleopatra emerges. From the Egyptian point of view, she was a monarch who tried to retain Egypt's independence in the face of Roman imperialism and who respected Egyptian traditions. Cleopatra's royal titles included *Philopatris*, 'Lover of her Homeland', and she seems genuinely to have cared for her country.

Egyptian documents from the last years of her father's reign paint a gloomy picture. There were widespread complaints about the corruption of government officials, extortion and impossibly high taxes. In some places economic pressures were so bad that people fled from their homes to avoid paying taxes, and temples were robbed. Once she had become ruler, Cleopatra sought practical solutions to some of these problems, devaluing the currency by one-third in order to increase revenue from exports, and ensuring that taxes were collected more efficiently and without extortion. Matters seem to have improved by 45 BC, when royal building projects resumed after being halted by shortage of funds, and there is other evidence of economic upturn. How far this can be attributed to the queen herself is debatable. It certainly seems that Cleopatra took government business seriously, reading petitions, meeting dignitaries and countersigning state papers herself. One such paper vividly evokes Cleopatra as a working monarch. It appears to have been read and authorized in the queen's own handwriting: her one-word comment translates simply as 'make it happen'.

A black basalt statue recently identified as Cleopatra wearing the triple uraeus cobras, a rare attribute distinguishing her from other queens. It was originally gilded to show Cleopatra's divinity. Images like this one have been used to argue that Cleopatra was black, or partly so, perhaps via her unknown grandmother.

Right *Relief from the south wall of the temple of Hathor at Dendereh, showing Cleopatra (left) and Caesarion (second from left) offering to the gods who maintain their rule. Caesarion was about eight years old when the image was carved c. 40 BC, but he is shown as an adult and his mother's equal.*

Below *A taxation ordinance dated to 33 BC. Cleopatra's handwritten additional note may be seen at the bottom of the right-hand column of text.*

Originating in Greek-speaking Macedonia, Cleopatra's forebears had kept a distinct Hellenic identity throughout three centuries of ruling Egypt, and showed little curiosity about its civilization. Cleopatra was the first of the Ptolemies to learn the Egyptian language in order to communicate with her subjects, and issued her edicts bilingually in Greek and Egyptian. She was also more involved with Egyptian culture than the earlier Ptolemies, and gave thought to her representation in Egyptian art, which developed a unique iconography for her. Unlike the other Ptolemies, no Greek-style sculpture of Cleopatra has ever been found in Egypt itself, and it is possible that she was always portrayed there in Egyptian fashion. Cleopatra also honoured the traditional Egyptian cults by extending the shrines of the oracular bull-god at Armant and the temple at the ancient site of Koptos. Temple-building not only pleased the priesthood, but also gave Cleopatra the opportunity to promote the young Caesarion as the future king Ptolemy XV and the initiator of a glorious new dynasty. No pharaoh since Ramesses II, more than 1000 years earlier, had promoted the royal heir with such impressive monuments.

By 36 BC she had had three children by Mark Antony: twins Cleopatra Selene and Alexander Helios, and Ptolemy Philadelphus, and she had great ambitions for these too. She seems to have imagined herself, Mark Antony and the children ruling a new version of Alexander's empire – one that would rival Rome. At an elaborate ceremony in 34 BC, each child was allotted an area of Alexander's former dominions. This was a symbolic statement more than anything else, since most of these places were no longer under Egyptian control.

How strong a challenge Mark Antony and Cleopatra posed to Rome and Augustus is hard to say. Cleopatra certainly financed Mark Antony's military activities against Augustus, who took their opposition seriously enough to declare war on Egypt in 32 BC. After their defeat at the sea-battle off Actium in northwestern Greece, Mark Antony and Cleopatra retreated to Alexandria to await Augustus' arrival. Some 3000 years of Egypt's existence as an independent kingdom were about to end in Roman annexation. Antony and Cleopatra preferred suicide to a humiliating captivity.

Death and immortality

Cleopatra's suicide is one of history's great set pieces, immortalized by Shakespeare's play, several films and countless paintings. What exactly happened is unclear, as the ancient accounts are contradictory and were all written many years after the event. Some say that she poisoned herself, others give the more famous version that she allowed herself to be bitten by a snake. The latter theory is appealing because of the snake's divine and royal symbolism in Egyptian mythology, but presents too many practical difficulties to be convincing. The fate of Cleopatra's body is unknown too, though presumably she would have been honoured with an Egyptian-style burial.

After her death, Cleopatra became an obvious target for Augustus' propagandists, who mostly portrayed her in a negative light. As with the other great foreign woman who challenged Rome, the British queen Boudicca (Boadicea), Classical historians emphasized Cleopatra's threat to patriarchal Roman values. Their works vilified her as extravagant, indolent, self-indulgent and cruel – a woman who tested poisons on captives and dissolved pearls in wine simply to show off her wealth. She was the ultimate un-Roman.

In Egypt, however, quite different traditions about the queen were preserved. Her name was never erased from monuments and her statues remained in the temples, continuing to receive divine honours for centuries. Cleopatra even remained a popular name to give female children. The Egyptians remembered Cleopatra as a great ruler and something of a heroine. They also preserved her associations with wisdom and sexual attraction, attributing to her authorship a collection of cosmetic and medicinal lore, including a cure for baldness and a hair-restorer. Egypt too contributed to the myth-making about Cleopatra, helping to turn its most famous sovereign into a legend that would transcend history.

Death of Cleopatra *by Jean-André Rixens (1874). Cleopatra's suicide, and the imagery of the snake, summed up Egypt's associations with sex and death for Western artists.*

People & Places

Egypt has never existed in splendid isolation. Since prehistory, Egyptians have traded and exchanged ideas with Libya, Nubia and African lands beyond; the so-called 'Roads of Horus' have ferried travellers across Sinai to Palestine; and the seas have not been barriers, but highways to the Levant and East Africa. The ambassadors, gods and the gold of Egypt were known and welcome far and wide in ancient times. Among Egypt's earliest recorded trading partners was the kingdom of Yam. In the 6th Dynasty, the governor Harkhuf made four adventurous journeys there to bring back exotic goods such as ebony and ivory. Afterwards Yam seems to disappear from the historical record. Here we ask, where was Yam? The answer is crucial for our understanding of relations between the nations of North Africa at such an early date.

Egypt's most celebrated trading partner was Punt, where Egyptians obtained the produce best fit for offering to the gods. Egyptians and Puntites traded for at least 1500 years, but surprisingly we cannot be sure where Punt lay, except that it was along the Red Sea. Was it in modern Sudan, the Horn of Africa or across the water in Arabia?

The north of Egypt is a Mediterranean land, so relations with the Levant and the Aegean are well documented. Nevertheless, archaeologists did not anticipate the paintings found in the palaces at Avaris in 1991. Their style is distinctive and well known from palaces elsewhere, above all in Crete. So what do they tell us about relations between Crete and Egypt at the beginning of the New

Bearded chiefs, following the donkey which has carried their queen, come to trade with an Egyptian expedition in the land of Punt, the fabled African emporium. From reliefs in the temple of Hatshepsut at Deir el-Bahri, Thebes.

Representatives of other African nations were familiar participants in the Egyptian court, as shown in the tomb of Huy, the vizier of Tutankhamun.

Kingdom? That their respective rulers merely shared a world of ideas; or that Cretans were actually members of the royal family of Egypt? Without doubt Egypt had one important partner in the Mediterranean throughout the New Kingdom – Alashiya. Today, however, Alashiya, like Yam, seems to be a name without a place. So here again we can ask, where was Alashiya?

Familiarity with the wider world does not make it any less daunting for the traveller far from home. The hero of Egypt's greatest classic, the *Story of Sinuhe*, summarizes the hopelessness of an asylum-seeker in a single spare phrase: 'Foreign land gave me to foreign land'. The priest, Wenamun, recounts his own experience abroad more personally: 'I sat down and began to cry, and he said to me, "What is the matter?" So I said to him, "Have you not seen the birds which have made a second migration to Egypt? Look at them, travelling to the cleansing water. Until when will I be left here?"' Some authorities have debated whether Sinuhe and Wenamun were real adventurers or fictional heroes. Their question is not unimportant: the *Story of Sinuhe* is our most detailed picture of life in Palestine from the Egyptian Middle Kingdom; the *Report of Wenamun* is usually held up as a statement of the dramatic decline of Egypt's prestige in the international community at the end of the New Kingdom. How different the ancient world seems, if the landscapes these texts portray are landscapes of the imagination.

Of course, ancient Egyptians were not immune from the hostility of foreigners. In modern histories the definitive enemies of Egypt are the 'Hyksos', who 'burned our cities ruthlessly, razed to the ground the temples of the gods, and treated all the natives with a cruel hostility' – at least as reported around 1700 years later by the historian Josephus. This lurid account has inevitably coloured any modern interpretation of the Hyksos; but here we ask whether it sits easily with the work of modern historians?

Another mysterious group of invaders constitute a mystery whose ramifications reach out beyond Egyptology – the 'Sea Peoples'. This is the term used by modern scholars for a disparate bunch of peoples who attacked Egypt in the wake of the collapse of the Hittite Empire. Earlier generations of scholars presumed that the main force which drove the ancient world was the incessant migration of warlike tribes, who imposed 'advanced' ideas and practices on to 'inferior' local populations. Therefore, many have long since assumed that the 'Sea Peoples' were wandering marauders, the ancient equivalent of the Vikings. Indeed, these groups, such as the Peleset, Sherden, Shekelesh, Denyen and Akwesh, might have left a legacy of names across the Mediterranean: Palestine, Sardinia, Sicily, and even Danaoi and Achaioi, ancient names for the Greeks. But the question, *why* did these people ever leave their homelands suggests a different story. Perhaps the collapse of Hittite government generated crises in which many people were displaced from their homes. Certainly no one can doubt that the international politics of the ancient world were every bit as complex as they are today.

Where was the kingdom of Yam?

The person of Merenre … sent me along with my father … Iri, to Yam, to open up the route to that land.

FUNERARY INSCRIPTION OF HARKHUF, *c.* 2225 BC

The mysterious land of Yam features in Egypt's oldest narrative of foreign travel, dating to the 23rd century BC. Inscribed on a tomb façade, it describes the adventures of Harkhuf, governor of Elephantine (Egypt's southernmost town) during the 6th Dynasty. Harkhuf led four trading expeditions to Yam, located somewhere in Nubia, south of Egypt. Donkey caravans were used there and back, and the exchange of Egyptian goods for products found in Yam was quite substantial. On one trip, 300 asses brought back 'incense, ebony … leopard skins, elephant tusks and boomerangs'.

Harkhuf's trips were not always routine. Once, he found trading threatened by the departure of the ruler of Yam in order to 'smite the Tjemeh-people to the western corner of heaven' and had to pursue and pacify him. Then, as he returned to Egypt, Harkhuf used his strong Yamite escort to avoid the exactions of another Nubian ruler, who instead 'gave me oxen and goats and conducted me over the heights of Irtjet'.

Finally, on his fourth trip to Yam, Harkhuf obtained a pygmy (*deng* in Egyptian), stimulating the boy-king of Egypt at that time, Pepy II, to write a feverishly excited letter to the returning governor. Promising him rich rewards, the boy-king orders Harkhuf to bring the pygmy immediately and safely to Memphis, the royal capital: if by ship, 'get stalwart men who shall be around [the pygmy] on the deck, beware lest he fall in the water.… My majesty desires to see this [pygmy] more than the tribute of the Mine-land and Punt [lands that were rich in minerals and incense respectively]!'

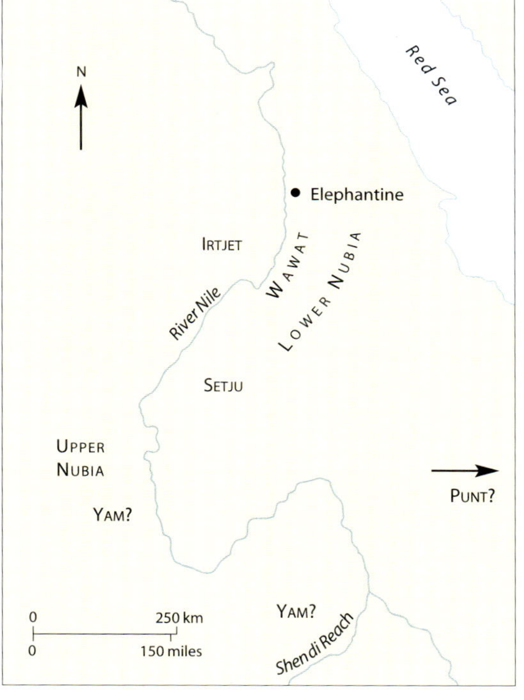

Map of the regions relevant to Yam and Irem.

Other sources show the importance of Yam to Old Kingdom Egypt. Remote enough that its ruler did not formally have to submit to the Egyptian king (other Nubian rulers did), Yam sent men for Egyptian-ordered labour and military levies. Potentially, its hostility was also feared. Yam was included among other Nubian lands in the 'Execration Texts', inscribed on figures of bound enemies deposited in cemeteries and elsewhere to abort or prevent, through magic, any attack upon, or resistance to, Egypt.

Below *Part of the travel narrative of Harkhuf, carved on the rock façade of his tomb; this section includes the determinative of the word for pygmy.*

Locating Yam

Yet where was Yam? This question inspires considerable scholarly debate and is important not only to determine the depth of Egyptian penetration into other parts of Africa, but also to assess the relative size and strength of various Nubian polities vis-à-vis Old Kingdom Egypt. Especially significant here is Harkhuf's narrative.

Harkhuf's first and second journeys to Yam took respectively seven and eight months there and back. Moreover, he once returned to Egypt via 'the neighbourhood of the house of the ruler of Setju and Irtjet', and another time via the frontier between the land of Setju and its southern neighbour Irtjet. By this time the ruler had added a third polity, Wawat, to the other two. These, and other references, have led to different concepts of early Nubian geopolitics. Some scholars assume Harkhuf's donkey caravans started their land journey at Memphis, and returned thence. The length of time taken then indicates Yam lay in Upper Nubia, and Wawat, Setju and Irtjet (all north of Yam) in Lower Nubia. An opposing interpretation sees Elephantine as the starting and end point for each caravan, with goods from or to Memphis then travelling on by ship between the two towns. In this case, Yam lay further south, perhaps on or near the Shendi Reach of the Nile. These circumstances permit Wawat to comprise all Lower Nubia (as it always did in later times) and Setju and Irtjet to be in Upper Nubia.

The implications of the two theories are substantial. According to the first, Wawat, Setju and Irtjet would each be territorially small, best interpreted as 'chiefdoms'. Even when combined under a single ruler, as Harkhuf once found to be the case, they would form at best a fairly small kingdom. The second hypothesis, however, would make each territorially large, and – once combined – a substantial kingdom, possibly quite threatening to Egypt, especially insofar as direct access to the desirable goods available in Yam was concerned. These goods, in some cases, may well have been obtained by Yam from other, even more southerly locales.

Can this mystery ever be solved? Probably: the Shendi Reach and its environs are archaeologically under-explored, and in the future may provide textual and archaeological evidence showing whether Yam was there or not.

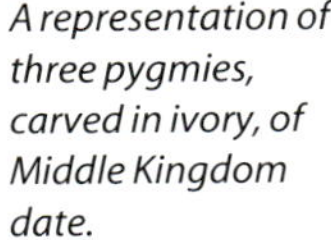

A representation of three pygmies, carved in ivory, of Middle Kingdom date.

A scene from the tomb of Huy, Viceroy of Nubia for Tutankhamun. Nubian officials (lower register) are presenting typically Nubian products, including gold ring-ingots and a giraffe.

Yam in the New Kingdom?

Relevant here is another Nubian land, Irem. Attested in the New Kingdom and later, Irem may be the then equivalent to Yam, the name having undergone linguistic or orthographic change. Irem was significant to New Kingdom Egypt, which for over three centuries controlled all Lower and much, if not all, of Upper Nubia. During the 19th and 20th Dynasties, and even earlier, Egypt and Irem were periodically in conflict, sometimes on a large scale, while more pacific contacts, such as trade and even tributary relationships, probably went on as well.

As with Yam, scholars disagree about Irem's location, an issue with serious geopolitical implications insofar as Egypt's relations with Nubia are concerned. Some place Irem in Upper Nubia, along with other polities, as one of several occasionally rebellious lands which nevertheless lay within the Egyptian empire. However, a campaign record of Sety I indicates that Irem lay south, or at least outside, of Egyptian-controlled Upper Nubia.

Here again travel narrative provides intriguing, but not conclusive, indications about Irem's location. A large sea-going trading expedition was dispatched by Queen Hatshepsut to Punt, an incense-yielding country on the African shore of the Red Sea. While its location is also debated (p. 173), Punt may have been in the general region of the modern frontier between Sudan and Eritrea.

One aspect is especially important. A combined Egyptian-Puntite party which went inland to collect the desired products traversed a region shown in the reliefs recording the expedition at Deir el-Bahri as consisting of two zones. One included natives different in appearance from Puntites, and fauna (giraffe, rhinoceros) more typical of savannah lands closer than Punt to the Nile Valley. Since the 'tribute' acquired by the expedition was produced by the lands of Irem and Amu as well as Punt, the first two might include the savannah region shown, and be closer to the Nile, or even on it. Given Punt's possible location, this could place Irem – like earlier Yam – on or near the Shendi Reach, although some scholars dispute this reading of the relevant scenes. Again, archaeological exploration might one day solve the mystery.

36 Sinuhe: literary hero or real-life deserter?

Of course, I am like the bull of one herd in the midst of another herd.
THE *STORY OF SINUHE*, *c.* 1800 BC

Opposite *Painted wooden statue from the tomb of Imhotep at Lisht, believed to represent Senwosret I. At the end of his tale, Sinuhe is reconciled with Senwosret, and makes an emotional return to his homeland.*

Below *Fragment of a New Kingdom ostracon with the* Story of Sinuhe, *which was read and copied for many centuries after it was first composed in the 12th Dynasty.*

The *Story of Sinuhe* is a classic. The ancient Egyptians certainly thought so – it was still being used to train scribes nearly a thousand years after its composition. For modern Egyptologists, too, it is a classic, though more for its themes relating to Egyptian values, the nature of being Egyptian and of the predicament of individual life among the dangers and forces of the wider world, and for its exquisite phrasing and careful structure.

The plot of the story is relatively straightforward. Set in the early 12th Dynasty, Sinuhe is taking part in an expedition abroad led by the King's Son Senwosret I. In the early part of the story, Sinuhe accidentally overhears of the death of the old king, Amenemhat I, back in Egypt. He breaks down under the gravity of the knowledge (the text has: 'my heart was distraught and my arms thrown out, and trembling spread through all the parts of my body') and flees. The remainder of the text comprises his search to regain and reground his self-identity. His flight takes him to other countries and leads him to a life of success and plenty in the lands of the Levant.

Again, external circumstances intrude – a powerful warrior of a neighbouring tribe challenges Sinuhe to single combat. Sinuhe faces up to the challenge and wins through, killing the warrior. None the less, the episode forces Sinuhe to realize that he can never be fully accepted in this foreign land, nor will he ever be truly at home there (the text captures this in one of its many poetical images: 'What can fix a papyrus-plant to a mountain?'). His predicament reaches the ears of King Senwosret I and after an exchange of letters, Sinuhe eventually returns to Egypt and lives out a happy old age in the favour of the king.

The story is crafted within a careful overall structuring of the shape and flow of the text, for instance episodes of Sinuhe's life are interspersed with eulogies of Senwosret I, creating a clear structure to the story. The phrasing shows a strong favouring for the poetic and is expressed within a clear verse structure throughout the text.

Fiction or reality?

But some Egyptologists have spilt metaphorical blood in print over Sinuhe himself. Is he just a literary creation of an imaginative ancient Egyptian author (who, like so many Egyptian authors, remains unnamed and unknown). Or was he a real person, whose stirring adventures have formed the basis of the literary composition as we now have it?

The case for Sinuhe being a real character is not one founded on clear evidence – there is no trace of such a person in the (admittedly incomplete) material from the Middle Kingdom. This line of argument is founded on a desire to authenticate the historical details in the story (such as the date given for the death of King Amenemhat I at the start of the story, or the details of Levantine society). A recent, cogent attempt to ground Sinuhe in reality has been based on stressing the similarity between the story and autobiographies – a common kind of inscription found in elite tombs of the period (p. 211).

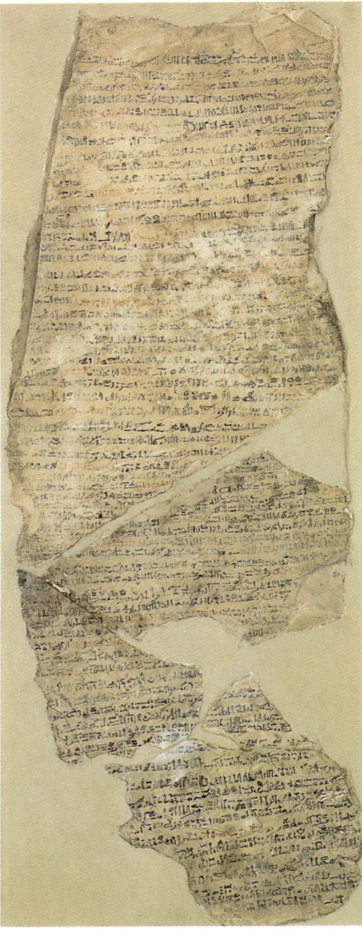

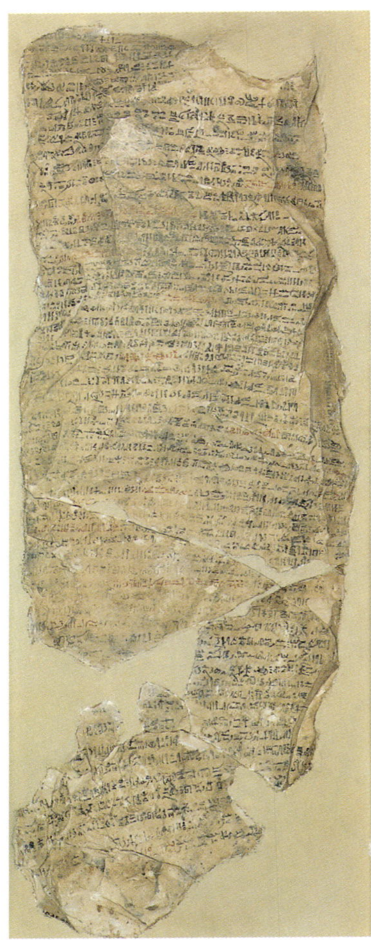

Both sides of an ostracon in the Ashmolean Museum, Oxford, which is the fullest copy of the Story of Sinuhe *surviving from the New Kingdom (see also p. 212).*

In contrast, the case for Sinuhe being a literary character is one which requires little justification. The numerous surviving versions of the story are all clearly literary and derive from the same archetype. Although the story draws strongly on autobiographical themes and is structured around these, it develops and explores them in ways which overlap little with other autobiographies, but share instead a strong common thread with other indisputably literary texts of the period.

Since the story uses autobiography as a compositional device from which to emerge and return (just as the *Story of the Shipwrecked Sailor* makes literary play with the common genre of inscriptions relating to expeditions), it is hardly surprising that it draws heavily on the forms of that genre. Seen from the literary angle, the story explores the parameters of the human condition: it is a story about the nature of being human – a common theme in Middle Kingdom literature, but one hardly to be found within the usual autobiographies. This is unsurprising since autobiographies, being tomb inscriptions, have a specialized mortuary setting and stress the success and achievement of the deceased without focusing on other aspects of human life, such as problems, failures and weakness.

In particular, Sinuhe's story deals with reactions to contingencies and predicaments beyond individual control, dramatized around the central elements of the flight, the single combat and the return. In this way, the device of a geographical journey is used literally to plot Sinuhe's move away from and return to Egypt, but also metaphorically to shape his journey of self-

Asiatics arriving to trade in Egypt, as shown in the tomb of the governor Khnumhotep II at Beni Hasan. The detail of their chief, Absha, is shown larger below. During the Middle Kingdom there was close contact between Egypt and the Levant, reflected in this painting and in the story of Sinuhe.

identity and belonging. In facing up to the predicaments which threaten to overwhelm him, he has only his own resources to use – the resources of ordinary humanity. Sinuhe has no magical weapon to call upon; he is not visited by a god who advises him how to act; he does not have superhuman strength or insight. In this he shares much in common with other 'heroes' of the Middle Kingdom literary pantheon – such as the Shipwrecked Sailor and the Eloquent Peasant – who, too, have only the resilience, fortitude and skill of ordinary human resources to fall back upon. This journey of self is cast within more general (but culturally specific) themes of interrelationships, primarily with the king and the divine, but also of social belonging.

Does the reality or fictionality of Sinuhe matter very much? Probably not. Literary texts still give us useful information about the life-world within which they were written (fiction doesn't necessitate untruth). On the other hand, if Sinuhe was a real character, then he's been given a literary make-over to such an extent that little remains in the story other than his literary self. This is the case even if the story does turn out to be based on an (and one that must be rather different) original autobiographical text or, more hypothetically, on the oral story of the misfortunes of a real person.

In terms of evidence, the literary camp clearly have the easier case to defend: the sole evidence is the story, and this is indisputably a piece of literature. For the realists, only clear evidence of a non-literary kind, preferably the tomb which might be claimed to have been the source for the literary text, will do. We are still waiting.

Who were the Hyksos?

... and unexpectedly, from the regions of the East, invaders of obscure race marched in confidence of victory against our land. By main force they easily overpowered the rulers of the land, they then burned our cities ruthlessly, razed to the ground the temples of the gods, and treated all the natives with a cruel hostility.

MANETHO, ACCORDING TO JOSEPHUS, *AGAINST APION*, 1ST CENTURY AD

In Egyptian tradition, the Hyksos gained a lurid reputation as bloodthirsty conquerors. In reality, despite the large number of texts and archaeological sites which can be linked to them, the identity of the Hyksos is far from clear. Apart from the contemporary texts – dating from the 15th and 16th Dynasties and the transition between the Second Intermediate Period and the New Kingdom – our most important documentary source is Manetho's *History of Egypt*, from the Ptolemaic period. Although written at a much later date, Manetho's is the most detailed account we have of the Hyksos. However, it is not without its problems: the original does not survive and the excerpts in

A sphinx of Amenemhat III, from Tanis, later usurped by the Hyksos king Nehesy.

Left *Scarabs with the names of Apophis (left) and Sheshi, two rulers of the 15th Dynasty, the major line of Hyksos kings.*

subsequent writers such as Josephus are questionable, and often treated with scepticism by Egyptologists. These excerpts refer to a race of foreign kings who had a power base in the Nile Delta, centred on a capital at Avaris. 'Hyksos' is a later Greek form of the Egyptian name used for several rulers of the Second Intermediate Period: *heqa khasut*, or 'rulers of foreign lands'.

The information we glean from Manetho suggests that, during the Second Intermediate Period, the Hyksos were the pre-eminent power in the land, and that at times their rule even extended as far south as Thebes and Nubia. Manetho also describes the cruelty of these overlords, though this is possibly a case of the victors rewriting history – the Hyksos were eventually overthrown and, according to tradition, expelled from Egypt. Inscriptions on two stelae recount how, around 1540 BC, Kamose, ruler of Thebes, threatened the walls of Avaris with his armies; he taunted the Hyksos king Aauserra Apophis as being neither a true Egyptian, nor one who could carry out brave deeds.

Although Kamose failed to take Avaris, he returned home to Thebes in triumph, leaving Aauserra cowering in his palace, too frightened to come out and fight. Later, around 1520 BC, Kamose's successor, Ahmose succeeded in taking Avaris and went on to found the New Kingdom – a period which saw Egypt rise to pre-eminence in international affairs in the Near East.

Where did the Hyksos come from?

The ethnicity of the Hyksos is particularly ambiguous. The phrase *heqa khasut* may suggest foreign rulers rather than those officially recognized as pharaoh, and was perhaps tinged with a certain pejorative connotation. And yet this is the term employed by contemporary Egyptian seal-makers working for their Hyksos overlords – it seems there was a degree of internal resistance to the authority of the rulers of the 15th Dynasty. Documents of the Second Intermediate Period refer to the Hyksos as *aamu*, or 'Asiatics', and analysis of their personal names suggests a Semitic origin. However, these texts do not use 'Hyksos' to indicate an ethnic group resident in the Nile Delta, but refer specifically to the rulers.

The question of the origin or ethnicity of the Hyksos has more recently been approached through archaeology, and in particular the excavation of two important Middle Bronze Age sites in the Nile Delta: Tell el-Dab'a (p. 166), excavated since the 1960s by an Austrian team directed by Manfred Bietak, and Tell el-Maskhuta, excavated between 1978 and 1985 by a team from the University of Toronto led by John S. Holladay. These excavations have revealed the remains of an apparently intrusive population, whose material culture shares many aspects with the Middle Bronze Age cultural tradition of the southern Levant. Canaanite influence can be discerned in architecture, burial customs, personal adornment, weapons and pottery.

Below *Detail from the 'Carnarvon Tablet', on which a New Kingdom scribe has copied the text of a stela recording Kamose's campaign against Apophis.*

Above *Ramesses III and his army fighting in chariots; drawing by Champollion of a relief at Luxor. It has often been suggested that chariots were brought to Egypt by the Hyksos, who used them to overwhelm the local population. In fact, there are indications that the chariot was used in Egypt decades before the Hyksos.*

The Hyksos have also been credited with introducing new military techniques to Egypt, most notably the horse-drawn chariot and the composite bow, both typical of Middle Bronze Age warfare in Syria and Palestine. It seems it was a two-way process, however, and there is also evidence for Hyksos assimilation of certain aspects of Egyptian culture, such as the apparatus of government and language, religious practices and beliefs. The archaeological evidence, therefore, appears to suggest the overlay of an intrusive Levantine population in the Egyptian Nile Delta, which might be equated with the Hyksos of Egyptian historical documents. An alternative explanation is that the material record might reflect an indigenous Egyptian population of the Nile Delta that was distinct from the population of the Nile Valley and that chose to identify itself culturally, and possibly politically and economically, with its close neighbours to the northeast – the population of Syria-Palestine.

International relations

Contacts between Egypt and the Levant stretch back into the mists of time, to the foundation of the Egyptian state or even earlier. A period of expansion during the Middle Kingdom is marked by greater contact with the Canaanite population of the southern Levant, perhaps best illustrated by the representation of Asiatics in the tomb of Khnumhotep II at Beni Hasan (p. 161). But conventional histories of Egypt suggest that it is not until the decline of Egyptian power during the 13th Dynasty that nomadic peoples from Canaan settled in Egypt, becoming traders, farmers and craftsmen. It is these settlers who are believed to be the ancestors of the Hyksos.

In traditional schemes of the chronology of ancient Egypt, the Hyksos period is usually designated as a period of internal collapse between the high-points of the Middle and New Kingdoms, but in fact the archaeological evidence argues for

Right *One of a pair of stelae (the other now lost) erected by Kamose in the Temple of Amun-Re at Karnak. This one continues the account copied in the 'Carnarvon Tablet'.*

a cosmopolitan period characterized by diverse trading contacts stretching well beyond the borders of Egypt. The Hyksos rulers appear to have played an integral role in the development of these long-distance trading ventures. A characteristic element of Middle Bronze Age pottery is the distinctive Tell el-Yahudiyeh ware – with its grey surface and incised and punctured decoration – usually used in the manufacture of small perfume bottles. This ware is widespread throughout the Nile Delta, as well as in Palestine and Cyprus, arguing for extensive trading contacts in the region, particularly the widespread movement of desirable commodities.

Alongside these trading ventures there is also evidence for high-status gift exchange between rulers. Luxury vessels (the calcite lid of a perfume vase and an obsidian vase) inscribed with the name of the Hyksos ruler Khyan have been identified as far away as Knossos on Crete and Hattusas in central Anatolia – the capitals of Minoan Crete and the Hittite world. Both these regions were to play an important economic or political role in the East Mediterranean during the later 2nd millennium BC. Although the full significance of these pieces is unclear, they certainly demonstrate Hyksos initiative in the development of diplomatic and trading contacts far beyond the limits of earlier Egyptian trading activity.

This cosmopolitan aspect of the Hyksos – be they the political rulers or simply the inhabitants of the Nile Delta – is perhaps further illustrated by the decoration of the palace at Avaris. This includes wall paintings in Minoan style – perhaps dating to the Hyksos period although just as likely a few decades afterwards – which are otherwise unknown in an Egyptian context (p. 166).

In contrast to the insular world of ancient Egypt, the Hyksos actively looked beyond their borders and eagerly consumed the exotic. Ultimately, however, the Hyksos remain an enigma, illustrating the peculiar problems often encountered in relating archaeological evidence to textual sources. An Egyptian political – and possibly derogatory – phrase has been applied to an apparent population group, and as a result 'Hyksos' today represents an uneasy conflation of archaeology and Egyptian historical documents.

The brutal wounds and partly decomposed body of Taa, Kamose's predecessor, are consistent with death on the battlefield, although we cannot be sure how he died or who he might have been fighting.

Right *Calcite alabastron lid inscribed with the cartouche of the Hyksos ruler Khyan. This was found at the Minoan palace of Knossos on Crete.*

Left *Small juglet of Tell el-Yahudiyeh ware, a type widely traded in Egypt, Cyprus and the southern Levant during the Hyksos period.*

38 The Minoan paintings of Avaris

The people of Crete ... make more history than they can consume locally.
SAKI, 1911

Contacts between Egypt and the island of Crete were very close in the early 2nd millennium BC. This was the first peak of the Minoan civilization on Crete, the so-called Old Palace period, with magnificent palatial compounds at places such as Knossos and Phaistos. The Cretans imported luxury items and probably exotic animals and plants such as monkeys and palm trees. In return they exported colourful woollen textiles, vessels of silver, unidentified commodities in pottery containers and the finest tableware of the ancient world – known as Kamares ware. There was also considerable Egyptian influence on Minoan art and religion, including the adoption of Egyptian symbols such as the sphinx, the griffin and the goddess Taweret. However, three centuries later – in the New Palace period – Minoan civilization, by then expanding across the Mediterranean, reappeared in Egypt in a way entirely unexpected by modern scholars. As a result of a major new discovery in Egypt, our understanding of the relationship between these two great civilizations has been transformed.

Plan of the palace precinct of the 18th Dynasty at Avaris, combining geophysical survey information with the excavation plan.

The paintings at Avaris

Austrian excavations at the village of Ezbet Helmy (part of the site of Tell el-Dab'a, ancient Avaris) have uncovered palaces within probably the biggest Egyptian military and naval headquarters of the 15th century BC. Two palaces, F and G, have a wide courtyard between them, and a third palace, J, is attached to G. They were constructed on platforms with access ramps, and were surrounded by a wall: the whole district covers about 4 ha (10 acres). Remarkably, palace G and especially Palace F were decorated with Minoan wall-paintings, recognizable from the artists' technique (applying fresco and secco to a hard lime-plaster prepared with crushed murex-shells) as well as distinctive conventions and motifs.

The hard plaster, suited to Aegean stone architecture with bedrock foundations, proved unfit for Egyptian mud-brick walls built on soil.

Because mud-walls shrink, the plaster soon fell down. The resultant fragments were apparently collected and dumped beside a ramp and other adjacent areas, where the archaeologists have found them by the thousand.

Reconstructing the scenes is painstaking and difficult work because only about 10 to 15 per cent of the paintings are preserved. The first reconstructed panel shows yellow skinned bull-wrestlers and bull-leapers against a maze pattern, which apparently represents a courtyard and terminates above in a red undulating void. A few fragments of inverted landscape suggest mountains in the distance, and at the base is a frieze of half-rosettes. The inverted landscape and half-rosettes suggest exceptional acquaintance with Minoan visual codes. More specifically, the half-rosettes have close parallels in architectural features from the façade of the palace of Knossos. Other Minoan conventions include the use of blue for vegetation and for natural grey (such as in horns, hoofs and bull-hide speckles), and the use of red backgrounds. Characteristic also is the duality of the blue-black and reddish yellow speckled

Part of the reconstructed frieze with bull-wrestlers from Palace F **(top)**, *and the bull-leapers' frieze from Knossos* **(above)**.

Fragments depicting robed men **(right)** *and a running athlete in front of an architectural façade* **(below)**.

animals, as well as the palm tree with blue crown dividing this scene from the adjoining one.

Fragments of more bulls and bull-wrestlers appear in the same frieze to the left. One of the animals has broken down with his tongue hanging out and a bull-wrestler clings to his neck while another in front of the bull is jumping up and down. This is evidently a scene of human triumph over the bull. Several acrobats (not yet reconstructed) belonged to this frieze, and an entire programme of male athletics was apparently depicted. A further frieze shows lions and leopards chasing ungulates. Finally, hunters with collared dogs hunt ungulates, among which a wild goat is certainly a victim. Other fragments in a less refined style show a typical Aegean stone façade with windows against which a robed man and a runner are shown.

These friezes are on a small scale, but there are also full-scale figures of males and females, which may have been painted on the sides of windows and wall-niches. Fragments of humans and animals worked in relief constitute a further parallel to Knossos. A painted floor with a maze-pattern framed with a striped border and zones with running spirals and other complex motifs is also typically Minoan. Of special significance are large fragments with spiral patterns that can only have belonged to a huge griffin of the same size as one in the throne room of Knossos, and with wings exactly the same as a griffin from Xeste 3 on the island of Thera. It is likely also that the throne room of Palace F was furnished with emblematic griffins. Moreover, the friezes were planned in Minoan fashion by impressing strings into the wet surface of the plaster.

Below *A lively scene of a dog wearing a collar hunting ungulates.*

Above *Cretans bringing merchandise (tribute in Egyptian terminology). From the 18th Dynasty tomb of the Vizier Rekhmire (TT 100) at Thebes.*

Below *Part of a floor painting, from Palace F, with a border and maze pattern.*

The significance of the paintings

The Minoan paintings at Avaris are not the only ones to have been found outside the Aegean. In the palace at Alalakh (lower Orontes Valley), typically Minoan borders and the wings of a griffin have been identified. Parts of a small griffin were also found in Kabri, near the coast of Galilee, where the floor of a throne room was painted in imitation of a pavement, and paintings on the walls show buildings and probably ships in Minoan style.

More recently, the larger palace of Qatna (upper Orontes valley) has also yielded paintings which show distinct Minoan influence. Such features can be explained as a fashion spread by itinerant artists from the Aegean. However, a different explanation can perhaps be suggested for the paintings at Avaris.

The paintings can be dated to the early phase of the palaces in the reign of Thutmose I or, more likely, the joint reign of Thutmose III and Hatshepsut. Scenes from this same period in tombs at Thebes undoubtedly depict Minoan envoys arriving at the Egyptian court, demonstrating that contact was conducted at the highest level. According to the archaeological evidence, the site of the discovery at Tell el-Dab'a can most likely be identified as a part of *Perunefer*, the major military and naval base for the campaigns of Thutmose III and Amenhotep II to Syria and Palestine, which until now was known only from texts. In the dockyards of *Perunefer* seagoing boats were built and repaired, including Keftiu – 'Cretan' – boats. It seems entirely plausible that a connection can be made between the paintings, the Minoans shown in Thebes and the Keftiu-boats of *Perunefer*.

More specifically, Egypt was a land power in the early 18th Dynasty and it is possible that with its increasing military engagement in the Near East it needed a sea-going fleet. A political *rapprochement* with the leading sea-power at that time, the Minoans, would seem to be a sensible move. The palatial Minoan emblems, such as the half-rosette frieze and the griffin, in an Egyptian palace of royal dimensions suggests contact, perhaps even a political alliance, between those two major powers in the Eastern Mediterranean. How it came about is still a mystery to be debated.

39 Was Alashiya Cyprus?

My brother, do not be concerned that your messenger has stayed three years in my country, for the Hand of Nergal is in my country and in my own house. There was a young wife of mine that now, my brother, is dead.

LETTER FROM THE KING OF ALASHIYA TO THE KING OF EGYPT, *c.* 1350 BC

The coastal kingdom of Alashiya was renowned in the ancient world for its rich copper resources, but today its actual location is unknown. Numerous references to the land appear in texts of the 2nd millennium BC, from Egypt and also across Syria and Anatolia, but none have been uncovered in a region actually claiming to be Alashiya. However, Cyprus, or at least a part of it, may be a strong candidate. The island of Cyprus was very familiar to the large empires of the East Mediterranean – Egypt and the Hittites – and to the smaller city-states of the Levant, and there is plentiful archaeological evidence for contacts between Cyprus and the surrounding regions. But although written documents have been found at a number of the important coastal centres on Cyprus, such as Enkomi and Kalavasos, these cannot yet be read and so we do not know the indigenous name of the island at the time.

Right *Copper oxhide ingot from Enkomi, Cyprus. The texts mentioning Alashiya refer to the kingdom as a major copper-producer, which correlates with the archaeological evidence from Cyprus.*

Opposite above *View of the Late Bronze Age town of Enkomi, showing the sanctuary of the Horned God. If Alashiya was Cyprus, or part of it, was Enkomi its capital?*

The earliest references to Alashiya are found in the archives of Mari, Babylon and Alalakh, dating to the 18th–17th centuries BC, and possibly even as early as the 19th century BC. Unfortunately, these provide no information as to the exact location of Alashiya, but they do tell us that it was a town and that it had important copper sources in the mountains.

Between the 15th and 12th centuries there are many more references to Alashiya, largely from Egypt and the Hittite archives. The Annals of Thutmose III, recorded in the Temple of Amun at Karnak, inform us that the chief of Alashiya paid tribute of lapis lazuli, wood, horses and copper to Egypt. Although there is no clear indication as to the location of Alashiya, the text places it with Keftiu (which may be Crete), indicating a Mediterranean location.

Also dating to the 15th century is a text in the Hittite archives which recounts that Maduwatta (a chief of Ahhiyawa and a vassal of the Hittites) attacked Alashiya. The Hittites, claiming that Alashiya belonged to them, rebuked him. This text places Alashiya within the Hittite political orbit, although the exact geographical location still remains obscure. While the chief of Alashiya probably paid tribute to the Hittites, it is unclear how extensive Hittite political control was.

The Amarna archive

Probably the most informative documents referring to Alashiya are the archives dating to the 14th century BC found at Amarna in Egypt. These texts, written in the cuneiform script using the Akkadian language, are letters recording diplomatic and economic relations between the rulers of Syria-Palestine and the Egyptian pharaoh. In particular, they illustrate the movement of luxuries in high-status gift exchange. The vocabulary used by the participants in these transactions indicates their relative social standing. The Late Bronze Age super-powers (Egypt, the Hittites and Mitanni) refer to each other as 'my brother'; the lesser rulers of the Levantine city-states address the pharaoh as 'my father'. The king of Alashiya certainly regarded himself the equal of the pharaoh, addressing him as 'my brother'. Moreover, unlike the vassal kings of Syria-Palestine, the king of Alashiya was involved in major gift exchange with Egypt. He had some control over production of copper, but also gave the pharaoh horses and timber.

The Amarna Letters are very illuminating. They comprise a regional archive dealing specifically with the western Asiatic mainland, firmly placing Alashiya within the vicinity of Syria-Palestine. Even so, it is unlikely that the ruler of a humble city-state on the Levantine coast would address the pharaoh as 'my brother'. This might indicate that Alashiya was located beyond Syria-Palestine, perhaps in Anatolia – or possibly on the island of Cyprus. Given the earlier association between Keftiu and Alashiya in the Annals of Thutmose III, perhaps the latter is more plausible? Certainly, it seems extremely improbable that there was an independent state (Alashiya)

Clay tablet from the Amarna archive, written in Akkadian. This archive records a series of economic and diplomatic transactions between pharaoh and various rulers in the region. This one is from a king of Alashiya to Akhenaten.

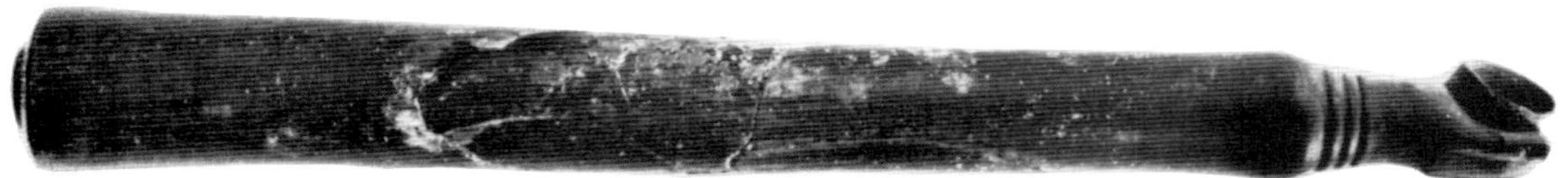

Red lustrous arm-shaped vessel from Enkomi, probably a container for perfumed oil. The correlation between texts and archaeology suggests Cyprus as a possible source for this luxury commodity.

Below *Egyptian high-status goods, such as this faience vase, were imported to Cyprus in small quantities, but significant concentrations have been found at Enkomi. This supports the identification of the site with (part of) Alashiya.*

on the Anatolian coastline which could maintain itself as the equal of the major Late Bronze Age powers. This has been supported by recent chemical analyses of tablets from the Amarna archive, which demonstrate that the Alashiya tablets derive from western Cyprus.

Later mentions

Early 19th Dynasty texts illustrate the economic importance of Alashiya, mainly as a source of copper. Contemporary (13th-century BC) Hittite and Ugaritic documents also refer to Alashiya as a copper producer, with sources in Mount Taggata. Hittite texts attest to close political relations with Alashiya, which continued to pay the Hittites tribute and received their political outcasts. A close asymmetrical political relationship is similarly apparent with the kingdom of Ugarit (in modern Syria) during the 13th and early 12th centuries BC. Hittite and Ugaritic texts also indicate that Alashiya was an important naval power.

From the 12th century the only references we find to Alashiya are in Egyptian texts. The most important of these is on Ramesses III's mortuary temple at Medinet Habu, which recounts that the 'Sea Peoples' (p. 176) conquered Alashiya. The last reference to Alashiya is found in the late 11th-century tale of Wenamun, who was shipwrecked there while on an expedition to obtain cedar wood from Byblos (p. 181). This tale confirms that Alashiya had survived the turmoil of the 12th century, including the destructions of the Sea Peoples, and also that it was a coastal (possibly an island) power. The disappearance of Alashiya from later documents mirrors the changing political configuration of the East Mediterranean at the beginning of the 1st millennium BC. Possibly the important state of Alashiya was replaced by the smaller city-kingdoms characteristic of the Cypriot Iron Age.

So we learn from the texts that Alashiya was a state with an urban nucleus and control over copper resources in the mountainous hinterland. This was a coastal state that maintained a naval fleet and was ruled by a king who was the equal of the Egyptian pharaoh. The ruler of Alashiya participated in gift exchange with the major Near Eastern powers, and from the 14th century had scribes versed in Akkadian at the same time that it emerged as an important diplomatic power.

Much of this is resonant with the Cypriot archaeological record. Late Bronze Age Cyprus certainly imported luxuries from Egypt, Syria, the Aegean and Anatolia, and appears to have been a major sea-trading power. Particularly interesting are the close economic and cultural links manifest between Ugarit and Enkomi during the 13th century BC, which is consistent with the textual data. The identification of Cyprus with Alashiya might imply that during the Late Bronze Age, Cyprus was a single centralized state. While at present this cannot be supported by the archaeological evidence, it remains plausible that part of Cyprus might be identified with Alashiya.

Sceptre head of faience with the cartouche of Horemheb, last ruler of the 18th Dynasty. This was found at the Late Bronze Age town of Hala Sultan Tekke, Cyprus, and illustrates the close cultural and economic ties between Egypt and Cyprus at this time.

Punt and God's Land

40

Turning my face to sunrise I performed a miracle for you, I made the lands of Punt come here to you, with all the fragrant flowers of their lands to beg your peace and breathe the air you give.

THE GOD AMUN-RE ADDRESSING AMENHOTEP III IN A STELA FROM THEBES, *c.* 1353 BC

The mysterious land of Punt, a source of aromatics and other exotic products, is referred to in Egyptian texts from the Old Kingdom to the Late Period. Visits to Punt were always quite rare, and the products that were brought from there were therefore regarded as 'wonders'.

The first documented expedition to Punt was during the 5th Dynasty, in the reign of Sahure. The last was in the reign of Ramesses III, although Punt continues to be referred to until the Ptolemaic period. Our most detailed account of a voyage to Punt is that recorded in the reliefs at Hatshepsut's temple at Deir el-Bahri. The fine sculptures illustrating the voyage provide a great deal of information on the fauna and people, and were certainly the work of an official artist who had accompanied the expedition. Unfortunately, however, the accompanying texts do not give any indications of the distances and journey times involved. Such is the level of detail and accuracy of the depictions that we can identify the varieties of fish, and these show that this particular expedition sailed along the coast of the Red Sea.

Although not illustrated in the same way, an expedition in the reign of Ramesses III is said to have travelled to and from the Red Sea port near Quseir by the Wadi Hammamat. A Middle Kingdom port called Sawu is known at Mersa Gawasis, to the north of Quseir, and inscriptions there also refer to Punt; so it seems the usual way of reaching Punt was by sea.

Produce and people of Punt

Because one of the main products of Punt was *antyu*, a resinous material which came in large lumps and which has long been understood to be myrrh, early Egyptologists thought that Arabia was the location for Punt. Following the uncovering of the Deir el-Bahri reliefs, however, it was clear that Punt was not in Arabia, but in East Africa, and it was initially equated with the Horn of Africa (Somalia and Eritrea).

Puntites bringing produce to the Egyptian expedition, from the scenes in Hatshepsut's temple at Deir el-Bahri.

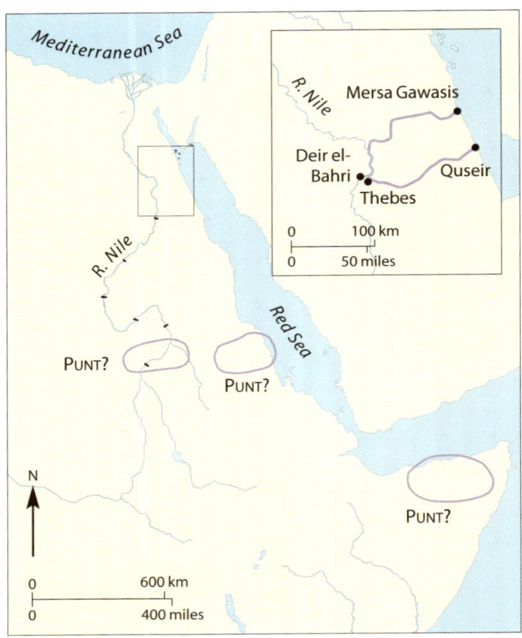

Map showing the suggested locations for Punt in Somalia, Ethiopia and Sudan. The inset shows the location of the Red Sea ports known to have been used for expeditions to Punt.

In fact, a slightly different location now seems more likely, and the types of products that the Egyptians brought back place Punt instead in the region of Ethiopia and eastern Sudan. The Egyptians would first have sailed along the Red Sea coast and then had to travel inland to reach Punt itself. Giraffes, dom palms, baboons and rhinoceros are shown in the reliefs, and gold and electrum (a natural alloy of gold and silver) were also brought from Punt. The 'gold of Amau' came to Egypt through Punt, but could also form part of the tribute from the kingdom of Kush, in Nubia. This again points to a location in eastern Sudan for Punt, and also to the possibility that it could be reached along the Nile routes, but no Egyptian expeditions are ever said to have used those routes. It seems likely that some of the exotic products that came to Egypt via Kush originated in Punt.

Right *The chief of Punt, Parehu, and his obese wife, from the relief scenes in Hatshepsut's temple at Deir el-Bahri.*

Opposite above *The landscape of Punt, with beehive-shaped houses on stilts in a marshy or watery terrain.*

Opposite below *Rowers on Hatshepsut's large sea-going ships.*

The Puntite houses are beehive shaped and built on stilts, suggesting a marshy terrain. A text of the 26th Dynasty states that rainfall in Punt drained into the Nile, indicating a location in Ethiopia. The people of Punt are shown as rather like the Egyptians in appearance, and are distinct from the typical Egyptian representations of Nubians. One famous relief depicts the wife of Parehu, the chief of Punt at the time of Hatshepsut's expedition. She is shown as obese and some Egyptologists suggest that she suffered from Dercum's disease, although others relate her appearance to an East African ideal which equates size with beauty and wealth.

Identifying Punt archaeologically

Despite the fact that the temple scenes and texts enable us to place Punt in Ethiopia and eastern Sudan, identifying Punt archaeologically is much more difficult. The Egyptians travelled to a place that they knew as Punt over a period of 2000 years. This 'Punt' no doubt occupied roughly the same geographical area over that span of time, but that does not mean that politically, or even culturally, it was the same in the Old and New Kingdoms. Recent archaeological work in the Gash Delta of eastern Sudan has raised the possibility that it is the location of the Punt of the Egyptian New Kingdom.

'God's Land' is a much more general term that seems to have included Punt but also other regions to the east of Egypt, from western Asia, the Eastern Desert to parts of Nubia and Sudan. It may be that the name 'God's Land' is applied to these places because of the role of their products in temple ritual. Punt provided incense and resins, as did parts of north Sinai and Arabia. Lebanon was the source of the fine timbers that were used for the sacred barques and shrines that housed the gods, and the flagstaves that marked the entrances to temples. Punt and Nubia were also the source of the wild animal skins that priests wore when performing rituals.

Although 'Punt' survived only in ritual texts after the reign of Ramesses III, new kingdoms and cultures developed in the region and the Ptolemies still sent expeditions from their port at Berenike to this part of Africa to hunt elephants and acquire other exotica. In the Roman period this region came under the authority of the powerful trading kingdom of Aksum.

The 'Sea Peoples': raiders or refugees?

All at once the lands were on the move scattered in war. No country could stand before their arms.... They were advancing on Egypt while the flame was prepared before them. Their league was Peleset, Tjeker, Shekelesh, Denyen and Weshwesh, united lands.

INSCRIPTION FROM THE MORTUARY TEMPLE OF RAMESSES III, *c.* 1186 BC

The end of the Bronze Age witnessed a dramatic reconfiguration of the social, political and economic organization of the East Mediterranean. Around 1200 BC there was a horizon of violent destructions throughout the region, stretching from the palaces of Mycenaean Greece to the Anatolian centre of the Hittite empire and along the coast of Syria-Palestine. Subsequent to this devastation the palatial civilization of the Aegean vanished, as did the Hittite Empire. Yet, while the large city-kingdom of Ugarit in Syria disappeared in flames, the urban centres of the southern Levant and Cyprus went on to flourish. These disruptions entailed

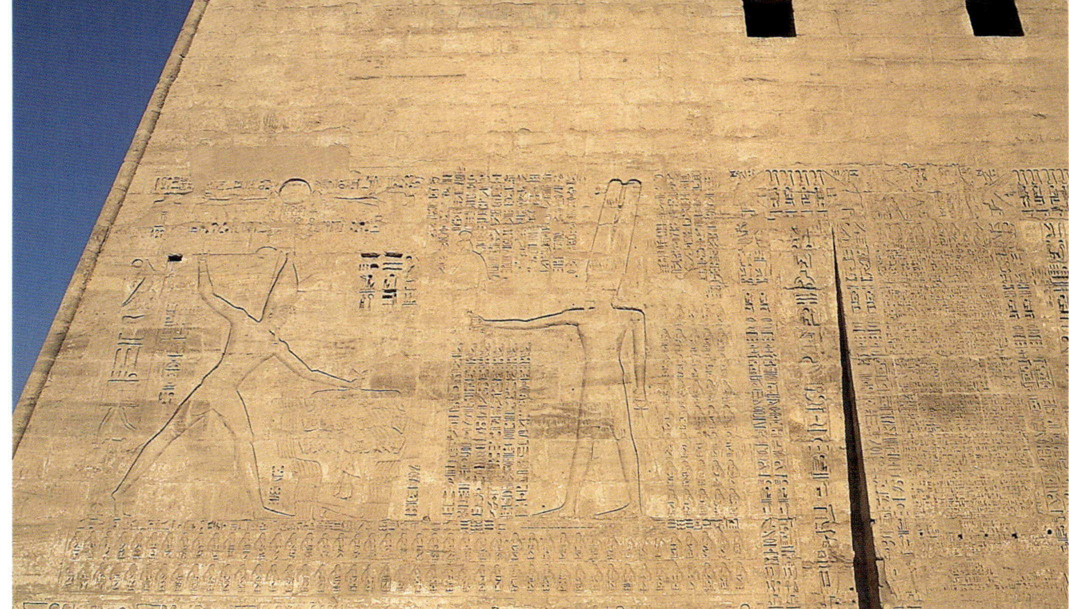

Detail of the pylon at Medinet Habu showing Ramesses III smiting his enemies.

massive population movements, most clearly charted by the settlement of the Philistines in the southern Levant and apparent Mycenaean migrations to Cyprus. Although there is increasing evidence for long-distance trade-networks linking Cyprus and Italy during this period of change, by the 11th century the economic basis of maritime trade that had supported the civilizations of the East Mediterranean basin had collapsed. The cultures of the Mediterranean moved into the brave new world of the Iron Age.

Left *The mortuary temple of Ramesses III at Medinet Habu.*

Reverberations in Egypt

Egypt was not immune to the situation: contemporary textual data from there throw intriguing light on the disruptions that characterize the end of the Bronze Age. Ramesses III, second ruler of the 20th Dynasty, recorded on his mortuary temple at Medinet Habu the tumultuous events that shook Egypt during his reign. In Year 8, Egypt was faced with attack by a coalition from the sea, known to modern scholars as the 'Sea Peoples'. Following a mass migration wreaking devastation throughout Anatolia, Cyprus and Syria-Palestine – the texts in this instance being in close agreement with the archaeological record – the 'Sea Peoples' attacked Egypt. Whether this was a single force or small skirmishes between various groups of peoples at different times has been disputed, though the latter seems more plausible. Ramesses III claims to have defeated this confederation – identified as the Peleset, Tjeker, Shekelesh, Denyen and Weshwesh – in both land and sea battles, possibly conflating accounts of the smaller skirmishes in the description of a single cataclysmic event. The scale of Ramesses' victory also appears greatly exaggerated; indeed, Ramesses III records settling the Peleset along his northern borders in Canaan (modern Palestine) and the Tjeker turn up in later texts such as the Report of Wenamun (p. 181).

Detail of reliefs from Medinet Habu, showing captured prisoners, possibly to be identified as the Peleset.

Who were the 'Sea Peoples'?

So who were the 'Sea Peoples' and what were the causes of these great population movements? The reliefs that adorn the walls of the temple at Medinet Habu are an important source of visual evidence for the identification of the 'Sea Peoples'.

The different groups of attackers are illustrated in great detail, and are distinct from other Egyptian enemies. The care taken in portraying the elements of their costume is particularly informative. Three main groups can be distinguished according to their headdress. The Peleset, Tjeker and Denyen all wear distinctive *feathered* crowns which are paralleled by contemporary representations from Enkomi in Cyprus. This group has been identified with the Philistines by Trude Dothan. The Sherden wear *horned* helmets, reminiscent of the helmets worn by the warriors marching in procession around the Warrior Vase from Mycenae, also dating to the 12th century BC, and the headgear of two bronze statuettes from Enkomi. The Shekelesh wear *fillet* headbands. Other aspects of their costume clearly refer to the

Aegean world, suggesting that the attacking hordes ultimately came from the central Mediterranean. The distinctive kilt with wide hems and tassels recalls the kilts worn by the people from Keftiu depicted on Theban tombs (see pp. 168–69) and the costume worn by the men on the Procession Fresco from Knossos.

The armour and weapons of the 'Sea Peoples' also refer to the Aegean and Cypriot world. In the sea battle the Sherden warriors wore a ribbed corselet, similar to that worn by warriors carved on ivory mirror handles from Cyprus. The Sea People warriors brandish round shields, pairs of spears and large, tapering two-edged (or cut-and-thrust) swords – military equipment current in the Mycenaean world from the late 13th century and introduced to Cyprus during the 12th century BC. Scholars have also linked the ships depicted in scenes of the sea battle with the Aegean world. The prow carved in the form of a bird's head, for example, recalls a boat painted on a Mycenaean pot from Skyros.

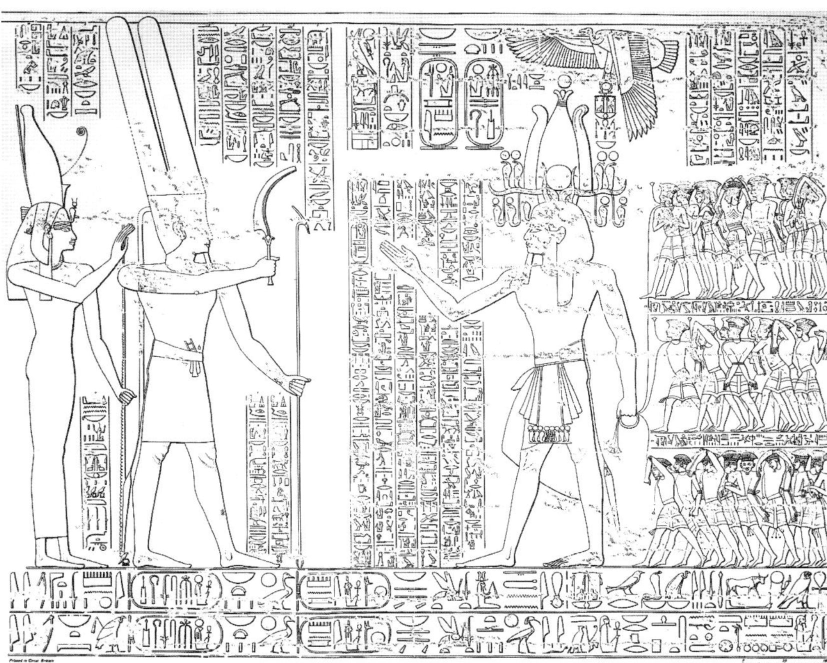

Detail of the Medinet Habu reliefs showing Ramesses III presenting prisoners to the gods of Karnak, Amun-Re and Mut.

Left *A battle somewhere at sea or in the Nile Delta between the armies of Ramesses III and various 'Sea Peoples'. From the reliefs at Medinet Habu.*

The Egyptian sources are supplemented by contemporary documentary evidence from Ugarit, detailing the catastrophes that afflicted the town prior to its destruction *c.* 1200 BC. Excavations at Ugarit uncovered a series of letters written on clay tablets between Hammurabi, the last king of Ugarit, and the king of Alashiya (p. 170). The letters refer explicitly to a sea-borne threat. The final letter in the exchange was never sent, but found in the kiln at the palace at Ugarit. In this the King of Ugarit writes, 'My father, the enemy ships are already here, they have set fire to my towns and have done very great damage in the country ... did you not know that all my troops were stationed in the Hittite country and that all my ships are still stationed in Lycia and have not yet returned?' These letters are witness to enormous disruptions throughout the region, with large-scale military manoeuvres to counteract an enemy threat from both land and sea. Ugarit was destroyed before the King of Alashiya could send help. The archaeological evidence suggests that Cyprus too was facing similar problems at this time.

Ivory gaming box from Enkomi, Cyprus, showing a warrior (extreme right) wearing a feathered headdress and kilt, similar to the costume of the Peleset, and carrying a double axe.

Below *Domed seal from Enkomi, showing a warrior in a feathered headdress and holding a round shield.*

Certainly the archaeological evidence and the textual data argue coherently for human involvement in the collapse of the Bronze Age centres of the East Mediterranean, detailing widespread population movements and numerous skirmishes, battles and raids. Moreover, the direction of attack appears to be from the west, and many scholars believe that the peoples of the Aegean world played a significant role in the events that shook the Mediterranean around 1200 BC. One remarkable image from the Medinet Habu reliefs shows women and children in ox-drawn carts in the midst of the land battle. This image testifies to the scale of the events recorded by Ramesses III. Rather than simply a military endeavour, the phenomenon of the 'Sea Peoples' is clearly that of a massive population movement, uprooting whole families – men, women and children – in search of a new home.

The clearest case for the settlement of Aegean migrants in the east has been argued for Cyprus and the southern Levant. Many scholars believe that there was a massive influx of Mycenaean settlers on Cyprus during the 12th century BC. They argue that these settlers were responsible for the destruction of the Late Bronze Age towns of Cyprus and that they brought with them many elements of their own cultural tradition to the island. These include the introduction of new pottery styles, funerary customs and religious practices, and changes in domestic architecture – most notably buildings with hearths, very much in the tradition of the Mycenaean megaron based on a hall with a central hearth. Similar changes are recorded for the southern Levant, where they are attributed to the Philistines.

The heartland of the Philistines is centred around Gaza and Ashkelon in the extreme southern limits of the Levant. The salient feature of the Philistine archaeological record is the characteristic pottery, clearly of Mycenaean inspiration, with bichrome painted decoration, typically of birds. Shapes include deep bowls and kraters (large open vessels for mixing wine and water), and side-spouted jugs – shapes associated with feasting and in particular consumption of wine and beer. New cooking vessels in both Cyprus and the Levant might indicate changes in diet. In Philistia this is supported by the apparent introduction of pork, as indicated by large quantities of pig-bones from sites such as Ashkelon. Hearth buildings have also been identified in Philistia, at Tel Miqne (ancient Ekron).

The events surrounding the collapse of the Bronze Age empires and the settlement of Aegean peoples in the east are very much the focus of ongoing archaeological research. Medinet Habu still remains the main source for interpreting these events and providing some sort of context for the dramatic population movements and destructions that afflicted the region at this time. As such, this is one case where the textual data, visual imagery and archaeological record are complementary.

The Report of Wenamun: fact or fable?

42

I saw eleven ships that had come in from the sea and belonged to the Tjeker, saying 'Arrest him! Let no ship of his leave for Egypt!' Then I sat and wept ... 'Do you not see the migrant birds going to Egypt ... Until when shall I be left here?'
THE *REPORT OF WENAMUN*, *c.* 1075 BC

The text known today as the *Report of Wenamun* is one of the key historical sources for our understanding of Egypt's foreign relations at a crucial time in its history, around 1000 BC. Papyrus Moscow 120, the only surviving copy of the text, was published in 1898 by the Russian scholar Vladimir Golenischeff, who had purchased it along with some other papyri that seem to have been found in a clay jar in a tomb near el-Hiba. When the *Report* was written, el-Hiba was the frontier between the two kingdoms into which Egypt was divided during the 21st Dynasty. The *Report* attracted the immediate attention of scholars, not only because of the beauty of its composition, but also because it seemed to illustrate the apparent decline of Egyptian influence and power, and the growth of Phoenician authority in the Iron Age.

At first, nobody doubted the veracity of the *Report*, nor the possibility of it being a faithful account of a real adventure that had happened to Wenamun, the main character in the story. Wenamun epitomized the determination, faith and tenacity of an Egyptian priest carrying out his duties, inspired by higher, religious motivations. In contrast to him the story also portrays Djekerbaal, the Phoenician ruler of Byblos, whose name points to a Semitic origin. He

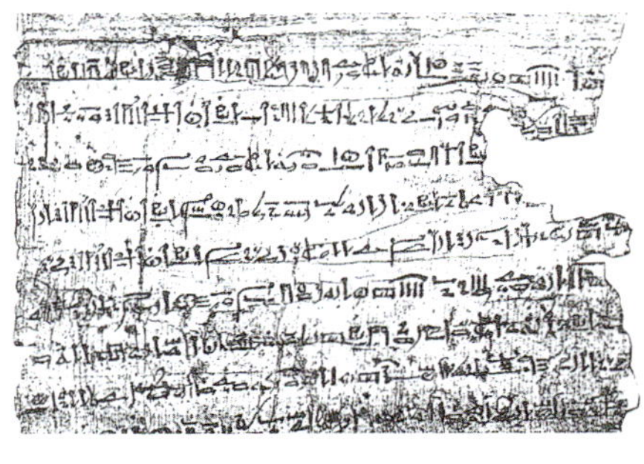

Above *Papyrus Moscow 120, containing the* Report of Wenamun. *Only one copy of this document exists and some of its characteristics could indicate an administrative origin. The nature of the text and its literary quality, however, seem to point in a different direction.*

Left *The site of el-Hiba, where the papyrus may have been found.*

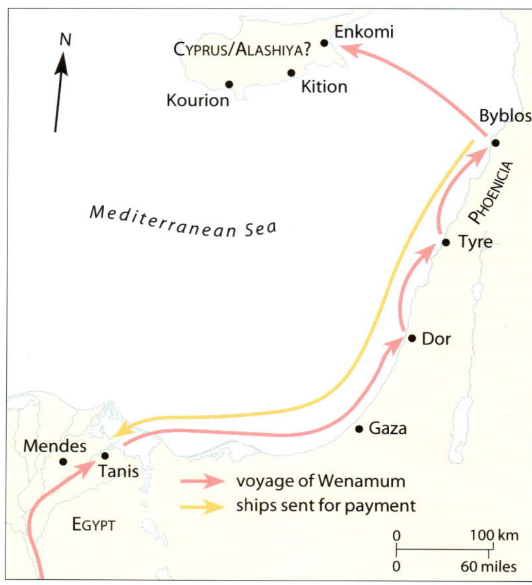

Map to show the possible route of Wenamun and the ships sent back to Smendes in order to obtain payment after Wenamun had been robbed.

seems interested only in business, trade and money, and is unimpressed by Wenamun's religious views. At the time of publication he looked very much like an early instance of an offensive racial stereotype in the European cultural atmosphere of the late 19th century – the Shylock.

The Story

Wenamun's *Report* narrates his adventures as an envoy of Herihor, the priest-king of Thebes. Wenamun sails to Byblos, to purchase cedar for the sacred barque of the god Amun-Re. In this task, the support of the king in the Delta, Smendes (p. 140), is essential because he provides the ship and crew for the journey. However, Wenamun is robbed of the gold and silver he is carrying by a member of his own crew. In response (although the papyrus is broken at this point), it seems that Wenamun steals the goods he needs for trade from a ship of the same nationality as the robber, the Tjeker confederation.

Because of his piratical act he is not received amicably at Byblos by the king, Djekerbaal, and is left stranded on the beach together with a statue of Amun-Re he has carried from Egypt. Nevertheless, a man in the entourage of Djekerbaal, in a vision, tells the king to bring Wenamun to his presence. When the Egyptian arrives a tense dialogue follows: the king, in angry mood, makes clear to Wenamun the shortcomings of his behaviour. Wenamun argues that he is not a simple trader but a divine envoy. Since he can present neither credentials nor money, they agree to send a messenger to Smendes so that the latter can forward payment. So it is that Smendes eventually saves the mission.

When Wenamun is about to return to Egypt with the cedar, some vessels of the Tjeker suddenly appear in the harbour, prevent his exit and demand that Djekerbaal arrest him. The king allows Wenamun to flee his harbour, but agrees not to interfere with whatever may happen on the open seas. So, chased by the Tjeker, Wenamun arrives at the coast of Alashiya, possibly Cyprus (p. 170), where a mob threatens to kill him. The local queen intervenes and seems to treat him well, but at this point the papyrus ends abruptly.

In 1952 Professor Černý, the foremost authority on ancient Egyptian documents, confirmed the importance of the *Report* by pointing out its formal similarities with known administrative documents. The arrangement of the text and the treatment of the papyrus implied, in his view, that the *Report* was such an administrative document, and therefore a first-class historical source. Nevertheless, the language of the text displays unequivocal literary, almost poetic, features, making it hardly compatible with the concise, unembellished prose expected of official documents. A literary reinterpretation of a real report could be one explanation of this conundrum, and the papyrus does have written on it an abbreviation generally interpreted as the clerical expression 'copy'. Even so, an Egyptian scribe prided himself on his skill in reproducing a document faithfully, and so an interpretation would never be considered a copy. Indeed we do not have any other example of a literary variant of an administrative report.

The world of Wenamun

It is true that the story of Wenamun presents a remarkably detailed account of the international situation in the eastern Mediterranean at the end of the Ramesside period. The crews of the cargo ships seem to have been mainly Syrian or Phoenician, and treaties of friendship existed among the different ports providing for the protection of both sailors and goods. An efficient network of couriers ensured swift communication between the various centres, facilitating the payment for goods from one to another. Written credentials were presented by the trader to the person with whom he intended to do business, in order to establish both his own identity and that of the lords in whose names the trade would take place.

The small principalities of the Syrian coast sustained a cosmopolitan culture of exchange, at a time when no particular territorial power threatened their prosperous independence. It is in this context that Wenamun turns up to demand cedar from Byblos without any of the usual procedures, arguing that he is entitled as the envoy of the god Amun-Re. Inevitably he is received with irritation

Detail of the decoration of the sarcophagus of King Ahiram of Byblos (c. 13th century BC), showing a scene of remarkable Egyptian influence. The dialogue of Wenamun and Djekerbaal could be visualized in a similar way.

by Djekerbaal, who even shows Wenamun his accountancy records (another historical detail) to demonstrate to him the proper way to carry out such transactions.

This inadequacy of Wenamun seems to be one of the pillars of the narration. He behaves like a devoted priest – but also an incompetent diplomat. His performance is full of miscalculations, which, in the carefully established international context he moves through, spells the probable failure of his mission. Perhaps Wenamun's performance was intended to serve as a warning to other Egyptians travelling beyond the established limits of Egypt. It is also interesting to note the way in which Wenamun seems to embody the Theban world – a world far from the sea, centred on religion and adhering to the fundamental conceptions of Egypt as a valley isolated by the deserts. To this world, the Egypt represented by Smendes, king of the Delta (p. 140), offers a stark contrast: a world open to the Mediterranean, a thoroughfare for Phoenician vessels and a first-hand witness to the eventual expansion of Greece and Rome, in which Egypt will slowly dissolve.

Whether Wenamun the priest and trader actually existed or not is extremely difficult to establish in the absence of other sources of information about his role in the hypothetical mission to Byblos. The Wenamun who certainly existed – and still exists – is the literary character. He is an Egyptian who incorporates an ideal of service to gods in a strange, incomprehensible and increasingly threatening world, in which he feels like a stranger. He is, after all, a man whose life is a reflection of the age-old idea of existence shared by the ancient Egyptians: a dangerous journey towards a final communion with the sun in its eternally repeating voyage.

Stela of Hahap, a Phoenician person represented in an Egyptian stela. Although later than the Report of Wenamun, *this stela shows two different scripts, Egyptian hieroglyphic and Phoenician. The* Report of Wenamun *seems to corroborate the bilingual character of the royal entourage of some Phoenician royal courts as a result of many generations of contact and trade.*

Ancient Wisdom & Belief

'To the spirit, Ankhiry. What wrong thing have I done to you that I should be brought to this evil state I am in? What have I done to you? What you have done is to hurt me, though I have done nothing wrong to you.' So begins the poignant letter of an unknown man to his wife, documenting one more loving relationship which has become embittered. At such moments the ancients seem closest to us in terms of our shared experience of what it is like to be human.

But then, look again: 'To the *spirit*, Ankhiry'. His wife, in fact, is dead, and has been, we find out later in the letter, for three years. Suddenly our shared experience seems to evaporate, and we are confronted with the other world of the ancients – a world seemingly inhabited by superstition, magic and an overarching belief in the presence of the dead and the power of the gods.

Some ancient beliefs and practices seem bizarre, even alienating, but it is the key task of Egyptology to engage with these mysterious customs and try to explain them. First among these, of course, is the fantastic and bestial pantheon of Egyptian gods. The art and literature of the ancient Egyptians, which we are so familiar with today, seems filled with curious creatures: partly human, partly animal, each one able to merge with others to form ever more mysterious hybrids. What do these fluid images of gods really mean?

Scene in a Book of the Dead *from the tomb of Horuweben, 21st Dynasty. This seemingly surreal composition mixes religious images with hieroglyphs to evoke a poetic vision in which our own journey into death, like the sun's journey into night, is just the preliminary to a bright new day.*

At the centre of the religious practices of the nation was the king. It was the king who led his people in worship, and the king who built and maintained Egypt's temples. From the very beginning of pharaonic history, the king's working life had been structured around a religious itinerary in order to allow him (more rarely, her) to officiate at the many rituals and festivals conducted by the far-flung communities of Egypt. The king was indeed foremost in importance in the community of the living, and yet was something else as well: 'the perfect god'. We need to consider why the king was worshipped by his people, not as 'first among equals' but as a god in this world of mortals.

In our own world of science, belief in magic may seem absurdly naïve. On the other hand, anyone who has said a prayer in times of trouble, or simply consulted their horoscope at breakfast, acknowledges that a belief in unseen guiding forces, which amount to much more than the vagaries of chance, is not too far removed from modern life. So why did the ancient Egyptians believe in magic?

Death is something mankind cannot avoid. None the less, Letters to the Dead are one indication that something shared and familiar to us meant something quite different to ancient Egyptians. Naturally we must wonder why they were written. A second point of difference is mummification. The modern world is quite familiar with the linen-wrapped remains we call 'mummies': but what do they really tell us about the pharaonic way of death and beliefs in the afterlife. Was mummification about preserving the body, or was it a process of purification by which the immortal soul could be freed from its mortal remains?

Other mysteries highlight specific ways by which ancient Egyptians recorded their reflections on what it is like to be human. For example, literature – meaning imaginative tales about fictional characters, or real characters in fictional situations – suddenly appears during the Middle Kingdom. Classics, such as the *Story of Sinuhe*, are already lyrical and mature, as if there was no need to nurture this new mode of expression. Why did such a literate culture not develop tales and poems before? Or do we have hints of older traditions of oral storytelling from which the earliest literature was developed?

Literacy also leads us to ask why ancient Egyptians used hieroglyphs as their principal script. Why persist for more than 3000 years with a script that seems so complex to learn and so cumbersome to write? One final mystery is a question of art: certain scenes used to decorate people's tombs over many centuries include standard images – mostly formal poses of couples seated together – whose relevance to death and burial is not obvious to a modern audience. Several scholars have suggested that these contain veiled references to sex as a symbol of new life; others simply find this suggestion crude. Can we be dogmatic about the meaning of art?

A scribe shown beneath an image of Thoth, god of wisdom. Thoth's esoteric knowledge is encapsulated in the crescent moon on his head – symbol both of a light in the darkness and of his junior relationship with the sun god. Here Thoth is a baboon, but, as with other gods, his appearance may be quite fluid and he may appear in other forms, such as an Ibis or a man.

The mysterious gods of Egypt

43

He is the One who made everything and created the gods. He is Tatenen who gave birth to the gods . . . he placed the gods in their shrines . . . and so the gods entered their bodies [made of] wood, stone and clay.

HYMN TO PTAH FROM THE 'SHABAKA STONE', *c.* 710 BC

The apparently boundless multiplicity of gods worshipped by the ancient Egyptians has bewildered non-Egyptians from Classical times onwards. Their bizarre – often bestial – forms seem perhaps most mysterious to people whose experience of religion falls within the major faiths of Judaism, Christianity and Islam. Followers of these share two fundamental beliefs that set them apart from the ancient Egyptians, and explain why so much of the religious thinking of ancient Egypt seems perplexing and impenetrable today.

The first of these beliefs is a dogmatic insistence on monotheism, which stresses the uniqueness and omnipotence of one god ('thou shalt have no god but me', 'there is no god but god'). The ancient Egyptian view was very different. To begin with, while the most common Egyptian word for 'god' (*netjer*) does imply unlimited cosmic power, it can refer to beings who have varied levels of divinity, including the king himself. And the existence of a particular god was not seen as a threat to other gods, so that the implication of monotheism – 'if my belief in god is true, then your different belief is heresy' – would not have occurred to most Egyptians before the arrival of Christianity.

One reason why the Amarna period was so unusual was not the promotion by the king of a particular god, Aten, to be the pre-eminent state deity, but that this was allied with the rejection and persecution of at least one 'rival' deity, Amun-Re.

The second significant difference in belief is that, for the ancient Egyptians, there was no text of divine revelation explaining what god expects from humans. The gods of Egypt seemed to have very little interest in the behaviour of the people who worshipped them. The only substantial information on behaviour which might cause divine disfavour comes in the 'Negative Confession', where individuals standing before a tribunal of the gods and seeking admission to a pleasant afterlife state that they generally behaved well and did not cheat any god of offerings. Protestations of faith in a god as a personal saviour are notably lacking.

The multiplicity of gods associated with specific regions had its roots in Predynastic Egypt, but such divine proliferation had few negative political implications. Although, with the unification

Statue of the sun god Horus, wearing the crown of the king of Egypt, in the temple at Edfu.

Ramesses II offers an image of the goddess Maat, symbol of divine order, carved on a column at Tanis.

of Egypt in the 1st Dynasty, Horus of Hierakonpolis became the god particularly associated with kingship, cults of other gods popular in different parts of Egypt were respected by Egyptian kings, not suppressed. This respect was perhaps seen as a unifying force, and the relationship between the king and the gods of Egypt is fundamental to royal authority. Other deities important to the king included divine personifications, such as the goddess Maat who represented cosmic order.

For the vast majority of Egyptians, the most significant god was their own 'town god' (*netjer niwty*), who resided in the local temple, but other times they might be more concerned with invoking the help of specialized deities. Examples are Taweret and Bes, who were particularly associated with childbirth.

On a quite different level are deities associated with various forces of nature, the most obvious and powerful of which – the sun – was always of crucial importance, principally in the form of the god Re and, for a short period, Aten.

Divine iconography

With so many deities it was important that they could be clearly recognized. For deities who were primarily human in appearance the most common technique was a suitably distinctive headdress. Amun-Re, for instance, is usually shown as a male anthropoid figure with a crown of two tall plumes. Other deities were differentiated in appearance by having attributes taken from the natural world, and gods could be shown as animals, or as animal-headed humans.

It was important that divine iconography was appropriate. Images of powerful animals would obviously enhance the aura of divine authority – hence the selection of the crocodile for gods such as Sobk. For the goddess Sakhmet the combination of name 'the (female) powerful one' and image – a fearsome lioness – is unambiguous. On the other hand, the jackal or jackal-headed forms of Anubis and Wepwawet seem apposite for deities concerned with funerals and the passage of the individual from this world to the afterlife because jackals were mostly encountered beside cemeteries, skulking at the desert-edge.

Right *Amun-Re, the god of Thebes (right), embracing an 18th Dynasty king as his equal.*

The god of Elephantine, Khnum, is typically shown with the head and horns of a ram, but with the body of a man so that he can interact with the king. A wig eases the transition from animal's head to human body.

These artistic associations could create problems of harmony in iconography. The application of a large wig to hide the visual oddity of, in the case of Thoth, a thin ibis' neck rising from a man's shoulders, is a useful visual device. On other occasions, the application of an animal's head may have seemed just too odd, so other solutions were found, such as the god Geb having not a goose's head but a goose *on* his head. The origin of Amun ('the hidden one') is as obscure as his name implies, but became appropriate in the New Kingdom when his statue was paraded during festivals at Thebes concealed from view within the cabin of his divine barque.

Powerful connections between the god and his/her iconographic representation might also lead to the animal itself being regarded as in some ways 'sacred'. It is easy – as the Greeks and Romans did – to overestimate the importance of these cults, particularly before the Late Period when they seem to flourish as an expression of Egyptian nationalism in a period of foreign domination. But the linking of divineness with economically unimportant animals did occur; for example the ibis and baboon were the sacred animals of Thoth. For larger, economically more important animals, the selection of a single, actual animal who was regarded as an incarnation of the god is best represented by examples such as the Apis bull at Memphis (p. 251).

Divine families

Perhaps somewhat paradoxically for a people renowned for their bizarre-looking deities and strange religious practices, a fundamental aspect of how the Egyptians viewed their gods is to treat them in ways informed by their own daily experience. Human beings, with their basic needs, desires and ways of behaving, were the model for the gods. The first problem faced by the Egyptians was, how are gods created? Using humans as a model the answer was obvious – sexual reproduction. Several of the varied myths of creation are genealogies of gods procreating in

The god Amun-Re carried in procession, concealed in his barque, from the Red Chapel of Hatshepsut.

Below *The divine couple Amun-Re and Mut, on the base of a Ramesside scarab.*

order to people the universe. By the New Kingdom the standard model for major deities was the divine family of father, mother and child – a triad. Hence Thebes was home to the family of Amun-Re, Mut and Khonsu; Memphis to Ptah, Sakhmet and Nefertum; and Abydos particularly – but everywhere more generally – to the model family of Osiris, Isis and Horus.

If gods are like humans they, too, need physical shelter. Egyptian temples were built not for congregational worship, but to provide houses for gods in a very real sense, since the god is present within the statue at the heart of the temple. The basic Egyptian word for 'temple' is simply that for a well-appointed, expansive 'mansion' (*hut*). The central activity within temples is the cult-service – if a god is like a human he/she will need to be fed, and the provision of offerings on a regular basis is the most important way a god is worshipped

Below *On this column from Tanis the Seth-animal has been altered to resemble the ram of Amun-Re.*

Myth

Although there was no clear explanation of divine will through a revealed text, ideas of the 'proper' order of the universe emerged in different ways. Myth was used as a way of illustrating important truths. The Osiris/Horus cycle of myths is particularly important as it provides a model of how people should behave (Isis as a model wife and mother) and should not (Seth as the murderer of his brother). It introduces the idea of Osiris as the dead, divine king who rules in the afterlife, and his son Horus the living, divine king who rightfully takes his father's throne.

Myths are dramas requiring a cast of actors, and a plurality of deities with individual characters is necessary. It is also important to note that, as with humans, gods can be a complex mixture of what we might see as 'good' and 'bad'. For example, Seth is a powerful deity who acts sometimes in 'bad' ways, sometimes in more positive ways, and always needs to be placated. He is also an important regional deity in the eastern Delta. It is only comparatively late in Egyptian history that Seth is seen as a more two-dimensional 'evil' deity and his image then comes under attack, foreshadowing intolerance to religious diversity unknown for most of Egyptian history.

Opposite *The god Geb, with his goose attribute on his head, from the tomb of Twosret in the Valley of the Kings.*

44 Was the king really a god?

How the gods rejoice, you have increased their offerings.
How your people rejoice, you have shaped their borders.
HYMN TO SENWOSRET III, *c.* 1820 BC

The temples of ancient Egypt assert unequivocally that the nation's king was a god. In art and texts pharaoh is shown in the company of other deities, either as their equal or as their unique child. However, one influential modern response insists that this is 'polite fiction': that the king himself was not a god, and that it was actually the office he held which was divine. Certainly the Egyptian language distinguishes 'king' (*nezu*) from 'kingship' (*nezyt*). Moreover, the king was obviously mortal, and – to judge from the abscess-ridden mouth of Amenhotep III – subject to excruciating pain like the rest of us. Some kings were erased from the official record, presumably for their failings in office, and at least two seem to have been assassinated by their own courtiers (p. 108). Moreover, although kings appear godlike in monuments of the state, in literature they may exhibit all too human frailties such as cruelty and lust.

However, we must avoid a biased interpretation of ancient Egypt based on our own expectations. Egyptian myths contain many references to the deaths of gods, sometimes assassinated by their own families. Evidently their

On the stela of Qahedjet, an obscure king who may be the 3rd Dynasty King Huni, the falcon-headed sun god Horus embraces him as an equal. The names written above identify the king further as an earthly incarnation of Horus.

Opposite *Chapel of Thutmose III from Deir el-Bahri. On the back wall the king offers water and incense to Amun, to obtain authority to rule this world. Amun's consort Hathor is represented as a cow, suckling and protecting the king in a statue added by Thutmose's son, Amenhotep II.*

beliefs did not presuppose that divinity was immortal. Likewise, unflattering stories about kings often turn out on closer reading to be allegories, which equate the desires of kings to those of the gods. Given that the literature was composed by a small number of people close to the king, criticism is perhaps not to be expected.

Qualities of a king

In fact, there seems no meaningful basis for separating the king from his office. Each day of his life was structured around duties, which were intended to defend *maat* (harmony) from the wrongdoing which would generate *khenenu* (chaos). Those who opposed him were dismissed as 'impotent', 'rebellious' or 'twisted of character'. To fulfil his responsibilities the king was endowed with exceptional qualities such as *sia* (understanding), *hu* (accurate speaking), *wedj* (command) and *heqa* (power to control). These are not attributes unique to gods, but they do distance the king from most of humanity. More importantly, the king inherited these attributes 'in the egg' because he was 'the son of Re, of his body', that is a child born from the very substance of the sun god – in other words, a king was born into this world, not created at his enthronement.

The king also carried the unique title 'perfect god' (*netjer nefer*), which again defies our own cultural expectations by suggesting that there are imperfect gods. Actually it seems to indicate that the king existed in a divine state like other gods, but also in a physical state like ourselves (but unlike other gods), and so embodied the experiences of both gods and people.

His principal duties were to worship the gods on behalf of his people, and to realize the will of the gods in the world. His other duties were connected with his obligation to reinforce *maat*. He would command new temples and further endow the cults of existing ones. He would make war on his enemies and expand Egypt's borders. It makes no sense to divide these activities into religion and politics because they have the same underlying purpose, and the typical scene decorating the outside of a temple was that of the king slaughtering his enemies. Even the act of quarrying the

Right *A limestone statuette of Reneferef from his unfinished pyramid complex at Abusir. He is depicted enthroned and embraced by the falcon of Horus, emphasizing the king's close relationship to the gods. Nevertheless, the statue was probably positioned to be seen from the front, so that the god would be invisible to any human observer.*

formless desert encircling Egypt for stone to build temples was an expansion of *maat*. All these responsibilities locked the king into reciprocal relationships with both his gods and his people, by which the success and protection of one would repay the trust and protection of the other.

On a stela from the temple of Armant, an unknown chronicler extols Thutmose III by offering 'a collection of instances of victory and might which this perfect god has performed', noting that, if we were to recall every instance, 'they would be too numerous to put in writing'. First, Thutmose crushes the mineral world by firing his arrow through a copper slab three-fingers thick. Then he slaughters the fiercest members of the animal kingdom: lions, bulls, elephants and even a rhinoceros. Finally, he overwhelms humanity itself by defeating a massive coalition of Egypt's enemies at the Battle of Megiddo.

Elsewhere Thutmose ascribed this success to his father, the god Amun-Re, adding 'it was not the act of men'. Nevertheless, the Armant chronicler credits above all the supernatural abilities of his king. A modern audience may find it hard to concede that such feats could actually be performed, but then we are dealing with a religious text and a question of faith. For believers, the king of Egypt was unequivocally a god.

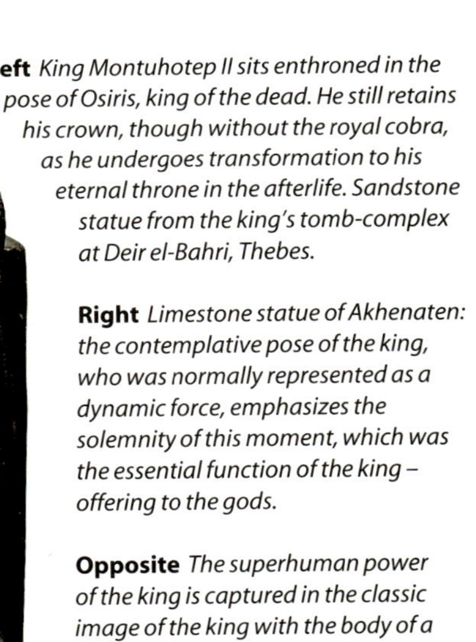

Left *King Montuhotep II sits enthroned in the pose of Osiris, king of the dead. He still retains his crown, though without the royal cobra, as he undergoes transformation to his eternal throne in the afterlife. Sandstone statue from the king's tomb-complex at Deir el-Bahri, Thebes.*

Right *Limestone statue of Akhenaten: the contemplative pose of the king, who was normally represented as a dynamic force, emphasizes the solemnity of this moment, which was the essential function of the king – offering to the gods.*

Opposite *The superhuman power of the king is captured in the classic image of the king with the body of a lion – confident and calm, but stern and far too dangerous to provoke. This particular granite sphinx of Amenemhat III is such a masterpiece that later kings reused it for 600 years.*

44

Mummification and the passion of Osiris

The best method of embalming was said to be that which was practised on one whose name I cannot mention in this context.
HERODOTUS, *c.* 430 BC

It seems to be a universal human instinct to treat the mortal remains of our fellows, however anonymous, with care and dignity, even in times of war or disaster. Accordingly, as long as people have settled in the Nile Valley they have sought to dispose of their dead with respect, but in pharaonic times the methods used often went to extraordinary lengths.

In the most sophisticated burials the body of the deceased was prepared using mummification – the artificial preservation of the corpse. This process entailed first removing the internal organs (evisceration), then cleansing and purifying the body, before desiccating it in natron-salt. The corpse was next washed and coated with oils and resins, wrapped in great lengths of linen, and finally placed in a coffin. In addition, the internal organs were often separately embalmed and deposited in the tomb in jars. We know that such practices persisted for more than 3000 years. Indeed, for many of us a linen-bound mummy is our first encounter with ancient Egypt, whether glimpsed in the half-light of a museum display-case or lurching across a movie screen. But why did the ancient Egyptians make such complex preparations for burial, and what beliefs lay behind them?

The origins of mummification?

In Predynastic times burials were normally simply laid in the hot, dry sands of the deserts that surround the Nile Valley. As a result, the body quickly became naturally desiccated and decay was arrested, so that the skeleton, skin, tissue and hair of the individual would often survive intact,

Right *The discovery of Tutankhamun's tomb in 1922 inspired modern media fascination with mummies, epitomized by Boris Karloff in the film* The Mummy *(1932). The film's credible imagery, based on mummies such as Sety I (opposite), perpetuated the myth that ancient Egyptians believed bodies remained alive after death.*

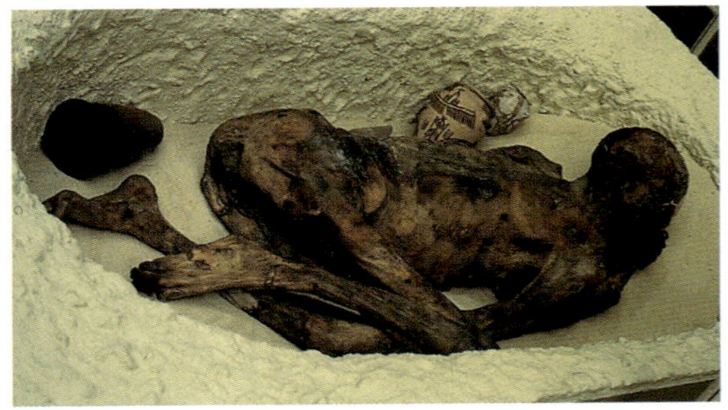

Far right *Reconstructed burial of a Predynastic man from Gebelein. His naked body was not embalmed but has been desiccated and discoloured by desert sand. Grave-goods with religious motifs suggest a belief in the afterlife.*

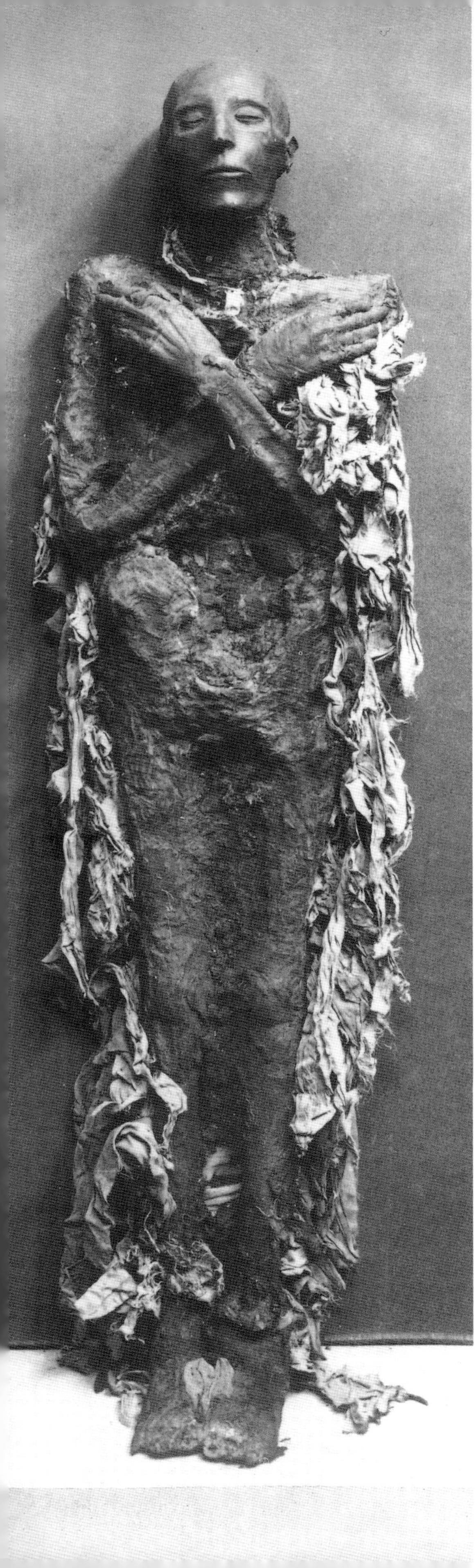

though their actual appearance in life would be lost as the bulk of the body, especially in the face, was stripped away, and the hair and skin colour were transformed. It has often been suggested that such burials, perhaps exposed by desert winds or scavenging animals, were the inspiration for mummification. According to this view, the Egyptians became intrigued by the preservation of the body, and the implications of this for the continuation of life after death. In later Predynastic periods, however, burials became increasingly elaborate – the corpse was placed in a container or the grave was lined in some way. In either case the body was no longer in contact with the desiccating heat of the sand and so would be susceptible to decay, unless it was artificially preserved before burial.

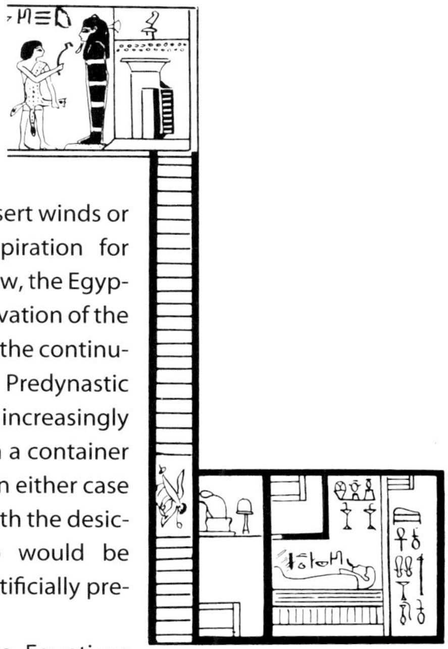

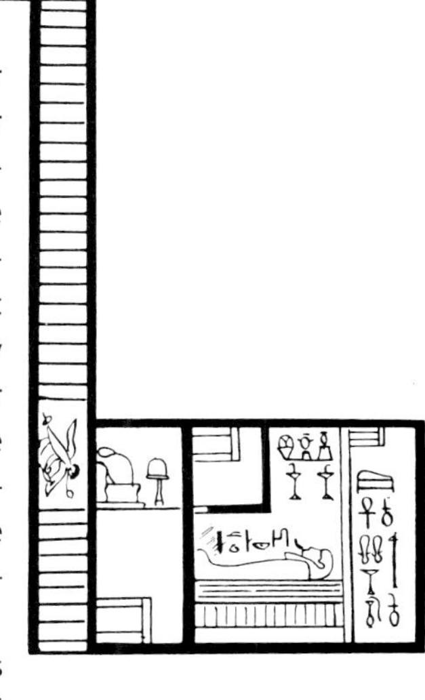

Above *Tombs in pharaonic times typically had two distinct elements, illustrated in this New Kingdom vignette. Below ground the mummy is laid in the burial chamber, while funerary ceremonies are performed in the chapel above. In the passage connecting the two chambers, the liberated soul of the deceased is shown flying free as a bird.*

We cannot be sure whether the Egyptians actually thought like this, and, even so, it would only tell us how they discovered the effects of embalming, not why it became so central to their funerary customs. Moreover, there are many differences between the main features of burial practices of prehistoric times and those of the pharaonic period. First, whereas most Predynastic burials were contracted, bodies were later normally laid out in an elongated position. Secondly, from the earliest pharaonic period, tombs consisted of both a burial chamber and a separate area for offerings – this two-part structure remained absolutely central to Egyptian burial customs for 3000 years. Thirdly, the body was not simply desiccated (as it could have been just by burying it in the sand prior to the burial), and in fact the most basic form of mummification – all that was available to most people – involved only the cleansing and purification of the body, rather than its desiccation. Finally, the burial itself

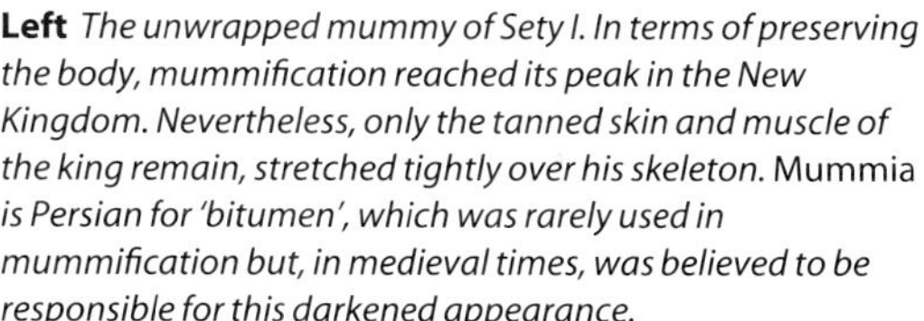

Left *The unwrapped mummy of Sety I. In terms of preserving the body, mummification reached its peak in the New Kingdom. Nevertheless, only the tanned skin and muscle of the king remain, stretched tightly over his skeleton.* Mummia *is Persian for 'bitumen', which was rarely used in mummification but, in medieval times, was believed to be responsible for this darkened appearance.*

Osiris enthroned as king of the dead, according to a Book of the Dead *(a funerary papyrus). He is worshipped by the dead man and his wife, who have successfully passed over to the afterlife by following in Osiris' footsteps.*

involved a series of rituals, for which we have no evidence in prehistoric times.

The myth of Osiris

The explanation for mummification given by the Egyptians themselves, in later periods at least, involved the god Osiris – the 'one whose name I cannot mention' according to Herodotus. The myth of Osiris is only known in full from very late versions, but fragments date as far back as the Old Kingdom. As the eldest child of Geb and Nut – the earth and sky gods respectively – Osiris was the first creature of this world and its first king. Osiris also became the first ever to die. Murdered by his jealous and unruly brother, Seth, his body was dismembered and scattered throughout Egypt. However, his remains were collected up and bound together with linen strips by his devoted partner, Isis, who through her magical attentions was able to bring him back to life, and then also conceive his son, Horus. In this way, death was doubly defeated in the moment that it first occurred, and Osiris became king in the west, the land of sunset. Osiris is therefore usually depicted wrapped in linen, with only his face and hands showing, wearing a crown and holding a crook and flail – the insignia of kingship. His kingly tomb was believed to be at Abydos (it was in fact the tomb of the 1st Dynasty King Djer), and became the focus for annual festivals celebrating his passion and rebirth.

By mummifying the body – painstakingly wrapping it in linen and often placing a mask over the face – the deceased was identified with the risen

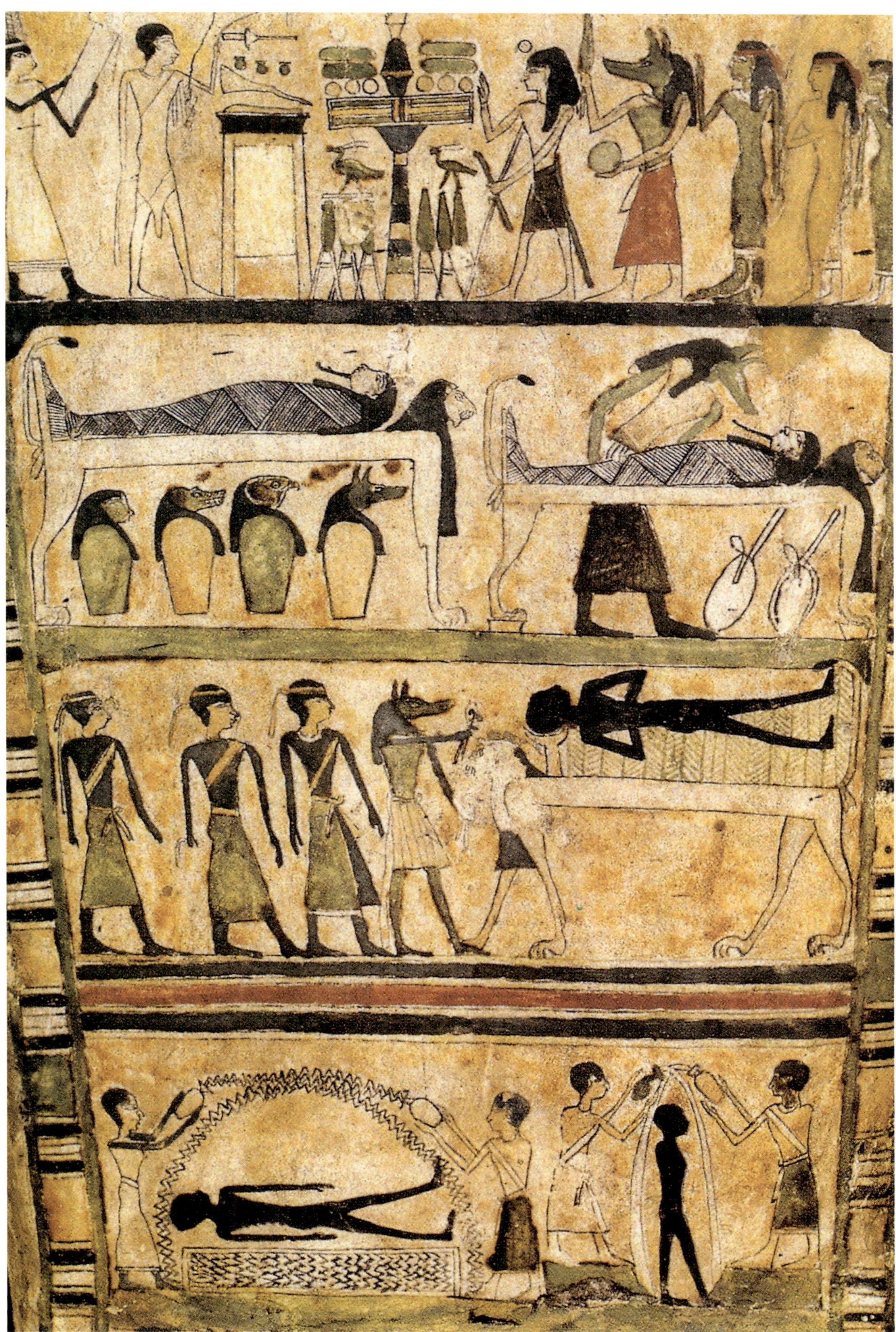

Scenes on the coffin of Djedbastiufankh from el-Hiba. Unusually, his vulnerable corpse is shown undergoing various embalming procedures. Also, the dog-headed god Anubis (or a priest adopting his role) is shown wrapping the corpse in linen to complete its transformation into the form of Osiris.

Osiris in the hope that he or she might also live a new life 'of millions of millions of years' as a transfigured spirit, or *akh* in Egyptian. In later periods, the embalming process took 70 days, corresponding to the length of time that Osiris lay dead.

Coffins originally represented a house or shrine in which the spirit of the deceased could flourish in security, but by the Middle Kingdom they too began to adopt the iconography of Osiris. Alternatively, coffins took the form of a body wrapped in the feathery embrace of Isis. who was often shown in art as a bird of prey (p. 75). From the New Kingdom on, the dead were often referred to as 'the Osiris so-and-so', just as we say 'the late so-and-so'. By then coffins were usually painted with scenes from Osiris' story, and texts were added which explicitly identified the deceased with the god:

Speaking of words by Isis:
I have come and embraced you,
O my brother, the Osiris, [Name], true of voice,
so that you shall not be inert,
so that these limbs of yours shall not weary,
so that you shall exist in your perfect changing forms of life,
so that your flesh shall grow no older than that of a god,
so that your words in your mouth you shall be true,
so that you shall walk upon your feet,
so that you shall raise yourself on your left side,
so that you shall put yourself on your right side, still living.

In fact, we should think of the mummy not simply as the preserved body but as the whole assemblage, of which the coffin is the outer face and the mortal remains the concealed core. Together they formed a *sah* – an image of the deceased, not as in life, but as an *akh* in the kingdom of Osiris. In fact, having served their earthly purpose, the mortal remains were not necessarily important, and many mummies, especially in the earliest and latest periods, although beautifully wrapped, contain only a jumble of bones.

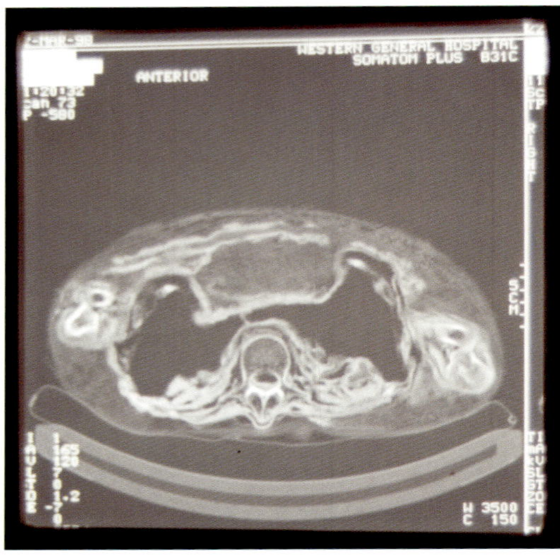

Through the cult of Osiris, mummification came to mean much more to Egyptians than a superstitious desire to preserve the physical body beyond death. From the Middle Kingdom, this identification with Osiris seems clear, but in the earliest historical periods Osiris is a shadowy figure, who seems to have grown in importance by absorbing the iconography and cults of other gods, such as Andjety and Khentyimentu. Nevertheless, there are clear allusions to the identification of the dead with Osiris in the Pyramid Texts, which were inscribed in royal tombs of the 5th and 6th Dynasties, and are the oldest surviving lengthy religious texts from Egypt. Likewise, the earliest mummies sometimes show the face of the deceased modelled with paint and gum in the linen wrappings, thereby creating what later became the standard image of Osiris. So, as for which came first – the myth of Osiris or the desire to mummify mortal remains – this is not so much a mystery as a chicken-and-egg conundrum. In other words, they evolved and grew together through the centuries.

Above *Scan of a mummy, showing that the chest (at top) has collapsed and then been packed during mummification. Very often the human remains inside a mummy are poorly preserved.*

Left *The 12th Dynasty coffin of Khnumhotep from Deir Rifeh exhibiting the iconography of Osiris: tightly wrapped in linen with only the face visible, sporting the beard and golden skin of the gods.*

Why write letters to the dead?

46

Mortals are they who can experience death as death.
MARTIN HEIDEGGER, 1959

Ancient Egypt holds a perennial fascination for us. On the one hand we encounter a society and culture which seems sometimes within our ready grasp – thoughts and beliefs, attitudes and values which resonate with our own. On the other hand, it is also a culture awash with what, for us, is the exotic and the unfamiliar – other values, other knowledge, other ways of life. These can seem enigmatic and strange, but it is one of the tasks of Egyptology to engage with these mysterious ways of life and to attempt to clarify them for us within their own cultural context.

One example is the practice of writing letters to dead relatives. Writing was special in ancient Egypt, its use specific – it was not as all pervasive in life as it is now for us. The ancient Egyptians did write letters, but most examples of early letter writing are for administrative purposes, dealing with bureaucratic problems. Personal correspondence remains a poorly attested area of writing, but where it does exist – as with the letters of Heqanakht (now dated to the early reign of Senwosret I of the 12th Dynasty), dealing with the family farm and relationships among the family – it emerges into bright light. Such are the Letters to the Dead. Formulated as letters, these were primarily written on pottery bowls (but also on cloth and offering-stands and the more usual medium for letters – papyrus) which were then left as offerings in the tomb-chapels of dead relatives.

The living and the dead

Writing letters to dead relatives might seem strange enough, but the content of the letters is even more surprising. These letters are not resumés of events in the family, nor do they ask how the deceased is getting on in the afterlife.

Letters to the Dead were typically written over bowls which were then filled with food and offered to the spirit of the person whose attention was required. Less often letters were written on linen or papyrus sheets, which were possibly then wrapped around a statuette.

Letter to the Dead (The Cairo Bowl)

A dispatch from Dedi to the priest Intef son of Iunakht [the deceased]:
Concerning the serving-girl Imiu who is ill, you are not fighting for her day and night, are you, with which ever (dead) male or (dead) female is acting against her? Why do you wish your 'gate' to be so desolated [the reference is obscure]? Fight for her today with renewed vigour, so that your household can be maintained and water will be poured for you [a reference to pouring water during the offering cult]. If nothing comes from you, then your household will be devastated. Can it be that you are not aware that the serving-girl is the one who, of all people, keeps your household going? Fight for her, watch over her. Save her from whichever (dead) male or (dead) female is acting against her. Then your household and your children will be maintained. It is good if you take notice [a standard letter ending].

Instead, they deal with problems which the living are having, such as those of debt, illness or childbirth – problems of ordinary life – and, what is more, the living expect the dead to be able to help them out. In fact, they sometimes chastise their dead relatives for not having done more already to assist them. Here is one example (the Berlin Bowl):

> You were brought here to the city of eternity [the cemetery] without there being any reason for you to be angry with me. If it is the case that these 'blows' [the problem is not made more specific] are being made with your knowledge, then look, the house is in the hands of your own children, yet even so misery has come anew [so, act for your children at least]. If it is the case that it is being done through hatred of you, then your (dead) father is great in the necropolis [i.e. get him to help out]. If it is the case that an accusation is in your own body [i.e. that you are the one bringing the troubles on us], then forget it for the sake of your children.

For the ancient Egyptians, many things lay outside the direct control of humanity – disease seemed to strike at random, problems could come out of the blue. Even now, we, in the age of science, are limited in our ability to tame nature and chance. The ancient Egyptians considered themselves to inhabit a world of directed force and power, where events were not mechanistic or blind (for example a bacterium invading the body and then multiplying), but could be directed by the invisible forces of the gods and the spirits. If a problem arose which could be set at the door of such an invisible malevolent spirit, then who better to bring on side than a beneficial spirit of your own – one of your own relatives who now inhabited that plane of existence?

The Berlin Bowl, inked over with a letter from a man to his deceased wife. Presumably it was then deposited in her tomb, although the stand may not originally belong to it.

The offering cult

In Egyptian belief, the blessed dead had passed on to an afterlife, but it was an afterlife where the bonds with the living were still maintained. At the centre of this reciprocal relationship was the offering cult. Members of the family maintained the memory of their dead relatives and made offerings to them at the chapel in the tomb. This was not simply a commemorative act – the *ka* (one of the ancient Egyptian conceptions of the 'spirit' of a person) of the deceased needed to be fed and sustained through the provision of offerings, both in the form of food, but also more general provisions, such as clothes. In the chapel of elite tombs, these offerings were enshrined in tomb paintings and inscriptions and also in the offering cult carried out by family members or priests contracted to undertake this service. In return, the dead, as *akh*-spirits (another of the ancient Egyptian conceptions of 'spirit') could intervene in aiding with those various problems which obviously have a cause, but one which is unseen or unknown. One letter even requests the dead relative to show herself in a dream fighting on the letter sender's behalf. This reciprocal relationship finds clear expression in one of the surviving Letters to the Dead (the Hu Bowl):

The very reason mortuary offerings are made to an *akh*-spirit is for watching over those still on earth.

The way in which the dead are expected to act is equally interesting, and reflects the afterlife beliefs of the time. It is not simply a case of alleviating discomfort, rather, the problems are seen as being caused by some unseen malevolent agent (for instance, a dead person with a grievance). It is the duty of the dead, in effect, to take on this malevolent agent, for example by bringing the case before the gods. So, the Hu Bowl, which dances around the particular problem being addressed, is quite explicit about what the dead relative is to do:

Get a judgment made about whoever is doing what is distressing to me – because I will be vindicated against any dead man or dead woman who is doing this against my daughter.

Letters to the Dead have a long history. The earliest examples come from the late Old Kingdom and the latest are from the late New Kingdom, about 1000 years later. However, by the end they were being superseded. In the New Kingdom, the cult of the gods developed a strong personal dimension, and more and more people began to think of themselves as having a close relationship with their gods. They thus began to solicit the help of the gods directly, not just by prayer and hope, but by writing to them for assistance with problems. When it came down to it, the dead served well, but the gods were even better.

Stela from the tomb of Montuhotep, a 12th Dynasty priest, with various scenes of the dead seated at tables loaded with offerings brought by the surviving family.

47

The power of magic

Sorcerers are too common; cunning men, wizards and white witches, as they call them, in every village, which, if they be sought unto, will help almost all infirmities of the body and mind.

Robert Burton, 1621

Ancient Egyptians made widespread use of magic. Magic can be found in many contexts, from formal uses, such as in temple rituals, through to everyday life, for instance in treating disease, in childbirth and in protecting children. But how did magic work? Can we really hope to find any sense in it now? An idea of what faces us can be gained from looking at a typical charm against scorpions:

Horus has been bitten, Horus the orphan has been bitten. Horus has been bitten, Horus has been bitten in the southern heaven, in the northern heaven. (Give) me breath, give me breath, oh herdsman! (Give) me breath, herdsman!

A shriek will go up from the malignant humours that are scattered through this body. Stretch out your right hand and your left hand and then make seven knots and set them before the poison. If the poison passes the seven knots which Horus has made in his body, I will not let the sunlight shine on the ground, I will not let the Inundation dash against the embankment, I will set fire to Busiris, I will burn up Osiris!

The main elements here are clear: the use of *words* to drive off the malignant effect of the sting, coupled with *ritual actions* in making the seven knots; the *analogy* with the god Horus, who similarly has been stung by a scorpion; and the *threat* to stop sunlight and the Nile inundation and to destroy the god Osiris. On first reading we might see some therapeutic benefits in the attempt to stop the spread of the toxins, but otherwise the spell probably seems gibberish.

However, we have to be careful to avoid the culturally loaded assumptions in our own ideas of magic, particularly those that regard it as superstitious, arcane or plain daft in opposition to the firm knowledge found, for example, in the sciences. In ancient Egypt, different conceptualizations of the problems of life were developed.

Left *Faience statuette of a type of 'friendly' demon known as Pataikos, shown treading upon crocodiles as symbols of malevolent forces. He is flanked by Isis and her sister, Nephthys, with the falcon, symbol of Horus, upon his shoulders.*

Opposite *Wooden statue of Hetepi, a 'chief magician' of the 11th Dynasty, carrying a bag presumably for his ritual implements.*

Magician's ritual knife, decorated with gods and hieroglyphs articulating the unseen forces affecting the human condition.

So, if we look at the concepts involved in magic, perhaps we can engage with it more sympathetically, and better appreciate how it fitted into people's lives.

Medical magic

Magic is particularly well attested in the treatment of diseases and afflictions, as well as in dealing with potential traumas such as childbirth or attacks by dangerous creatures. Here the distinction between what we term 'medicine' and 'magic' is one of degree: they are two poles of a spectrum of words and deeds concerned with protecting the body, which draw on a specialist body of knowledge and which were implemented by specialist practitioners. So, for example, in the famous Ebers Medical Papyrus, magical spells abound side by side with what we would consider straightforward medical treatments:

> A spell for drinking a medicine. The medicine has come; that which dispels the substances from this heart of mine, from these limbs of mine, has come. The magic is strong on account of this medicine – and vice versa. Have you indeed remembered that Horus and Seth were taken to the Great Palace of Heliopolis when an inquiry was held over the testicles of Seth with Horus? Thereupon he was flourishing like one who is upon the earth. He did all he wished like the gods who are there.
>
> Words to be said during the drinking of the medicine. A true means, proved an infinite number of times.

Some treatments are more clearly 'medical' in nature, usually because the cause is an obvious physical one (such as blows or falls) and the remedy is similarly physical. Other treatments, however, are more obviously 'magical'. Often this is because there is an invisible or unknown cause, or at least one that is difficult to establish – for example, the ancient Egyptians had no direct means of establishing the actions of microscopic agents such as bacteria or viruses. Or else it may be because the affliction results from the action of dangerous creatures, particularly scorpions or snakes, which can introduce toxins into the body through bites and stings. For these cases, the Egyptians developed a sophisticated conceptualization of the causes and effects of afflictions and of the resultant threat to the body, and thus worked out how to frame a reaction.

Human activity was understood to be situated within a broader world of forces dominated by the gods and other unseen agents, so that many things lay outside the direct control of humanity. Disease seemed to strike at random, a scorpion could sting in the dead of night, and both might introduce forces into the body intent on harm. These malevolent forces were often construed as the effects of demons or the malicious dead (p. 201), and thus required help from agents of similar power, primarily the gods. Mere physical treatment could not hope to be of use on its own.

Sympathetic and protective magic

Egyptian magical spells are often composed as follows: the human problem is considered as an analogy to problems encountered by the gods, particularly Re (as the primary god), Isis (especially for childbirth) and Horus (as the child of Isis). This is sometimes termed 'sympathetic magic'. The analogy is usually presented in narrative form as a mythological episode. The magician then attempts to compel these gods to act on behalf of the patient, even invoking a shared catastrophe threatening the entire cosmos should the treatment fail. Here the magician is not only trying to use the performative power of words, he is trying to tap into the very fabric of the cosmos on behalf of his patient.

The ancient Egyptian word for this activity is *heqa* – the force that was used by the creator god to bring the cosmos into being. On the other hand, *heqa* is not only available to the gods: the wisdom text the *Instruction to King Merikare* informs us that the creator provided humanity (his 'images who came from his body') with a world to live in, food and drink to sustain them, orderly society maintained by good rulers to live in, and *heqa* to ward off 'the blow of events'. The spoken element of the spell was accompanied by rites, often involving therapeutic practices and also methods of getting the magic inside the body through licking and swallowing, as well as rites performed by the magician, such as the use of the seven knots in the spell above.

Magic was used not only in treatment, but also for warding off potential harm. Protective amulets were a convenient way to ward off the malevolent. 'Amuletic decrees' provide a particularly interesting example – pieces of papyrus rolled up and put in containers around the necks of young children. The 'amuletic decree' invokes the protection of the gods against an astonishing range of dangers: ill-health, disease, bad dreams, ill-intentioned gods or people, dangerous journeys, the evil-eye, magic and its practitioners, dangerous creatures and demons, and accidents such as the collapse of a wall or the strike of a thunderbolt. In short, just about every conceivable harm that might befall a child.

Practitioners of magic

Finally, who were these magicians, who attempted to coerce the gods to act on behalf of their patients? Those who have left the clearest traces are elite magicians. Most have titles which associate them strongly with the temple: '(chief) lector-priest' (i.e. a priest who could read the ritual books), 'master of secrets', 'priest of Sakhmet' (goddess of disease and disaster), 'controller of Selqet' (goddess of scorpions and snakes) or 'amulet-man' (which also has the sense of 'protector'). However, there is every reason to see magic stretching into society beyond such learned specialists, and so, for example, there is evidence of a 'wise woman' at Deir el-Medina. We probably just see the top of this magical tree in the archaeological and textual record since this focuses on the highest echelons of society.

The interweaving of magic with other aspects of life is shown by the 'library', found in 1928, of Qenihirkhopshef, a scribe at Deir el-Medina in the late 19th Dynasty. Alongside his administrative work, Qenihirkhopshef collected a wide range of papyri including literary texts, hymns and ritual texts, as well as a range of magical-medical texts, including a book on dream interpretation. However, the most spectacular discovery is the late Middle Kingdom burial of a magician found by Egyptologist James Quibell in 1896 beneath storerooms at the Ramesseum (the mortuary temple of Ramesses II) in Thebes. This included a spectacular find of 23 papyri in a wooden box labelled as belonging to a 'master of secrets': most of the texts are magical-medical, but again there are also hymns and ritual and literary texts. Alongside were found magical statuettes, fragments of magical knives, ivory clappers, a segment of a magical rod and a magical wand (a bronze cobra). In other words, examples of the equipment needed to carry out magic. Equipped in this way, the magician was ready, both in word and deed, to engage with the dangers of the world around him.

Above *Amulets, often laid within the wrappings of mummies, depict deities and body parts which articulate the world as a connected whole, as if made up of the body parts of the creator god. Others depict hieroglyphs which write key words such as 'protection' and 'life'.*

Opposite below *A protective amulet, to be worn on the body, in the shape of a type of 'friendly' demon known as Bes.*

48 Why use hieroglyphic writing?

An offering which the king gives Osiris, lord of Djedu – a voice-offering for the governor, the overseer of priests, the guardian of the temple-cattle, Mereri.

FUNERARY STELA OF MERERI, *c.* 2200 BC

The most frequent misconception about Egyptian hieroglyphic writing is that it is picture writing, i.e. that each sign 'pictures' a word. This is not true, as can be seen on the stela of Mereri. The inscription (translated above) has nothing to say about lions, birds, hands or eyes, although each of these is clearly shown. In fact, hieroglyphs spell the sounds of words in Egyptian, and so are not unlike our alphabet. On Mereri's stela 𓂧 'hand' simply spells the sound *d*, and it is no more necessary to know why the ancient Egyptians used 𓂧 to write *d* than it is to know why we use the shape 'd' and modern Egyptians, using the Arabic alphabet, write د.

It is true that there are many more Egyptian hieroglyphs than there are letters in an alphabet, which is because hieroglyphs usually spell out

Limestone stela of the governor Mereri, from his tomb at Dendereh, 6th Dynasty.

sound-groups not individual letters. They did so by rebus: for example, if we wished to write English in hieroglyphs, we could put 'bee' and 'leaf' together to write 'belief'. The meaning of 'belief' has nothing to do with a bee or a leaf, but it happens to sound the same as 'bee-leaf'. Likewise, in Mereri's stela 'basket' is used to write 'lord' because the two words sound alike in Egyptian. As well as rebus, some hieroglyphs are used as *determinatives*, i.e. they do not write sounds but indicate the broad meaning of a word. For example, at the bottom right of Mereri's stela, the determinative 'god' is written at the end of the name Osiris, to show it is a god's name. In fact, most words are written using a combination of sound-signs and determinatives. For example, beside Mereri's staff the word for 'temple-cattle' is written as follows: *ṯ* (like 'ch' in 'church') plus *n* plus *t* plus *t*, which spell out the word *ṯntt*. This is followed by two determinatives 'animal' and 'more than one'. Notice that no vowels have been written in *ṯntt*, which is typical of hieroglyphic texts: it was assumed that a reader could recognize the word and so supply the missing sounds, just as we may use '10 Downing St' instead of 'ten downing street'.

Undoubtedly, hieroglyphic writing was not simple picture writing at the time of Mereri, so why did ancient Egyptians use pictures to write? After all, hieroglyphs are complex to draw and there are so many. One obvious explanation is that hieroglyphic writing was originally picture writing but became more 'sophisticated' over time. However, many texts have survived from the early pharaonic period and the writing principles used for these are the same as later. For example, on the label (*right*) for Den's sandals his name is written with the hieroglyphs *d* and *n*, which simply spell his name. At the right edge of the scene are the hieroglyphs 'grain', 'dagger', 'mat(?)' and 'decorated spear'. As pictures they convey nothing sensible, but as a rebus they spell out the Egyptian phrase 'the first occasion of striking the east'.

In fact, Den's label illustrates the real purpose of hieroglyphs: to clarify and enhance sacred art. The label was beautifully carved in ivory, then deposited in the king's tomb; and the hieroglyphs illuminate the scene and its relevance to sandals – they are the instruments with which the king trod on his enemies. Likewise, Mereri's stela explains who he was in life, and why future generations ought to remember him by offering to his spirit. The picture goes some way to provide this explanation: we see a man wearing symbols of authority and worldly success, including fine clothes, a staff and a sceptre. However, the text states specifically that he was a governor and a priest, and a man therefore who held crucial jobs within his community.

The idea that hieroglyphic writing was suited specifically to sacred art is confirmed in various ways. First, hieroglyphs were used only in sacred contexts, especially in temples and tombs. To write letters, accounts and other texts from everyday life, ancient Egyptians used a different script, which we call hieratic. (In the 6th century BC, hieratic was replaced by a similar script, demotic.) Hieratic signs are more stylized and cursive than hieroglyphs, enabling them to be written quickly using ink and a brush. The more complex hieroglyphs were carved or painted, usually on stone or on precious materials, such as ivory. Moreover,

Ivory label from a pair of sandals in the tomb of Den at Abydos. An early example of the archetypal representation of the king at war, this scene anticipates later assertions that enemies of pharaoh were scattered 'beneath his sandals'.

Ivory comb, from the tomb of Djet at Abydos. The king's name is written within a stylized palace or 'serekh', surmounted by a falcon, representing the sun god, Horus. At the top, the sun god is shown in a winged boat – symbolizing his daily journey through the sky.

hieroglyphic writing was first developed specifically for royal burials and royal dedications to the gods. Although many of these earliest texts accompany offerings in tombs, they are much more than mere labels: they record and articulate the involvement of the whole community in providing its best for the king's afterlife.

From royal tombs, hieroglyphic writing spread as a gift of the king to other graves, to temples, and to inscriptions on the borders of the king's realm, but rarely to other contexts. This was also true of education: few people outside the palace and the priesthood could read and write at all, still less by using hieroglyphs.

The final confirmation of the intimate link between hieroglyphs and art is the ease with which the two interact. For example, in the stela of Mereri notice how the text has been divided into four columns using vertical dividers. The text begins on the right and reads towards the figure of Mereri, but the third divider and his staff overlap to break down the differentiation between figure and text. The staff then isolates a small group of hieroglyphs next to his body, and these are the very ones which write his name.

Stela of Ty from his tomb at Dendereh, 11th–12th Dynasty. The inscription at the top reads: 'An offering which the king gives Osiris – a voice-offering for the controller of priests, the revered one, Ty. 1000 of bread, 1000 of beer, 1000 of alabaster, 1000 of linen, 1000 of fowl, 1000 of ox.' The inscription below reads: 'The courtier and controller of priests, the revered one before the great god, the overseer of the storehouse, the revered one, Ty.'

Hieroglyphs can also be written in different directions. For example, in the stela of Ty (shown left), there are two scenes: below, Ty is standing, so the text is written vertically to follow this upright composition. Above, Ty is seated in front of a table of offerings, so the hieroglyphs are written horizontally to emulate this broader format.

On the ivory comb of the 1st Dynasty King Djet (shown above), his name is framed by a pair of hieroglyphs and accompanied by another, which write the words 'authority' and 'life' respectively. Within this composition they seem to suggest that the world under the sun is defined and organized by the authority of the king, who thereby makes life possible.

If so, this is an early statement of an idea well known in the literature of later eras. Such interplay between images and words is integral to the religion of many cultures, which harness uniquely human resources – art and language – to articulate the deepest mysteries of life and death. Put simply, the ancient Egyptians used hieroglyphs because this beautiful pictorial script enhanced the elegance of their own sacred art.

The origins of Egyptian literature

Come, Neferti, my friend, tell me fine words and choice sayings which my person shall be entertained to hear.
THE *PROPHECY OF NEFERTI*, c. 1800 BC

According to the most recent research, Egyptian literature (as distinct from letters, religious texts and administrative documents) originated in the Middle Kingdom, more than a millennium after the invention of writing. We can assume that earlier generations told tales and sang songs which were not written down, although examples are known indirectly through workers' songs inscribed in tombs of the Old Kingdom.

There are also clearly poetic religious texts, such as the Pyramid Texts, which presumably were intended for magical or invocational purposes, and thus their linguistic beauty seems to be strictly related to their function. Furthermore, it seems certain surviving letters were meant to serve as entertainment, particularly examples from the reign of Djedkare Izezi (5th Dynasty), and so can also be understood as forerunners of Middle Kingdom literature.

In the early 2nd millennium BC, around the beginning of the Middle Kingdom, we can observe a wider use of writing across different areas of society from previously – representing perhaps a social and technical revolution that underpinned the appearance of literature in Egypt. Likewise, following the First Intermediate Period – an era of social change and accordingly a new social order (p. 228) – literature began to be written which did not serve immediately practical purposes. This new form of the written word was able to provide both intellectual adventure ('searching the heart', in Egyptian terms) as well as entertainment ('amusing the heart'). By its nature, literature is concerned with subjects beyond immediate, mundane matters, and problematic topics such as justice, cultural identity and origins, or god's influence on human destiny were dealt with in ways in which the imagination could roam freely. In fact, the earliest written literature can be described as 'problem-literature'.

Letter from King Djedkare Izezi to his vizier, Rashepses, copied on to the walls of the latter's tomb. It talks about the pleasure of words and anticipates later literary themes.

The purposes of literature

Literature therefore developed in the early Middle Kingdom because of the enormous social significance of writing and, alongside it, of story-

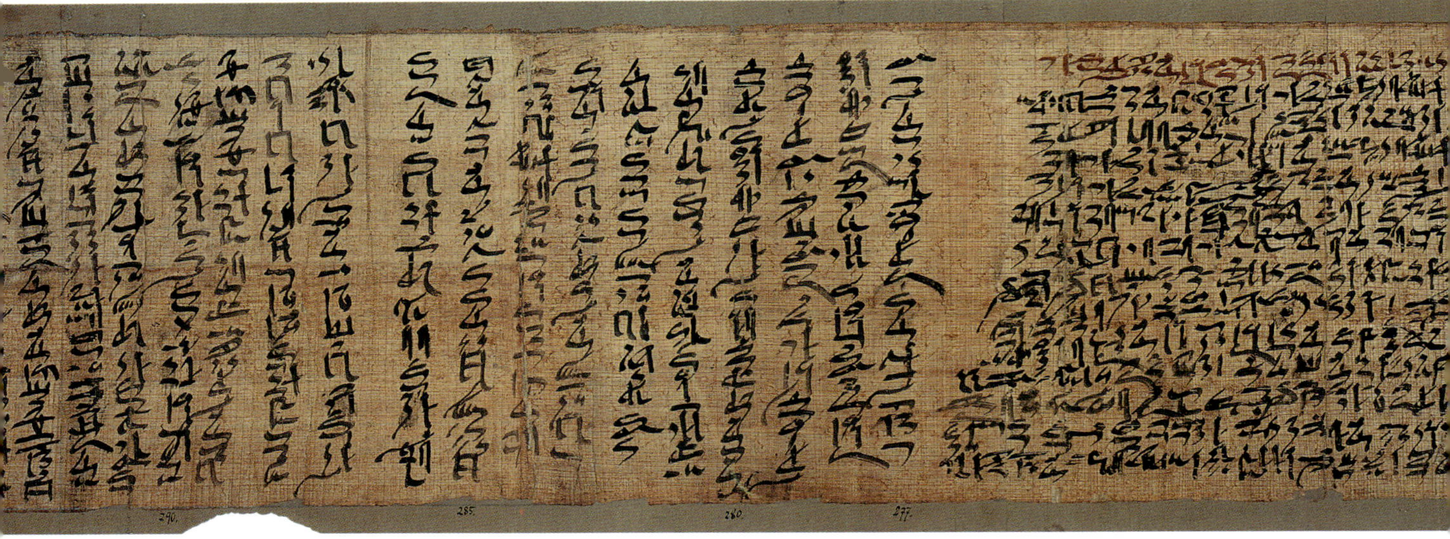

Manuscript B of the Story of Sinuhe *from the Middle Kingdom. The papyrus, now in Berlin, was found together with other literary manuscripts in a book-chest.*

telling. Literature 'altered one's vision', transported the reader and was perhaps even cathartic. When the characters of one story debate the relevance of 'fine speaking', a peasant says to a pharaoh 'in this way, surely, you wish to see me healthy', alluding to its therapeutic function. Likewise in the *Prophecy of Neferti*, the melancholy Snofru – a real king transformed into a literary character – is cured by 'fine words and choice sayings'. The 'blues' are also a key motif among the miracle-stories of Papyrus Westcar, in which Snofru is cured by the sight of beautiful, naked women singing. Equal measures of melancholy, literature and eroticism contribute to 'amusing the heart'. Literary texts were generally designed to be read aloud. In this respect, they stood near to the spoken word, and were normally written in the vernacular.

A particular highlight of literature from the early 2nd millennium BC is a portrayal of the life of a high-ranking courtier, Sinuhe (p. 158). In confusion at the death of his king, Sinuhe responds by fleeing to a foreign country. There he is very successful, but cannot be happy away from his homeland. The story ends with his return to Egypt, mercifully allowed by the pharaoh. In this text, three topics in particular are discussed: the high culture of Egypt in comparison to foreign barbarians; the relationship of the Egyptian people to the king; and the issue of personal destiny, including the immediate intervention of divinity. Here, a crisis is used as especially suitable material for story-telling, and many other literary works are founded on the idea of overcoming exceptional challenges.

The *Story of Sinuhe* can be understood against the background of a specific form of religious text. From the Old Kingdom, texts in people's burials were written in the first person and described their lives, or more exactly their social positions and careers. These functional texts were intended to establish the fact of a person's existence and continued *post-mortem* presence through self-presentation, for posterity and for eternity. This form of text, central to the Egyptian funerary cult, was parodied in the *Story of Sinuhe*.

In this sense, other literary texts can be understood as transformations of different functional texts. For example, when travelling into foreign parts, especially to quarry raw materials, it was usual to leave inscriptions on rock walls or stelae. The celebrated *Story of the Shipwrecked Sailor* adapts this form of text. Likewise, the *Tale of the Eloquent Peasant* is related to the genres of letters and court-protocol; the *Prophecy of the Neferti* can be seen as a version of prophecy texts; and the *Tale of a Herdsman* is a parody of myth.

In other words, the genres of literature in ancient Egypt were derivative. Moreover, literary texts were typically set in the distant (*Neferti*) or recent (*Sinuhe*) past. The authors disguised their fiction with reality, using historic clothing which was presumably recognizable to its intended readers. In other words, the reader was invited to a 'willing suspension of disbelief'.

Authors and their audience

Texts from the earliest period of literature became recognized as masterpieces. They were handed down over centuries, and during the New Kingdom became the basis of education in the school curriculum. However, it is noteworthy that at any period only a small part of the population participated directly in writing. All literary, and indeed any other, texts derive from the minds and concerns of a small group of *literati*. This is apparent in the limited range of styles, subjects and genres. Concrete information about the writers and their audience is only sparsely transmitted – biographies of authors cannot be written and the audience remain pale silhouettes. In a sense, however, this seems appropriate for a culture in which the wider community of human activity is more important than the individual.

On the other hand, many texts are set in the royal palace, where we can suppose the first steps in literature were taken. In fact, pharaoh is actually represented in two literary texts of the Middle Kingdom as the patron of writing 'fine words'. Likewise, the 'chief lector-priest' Neferti and the wise-man, Djedi, from Papyrus Westcar are obvious archetypes of the literate class.

Djedi is a teacher for whom books were an integral part of life. This wise old man, living far from the palace, with supernatural abilities and exuding knowledge, is recognizable as a fictional conceit. Neferti must also have been recognizable – if not historically real – as a typical character in Middle Kingdom Egypt. He is also a model of literary life in another sense: it was men like Neferti who read, composed and copied the literature of Egypt from its earliest beginning in the Middle Kingdom.

Right *Self-presentation texts (or 'autobiographies'), such as this in the tomb of Ameny at Beni Hasan, offer formulaic accounts of officials' lives.*

50

Hidden symbols of sex in Egyptian art

... ordinarily, run-of-the-mill, everyday sex relations in virtually all human societies are hidden, conducted away from the gaze of all but the participants ...

Ernestine Friedl, 1994

Below *A vignette from the Erotic Papyrus of Turin, demonstrating that Egyptian artists did depict explicit sexual activity in contexts other than the 'high art' of temples, mortuary chapels and palaces.*

Below right *A group sculpture dating from the Ptolemaic period, with overt sexual imagery which leaves nothing to the imagination.*

Egypt's 'high art', the reliefs and paintings on the walls of temples, elite mortuary chapels and palaces, almost never depicts explicit sexual activity. This might seem mysterious in itself, and all the more so in that other genres of Egyptian art are bluntly graphic about sexuality, leaving nothing to the imagination. Many figurines depict copulating couples, or males with enormous, sometimes erect phalli, and artists' sketches on flakes of limestone (ostraca) are equally explicit.

Papyri also convey explicit sexuality, most famously the Erotic Papyrus of Turin (*c.* 13th–12th century BC). Originally perhaps from Thebes, this papyrus displays 12 well-drawn vignettes showing sexually aroused if unkempt and older men having sexual relations (some highly improbable) with attractive, almost completely nude younger women. Some scholars believe these are scenes set in a brothel; others that they obscenely satirize the elite of a disintegrating society or, more subtly, provide an amusing ironic counterpart to the erotically charged but sexually restrained love poetry of the period.

Representing sexuality

In fact, sexuality was not completely excluded from temple art when it was central to the mythological themes rendered on temple walls. Nevertheless, these depictions were extremely restrained compared to the explicitness of the materials mentioned above. For example, sexual

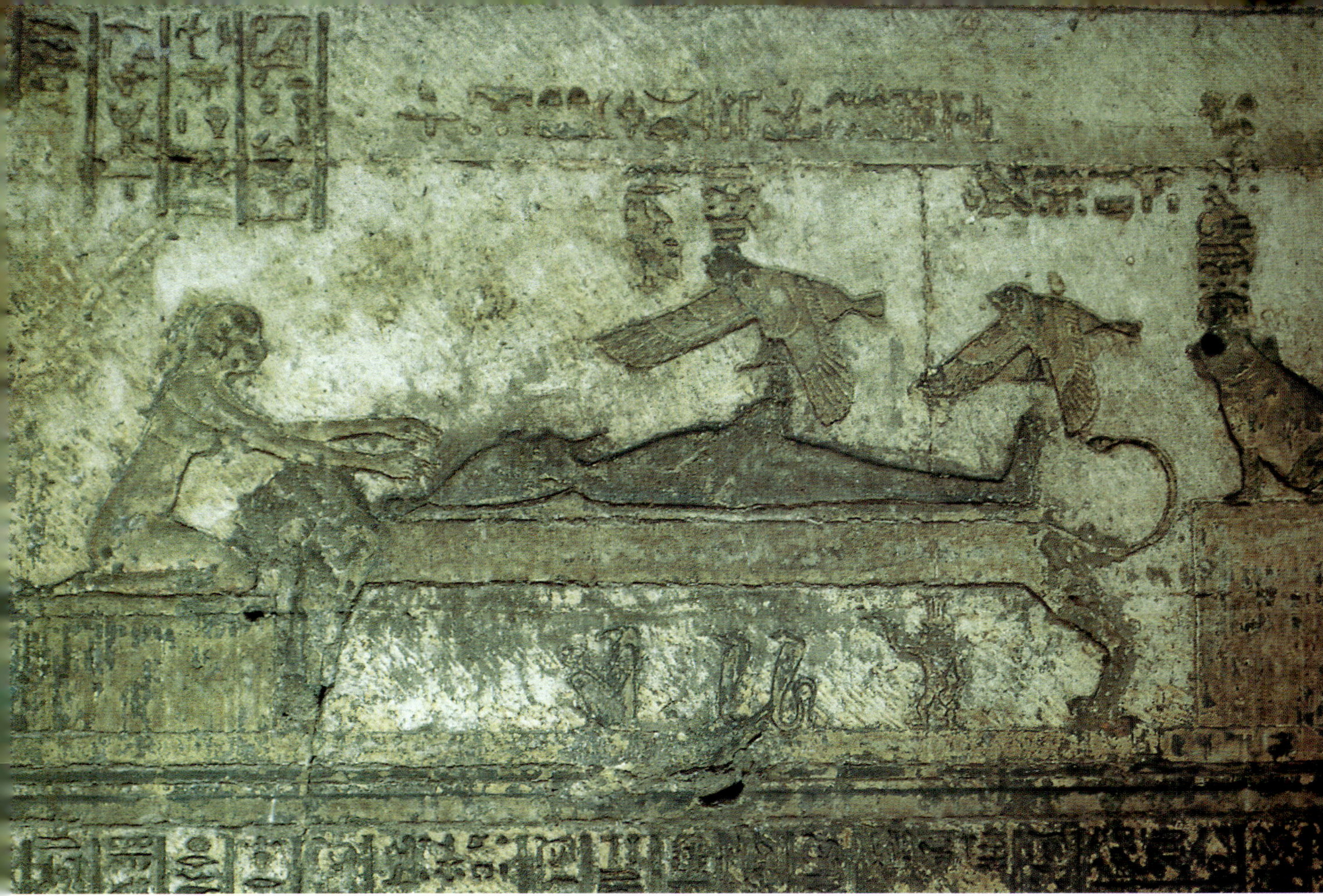

coupling between the god Osiris and his consort Isis was fundamental to a myth of regeneration and rebirth that energized both temple and mortuary cult. This sexual union was depicted in a number of temples but, in human terms, in almost unrecognizable form. Osiris, murdered but reassembled and provided with partial life, lies totally inert and passive, but his penis is erect. Isis, the active partner, descends in the form of a small bird upon Osiris' phallus in order to be impregnated. As a result, she will bear Osiris' son Horus, who will complete the regeneration of his father. Isis' bird form is mythologically appropriate, but also serves to soften the explicitness of her act.

Similarly, the cycle of the divine birth of the Egyptian king was depicted in several temples or chapels. According to this myth, every king was the product of a sexual union between his human mother, the queen, and a god; or between his human father, the preceding king, and a goddess. In this way each ruler had the half-divine, half-human qualities that made him the unique mediator between humanity and the divine. Texts are quite explicit and frank about this process, but art is more restrained. Thus the god and queen can be shown in an intimate, but only allusively sexual relationship. Seated in close proximity they face each other and partially overlap, an indirect reference to their coitus; while the bed upon which sex takes place is also depicted, but separated from the couple by a pair of goddesses supporting them from below.

This reticence about depicting the sexual act (certain genres excepted) relates in part to the ancient Egyptians' strong sense of decorum as to what could appropriately be shown in the 'high art' of temple and tomb. Other fundamental biological facts were also avoided – death (except for that of foreign foes) and birth (except for that of animals). Discretion might also relate to a broader universal, dubbed 'sex the invisible' by anthropologists, who note that the privacy of love-making is carefully maintained in virtually all human societies.

The conception of the god Horus is depicted in a veiled, non-explicit way in this relief from the chapel of Osiris, in the Temple of Hathor at Dendereh. Isis, in the form of a bird, descends on the erect penis of the dead Osiris.

Possible sexual encodement in mortuary art: a couple are shown seated together – under the wife's chair is a monkey. Symbolically monkeys are an allusion to sexual activity.

Encodement: Egyptian reality or Egyptological fantasy?

The temple scenes described above involve a kind of 'encodement' – they communicate an unambiguous sexual message while severely restricting its more explicit aspects. Many Egyptologists believe, however, that sexual encodement goes much further in Egyptian art, although others do not agree. The latter argue that scenes in mortuary art (the principal focus for this encodement theory) are to be read literally as depictions of dining, hunting or whatever, and not as conveying a hidden but easily decodable sexual message. Or, while not denying the possibility, critics find much of the sexual encodement read into Egyptian art is based on illogical premises or is overly subjective in its conclusions.

A relief from Hatshepsut's mortuary temple at Deir el-Bahri depicts the queen's divine parentage. The god Amun-Re is shown with the mother of Hatshepsut, their legs overlapping and their arms intertwined in an allusion to sexual intercourse.

The encodement theory was inspired by New Kingdom love poetry. Highly erotic and, rarely, sexually explicit in content, this poetry is also rich in metaphors and symbols which have sexual significance. Marshes are erotic because lovers meet in their seclusion for intercourse. Netting birds becomes a sexually charged image when a girl's lustrous long hair is identified as ensnaring her lover, arousing him to sexual interest and activity.

Many suggest similar symbolism is used to convey 'hidden' sexual messages in Egyptian mortuary art, and long before the New Kingdom, for two reasons. First, sexual pleasure was desired even after death (as also were eating and drinking); and second, the immortality of deceased Egyptian males was thought to depend, in part, upon repeated rebirths of the deceased, who regularly impregnated a female partner for this purpose. Allusions to both these concepts in mortuary art may have magically guaranteed their effectiveness.

The means of encodement were varied. Erotic symbols could infuse seemingly mundane or non-sexual scenes with sexual meaning. A couple seated side by side are accompanied by a pet monkey: but symbolically monkeys are an allusion to sexual activity. Other seemingly non-sexual scenes may display anomalous details intended to signal a hidden sexual message. A deceased couple are shown receiving offerings or prayers, yet the woman is having her hair dressed – hardly appropriate to the event. Elaborate wigs and hair treatments symbolize sexual accessibility and stimulation, so here again sexual union is indirectly conveyed. Verbal word play of a sexual nature may be transformed into a visual variant. On a shrine from his tomb, a seated King Tutankhamun is shown shooting an arrow at birds, his queen sitting on the ground beside him. But the scene also represents an Egyptian word which means both to shoot an arrow and to ejaculate, so here too a sexual meaning is inferred.

Yet these notions are open to criticism. Many scenes in elite tombs show a wife accompanying a husband hunting birds, but she sometimes explicitly hopes to secure an edible bird. And many apparent anomalies in Egyptian art are due to its conventions, rather than the creation of hidden sexual messages. Some degree of sexual encodement is recognized by most scholars, but what some see as a far-reaching system, others find merely extreme over-interpretation.

In a scene on a golden shrine from his tomb, Tutankhamun is shown shooting an arrow while his queen sits on the ground. A hidden sexual meaning may be encoded in this scene since it represents an Egyptian word meaning both to shoot an arrow and to ejaculate.

Historical Mysteries

The great historian Herodotus was the first European to write at length about Egypt, after visiting the country around 450 BC. He is our earliest tour-guide, from a time when pharaohs still ruled and the gods' temples were thriving. His overriding impression is amusing, if perhaps mischievous: 'Not only is the Egyptian climate peculiar to that land, just as the Nile behaves differently from other rivers elsewhere, but the Egyptians too, in their manners and customs, seem to do just the opposite of what people usually do.'

Despite Egypt's peculiarities, Herodotus was impressed by the achievements of this ancient nation. For example, he reports that Egyptian sailors circumnavigated Africa in the reign of Necho II – 2000 years before Europeans did so. Is there any truth in this tale? And if so, how do we explain some scholars' claims that ancient Egyptians – despite their reliance on overseas trade – were unwilling to set sail themselves? Could people so reliant on boats along the River Nile, really have been fearful of the sea? Herodotus also discusses the cult of the sacred Apis bulls. We know these bulls were venerated as far back as the 1st Dynasty, and, for some 1500 years from the 18th Dynasty, they were buried in tombs and underground vaults at Saqqara. Except, that is, for bulls in the years around 1100–900 BC, many of which seem to be missing. Is this a trivial archaeological detail, or could it mean, as some writers have suggested, that we have completely misunderstood the history of Egypt at this time?

Hittite warriors shown in the temple of Ramesses II at Abydos. They are streaming to the battlefield at Qadesh to engage the armies of Ramesses II in the defining battle for control of the Near East around 1275 BC. However, the outcome of the battle is not clear to modern scholars.

The removal of the royal tombs from the Valley of the Kings to Tanis marks the end of the New Kingdom. However, the exquisite workmanship of the golden funerary mask of Psusennes I, from Tanis, inlaid with imported lapis lazuli, belies the claim that the end of the New Kingdom entailed a sudden collapse in Egypt's wealth and international influence.

Given Egypt's reputation for wisdom and skill in ancient times, some of our most intriguing mysteries concern technology. The Egyptians largely ignored iron for many centuries after they first came across it. Why were they not enthusiastic about a metal which is today regarded as a defining stage in human development? Their apparent indifference seems all the more remarkable because Egyptians since prehistory had quarried and carved very hard stones, such as granite. What techniques did they have which made iron redundant? Another technological mystery arises from a long-standing claim by certain scholars: were the Egyptians the first to invent glass?

Herodotus was most keen to point out that nations are different. For modern scholars the most complex question is explaining why nations change. For example, some have argued that the Old Kingdom, which built the great pyramids of Giza, came crashing down in the aftermath of an environmental catastrophe. Others have argued that the state became top heavy with bureaucrats and vested interests, and eventually collapsed like a house of cards. Can we reach a definitive conclusion? Whatever happened, the following era, usually referred to as the First Intermediate Period, is one of the most problematic. Traditionally it has been portrayed as a 'dark age' in which government gave way to anarchy, and culture descended into chaos. Should we, however, pay more attention to evidence that this was really an era of dynamic cultural renewal? The Middle Kingdom came to an end even more emphatically than the Old Kingdom, with royal control fragmenting, albeit over a period of decades, until Egypt was eventually divided between dozens of kings. What social pressures brought about such a decisive end to central authority?

Ancient Egypt's most splendid era, in terms of wealth and prestige, was the New Kingdom, when Egypt was the most powerful nation in the world. But did it rule its neighbour, Palestine, as many have assumed? At the height of the New Kingdom, Ramesses II fought a disastrous battle at Qadesh and nearly lost his life alongside many hundreds of his soldiers. Undeterred, the king commissioned a massive record of the battle. Was he too vain to recognize the truth? Or was he more proud of his deliverance from his enemies than of any of his victories?

Appropriately, our final mystery concerns Herodotus himself. Egypt might have seemed to him a contrary place, but it was also a proud and ancient land, which he reported with humour and affection. Nevertheless, it is not easy to make sense of what Herodotus actually saw when he was there. Did this astute observer of other folk really see the Great Pyramid at Giza but miss the Great Sphinx just metres away? Or was the Great Sphinx simply just not interesting to earlier generations of visitors?

What did the Egyptians know of their history?

Because of the way they keep records of the past, the Egyptians who live around the sown parts of the country have made themselves the wisest people I have ever come across.

HERODOTUS, *c.* 430 BC

Herodotus, the first great historian, was clearly impressed with the record keeping of the Egyptians in the Nile Valley. There is plenty of evidence to support his view. For example, the accounts of temples and palaces were carefully dated, written in multiple copies and deposited in archives. And literate individuals – albeit a minority of the population – maintained their own family archives, like the scribe Thutmose, who around 1080 BC wrote to his son:

> Now, as for the documents rained upon in the house of the scribe Horsheri, my [forefather], which you brought out and we found not to have been wiped, and I said to you I will sort out again: you should take them away and we will put them in the tomb-chapel of Amunnakht, my forefather. Trust me because I have sworn.

Records of the past are also found in numerous ancient monuments, such as tomb-inscriptions describing a life in royal service. Genealogies in tombs and inscribed on statues may cover many centuries: the genealogy of one High Priest at Memphis lists members of his family who had held the same office as far back as the reign of Montuhotep II of the 11th Dynasty, a period of more than 1000 years in total. References to those who recorded the past can be found throughout this present book – from Harkhuf in the Old Kingdom to Manetho 2000 years later.

In a sense, some of these records can be understood as the testimony of a particular individual, but they are usually recorded in tombs alongside traditional religious and funerary texts, and so are embodied within a larger vision of Egyptian culture and its virtues. On the other hand, Herodotus makes an apparently contradictory statement while discussing Greek settlement in Egypt in the reign of Psamtek I in the 7th century BC:

> Because of our regular contact with these settlers in Egypt, the first foreigners to settle there, we Greeks have an accurate knowledge of Egyptian history *beginning with king Psamtek and ever since.*

Ahmose, son of Ibana, shown in his tomb at el-Kab. In his funerary inscription Ahmose records military service under three kings of the 18th Dynasty.

Above *The king-list of Sety I at Abydos, in which the past is embodied in the form of the names of 76 kings from Menes on.*

In other words, history – as we understand it today – only became possible when Europeans first settled in Egypt in large numbers. So how do we reconcile these statements of Herodotus?

The Egyptian concept of history

Essentially this is to do with the difference between how we understand the past now, and how the ancient Egyptians did so. For the Egyptians the past was organized not around the careers of politicians and the clashes between nations, but around the succession of kings and the festivals of gods. This is apparent even in the earliest written texts from Egypt, from the royal cemetery at Abydos (p. 24). These texts take the form of labels attached to jars in the kings' tombs, and are usually inscribed with a formulaic text recording the king's name, the contents of the jar (as an offering to the king) and the defining event of that year – typically a religious festival or a royal appearance.

Left *Statues and inscriptions of non-royal individuals, such as Nenkheftkai of the 5th Dynasty, are standardized in form, and tend to reveal little about their lives other than their social position and relationship to the king.*

From these early labels more extensive records developed, of which the most detailed is the fragmentary Palermo Stone (p. 227), a basalt stela originally over 2 m (6.5 ft) tall, cataloguing the major festivals in the reigns of the kings up to the 5th Dynasty. The list begins with the reigns of the gods, thereby confirming that our world, since the beginning of time, has been a kingdom with a divine ruler at its head. Likewise, documents were always dated to one day in the reign of a particular king, and no absolute calendar was created using a fixed starting point, such as the one commonly in use today which counts the years before or since the birth of Christ.

King-lists

From the New Kingdom we also have monumental lists of kings' names, most famously those from Abydos. A list in the temple of Sety I there contains 76 names stretching back to Menes, the first human king of Egypt (p. 33). The specific number of names seems to reflect a religious tradition known as the Litany of Re, so the names of many – probably most – kings have been omitted. However, a list at Karnak carved in the reign of Thutmose III, around two centuries earlier, gives a different list and includes several of the missing names, while the tomb at Saqqara of a priest named Tjunury provides others. It seems likely that these lists were associated with religious cults in which statues of earlier kings were carried in festival processions (Tjunury probably took part in these). Significantly, Abydos was believed to be the burial place of Osiris, the first mortal to sit on the throne according to Egyptian mythology; it was certainly the oldest royal cemetery in Egypt, and so the most appropriate place to reflect on the past as embodied in the succession of kings.

The monumental king-lists of the New Kingdom are less comprehensive and detailed than the Palermo Stone, but this certainly does not reflect increased ignorance at that time. We know, for example, that 'day-books' (*herut*) detailing the activities of kings were compiled on leather scrolls and then deposited in temple archives. These were used as the basis for monumental accounts of the achievements of kings, usually erected in temples – where, incidentally, few people actually had access to them.

In the 19th Dynasty an astonishing document was composed, written on papyrus, known today as the Turin Royal Canon. Although badly damaged, this seems to have been a complete list of the 300 or more kings of Egypt from the beginning of time until Ramesses II (13th century BC), with precise reign-lengths and summary totals for groups of kings. Like the Palermo Stone, it begins not with Menes but with the reigns of the gods. At present the Turin Royal Canon is a unique discovery, but similar documents were undoubtedly used around 300 BC by Manetho, a priest from Sebennytos, to compile a detailed history of Egypt. His task was to demonstrate the true antiquity of Egypt for the foreign dynasty of the Ptolemies. Sadly, Manetho's history has not actually survived and is only known from excerpts made by much later writers, which often appear inconsistent.

Taken together, these many and varied sources make plain that there is no contradiction in Herodotus' statements. For the ancient Egyptians, knowledge of the past was not what Herodotus – nor any other Westerner – would understand as history. Instead they organized their knowledge around the succession of kings, which they could trace back to the very beginning of time when Egypt was ruled by gods. Establishing this repetitious continuity of the world was important because it allowed the ancient Egyptians to establish an essential truth: to know the past is to foresee the future.

Detail from the fragmentary Turin Royal Canon, with kings' names listed in columns.

Below *Stela of Thutmose IV in a chapel between the paws of the Great Sphinx at Giza. The text mentions Khafre, responsible for the Sphinx, although the stela was erected 1000 years after his death, showing that later pharaohs knew and cared about their predecessors.*

52 The end of the great pyramid age

O, but the builders of pyramids have become fieldworkers; those who were in the divine barque are at the yoke.... There is only groaning throughout the land, mixed with laments.... Look, the beggars of the land have become the rich; the lord of property is a have-not.

THE *ADMONITIONS OF IPUWER*, *c.* 1700 BC

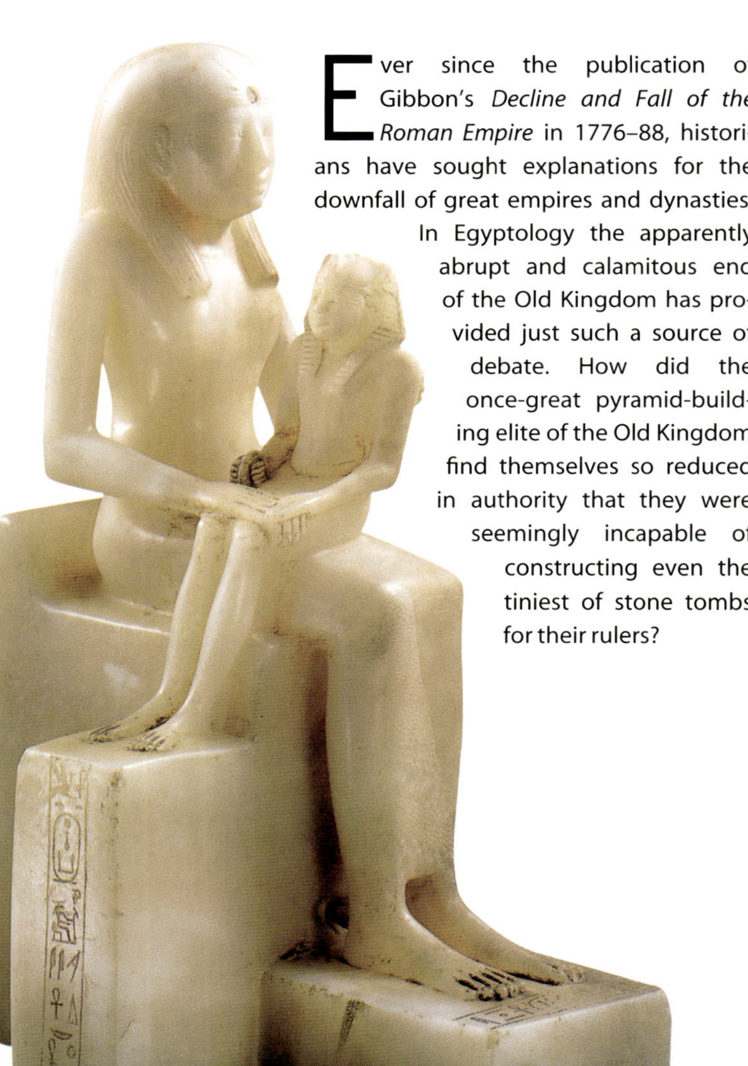

Ever since the publication of Gibbon's *Decline and Fall of the Roman Empire* in 1776–88, historians have sought explanations for the downfall of great empires and dynasties. In Egyptology the apparently abrupt and calamitous end of the Old Kingdom has provided just such a source of debate. How did the once-great pyramid-building elite of the Old Kingdom find themselves so reduced in authority that they were seemingly incapable of constructing even the tiniest of stone tombs for their rulers?

The Old Kingdom effectively concluded with Pepy II and his ephemeral successors at the end of the 6th Dynasty. Some historians include the 7th and 8th Dynasties as well, because Manetho indicates that the royal court remained at Memphis, and the only surviving royal tomb of this period – the unfinished pyramid of the 8th Dynasty ruler Ibi (p. 98) – is located in the Memphite necropolis. However, most scholars assume that the reign of Pepy II was the last of any significance.

Two factors above all have inspired Egyptologists to regard the First Intermediate Period (*c.* 2175–2045 BC), the 130 or so years following the 6th Dynasty, as a kind of dark age. The first is the almost total absence of monumental architecture, especially royal tombs. The second is a number of texts – most of which admittedly date from no earlier than the Middle Kingdom – that suggest that some great cataclysm turned the accepted social order on its head. Foremost among these are the *Admonitions of Ipuwer* and the *Prophecy of Neferti*. The various hypotheses and explanations concerning the end of the Old

Left *Pepy II as an infant, seated on his mother's lap. Some have speculated that the great length of his reign, up to 94 years, might have led to political tensions regarding policy and the royal succession.*

Opposite *The pyramids at Giza epitomize the economic power of the king and palace during the 4th Dynasty; but a shift to less centralized government began as a matter of policy before the end of the Old Kingdom.*

Literary texts, such as the Admonitions of Ipuwer *shown here, evoke a world in chaos and despair, and have coloured many modern accounts of the First Intermediate Period.*

Kingdom can be divided into three basic types: environmental, political and socio-economic. Nevertheless, experience tells us that historical events are rarely so simple and straightforward that they can be ascribed to a single cause rather than a complex mixture of factors.

Environmental disaster?

Since the 1970s a number of scholars have argued that the late Old Kingdom experienced an increasingly arid or unpredictable climate. Written sources, such as the Palermo Stone, as well as the geomorphology of the Nile, suggest that the amount of rainfall and the level of the annual Nile inundation decreased by the 6th Dynasty. At this time the agricultural land would have included not only the banks of the river, dependent on the inundation, but also strips of

Statuette of the 'revenue official' Hetepni. His titles, including 'counter of all that moves in water and in the marshes', reflect the increasing importance of non-royal officials in administration during the 6th Dynasty.

savannah on either side, which would have been severely affected by any depletion in rainfall. During the First Intermediate Period the Egyptians might therefore have been much more dependent on an unpredictable inundation. It has frequently been suggested that texts such as the *Admonitions of Ipuwer* describe social disorder resulting from demographic pressure and famine. Indeed, Barbara Bell has suggested that, like 'rainmakers', many of the pharaohs of the early First Intermediate Period may have been put to death by their subjects for their failure to produce good agricultural conditions.

More recently, however, flaws in this mixture of environmental and literary arguments have been pointed out. Jean Vercoutter has argued that a link between low rainfall and the Nile inundation is highly suspect, given that the Nile flood is much more influenced by the Indian Ocean than the Sahara. Many Egyptologists have also argued that the *Admonitions of Ipuwer* is not reliable evidence, given that it survives only from the New Kingdom. Although it is clearly 12th Dynasty in style, there is no guarantee that it describes events in the First Intermediate Period. It belongs with other misanthropic or pessimistic texts of the Middle Kingdom, such as the *Dialogue of a Man with his Ba* and the *Prophecy of Neferti*. Although this genre might have been partly inspired by environmental or social problems following the end of the Old Kingdom, it would be dangerous to treat any of the texts as if they were factual historical documents.

Too many bureaucrats and tax breaks?

A variety of factors may have brought about the fall of the Old Kingdom, including climatic change, an increase in the power of provincial rulers, whose posts became hereditary, the granting of too many tax exemptions to officials and temples, with a consequent decrease in royal wealth and authority, and possible loss of prestige by the last Memphite pharaohs (although the evidence for the last is a tenuous 18th Dynasty text describing a homosexual encounter between Pepy II and his general Sisenet).

The gradual decline in the size and quality of royal pyramid complexes may have been either a result or symptom of the above factors. Some scholars would certainly argue that the exorbitant construction of royal pyramids and sun temples might have bled the economy dry. However, this is hard to prove, since most of our economic evidence derives from funerary monuments, making it difficult to assess the nature of the entire Old Kingdom economy and the extent to which it was dominated by funerary expenditure.

Above *The tomb of the governor Ankhtify at Moalla, who attributed his own power to personal success not royal authority.*

On the other hand, the First Intermediate Period was not the chaotic dark age that excessively literal interpretations of the 'pessimistic' texts have suggested (p. 228). Certainly there was some political decentralization, and wealth was probably channelled into the production of funerary equipment for local rulers and their officials rather than being absorbed by royal pyramids. However, there are grounds to believe that the demise of the centralized culture of the Old Kingdom might actually have brought with it significant benefits, such as the development of a healthy cultural diversity in the regions, combined with a greater propensity for technological innovation. Wheel-made pottery, for instance, had been introduced in the Old Kingdom but it only became standard as a result of provincial experimentation during the First Intermediate Period. A wide range of new types of funerary objects also became popular in provincial burials. Previously the grave-goods belonging to poorer individuals had been selected entirely from the kinds of objects used in daily life, but in the First Intermediate Period many objects made purely for funerary use appear.

The end of the great pyramid-building epoch is only a total calamity if we look at it through the eyes of the pharaohs. Seen from the point of view of those who had been excluded from the favoured royal entourage during the 3rd to the 6th Dynasties, the demise of the Old Kingdom would almost certainly have represented an opportunity for social advancement and economic improvement, as power and wealth were more evenly distributed through the country.

The emergence of powerful local rulers such as Ankhtify of Moalla, however, would have ensured that this was not a democratic revolution. Political power remained in the hands of an elite, who were now simply spread throughout the country rather than clustered around the king at Memphis. In other words, the end of the Old Kingdom was probably more about devolution than revolution.

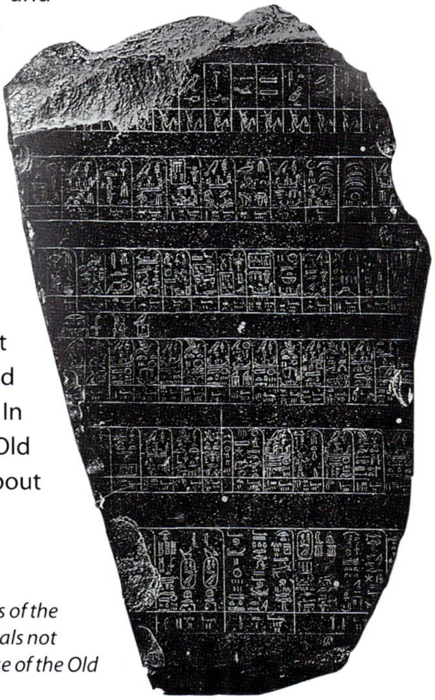

The Palermo Stone summarizes the reigns of the earliest pharaohs through religious festivals not politics, so it reveals little about the demise of the Old Kingdom.

53 The First Intermediate Period – a dark age?

See now the transformations in people.
THE *ADMONITIONS OF IPUWER*, *c.* 1700 BC

The end of the 3rd millennium BC in Egypt is usually known as the First Intermediate Period but should perhaps be called instead the 'Era of the Regions'. Long-standing developments gradually elevated local officials to the status of rulers over small areas, and individual towns and districts grew in importance, sometimes supporting their own armies. Artifacts from one region become distinct from those of others, whether in writing (both the forms of signs and structure of texts), in phraseology (references to local gods) or in archaeology (from ceramics to

tomb-architecture). At this time the kingship was probably defined not through a place of royal residence but through the ruling family, so the kings of Egypt, based in Herakleopolis, were known as the 'house of the Khety' after the first of their line. However, contemporary evidence indicates that local rulers felt more obligated to their own region. In the archaeological record and in tomb inscriptions of the time, an almost feudal system becomes apparent. Presumably therefore, the kings at Herakleopolis exercised only a loose sovereignty over much of Egypt.

Causes of change

Climate change and especially fluctuations in the height of the Nile flood are often suggested as being of great significance for the Era of the Regions (p. 224). Increasing aridity is linked to famine in the funerary inscriptions of local rulers, and is a ubiquitous metaphor, as seen for instance in the inscription from the tomb of Ankhtify at Moalla:

This whole country has become
As locusts in the drought:
One travels upstream, the other downstream.

Admittedly, personal interests and the conventions of writing colour these texts, but some genuine historical background to such images seems possible. Any climatic challenges were probably answered on the local level by local rulers through an intensification of the practice of storing reserves and the extension of the irrigation system. Certainly, the earliest references to the introduction of a type of farming known as basin-economy come from just this time.

Tomb models from Asyut showing the large military forces that were at the disposal of the local ruler, Mesekhty. On the opposite page is a troop of Nubian mercenary archers, below are Egyptian spearmen.

Right *Drawing of the stela of Sobknakht and his wife Khuyt from Gebelein. The hieroglyphic inscription contains just the offering formula and the names. The couple belong to a social group which had no funerary monuments in the Old Kingdom.*

Below *Montuhotep smiting foreigners and an Egyptian, probably his opponent from Herakleopolis, depicted in a frieze from the temple of Hathor in Gebelein.*

The three main chronological phases of this period can be summarized as follows: first, the end of the 6th to the 8th Dynasties – the end of the Old Kingdom and the beginning of the Era of the Regions (or First Intermediate Period); second, the 9th to mid-11th Dynasties (*c.* 2125–2000 BC) – the high-point of the Era of the Regions; and third, the 11th Dynasty, from the reunification of the country to the early 12th Dynasty (from around 2000 BC onwards), which marks the end of the Era of the Regions and the beginning of the Middle Kingdom.

In political terms these correspond closely to three significant developments: the death of Pepy II, and the division of Egypt into smaller domains with a loose kingship based at Herakleopolis; the promotion of the rulers of Thebes to the kingship of their local territory, and the subsequent rivalry between the two power-blocks – Thebes vs. Herakleopolis; and the victory of the Thebans and the reunification of Egypt under Montuhotep II between *c.* 2032 BC and 1994 BC.

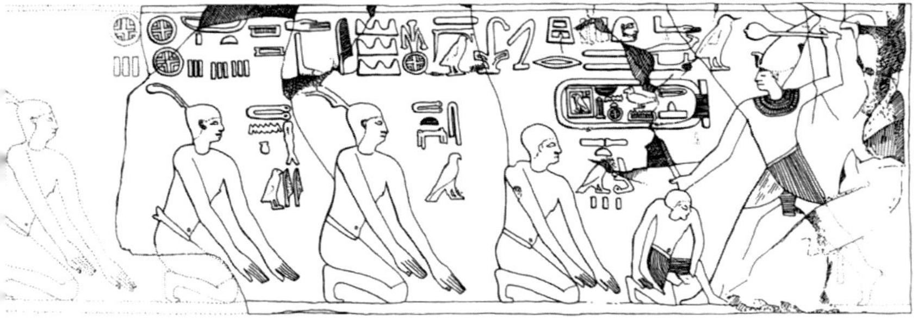

A dark age?

In later times, this era was remembered in history and literature as a dark age, as in the following couplet from a poem dating from the Middle Kingdom, the *Prophecy of Neferti* (possibly *c.* 1900 or *c.* 1700 BC):

The country is reduced,
Its rulers are increased.

While the implication here of the dissipation of power may correspond to the actual historical situation, it is obviously intended more to show that things were different – and better – at the time of the writer. It is important to recognize that the contemporary sources were written from the perspective of local power-brokers, whereas in later texts relating to this period it is central authority that came once more to the fore. Criticisms of the Era of the Regions are usually retrospective, as in the *Admonitions of Ipuwer*, *c.* 1700 BC:

In truth, the country spins round like a
potter's wheel,
The robber owns treasures,
[The servant becomes] the plunderer.

This partly mythical, partly historical statement can be understood as belonging to a tradition of writing which then stretches down as far as Manetho in around 300 BC. In his *Aegyptiaka*, Manetho records the following anecdote about the founder of the 9th Dynasty, in the middle of the Era of the Regions:

King Achthoes, behaving more cruelly than his predecessors, brought woes for the people of all Egypt, but afterwards he was smitten with madness, and was killed by a crocodile.

Clearly, an anti-Herakleopolis and pro-Thebes perspective has shaped the historical memory here: after all, it is the winners who write the history. Other influences also appear, in particular the Greek-educated Egyptian priest Manetho has combined an Egyptian motif (death by crocodile) with a Greek one (madness as divine punishment). Nevertheless, this passage belongs to a tradition of writing about the Era of the Regions reaching back more than one-and-a-half millennia.

Contemporary art and literature

Traces found in art and texts from the end of the 3rd millennium show that the way people saw themselves differs radically from the perception of Egyptians living later, especially in the Middle and New Kingdoms. Later authors, members of the elite, developed the tradition of the dark age for their own purposes: the Era of the Regions became a mythical representation of chaos, and served as a legitimization of the state with only Pharaoh at its pinnacle. Funerary inscriptions from the Era of the Regions, however, contrast chaos elsewhere with the security and maintenance of their own region, as for instance in the Stela of Merer of *c.* 2050 BC:

Though fear had arisen elsewhere,
Meanwhile I stabilized this town.

Nevertheless, occasionally major conflicts within Egypt are suggested, as in the Stela of Heqaib, *c.* 2050 BC:

I am a master of (my) heart in turmoil,
Whereas normally everyman shuts his door.

This formulation, however, assumes particular importance for this text because 'master (*heqa*) of my heart (*ib*)' is a pun on the name of this official – Heqaib.

For a long time Egyptologists adopted the view of the Egyptians of later periods. E. Meyer (1855–1930) first saw the period between the 8th and 12th Dynasties as an era in its own right, and understood it, on the basis both of the ancient sources and his own view of history, as a transitional dark age. Gradually, however, the tension has become apparent between the contemporary and the later sources relating to this time. In the light of present-day research, the 'Era of the Regions' seems less 'dark' and rather more diverse and interesting.

Measured by the standards of the Old Kingdom, the last two centuries of the 3rd millennium exhibit a decline in art and craft, and major monuments in the pharaonic tradition are certainly lacking. On the other hand, people from social groups that are nameless to us in the Old Kingdom emerge from the shadows.

This is not only a vagary of history but indicates a dramatic cultural and social transformation. In funerary inscriptions, changes in society are a key topic. So, the Era of the Regions, unspectacular at first sight, created genuine intellectual, economic and social currents which led to a lasting transformation of Egypt.

Relief from the tomb of Ankhtify of Moalla (p. 227). The tomb owner is shown with the attributes of the high elite (staff, sceptre, collar).

54 The end of the second pyramid age

... darkness descends upon the historical scene, leaving discernible in the twilight little beyond royal names ...
ALAN GARDINER, 1961

The pyramid of Amenemhat III at Hawara – the last major pyramid complex in Egypt.

The demise of the Middle Kingdom – the second pyramid age – occurred at the end of Manetho's 13th Dynasty, but Egypt had probably already been in a state of slow decline for many generations since the peak of the Middle Kingdom in the late 12th Dynasty, around 1860 BC. The study of the last two hundred years of the Middle Kingdom is highly controversial, involving the interpretation of a complex and often tenuous web of evidence.

Although the 13th Dynasty evidently continued to rule from the same capital as the 12th

Dynasty – Itjtawy, near Lisht – there appear to have been a large number of rulers with very short reigns, none of whom were in power for long enough to construct funerary complexes on anything like the same scale as their predecessors. Six 13th Dynasty royal tombs have survived: five of them are very small pyramid complexes at the southern end of the Memphite necropolis, while the sixth is merely a shaft-tomb located within the earlier pyramid enclosure of Amenemhat III. The names of numerous 13th Dynasty rulers are inscribed on stelae and statues throughout Egypt, as well as on blocks among the remains of Upper Egyptian temples, suggesting that many aspects of the centralized Middle Kingdom political system survived almost intact. In addition, the material culture and the administrative and social systems of the late 12th and 13th Dynasties seem to have been relatively homogeneous. However, there are also signs of change, heralding the arrival of the so-called Second Intermediate Period.

Viziers or kings?

It is indicative of the great uncertainty surrounding political matters in the 13th Dynasty that the American Egyptologist W. C. Hayes once argued that it was the viziers who held the real political power at this date, while the kings became temporarily less important. However, Stephen Quirke has pointed out that Iymeru Neferkare, one of the two most prominent 13th Dynasty viziers, along with Ankhu, was actually contemporary with the best-attested king of the dynasty, Sobkhotep IV. He also argues that Ankhu, although very powerful, still seems to have drawn his authority from the reigning king, and, contrary to Hayes, held this position for only two reigns and not five. Finally, Quirke points out that there were equally influential

Wooden statue representing the royal ka *(spiritual double) of the 13th Dynasty ruler Awibre Hor, who was buried in a humble shaft-tomb within the pyramid enclosure of Amenemhat III at Dahshur. The pair of arms on the statue's head form the hieroglyphic sign meaning* ka.

Below left *Gold and green jasper heart scarab of Sobkemsaf II of the 17th Dynasty. One of the better-known rulers of the somewhat obscure Second Intermediate Period, Sobkemsaf had a rich burial at el-Tarif, Thebes.*

families of viziers and other high officials in the 18th Dynasty, for instance, but Egyptologists have not suggested that there was any diminution of royal ascendancy at that time.

As an alternative explanation for the rapid turnover of kings in the 13th Dynasty, Quirke suggests that there was a circulation of power among an elite, and that at this time, unlike the First Intermediate Period (p. 228), the city of origin of each new individual ruler or ruling family may have been more important than blood-links. His argument is that the father-son succession was not necessarily the only means of passing on the kingship, and that dynasties were probably defined as much by the location of the royal court as by family relationships between individual rulers.

Little detailed information has survived concerning the 13th Dynasty kings apart from numerous names in the Turin Royal Canon, a 'king-list' recorded on a fragmentary papyrus (see p. 223). The first three names (Khutawyre Wegaf, Sekhemkare-Khutawy and Sankhtawy-Sekhemkare) were followed by a period when the records of annual flood levels were not recorded (or at least no records have survived), thus leading some scholars to argue that the country may have experienced some form of political crisis. It is notable that late Middle Kingdom records of Nile flood levels at the Nubian fortress of Semna appear to show abnormally high levels of flooding (over 7m/23 ft higher than average 'modern' levels prior to the building of the Aswan dams), raising the possibility that climatic change might have caused severe agricultural and economic problems. It is possible, then, that as with the end of the great pyramid age (p. 224), environmental problems might have been just as influential as man-made factors.

Principal Rulers of Dynasties 13–17

13th Dynasty *c.* 1755–after 1650 BC
(Awibre) Hor
(Woserkare) Khendjer
(Sekhemresewadjtawy) Sobkhotep III
(Khasekhemre) Neferhotep I
Sahathor
(Khaneferre) Sobkhotep IV c.1725

14th Dynasty *c.* 1750–1650 BC
Minor rulers probably contemporary with 13th or 15th Dynasty

15th Dynasty (Hyksos) *c.* 1630–1539 BC
Salitis = Sheshi(?)
(Merwoserre) Iakebher
(Sewoserenre) Khyan *c.* 1600
Ienses/Iannas
(Aawoserre) Apophis *c.* 1570–1530
Khamudy *c.* 1530–1520

16th Dynasty 1650–1550 BC
Minor Hyksos rulers contemporary with 15th Dynasty

17th Dynasty *c.* 1630–1539 BC
(Nubkheperre) Inyotef VII
Sobkemsaf II
(Senakhtenre/Seqenenre) Taa *c.* 1560
(Wadjkheperre) Kamose *c.* 1545–1539

Stela of Wepwawetemsaf, from Abydos. This late 13th Dynasty ruler is shown at the bottom left of the stela. He may only have ruled over Middle Egypt, since this is the only surviving text dated to his reign.

Political fragmentation

During the 13th Dynasty there is some evidence for deterioration in the control of Egypt's borders, resulting in a relaxation of the Egyptian grip over Nubia. Ironically, it was during the one phase of relative centralization and stability in the 13th

Dynasty (under Neferhotep I, Sahathor and Sobkhotep IV, *c.* 1750–1720 BC) that the first signs of revolt emerged in Lower Nubia, which soon afterwards was annexed by Kushite rulers based at Kerma. The border with western Asia also became vulnerable, and by the mid-17th century BC the 15th Dynasty, a sequence of at least six strong rulers of Asiatic origin known as the 'Hyksos' (p. 162), had evidently gained power in the eastern Delta. It was the Hyksos who sounded the death knell of the Middle Kingdom, no doubt rapidly driving the indigenous 13th Dynasty rulers out of Itjtawy. From this point until the beginning of the New Kingdom, Egypt was politically divided into northern and southern spheres, dominated by Hyksos and Theban rulers respectively.

Left *Gold coffin of King Nubkheperre Inyotef VII, from his tomb at el-Tarif, Thebes. He was the first 17th Dynasty ruler to begin to pose a threat to the Hyksos.*

The evidence for a gradual process of political fragmentation in the late 13th Dynasty takes the form of the surviving names of the 14th and 16th Dynasty rulers. Manetho's history always implies that dynasties run sequentially, one after the other, but it is clear that there are several periods in Egyptian history when dynasties overlap significantly. This seems to be the case with the many 14th and 16th Dynasty rulers either listed in Manetho's history and the Turin Royal Canon, or named on contemporary scarabs.

These lesser rulers, some of whom appear to have Asiatic names, are assumed to have controlled small city-states, probably mainly in the Delta region, at the same time as the 13th and 15th Dynasties (see chronological chart, opposite). Thus, both the Egyptian rulers of the late Middle Kingdom and the Hyksos rulers of the Second Intermediate Period seem to have tolerated the existence of many lesser kinglets, perhaps operating within a kind of federal system.

The precise mechanisms underlying the decline of the second pyramid age are not known, but what seems to have happened was a fairly rapid process of political fragmentation in the late 13th Dynasty, involving the division of the Delta and perhaps also part of Middle Egypt into a number of small independent kingdoms. This political disintegration probably weakened the 13th Dynasty kings to such an extent that they were unable to prevent the Hyksos 15th Dynasty from seizing power in the Delta (by invasion, long-term immigration or a combination of the two). This in turn caused the indigenous Egyptian court to move south to Thebes, where it was effectively re-invented as the 17th Dynasty, which would eventually become powerful enough to defeat the Hyksos and re-unite the country in the New Kingdom.

Red granite life-size seated statue of Sobkhotep IV, one of the last rulers of the Middle Kingdom. It was probably during his reign that the Hyksos 15th Dynasty established their capital at Avaris.

Did the Egyptians go to sea?

I had gone to the mining region of the sovereign.
I had gone down to the sea in a boat 120 cubits long and 40 cubits broad,
in which were 120 sailors from the choicest of Egypt.
They looked at the sky, they looked at the land,
and their hearts were stouter than lions.
They could foresee a storm before it came, a tempest before it happened,
but a storm came while we were at sea, before we could reach land.
THE *TALE OF THE SHIPWRECKED SAILOR*, c. 1850 BC

It has many times been claimed that the ancient Egyptians would not go to sea. But this is a question with a plain answer: the ancient Egyptians did indeed traverse the surrounding seas. In fact, they were very familiar with the water-borne environment, not least because pharaonic civilization was defined by the peculiar characteristics and dynamics of the Nile. Still, there are considerations to bear in mind in order to appreciate the complex relationship of attraction and rejection that the Egyptians maintained with the seas.

Typically, there are three motives which force a community to go beyond its borders. First is population pressure. Second is a lack of essential raw materials that are present in neighbouring areas, which will lead to the creation of stable commercial routes. Third is the threat of powerful enemies, forcing elements of the community to seek a less dangerous place to live. None of these apply to ancient Egypt, but this does not mean that the Egyptians did not embark on long-distance navigation.

A relief depicting boats from the temple of Sahure at Abusir (5th Dynasty). The experience with river navigation, necessary in a country where the main route was the Nile, served to familiarize the ancient Egyptians with the technical problems related to sailing in other waters.

Byblos and Punt

The Mediterranean route linking the Nile Delta with the Syrian coast was known and established at least from the Old Kingdom. Byblos in particular was the arrival point of important caravan routes from far-away lands (p. 181) and was also the provenance of most of the wood, particularly cedar, employed in Egypt in manufacturing crucial objects such as sarcophagi. This activity is evidenced as early as the Palermo Stone (see p. 227), which mentions 40 ships loaded with cedar reaching Egypt during the reign of Snofru (4th Dynasty).

Slightly later are the decorations of the funerary temple of Sahure at Abusir (5th Dynasty), in which seafaring ships are depicted in great detail with what seems to be a mixed crew of Egyptian and Asiatic sailors. In later times the importance of trade with Byblos resulted in seafaring ships being known as *kebnut* ('Byblos-boats').

In addition to the Mediterranean seaway, from the Old Kingdom Egyptians also frequented the route that took them southwards through the Red Sea to the almost-mythical land of Punt (p. 173) in pursuit of incense, precious woods, ivory and other luxury products. Mentions of these expeditions can be found from the reign of Sahure and Pepy II (6th Dynasty).

Middle and New Kingdom journeys

During the Middle Kingdom representations of naval expeditions are scarce, but there are literary tales such as the *Story of the Shipwrecked Sailor*. The sailor, shipwrecked during a storm in the Red Sea, arrives at a fantastical island where a gigantic talking snake prophesies his safe return home. The story emphasizes that seafaring in Egyptian mentality had gone beyond the mere transport of goods and had become an important cultural phenomenon. In this context, the author of the 12th Dynasty text known as the *Admonitions of Ipuwer* complained that nobody sailed anymore to Byblos to bring the precious merchandise normally imported from there.

During the Middle Kingdom, the abundance of elements made of quality wood points without doubt to increasing contact with the Byblos. This may be reflected in the later myth of Osiris

The expedition to Punt: a relief from the mortuary temple of Hatshepsut at Deir el-Bahri. The ancient Egyptians reached distant countries which provided them with products they needed or desired, as long as they could reach them without losing sight of land.

floating all the way to Byblos inside the wooden coffin which Seth has tricked him into entering. Also from this period a port has been identified in the Red Sea at Mersa Gawasis, where anchors, shrines and remains of ship-building activities have been found. This port was very probably used as the departure point for the expeditions to Punt.

Ahmose, son of Ibana, portrayed in his tomb at el-Kab. Ahmose was an officer in the Theban navy at the time of the defeat and expulsion of the Hyksos at the beginning of the New Kingdom, during the reign of the pharaoh Ahmose.

During the Second Intermediate Period contacts between the Nile Delta and the Syrian-Palestinian coast probably increased due to the cultural and ethnic affinity between the elites of both areas, now that the Hyksos kings controlled access to the eastern Mediterranean from Egypt (p. 162). A reflection of this is the claim of the Theban king Kamose, on a stela in which he narrates a military campaign against Avaris, to have looted hundreds of ships loaded with cedar, lapis lazuli, silver, turquoise and 'all the precious products of Asia'. For the Theban kings at the beginning of the New Kingdom, the seaways were a priority, and Thutmose I reopened the Egypt-Byblos route, campaigning aggressively in Syria to achieve this. Likewise, his daughter Hatshepsut reopened the route to Punt, according to the decoration of her funerary temple at Deir el-Bahri showing a flotilla of five sea-going ships in a series of magnificent scenes.

A watery chaos

Evidence of long-distance navigation from the New Kingdom and later periods abounds. Although it is usually restricted to the two key destinations of Byblos and Punt, there is the intriguing story in Herodotus of the 26th Dynasty pharaoh Necho sending a fleet to circumnavigate Africa (p. 254). This raises the question, why did the Egyptians not establish overseas colonies? This is best answered by the great reluctance of ancient Egyptians to stay away from their country, and this has an unexpectedly profound dimension. Religious texts maintained that the world was created out of a watery chaos. Hence an Egyptian would be afraid of the sea, just as he would be terrified of dying without a tomb, because water is completely the opposite of a grave: it is an ever-changing realm without precise location or co-ordinates. Criminals and enemies would be cast in the waters of the river, and so denied the possibility of an eternal, ongoing existence offered by the rock-cut tomb.

The experience of navigation for the ancient Egyptians began with the Nile and riverine navigation – constant, predictable, controllable and, above all, always in sight of land. Their maritime routes were simple and essentially point to point, so their voyages apparently tried not to lose sight of the coast. The simple possibility of vanishing in this aquatic environment and dying without a tomb in the solid ground of Egypt was one which surely shaped their naval activity abroad. Nevertheless, despite claims to the contrary, it never did keep the ancient Egyptians off the seas.

Did Egypt rule Palestine?

56

His Majesty marched on a foreign land – Shechem is its name.
STELA OF KHUSOBK, *c.* 1830 BC

From the 4th millennium BC onwards relations between Egypt and Palestine were frequently close, though they varied dramatically in nature and intensity through time. The quality of our sources and the limited amount of information, however, available make it difficult to paint a complete and systematic picture of Egyptian and Palestinian relations, and the question of whether Egypt directly ruled Palestine is a difficult one.

Trading partner and cultural model

By the late 4th millennium there is evidence of widespread trading between the two countries. Egyptian finds in Sinai and southern Palestine in particular suggest a trading network with key centres in Palestine such as En-Besor. In the other direction, many ceramics imported from Palestine have been found in the tombs of early Egyptian rulers.

On the threshold of the 3rd millennium, it was Egyptian culture that provided the model for southern Palestine, and there are even sporadic examples of hieroglyphs being used in the region. One particularly interesting find is a limestone fragment from the Early Bronze Age city of Arad in the Negev, on which a swallow has been carved into a piece of local stone: this may be interpreted as the Egyptian hieroglyph for 'chief' (Egyptian: *ur*). If so, the symbol used for a local ruler was borrowed directly from the Egyptian model. There are other examples of this cultural dependence – for instance, imitations of Egyptian hieroglyphs in local pottery, such as inscriptions with the name of King Narmer (p. 28). It is clear, then, that during the Predynastic and Early Dynastic periods, Egypt was not only a trading partner with Palestine, but was also a cultural model.

Early military campaigns

Thanks to royal mortuary temples and various other funerary inscriptions, we have evidence of Egyptian trading expeditions to Palestine as well as isolated military campaigns. There are two areas of activity that are of particular interest. Mining, which the Egyptians carried out in the Sinai Peninsula, might have led to intensified conflicts with the peoples they called 'Asiatics' (*aamu*) and 'sand-dwellers' (*heru-sha*). And second is the earliest evidence of trade by sea to northern Palestine, with Byblos the most prominent port of call. There must have been many

Pottery fragment from Arad, in Palestine, inscribed with the name of Narmer, the 1st Dynasty king of Egypt.

Opposite above *Thutmose III of the 18th Dynasty shown slaughtering his enemies in the Temple of Amun-Re at Karnak. Thutmose extended Egypt's military influence in the wider world far further than any previous king.*

dramas arising out of these Egyptian activities, but there are few specific records. However, the funerary stela of Pepyankh (6th Dynasty) tells of a dead Egyptian being transported home from southern Palestine, and of a punitive expedition against a group of 'Asiatics'. One couplet gives a laconic description of the cause:

Moreover, the Asiatics among the sand-dwellers butchered both men,
together with the troops who were with them.

The Palestinian connection is even reflected in names – for instance, a man from the eastern Nile Delta called his sons 'the Asiatic' and 'He who strikes (the land of) *rtnnw*'. The latter presumably refers to an Egyptian military campaign, and we may assume with some confidence that *rtnnw* is the oldest evidence we have of the name by which southern Palestine would later be known – Retjenu. However, for the subsequent First Intermediate Period, no evidence has so far come to light that the Egyptians were politically engaged in Palestine, which may well be due to the changed social and political situation in Egypt at that time (p. 228).

Diplomatic contacts

Under the rulers of the 12th Dynasty, Egypt turned its attention to Palestine once more. In addition to trade, there must also have been diplomatic contact, reflected by such diverse sources as the *Story of Sinuhe* – partly set in Palestine (p. 158) – and the 'execration texts'. These texts list the names of foreign places or people, and were often inscribed on pieces of pottery which were then smashed as a magical defence against any threat those places might have posed. There were also individual military campaigns, such as the one mentioned in Khusobk's report from the time of Senwosret III:

His Majesty marched on a foreign land – *skmm* is its name. Then *skmm* fell together with wretched Retjenu.

The idea that *skmm* may be identified with Shechem in central Palestine is made all the more plausible by the fact that this place-name is also mentioned in a more or less contemporary execration text. Evidently this must have been a fairly large city-state that also owned the surrounding territory, which was inhabited by a single tribe.

This is one of the few insights we have into the ruling structure of Palestine during the Middle Bronze Age, and also provides evidence of the temporary but direct influence now exercised by Egypt in central Palestine. It is not easy, however, to make complete sense of the execration texts, although they refer to other Palestinian cities and occasionally individual tribes. They do indicate precise geographical knowledge of Palestine, and denote both a degree of Egyptian ambition and fear of possible resistance. The monumental Annals of Amenemhat II also provide evidence of intercultural contact and Egyptian pretensions to rule there, while Egyptianizing scarabs found in Palestine are further archaeological proof of Egypt's cultural influence.

In the Middle Kingdom the city of Byblos was increasingly important to Egypt, through trading and possibly other interests. Egyptians did not have direct control over the Levantine coast, but the upper echelons of local society were strongly influenced by Egyptian culture in matters of language, art and architecture. The rulers of Byblos were portrayed in the classic Egyptian artistic style, and their names and titles were written in the Egyptian language using Egyptian hieroglyphs. The dependence of the upper classes of Byblos on Egyptian 'high culture' was considerably greater than elsewhere in the ancient world.

Statue of Ramesses II found at Beth Shean, the main centre of Egyptian administration in Palestine.

War and peace

The era of the Hyksos brought the rule of 'Asiatics' over a large part of Egypt (p. 162). It is likely that their dominance also spread as far as southern Palestine, although the adjacent northern part of Palestine had little more than a trading relationship. In Egypt, the rule of the Hyksos collapsed after war with the native Thebans in the second half of the 16th century, and left the way clear for Egyptians to march on Palestine.

During the Late Bronze Age Syria-Palestine consisted of a network of fortified city-states, in the midst of which outlaws (*'abiru*) formed themselves into gangs (p. 283). There was Egyptian authority of some kind in the region, although the archaeological, pictorial and textual material is not sufficient to allow us any detailed knowledge of its nature and extent.

In prolonging the wars against the Hyksos for military and – not least – ideological reasons,

Left *Base of a statue from Megiddo, inscribed in Egyptian with the names of Ramesses IV. What such a monument implies about Egyptian control of that city is disputable.*

the Egyptians of the 18th and 19th Dynasties launched many campaigns against Syria-Palestine. These took Thutmose III as far as the River Euphrates in Syria, and he led a large number of incursions into Palestine. There are innumerable representations of battles waged during the 18th and 19th Dynasties, demonstrating Egypt's military supremacy in the Levant. However, the region was never integrated into the Egyptian state. Diplomatic relations are shown in a very different light by the Amarna archive, the correspondence between the pharaohs and the other great powers of the day, as well as local Palestinian rulers.

The Egyptians did build bases in Palestine, especially in Beth Shean, where there was an Egyptian governor whose palace is still preserved today. Two royal stelae of Sety II have also been excavated in Beth Shean. Their lengthy carved inscriptions contain – with very different emphases – a eulogy of the king as well as a sort of historical report. The latter gives a stereotyped account of the Egyptian troops crushing a local rebellion.

Stela of Sety II from Beth Shean. The king is shown presenting an offering to the sun god Re-Horakhty. The text contains royal propaganda with reference to local events.

Even if the region of Palestine was not incorporated into the Egyptian state, it is certainly possible to say that during part of the 18th and 19th Dynasties Egypt did rule over Palestine. As a defining moment, in the 13th century the interests of Egypt and of the increasingly powerful Hittites came into direct conflict in Palestine. Eventually the borders of the influence of the two empires were fixed by treaty in the aftermath of the Battle of Qadesh (p. 243).

In Egyptian perception, as well as in that of outsiders, Egypt by the reign of Ramesses II was a great power, with a pre-eminent political and cultural influence over Syria-Palestine. Under the later Ramessids, however, this declined considerably. There are a few places in Palestine where inscriptions bearing the name of Ramesses VI suggest the last remnants of direct pharaonic influence .

Waning influence

The invasion of Palestine by Shoshenq I in the late 10th century BC is apparently mentioned in the Old Testament (p. 289). His great victory stela erected at Megiddo is the main evidence of his campaign, but it is actually difficult to evaluate its importance. Certainly there was rich booty (especially the treasures from the king's house and the temple in Jerusalem), which was taken back to Egypt and helped to finance a major building project in Karnak. But it remains a mere episode and did not result in any lasting Egyptian dominance.

Egypt plays an important historical role in the Old Testament, and is referred to more than 700 times. These references are predominantly to an aggressive and dangerous superpower, which is accordingly symbolized as a crocodile. Soon, however, Egypt's influence lagged behind that of the other great powers of the day – the Neo-Assyrians, and subsequently the Babylonians.

Who won the Battle of Qadesh?

57

I found that Amun came when I called him, and gave me his hand, and I rejoiced; he called from behind, as if next to me: 'Forward, I am with you!'
RAMESSES II, FROM PENTAWER'S POEM ON THE BATTLE OF QADESH, c. 1275 BC

In the spring of his fifth year as king, around 1275 BC, Ramesses II led his African army to a showdown with an Asian coalition mustered by Muwatalli, the king of Hatti (the Hittites). The battle was to be fought at the crucial city of Qadesh, which controlled both the Orontes and the Beqaa valleys, the key routes along which trade flowed between the Mediterranean coast and Syria. Qadesh also lay at the most distant limit of influence for both Egypt and Hatti, and so, for sixty or more years, back to the reigns of Akhenaten in Egypt and Suppiluliuma I in Hatti, it had been the principal cause of conflict between the two superpowers of that era.

Crucially, on the eve of the battle, captured spies tricked the Egyptian generals into believing that the enemy coalition's forces had failed to turn up – for fear of Ramesses. As a result, the four brigades of Ramesses' army were strung out fording the Orontes, while the king, with his vanguard, was ambushed in camp by the full onslaught of the enemy. In the ensuing slaughter the tragedy for Egypt was near complete; but Ramesses' leadership, and the timely arrival of reinforcements, allowed him to fight out a brutal stalemate. Muwatalli too lost many of his people, including sons and his chiefs, and eventually, on the evening of the second day of the struggle, he

Ramesses II in hand-to-hand combat during the Battle of Qadesh, from his temple at Abu Simbel in Nubia. Although the king's courage is undoubted, his decision to trumpet this near defeat to the far ends of his domain has often perplexed modern commentators.

was obliged to let Ramesses and his troops withdraw. Nevertheless, Qadesh was lost from Egyptian control forever.

Ramesses' record of the battle

Qadesh is the first battle in history about which we have detailed knowledge, but therein lies the mystery. No account of the battle has survived from either Hatti or from Qadesh itself, whereas Ramesses II commissioned a monumental record for the walls of six of his greatest temples, and presumably others which have not survived. In addition, a poem was composed in celebration.

Seal of Muwatalli: he sought to consolidate Hittite territorial gains in Syria, and fought Egypt to a standstill at the Battle of Qadesh.

Below *Expansion of the Hittite empire from the reign of Suppiluliuma I until the Battle of Qadesh.*

Why did Ramesses wish to immortalize a battle in which he had nearly been killed, alongside hundreds of his countrymen, in which the judgment of his generals had been dangerously inadequate, and from which his army had scrambled to an undignified withdrawal? Did Ramesses really suppose that he had won the day? If not, why did he pay so little attention to the many victories he undoubtedly won in the years before and after Qadesh?

One traditional explanation has been to regard Ramesses' response as petulant bombast and vainglory. Unable to countenance humiliation, Ramesses believed he could rewrite history by proclaiming over and again that the battle had been a personal triumph. This conceit would seem to accord with a king who erected massive statues of himself throughout Egypt, perhaps most notably at Abu Simbel, and was – according to an entirely unproven popular tradition – the pharaoh who enslaved the Israelites (p. 277; as embodied by Yul Brynner in Cecil B. De Mille's 1956 film *The Ten Commandments*). In John Wilson's influential opinion 'the arrogant bellowing of victory comes as an insincere ostentation similar to the bloated bulk of Ramesses II's monu-

ments or to his shameless appropriation of the monuments of his ancestors'. A more measured response is that the public proclamation was intended to embarrass the military who had so failed the king, a policy that could perhaps have been politically advantageous in the years following the end of the Hittite wars. However, both explanations fall down on many counts, not least because the Qadesh reliefs were inscribed in sacred precincts, where very few people would actually be able to see or make sense of them.

As Boyo Ockinga has pointed out, a more generous explanation would accept that the king's personal valour and leadership were genuinely heroic, and especially that there is sincere humility in his thanksgiving to the god Amun-Re for his deliverance on the battlefield. After all, this relationship lay at the heart of what kingship meant during the New Kingdom: the king was the brave and loyal child of the gods on this earth, and in return he was granted their unfailing protection (p. 192). The Battle of Qadesh proved to be a dramatic demonstration of the truth of this belief, for only Ramesses' faith and the intervention of Amun-Re could explain his escape from such a hopeless situation. This profound demonstration of religious truth is the obvious explanation of why the battle was enshrined in Ramesses' temples in preference to the king's many straightforward victories. Accordingly, the humiliating distress of pharaoh's army could not be whitewashed because it was integral to the story.

The terrible slaughter of men and horses – Hittite and Syrian – beside the River Orontes at Qadesh, as depicted in Ramesses' temple at Abydos.

The new order

So who did win the Battle of Qadesh? In an obvious sense, the clear victor was Muwatalli, who gained control of Qadesh, albeit at heavy cost. In the following years, Ramesses' armies were able to capture or recapture crucial regions, such as Amurru, as well as towns throughout the Orontes Valley, but Qadesh always eluded his grasp. However, both Egypt and Hatti recognized that the stand-off established at Qadesh was ultimately immovable. The largest, richest and most centralized nations in the known world had locked horns and could not be budged. Moreover, the Syrian and Palestinian chiefs skilled at exploiting political confusion were stirring up dissent, and the expansionist regime of Shalmaneser I in Assyria had emerged as a mutual threat.

Above *The Egyptian version of the peace treaty with Hatti, surrounded by images of war, in the temple of Karnak.*

Right *Tablet bearing the Hittite version of the peace treaty with Egypt, from the archives of the Hittite palace at Hattusas.*

In the 21st year of his reign, Ramesses II therefore agreed with the new Hittite king, Hattusili III, to divide their areas of influence over the Syrian trade routes, an agreement formally recognized in a written treaty. In later years Ramesses II also took two Hittite princesses as wives, according to the established protocol of diplomatic alliances: the kings of Egypt and Hatti were thereby confirmed as brothers. The Egyptian version of the peace treaty was inscribed on a monumental wall in the Temple of Amun-Re at Karnak, surrounded by the Qadesh reliefs, in order to celebrate the intervention of the gods in the affairs of men. In a sense, the treaty confirmed that Ramesses II had lost a battle but not the war: the crucial trade routes, including those passing through Qadesh, continued to convey the economic goods Egypt required without interruption. Above all, the divinely inspired peace on which this new order was founded would last for a century, until the collapse of the Hittite empire.

What became of Egypt's Golden Empire?

58

As for Pharaoh, how will he get to this land?
Because, as for Pharaoh, whose boss is he anyway?
LETTER FROM THE EGYPTIAN GENERAL PIANKH, *c.* 1080 BC

Under the glorious rulers of the New Kingdom, Egypt was once more reunited after the period of Hyksos rule (p. 162) and soon rose to become the richest and most powerful nation on Earth. Its kings believed that their rightful domain was a kingdom along the entire length of the Nile, which they called 'Black Land' (*kemet*). So the kingdom of Kush to the south – Egypt's only genuine rival along the Nile – was repeatedly battered, first by Kamose in the mid-16th century BC and then by every pharaoh for a hundred years, until it finally capitulated to Thutmose III. As a result, Nubia fell under Egyptian control for more than four centuries, and Egypt's armies exploited its gold-laden deserts on a scale far beyond anything attempted previously.

The armies of Thutmose III and his son, Amenhotep II, then demonstrated by force of arms that Egypt also intended to take full advantage of the crucial sea-borne and overland trading routes across the Levant. Egypt's rivals in the region, Mitanni and Qadesh, were humiliated on battlefields across Palestine and Syria, and caravan routes transporting goods from Byblos, Babylon,

The temple of Ramesses II at Abu Simbel in Nubia, symbol of Egyptian occupation during the New Kingdom. Ancient Nubia shared many patterns of life with Egypt, and its deserts were the richest gold-fields of North Africa.

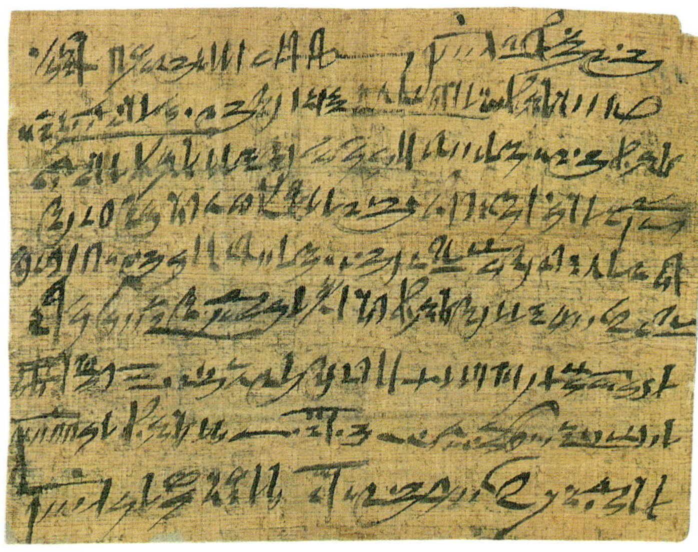

Left *Letter, quoted at the beginning, from Pharaoh's General, Piankh, to Thutmose, a scribe at Deir el-Medina, regarding the plot to murder policemen.*

Opposite *Silver and gold coffin of Psusennes I found at Tanis. This masterpiece might have been reused from the Valley of the Kings, but demonstrates that valuable materials were still available to Pharaoh even after the loss of Nubia.*

Below *Fragmentary statue of Osorkon I, also inscribed in Phoenician for Elibaal, king of Byblos. Relations between Egypt and Byblos outlasted the New Kingdom.*

Assyria and the world beyond were flung 'beneath the sandals' of the pharaohs.

In the 19th Dynasty a greater political and military threat to New Kingdom Egypt emerged in the form of the Hittite empire of Hatti, which nearly humiliated Ramesses II at the Battle of Qadesh (p. 243). However, in the end the two immovable superpowers were obliged to coexist peacefully until the 20th Dynasty when, during the reign of Egypt's Ramesses III, internal political tensions shattered the Hittite empire into its component states, like the Soviet Union at the end of the Cold War. Seemingly at this moment Egypt should have assumed the mantle of undisputed superpower. Instead, within a century she had lost control of Nubia and the mines which lay at the heart of its Golden Empire, the single event which can be said to mark the end of the New Kingdom. Why?

Collapse or decline?

Nubia was lost as the result of a civil war involving the most powerful figures in government at the end of the 20th Dynasty. In the reign of Ramesses XI, at the end of the 11th century BC, the armies of Panehsy, the Egyptian Viceroy of Nubia, occupied Thebes and confiscated temple-lands. We do not know whether or not Panehsy was originally acting with royal authority, but some seven years later the Pharaoh's General Piankh chased Panehsy's armies back to Nubia. Thereafter, Panehsy disappears from history, taking Nubia with him (p. 142). So was the loss of Nubia a political aberration or the result of a gradual decline in the authority of Egypt?

The monuments of the 20th Dynasty do seem unimpressive in comparison with the earlier New Kingdom, but this is not necessarily indicative of a decline in wealth or authority. Egyptian temples in Nubia, for example, were created for the threefold purpose of worshipping Egyptian gods, of enshrining the authority of kings, and of subjugating local territories to the Egyptian administration. This last point is crucial: Egyptian temples were powerful economic institutions with responsibility for administering huge swathes of the king's domain. The proliferation of temples in Nubia during the 18th and 19th Dynasties is the most dramatic archaeological testament to the expansion of Egyptian control. Nevertheless, by the 20th Dynasty, the infrastructure of control in Nubia had been effectively completed, and there was presumably little more to be added. Undoubtedly a vigorous Egyptian administration continued to govern Nubia right up to the war of Panehsy.

Some scholars also point to the absence of Egyptian monuments in Palestine during the 20th Dynasty, whereas in fact there had rarely been any such building. For example, putative Egyptian temples at sites such as Tell es-Saidiyeh and Lachish are actually local constructions. Certainly, no Egyptian temples were built in the Levant on the scale of those which towered over Nubia, and isolated Egyptian finds at places such as Byblos and Jerusalem can easily be explained

on the basis of cultural and diplomatic exchange. Hence a lack of Egyptian building in the Levant during the 20th Dynasty is not unexpected. The charming *Report of Wenamun* is also cited as proof of a decline in Egypt's prestige because it portrays a Theban priest at this time tormented by Levantine potentates. However, this work can also be interpreted as a fictional comedy about one man's mishaps abroad (p. 181).

Disunity or continuity?

Following the death of Ramesses XI two separate lines of kings emerged: in the north, the 21st Dynasty claimed the throne but abandoned the New Kingdom royal cemetery, the Valley of the Kings, opting instead to be buried in the temple of Amun-Re at their capital, Tanis (p. 95). At Thebes meanwhile the high-priests at Karnak occasionally assumed royal titles as well.

This situation can be – and usually is – explained as the breakdown of central authority in Egypt in the aftermath of the civil war of Panehsy. However, earlier generations of scholars did not appreciate that both lines of kings were often members of the same family, and that the Theban priests did not claim royal authority outside the sacred city of Thebes. Indeed, this ambiguous state of affairs was simply ended when a new family ascended the throne as the 22nd Dynasty.

The ruined temple of Amun-Re at Tanis. At the end of the New Kingdom, Tanis was created as a new royal residence and then royal cemetery. This marked a positive new beginning, not necessarily the decline of a nation.

In fact, if we disregard the Theban priest-kings, there was essentially one single line of kings in Egypt for 250 years after the end of the New Kingdom. Indeed, the most striking aspect of this era is that the 22nd Dynasty, who were Libyans by descent, ruled Egypt in the pharaonic manner, while their contemporaries as kings of Nubia, who were indigenous Nubians, also ruled in the pharaonic manner. The New Kingdom model of kingship thus held sway along the Nile long after the New Kingdom had passed away.

Likewise, the major achievement of an Egyptian army for which we have detailed evidence after the New Kingdom is strikingly reminiscent of the celebrated campaigns of Thutmose III and Amenhotep II. The list of 50 or more Palestinian towns defeated, according to reliefs at Karnak, by Shoshenq I (p. 289) can easily be interpreted as an attempt to confirm Egypt's long-standing authority over the trading routes of Palestine. Hence there is no compelling reason to suppose that royal authority in Egypt declined irretrievably during the 20th Dynasty, nor that Egypt's international prestige fell apart after the loss of Nubia at the end of the New Kingdom.

So how to explain the apparently seditious questions from General Piankh, quoted above, which is often cited as proof of the contempt in which Ramesses XI was held even by his own officials? In fact Piankh is writing about the need to murder two policemen at Thebes (the reason why is not made clear). Accordingly, he is simply pointing out to his – presumably anxious – co-conspirators that he is the king's representative in Thebes. In other words, if their crime is discovered, the king will ask Piankh himself to investigate it. So why worry? He is not confessing that Pharaoh no longer controls the land: only that some of his trusted officers have dark secrets.

The missing Apis bull burials

The operation had, however, the result that we were able to prove that the lower vault had been inhabited by three Apis whose graves, constructed with the same negligence as the upper chamber, supplied the only data on which to rely to assign the construction to a date near that of the Apis of Ramesses [XI].
AUGUSTE MARIETTE, 1855

Worship of the sacred Apis bull was an ancient cult at Memphis. Regarded as an incarnation of the creator-god, Ptah, only one sacred bull existed at any time. Each new Apis was identified by unique markings on its black hide, resembling a diamond on its forehead and a vulture on its shoulders. Apis also played a key role in the major festival of kingship, the *sed*-festival, during which the king would apparently run alongside the bull. This festival can be traced to the very beginning of Egyptian history, and so provides one of the oldest and most enduring images of the relationship between the king and the gods of Egypt.

Despite the antiquity of this cult, nothing is known about what happened when the sacred Apis died until the reign of Amenhotep III, in the first half of the 14th century BC. His eldest son, Thutmose, interred a bull at Saqqara, the royal cemetery of the city of Memphis, and the next seven Apis bulls were buried individually nearby. Then, on the same site, Ramesses II initiated the first phase of a massive underground complex of burial chambers for the Apis. Known to us as the Serapeum ('place of the Osiris Apis') – not to be confused with the Ptolemaic temple of the Hellenistic god Serapis – each bull was buried in royal splendour. Thereafter, the Serapeum vaults contain an almost unbroken sequence of bull

Life-size limestone statue of an Apis discovered by Mariette at Saqqara in 1851.

burials for more than one thousand years – until the very end of Egypt's independence under Cleopatra VII.

The missing burials

Almost unbroken – there seems to be a glaring gap of around two centuries, from Ramesses XI in the middle of the 11th century BC until Osorkon II in the early 9th, during the 21st and early 22nd Dynasties, a period for which we have no definite burials. Other sources indicate that the cult of Apis was still active at this time: so where are the bulls' burials? Intriguingly, this is also the time when there are breaks in the sequence of royal tombs at Tanis (p. 95). This coincidence has led certain authors to suggest that there might be major problems with the accepted chronology of this period.

Above *A block from the 'Red Chapel' at Karnak showing Hatshepsut running with the Apis. This formed part of the Jubilee ceremonies and seems to go back to 1st Dynasty times.*

Apis	Tomb	Date
I	A	Amenhotep III
II	B	Amenhotep III/IV
III	C	Tutankhamun
IV	D	Horemheb
V	E	Horemheb
VI	F	Sety I
VII	G	Ramesses II – Yr. 16
IX	G	Ramesses II – Yr. 30
	H	(canopic jars of Apis IX)
X	I	Ramesses II
XI	I	Ramesses II
XII	1 (?)	Ramesses II
XIV	K	Ramesses II
XIII	K	Ramesses II
19.9	2 (?)	Siptah
20.1	3 or L (?)	Ramesses III?
XV	L	Ramesses III
XVI	L (?)	Ramesses VI
XVII	M	Ramesses IX
XVIII	M	Ramesses XI (*c.* 1099–1069)
Problem Area		
XXI	N	Ramesses XI (?)
XXII	N	Ramesses XI (?) *Only 8 bulls for*
XXIII	N	Ramesses XI (?) *220–250 years*
XXIV	O	?
XXV	O	?
XXVI	O	?
XXVIII	?	Takelot I? – Yr 14? (*c.* 875)
XXVII	3?	Osorkon II – Yr 23 (*c.* 850)
22.x+3	3?	Shoshenq III
XXIX	P	Shoshenq III
XXX	P	Pimay
XXXII	Q	Shoshenq V
XXXIII	R	Shoshenq V
XXXIV=XXXV	S	Bocchoris/Shabaka
25.1	4?	Shabaka
	5?	Taharqa
XXXVI	T	Taharqa
XXXVII	T	Psamtek I
XXXVIII	U	Psamtek I
XXXIX	V	Necho II
XL	X	Apries
26.5	W	Amasis
XLI	Y	Amasis
XLII	Z	Cambyses
XLIV	B′	Darius I
XLV	C′	Darius I
XLIII	A′	Darius I
27.5	E′	Xerxes I or Artaxerxes I?
27.?	F′	Darius II
29.1	G′	Nepherites I
29.2	H′	Hakoris
30.1	I′	Nectanebo I
30.2	D′	Nectanebo II
XLVI	J′	Khababash
XLIX	L′	Ptolemy I
L	M′	Ptolemy II
LI	N′	Ptolemy II
LII	O′	Ptolemy III
LIII	P′	Ptolemy IV
LIV	Q′	Ptolemy V
LV	R′	Ptolemy VI
LVI	S′	Ptolemy VIII
LVII	T′	Ptolemy VIII
LVIII	U′	Ptolemy IX
LIX	V′	Ptolemy XII
LX	W′	Cleopatra VII
LXI	K′	Augustus?

Fourteen centuries of Apis burials.

Over the course of six centuries the original catacomb of Ramesses II, the 'Lesser Vaults', was extended northwards, with rooms opening on each side of a central corridor serving as burial chambers. The attribution of chambers to individual particular bulls seems straightforward until the end of the 20th Dynasty. Unfortunately, the loss of many of the records of Auguste Mariette, the discoverer of the Serapeum, makes it difficult to verify some of his attributions, and some seem certainly wrong. The problem becomes acute during the 30-year reign of Ramesses XI (*c.* 1099–1069 BC), to which Mariette allocates no fewer than four bulls. This sits uncomfortably with the 16- or 17-year average (and 26-year maximum) life-span of an Apis bull derived from later data, and it is therefore not unlikely that some or all of these bulls actually belong to the 21st Dynasty. Reattributing some of the burials could bring us into the reign of Psusennes I (*c.* 1040–995 BC), but would still leave some 130 years until the next firmly dated interment in Year 23 of Osorkon II.

Of the 'missing' burials, three were alleged by Mariette to lie in a mysterious chamber underneath chamber 'N', labelled by him as 'O', the excavation of which he abandoned because of its dangerous state. If these three problematic burials are the only ones unallocated, and if it is assumed that Apis XVIII died around the end of the first decade of Ramesses XI's reign, there would still only be seven or eight bulls for a period of approximately 225 years. These bulls would then have had an average life-span of over 28 years – rather in excess of possibility.

So there are certainly bulls missing from the record, and it seems unlikely that they were buried in any of the known chambers. It is not impossible that further rooms open from chamber 'O' since it lies below the level of the Lesser Vaults, but until this area has been properly investigated the suggestion remains speculative.

It is also possible that there was a temporary move of the bull cemetery during the 21st and 22nd Dynasties. Furthermore, four intact Apis burials were reported to have been found in the early 18th century, which it could perhaps be argued are evidence of a new vault. However, they had canopic jars, otherwise only known for Apis burials prior to the end of Ramesses II's reign, which suggests that they were actually chambers of the known Serapeum. Various deposits of bovine bones have been found at Saqqara, but none seems compatible with the 'lost' Apis bulls, which, for the time being at least, are destined to remain missing.

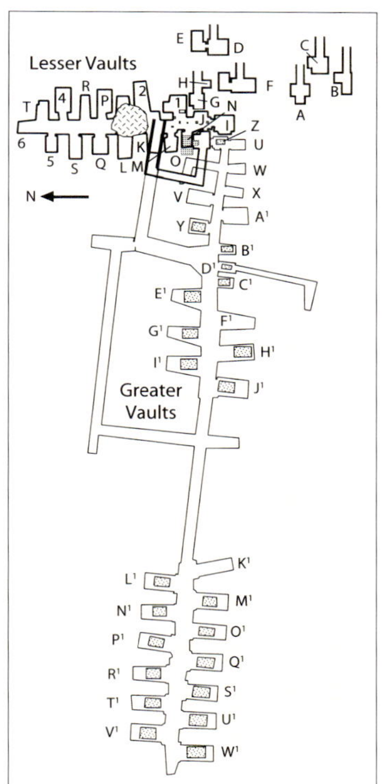

Above right *Plan of the galleries of the Serapeum at Saqqara. The Lesser Vaults were used from the time of Ramesses II down to the reign of Psamtek I.*

Right *Limestone stela marking the burial of Apis XXXVII in Year 21 of Psamtek I (642 BC), the last bull to be buried in the Lesser Vaults.*

60

Did Necho send a fleet around Africa?

As for Africa, we know that it is washed on all sides by the sea except where it joins Asia, as was first demonstrated, as far as I am able to tell, by the Egyptian ruler Necho.
HERODOTUS, *c.* 430 BC

The most famous legacy of the 26th Dynasty pharaoh Necho II is a tantalizingly brief story told by the Greek historian Herodotus of the mid-5th century BC, in which he says that Necho's fleet completed a circumnavigation of Africa – 2000 years before the Portuguese mariners of Vasco da Gama. Herodotus' anecdote is a favourite with those who claim that Columbus was not the first foreign explorer to reach the Americas. They argue that a ship or ships could have been separated from Necho's fleet and blown westwards across the Atlantic's narrowest part to the Brazilian coast. From there it was possible to sail north to the Mexican Gulf. On landing, colonies were set up that gradually dispersed Egyptian culture throughout Central and South America. This supposedly explains why ancient Egypt and some pre-Columbian civilizations have coincidental similarities, such as elaborate pyramid complexes and a 365-day solar calendar. So can there by any truth in Herodotus' anecdote?

Herodotus' story

According to Herodotus, Necho II ordered his Phoenician-crewed fleet to leave Egypt from the east via the Gulf of Suez, but to return via the Straits of Gibraltar at the Mediterranean's western mouth – in effect, to sail all the way around Africa

Relief of a Phoenician sea-going ship with two banks of oars (bireme), from the palace of Sennacherib at Nineveh, c. 700 BC. Did Necho's fleet consist of a similar kind of ship?

anticlockwise. The fleet duly sailed south into the Red Sea and down Africa's eastern coast. To support themselves on the long voyage, the sailors established temporary settlements on land and cultivated crops. Eventually, 'after two full years the Phoenicians rounded the Pillars of Hercules [the Straits of Gibraltar], and returned to Egypt that way in the course of the third'.

Herodotus wraps the story up with a surprising conclusion: 'the Phoenicians made a statement which I myself do not believe (though others may if they wish) to the effect that as they sailed west around the southern end of Africa, they had the sun on their right.' This is exactly what they would have seen going west around the Cape of Good Hope at the southern tip of Africa, because the sun appears to the right when travelling westward in the southern hemisphere. How could Herodotus have known this, unless the circumnavigation story was true?

For and against Herodotus

Superficially, most of Herodotus' story is plausible. The Phoenicians had been in contact with the Atlantic since the trading port of Gadir (modern Cadiz) was founded in about 800 BC. They had ships capable of sailing through the Straits of Gibraltar and along the North African coast, so a sea voyage around Africa would have been technically possible, especially since winds and currents favour east–west circumnavigation. Complex navigation would be unnecessary if the fleet kept the coast in sight, and the Egyptians certainly undertook sea journeys to Byblos, on the Levantine coast, and to Punt, via the Red Sea (p. 173). A two-and-a-half-year journey time sounds reasonable, too: the first historically documented circumnavigation of Africa under Vasco da Gama, who sailed from Lisbon in Portugal to Calicut in India, took 10 months in 1497–98.

Herodotus' story is also consistent with Necho II's foreign policy, which sought to benefit Egypt economically by improving access to sea-routes. Necho probably started the construction (or restoration) of a canal, 85 km (53 miles) long and wide enough for sea-going craft, connecting the Nile Valley with the Red Sea. This canal (a forerunner of the Suez) later became an internationally important trade route. There is also some evidence that Necho wanted to develop and consolidate Egyptian influence in lands to the south and east of Egypt.

None the less, the evidence for Herodotus is mostly circumstantial. It does not prove that Necho's fleet did circumnavigate Africa, merely that it would have been possible for it to do so. Other doubts creep in when one remembers that Herodotus' *Histories* is an elaborate piece of rhetorical writing. It is not an objective history, but a highly literary (and partisan) analysis of the culture clash between the Greek and Persian worlds. Herodotus has some respect for the Persians, but is convinced of Greek cultural superiority. His favourite technique for showing this is to devalue Persian achievements by emphasizing what other non-Greeks, especially Egyptians, can achieve, and the Necho story is an example of this. It comes directly after an account of a Persian king's failed expedition, and the message is clear: the Egyptians can do what the Persians cannot.

Herodotus also loves recounting stories of pharaohs solving difficult problems, thereby showing the depth of Egyptian wisdom – again, something the Persians could not match. Even the factoid of the sun appearing on the right instead of the left is characteristic of Herodotus' literary method, because one way he expresses non-Greekness is as the direct opposite of what is normal in Greece. Another example of this is his description of Egypt, in which he tells how Egyptian 'manners and customs seem to have reversed the ordinary practices of mankind' and gives many examples: such as writing from right to left instead of left to right, or doing in private what the Greeks do in public.

So there is as much evidence against Necho's fleet having sailed round Africa as there is for it; and taking Herodotus' account at face value shows the dangers of writing history using literary anecdotes taken out of context.

Bronze statue of Necho II. Few images of him survive because after his death he seems to have undergone some kind of execration. In the Bible, Necho is a warlike pharaoh who slays Josiah at Megiddo.

61 How did the Egyptians work granite?

... it is built of black stone ... which is brought from a great distance; for it comes from the mountains of Ethiopia, and being hard and difficult to be worked, the labour is attended with great expense.

STRABO, *c.* 20 BC

The ancient Classical authors all agree that one of the great achievements of the ancient Egyptians was to have gained mastery over so hard a stone as granite at such an early period in their history – the granite slabs paving the burial chamber of King Den at Abydos date back to the beginning of the 3rd millennium BC. Granite was the only one of the hard stones available in pharaonic Egypt for large-scale building projects (limestone and sandstone, used as widely, are softer).

From the 2nd Dynasty onwards granite was frequently used in temples (for door frames, columns and wall linings) and in royal tombs. The burial chambers and corridors of many pyramids, from the 3rd to the 12th Dynasty, were lined with pink granite. Some pyramids were also given granite external casing, such as that of Menkaure at Giza, as described by Strabo, above, or granite pyramidia, such as those of kings Amenemhat II and Khendjer at Dahshur and Saqqara. Granite was also regularly used from the Early Dynastic period onwards for many other purposes, such as statuary (from statuettes to colossi), sarcophagi, stelae, naoi (shrines), obelisks and small funerary vessels.

Granite is an igneous rock primarily made up of quartz and feldspar, and different types are distributed throughout the Eastern Desert and in the Nile Valley. Indeed the Nile 'cataracts', six rocky, fast-flowing sections of the river between Aswan and Khartoum, consist of granite outcrops. In the Nile Valley there are surviving traces of ancient granite quarries at Aswan and Tumbos. The Aswan quarries were worked from the Early Dynastic period to the Roman period, but most of the visible remains appear to be Ptolemaic or Roman. Numerous unfinished objects were abandoned in the quarries, including an 18th Dynasty obelisk and three colossal statues of apparently New Kingdom date. The Tumbos quarries, in modern Sudan, date from the 18th Dynasty through to the Meroitic period. An unfinished granite statue of an unidentified 25th Dynasty ruler still lies in situ at Tumbos.

Quarrying granite

The Aswan quarries are the only Egyptian hardstone workings that have been studied in any detail. It has been estimated, on the basis of surviving buildings and monuments, that around 45,000 cu. m (1,590,000 cu. ft) of stone were removed from the Aswan quarries during the Old Kingdom, though it seems likely that loose surface boulders would have been exploited in this period. It was in the New Kingdom, however, that the largest quantities of granite seem to have been quarried.

The most important source of information on Egyptian granite-quarrying for the pharaonic period is an 18th Dynasty 'unfinished obelisk', still lying in the northern quarries a few kilometres to the southeast of modern Aswan. The ancient quarrying force had already invested many thousands of hours in the extraction of this obelisk, nearly 42 m (138 ft) long, when it had to be abandoned because of the appearance of significant cracking.

This accident, however, means that the basic stages in the process of New Kingdom granite-quarrying are preserved for us. It appears that the workers began by removing the weathered upper layers of the granite, then cut a trench around the rough outline of the object, which would at this stage still have been attached to the bedrock. The trench is about 75 cm (30 in) wide and is divided into a series of 60-cm (24-in) wide working areas, each delineated by vertical red lines down the side of the trench. As many as 50 workmen could have been accommodated around the obelisk at any one time. The depth of the trenches was periodically assessed by overseers, who lowered cubit rods down the side of the trench, marking the tops of the rods with red triangles, most of which are still visible. Having achieved the required depth, the workers then began to undercut the object, but it is clear that this was only just beginning in the case of the unfinished obelisk. Presumably, the final stage would have been to quarry out the lower end of the obelisk completely, so that it could be pushed or pulled horizontally away from the bedrock (this is much easier than attempting to pull it vertically upwards out of the quarried trench).

Tools

There is some uncertainty as to the kinds of tools used for the quarrying of hard stone during the pharaonic period. Tool marks preserved on many soft stone quarry walls (such as the sandstone quarries at Gebel el-Silsila) suggest that some form of pointed copper alloy pick, axe or maul was used during the Old and Middle Kingdoms, and from the 18th Dynasty onwards a mallet-driven pointed chisel came into use. This technique, however, would have been unsuitable for the extraction of harder stones such as granite.

It was once thought, on the basis of long sequences of rectangular wedge holes at the Aswan quarries, that the granite was removed by inserting wetted wooden wedges into the holes and levering the blocks away from the bedrock. There are now two fundamental objections to this theory: first, wooden wedges, even when expanded by soaking them in water, would almost certainly not have the strength to fracture granite, and second, the wedge holes have never been dated any earlier than the Ptolemaic period, by which time iron wedges would have been available. Judging from various studies of the quarries at Aswan and experimental projects, the actual process of extraction in the pharaonic period seems to have involved the use of stone pounders (often dolerite, gneiss or basalt) gradually to remove the stone from the surface downwards in opencast quarries.

Opposite *Head and torso of a colossal statue of Ramesses II from the Ramesseum at Thebes (height 2.67 m). The head is cut from fine pink granite and the torso from black granodiorite, with a vein of the former cutting through the latter.*

Below *The unfinished obelisk at Aswan, showing the trenches of quarry-workers on either side, and, at the far end, the major flaw that caused it to be abandoned.*

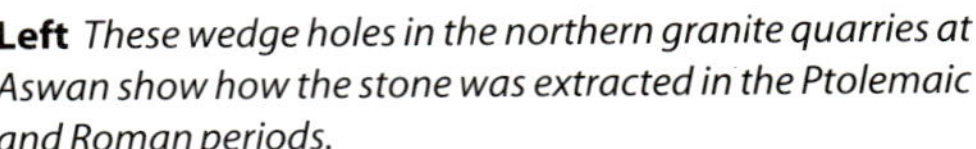

Left *These wedge holes in the northern granite quarries at Aswan show how the stone was extracted in the Ptolemaic and Roman periods.*

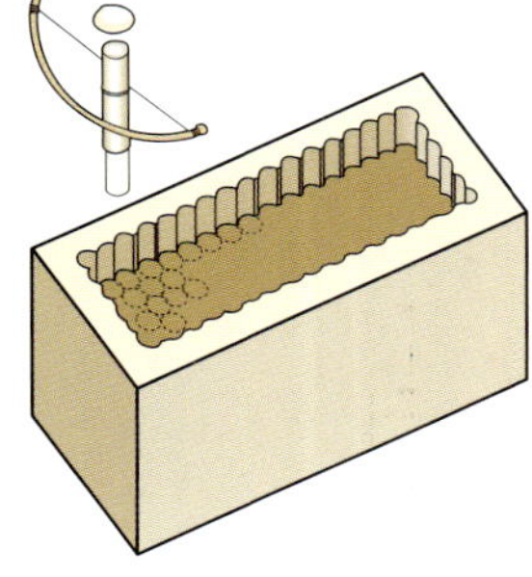

Reconstruction drawing showing the way in which the interior of Khufu's granite sarcophagus was drilled out using a copper drill, aided by copious quantities of sand.

Shaping granite

For many years there has been great debate concerning the techniques used by the ancient Egyptians to transform granite boulders or rough quarried blocks into fine objects such as sarcophagi or statues. Petrie found evidence of working with a combination of copper alloy saws and drills, some of which must have been huge: the copper tube used to drill out the interior of Khufu's granite sarcophagus, for instance, would have been 11 cm (4.3 in) in diameter. However, Petrie was at a loss to understand how these metal implements were given a sufficiently hard edge to cut through granite. He suggested that the saws and drills might have been provided with teeth of corundum or emery. The chemist Alfred Lucas, who analysed many of the objects in the Egyptian Museum, Cairo, in the 1920s and 1930s, was the first to advance the alternative theory (rejected by Petrie) that some kind of abrasive powder was used in combination with the metal cutting edges.

Because no actual drilling equipment or saws have survived, Egyptologists have until recently only been able to hypothesize on the basis of tomb-scenes or the marks left on surviving granite items. During the 1980s and 1990s, however, experimental work was undertaken by a British Egyptologist, Denys Stocks, which demonstrated clearly how the stone was worked. Recognizing that copper alloy alone would have worn away rapidly, Stocks experimented with the addition of quartz sand, poured in between the cutting edge of the drill and the granite so that the sharp quartz crystals gave the drill the necessary 'bite'. No special teeth were needed, only a steady supply of desert sand.

What tools did the Egyptians use for the finer carving, such as facial features on statues or the hieroglyphic inscriptions on the exterior surfaces of sarcophagi? Further experimental work undertaken by Stocks and other researchers has demonstrated beyond any reasonable doubt that such delicate carving was achieved with flint chisels, punches and scrapers, a good example of the way in which 'Stone Age' tools were still regularly used during the Bronze and Iron Ages.

The final polishing of carved stone items is depicted in tombs of various dates showing sculptors' workshops, such as the 5th Dynasty tomb of Ti at Saqqara and the 18th Dynasty tomb of Rekhmire at Thebes. The craftsmen are shown using large pebbles of hard stone, such as quartzite, in combination with abrasive quartz powder to achieve a smooth surface. As with the large-scale drilling and sawing of granite, it was the desert sand – something which the Egyptians had in abundance – that provided the most effective means of cutting through the stone. Egyptian agriculture has constantly been described as the gift of the Nile, but their precocious stone working was, in a sense, a gift of the desert.

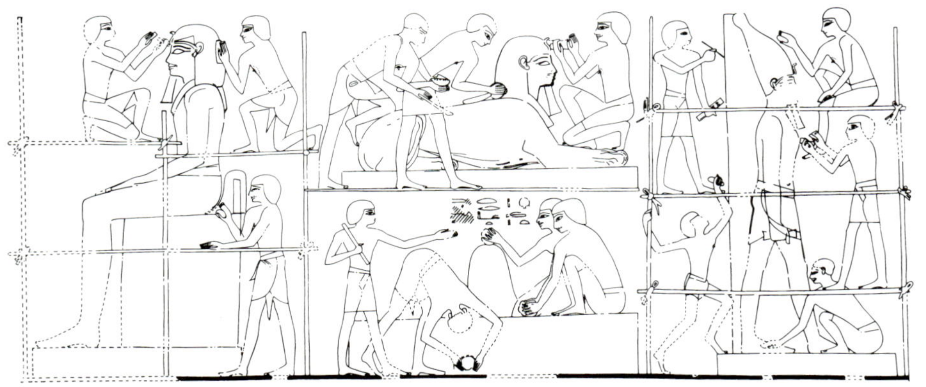

Below *Detail of a depiction of a New Kingdom sculptors' workshop in the 18th Dynasty tomb of Rekhmire at Thebes (TT 100).*

Did the Egyptians invent glass?

The new capital of Akhenaten needed a large amount of decorative work, and suitable factories sprang up.... The glazes and glass were the two principal manufactures, and in those lines under the impulse of the new art a variety and brilliance was attained, which was never achieved in earlier or later times.

W. M. Flinders Petrie, 1894

The simple answer to this question is 'no'. More interesting, however, is why did the question arise in the first place? Several factors are significant, one of the most important of which is the fascination for all things Egyptian among early scholars, and indeed the public. Here was an ancient civilization whose script had been deciphered, and which – for a time – was popularly regarded as inventing almost everything. In addition, tomb scenes from the Old Kingdom onwards seemed to show glass-blowers at work. So surely glass must have been another Egyptian invention.

It should be borne in mind that the accidental production of glass can occur at almost any time as a result of the fusion of suitable materials during metalworking or faience production. The key question here is the origin of deliberately produced glass. And it is specifically *making*, not simply *working*, glass that is important: glass-making requires the production of glass from its raw materials (essentially silica, soda and lime) whereas glass-working is merely the shaping of glass which has already been made elsewhere. Glass-making is much more technologically demanding.

Egypt or Mesopotamia?

In 1891–92 Flinders Petrie excavated at Amarna, where he found the remains of what he described as several 'glass and glazing works'. His opinion was that glass was being *made* here – he does not say in his publication that the Egyptians invented glass, simply that it was being made by the time of Akhenaten who had established his capital at

One of the earliest datable glass vessels from Egypt, a juglet inscribed for Thutmose III. The blue glass body with added decoration in powdered yellow glass was made by the core-forming technique as glass-blowing was unknown at that time.

An example of early glass from outside Egypt: a piriform bottle from Alalakh (Syrian-Turkish border), probably itself an import from Mesopotamia. The translucent brown glass has discoloured, and the colour of the thread decoration is uncertain. The poor condition of the piece is typical of early glass from the region, and contributed to the view among scholars that Egypt, where well-preserved glass was found, was probably the source of glass.

Glass furnaces at Amarna, site O45.1. Note the large size and thick walls of these furnaces, currently the earliest excavated.

Opposite above
Although the ancient Egyptians do not appear to have invented glass, our present evidence suggests that they may have been the first to use it for making sculpture in the round. This head of Amenhotep II of the 18th Dynasty is an early example.

Amarna. Indeed, by the 1920s Petrie is explicit that glass was not an Egyptian invention.

In the early years of the 20th century, scholars of glass such as Anton Kisa and F. W. von Bissing, probably influenced by Petrie's work at Amarna, and by a view that Egypt was supreme, did not believe that a glass industry existed in Mesopotamia. Assyriologists such as B. Meissner and R. Koldewey, however, recognized that glass was manufactured there and that it was probably at least as old as that in Egypt. We now know that glass from Tell Brak (Iraq), Nuzi (Yorgan Tepe in Iraq) and Alalakh (Tell Atchana on the Syria-Turkey border), and elsewhere, predates the earliest deliberately manufactured glass in Egypt. By how much is debated, although the glass from Tell Brak dates to the late 3rd millennium BC.

The reigns of Thutmose III and Hatshepsut in the 15th century BC seem to mark the arrival of deliberately produced glass in Egypt, possibly as a result of Thutmose's conquests in the Near East bringing captive glass-makers to Egypt. It is often said that the industry seems to arrive 'fully fledged' and this is marked by technically advanced pieces such as a colourless bead of Hatshepsut. The foreign workers probably initially established the industry on a small scale, which was subsequently developed by Egyptian craftsmen. However, the Egyptian 'glass-blowers' in tomb paintings are actually metalworkers using blow-pipes to intensify their fires; glass-blowing was not discovered until the 1st century BC, long after the invention of glass.

Egyptian glass-making

So how early did the Egyptians make their own glass? This is an important question in view of Egypt's relations with her neighbours, and in terms of the ability of her craftsmen to take on and Egyptianize a foreign product. The question has become more important in recent years because, as scholarly opinion has recognized Mesopotamia as the origin of the earliest glass, some have questioned whether the Egyptians ever actually made glass at all, or whether they simply worked imported material. The Amarna Letters, some of which refer to imported glass, have been used to support this view. But to argue for Egyptian dependence on foreign glass is to ignore much of the evidence – if Petrie was right that Amarna was a glass-making site, then that would make it the oldest excavated workshop.

New excavations at Amarna have located what is believed to be a glass and faience workshop. Large furnaces, of a type unknown for pottery or metal production, have been shown experimentally to be capable of making glass from local raw materials. Finds of raw glass and of cylindrical pottery vessels associated with glass-making tend to support this view.

Furthermore, these cylindrical vessels are of the same dimensions as a series of glass ingots that were found in a shipwreck at Uluburun, off the Turkish coast, dating to *c.* 1316 BC. These glass ingots are of the same composition as 18th Dynasty Egyptian glass, and may well have been made in Egypt. It is therefore quite likely that the Egyptians were not only making glass from at least as early as the reign of Akhenaten but they may even have been exporting it from around the same time.

Finds from Qantir in the Nile Delta also support the view that glass was actually made in Egypt. A glass ingot in the Egyptian Museum, Cairo, has been found to fit into the typical cylindrical vessels known from that site. The ingot is of red glass, now discoloured to green, and suggests a high level of competence in glass production by Ramesside times. So although it seems the Egyptians did not invent glass, they did develop it independently and certainly excelled in its working.

Left *An example of the high-quality workmanship achieved by Egyptian glass producers is this unusual vessel in the shape of a fish. The piece is core-formed, and dates from the 18th Dynasty.*

Why was there no Egyptian Iron Age?

The importance of metallurgy throughout history is underlined by our habit of dividing the past into Bronze and Iron ages, with various subdivisions of these....
JACK OGDEN, 2000

In the mid-19th century Christian Jurgensen Thomsen invented the so-called Three Age System when he organized the prehistoric artifacts in the National Museum of Antiquities in Copenhagen, Denmark. He arranged them into a chronological order that corresponded to a sequence of three cultural stages distinguished by the use of stone, bronze and iron respectively. Thomsen's work laid the foundations for the chronology of European prehistory, and the Three Age System has subsequently been applied by European historians to many other parts of the world. However, not all cultures can be equally easily defined according to the use of different materials for tool-making, and the Egyptian 'Iron Age' is a good example of the problems inherent in attempting to use a material-based chronological system of this type.

The title of this article might be less succinctly – but more accurately – re-worded as 'Why was iron not widely used in Egypt until the late 1st millennium BC, when the rest of the Near East had been experiencing a full-fledged Iron Age from at least the middle of the 1st millennium?' We certainly should not take the apparent slowness of the Egyptians to adopt iron as implying some kind of cultural vacuum between the Egyptian Late Bronze Age and the early Ptolemaic period, or that Egyptian culture was technologically backward in all or most respects during this period of seven centuries. The material culture of Late Period Egypt is full of vibrant and innovative developments in the working of materials and manufacturing of artifacts. Nevertheless, there seems little doubt that iron took an unusually long time to become a core element of the Egyptian economy.

Cuneiform tablet bearing the letter in which Tushratta of Mitanni mentions sending a 'dagger whose blade is of steel' to Amenhotep III.

Iron technology

The widespread use of iron throughout the ancient world was generally delayed not by lack of access to supplies of iron ore (which is often more plentifully available than copper or tin) but by the fact that iron smelting and manufacturing techniques took some time to be developed. Although iron melts at a much higher temperature than most other metals, such as copper, tin, silver and gold, it can be smelted (i.e. released from the ore) at similar temperatures to copper (1100–1150°C).

The real problem is that the smelting techniques are much more complex, and that the subsequent stages of processing (e.g. forging, hammering and carburization) only emerged after long periods of experimentation. However, once these technological developments had appeared, the Iron Age would have had several clear advantages over copper alloy-based economies. For instance, the wider availability of iron ore meant that metal artifacts could be produced locally and therefore often more cheaply; also, the blades of iron tools and weapons usually had a tougher, sharper cutting edge than their copper alloy equivalents.

There has been much debate about the possible stages in the transition from the use of copper alloy to iron, and the speed with which this is supposed to have taken place in the Mediterranean region. One suggestion, though not all scholars agree, is that the greater use of iron (and its increasing cheapness) was caused at least in part by a growing shortage of copper and tin. There has also been much discussion as to whether Cyprus and the Aegean were central to this change, or whether they were peripheral to major innovations that took place first in Mesopotamia. In other words, the problem of Egypt's late arrival in a true Iron Age is exacerbated by considerable uncertainty as to how, why and precisely when iron-working appeared elsewhere in the eastern Mediterranean.

Iron-working in the Near East

The evidence for iron-working in the Near East during the 2nd millennium derives mainly from textual sources. It is clear from such documents that at this time iron was worth about five times as much as gold and was among the high prestige materials that the great kings of the region were sending to one another as gifts.

A few New Kingdom examples of such gifts have survived in Egypt, including the golden-hilted iron dagger found in the tomb of Tutankhamun, which is thought likely to have been presented to him by a contemporary Hittite ruler. The most important implication of Tutankhamun's dagger is that iron was at this date (*c.* 1330 BC) still very much an exotic and precious material. It was in fact not until the very late 1st millennium BC that iron was widely used in Egypt.

Throughout the Near East, iron seems to have been more frequently produced from about the mid-1st millennium BC onwards, thus suggesting that this was technically when the Iron Age began in the region as a whole. The one country where this did not happen was Egypt, and it is sometimes suggested that the Egyptians' lack of iron weapons might have played a large part in their conquest by the Persians. The absorption of Egypt into the Achaemenid (Persian) empire took place in about 600 BC, just around the time that iron became so common in Mesopotamia that it replaced copper as the cheapest metal.

So why did the Egyptians take some 300 years longer to adopt iron-processing technology than their neighbours in the Near East? One very practical consideration might have been the fact that hafted hammers seem not to have been introduced into Egypt until the Late Period – this would potentially have been of great significance since the process of hot-working iron would have been far less comfortable using unhafted hammers.

The largest surviving set of iron artifacts from Achaemenid Egypt is a group of 23 iron wood-working tools excavated at Thebes by Flinders Petrie. Petrie dated them to the 26th Dynasty (7th century BC), although some archaeologists have suggested that they are no earlier than the Ptolemaic period (4th–1st century BC). So the reasons for Egypt's reluctance (or inability) to convert to the brave new world of iron remain unclear. We can only assume that there was some as-yet unidentified trend of social or economic conservatism that acted as a disincentive to metallurgical innovation in Late Period Egypt.

Right *Drawings of Tutankhamun's gold and iron daggers, and the iron dagger itself,* c.*1330* BC. *Both were found within the linen wrappings of the king's mummy.*

64 What did Herodotus see in Egypt?

Anyone who finds such things credible can make of these Egyptian stories what he wishes. My job, throughout this account, is simply to record whatever I am told by each of my sources.
HERODOTUS, *c.* 430 BC

The older something is the more inclined we may be to believe it. The same can be said of Herodotus, the Greek historian of the 5th century BC who is justifiably placed at the head of the western tradition of history and of interest in Egypt. Volume Two of his nine-volume *Histories* is entirely devoted to Egypt and Herodotus actually visited the country, probably some time between

449 and 430 BC. Egypt was at this period part of the Persian Empire – with which the Greeks were in the midst of a long and bitter conflict.

Herodotus' account of his visit constitutes most of what the Classical world has to tell us about ancient Egypt, true or otherwise. The fact that this foremost Classical historian pays so much attention to a country which, despite some ironic observations, he treats with obvious respect, not to say reverence, has inspired and influenced all later historical writing about Egypt.

Bust of Herodotus, the Greek historian and traveller, whose description of Egypt marks the beginning of the West's fascination with the world of the pharaohs.

The problem with Herodotus

In his own words, Herodotus' account is based on his personal observation – or *autopsy* – of the land, albeit freely mixed with elements from tales and traditions told to him by Egyptian informants. Since he insists on personal experience in collecting his information, numerous modern studies have tried to establish the truth of the details of the journey he says he made, and the reliability of the sights he claims to have seen. Many scholars have concluded that his account is an unreliable cocktail of hearsay and make-believe; others object to this as a slur on a great writer. However, it is true that some of his descriptions do cast doubt on his supposed *autopsy*.

Perhaps the most surprising case is the lack of any reference to the Great Sphinx in his description of Giza. Could anyone who really had visited a place as singular as Giza overlook a monument which has so fascinated visitors before and since? This is particularly hard to explain since his descriptions are usually keen to highlight sights to which he applies the term *thómata* – a marvel. And Herodotus does describe his own exploration of the Great Pyramid, as well as the measurements of another nearby.

Herodotus' descriptions leave room for speculation about his real motivations. After all, his overall purpose in the *Histories* is actually to produce a global interpretation of his troubled times, rather than accurate descriptions of

Opposite *The Sphinx at Giza, from the* Description de l'Égypte *(1822), the monumental report resulting from Napoleon's expedition to Egypt. The absence of any mention of this giant carving by Herodotus has been used as an argument against the veracity of his personal exploration of Egypt, though it was for long periods almost buried by the desert sands.*

foreign lands. He is a historian not a travel writer. This presumably also applies to the expectations of his audience, since Herodotus aims at defining the radical differences between the Greeks as a race on the one hand, and the many and varied peoples who formed the mosaic of their enemy, the Persian Empire, on the other. To this end, his work can be read on at least two levels, the first of which – showing that the conflict between the Greeks and the Persian Empire is inevitable because of their irreconcilable antagonism – is the more sophisticated. The simple description of these differences, therefore, is the secondary level. Nevertheless, it is still a colourful tale whose good reception is ensured by describing weird and wonderful things foreign to Greeks.

The truth of Herodotus' account can only be checked for sites that still exist. Alan B. Lloyd, for example, has taken the buildings described in the *Histories* as the touchstone for a modern *autopsy*. Lloyd's conclusion is revealing: Herodotus suited his own interests when choosing which buildings to describe. His choice was based on whether the building illustrates his argument, never just because the building itself is interesting. Presumably this is why the Great Sphinx did not make it into his description of Giza. This does, however, allow us to accept that Herodotus did go to Giza, despite this glaring omission. And presumably he really did go to every other place he says he went.

Who did Herodotus talk to?

One important feature of Herodotus' account is the distribution of the Egyptian monuments he claims to have seen. They are concentrated in the north, from the Mediterranean coast to the Faiyum. This is precisely the area in which the immigrant Greek population of Egypt was mostly settled. The Temple of Ptah at Memphis is the Egyptian building most often mentioned in his work. Interestingly, our modern name 'Egypt' comes from the Greeks through their corruption of *Hikuptah* ('Mansion of the Soul of Ptah'), which was the district where this temple was located.

The proximity of the monuments Herodotus describes to the main areas of Greek settlement is

The scattered remains of the colossal statues of Amenemhat III at Biahmu, which Herodotus described as part of his account of Lake Moeris (Faiyum), in turn related to the Labyrinth at Hawara.

probably more than coincidence. It is not hard to suppose, therefore, that Herodotus' informants were mostly Greek settlers. Nowhere in his work does he mention being able to read the Egyptian scripts or to speak the Egyptian language. One can only speculate on the number of Egyptians, even of the priestly class, sufficiently fluent in Greek to be able to conduct a meaningful conversation with him. He also states that the Greeks had understood Egyptian history much better since the reign of Psamtek I (p. 221) , because he was the king who first encouraged Greeks to settle in Egypt in significant numbers. In other words, from that time on a Greek-speaking audience had more detailed information because it could count on the testimony of other Greeks in Egypt.

Finally, we can turn the question round and ask what would the Egyptians have seen in Herodotus? He was, after all, a foreigner speaking a foreign language in a country then under the yoke of foreigners. By the time of his visit this nation, once powerful and prestigious, had been defeated and humiliated by the Persian Empire, which was heir to Assyria, Egypt's long-standing enemy. One can suppose that, even if the priestly elite did talk to Herodotus, they would not have understood the motivation for the sort of questions he asked in compiling the *Histories*. His thesis, presenting Persia and its subjects (including, of course, the Egyptians) as something fundamentally different from the Greeks, would have fallen on deaf ears.

For Herodotus, the Egyptians were part of a different and distant world. Likewise, the Egyptians would have seen no more than a foreigner with odd and inexplicable interests.

Herodotus described the subsidiary pyramids at Giza, ascribing the construction of one to a daughter of Khufu (Cheops), who sold her favours to build it. The story is evidence of an anti-Khufu tradition, which seems to be the main reason Herodotus included a description of the monument.

Egypt & the Bible

Egypt plays a crucial but ambiguous role in the Bible. In the Book of Genesis, the banks of the Nile provide a safe haven for asylum seekers, such as the sons of Jacob, where members of ethnic minorities, among them Joseph and Moses, thrived. Joseph himself found safety and eventually worldly success at the court of an unnamed pharaoh, after being sold into slavery by his own brothers. (According to Middle Eastern tradition, many centuries later the Holy Family also fled to Egypt with the baby Jesus in order to escape the murderous attentions of King Herod.) On the other hand, Joseph's descendants were reduced to slavery by a tyrannical pharaoh, and the great formative moment for the Israelite nation came about when Moses boldly marched his people out of 'the house of bondage'. Thereafter, amidst the to-and-fro of the Old Testament, Egypt is by turns a friend and an enemy of the ancient kingdoms of Israel and Judah.

In a historical sense, however, the relationship between Egypt and the Bible is a singular mystery: not one scrap of evidence has ever been found in Egypt which confirms beyond doubt the earliest stories about the Israelites. A stela of King Merenptah first mentions the name Israel in a list of Egypt's defeated enemies, but only in the unrevealing phrase 'Israel is desolate, and has no seed'. (The name does not appear again in ancient sources for many centuries.) Since the first great Egyptologist, Jean-François Champollion, visited the temples of Karnak in 1828, it has

The Sinai desert, which lies between Egypt and Palestine, has sustained various populations since prehistoric times. In the Bible it is portrayed as the home of the Israelites for 40 years after they fled Egypt, although the identification of these peaks with the mount on which Moses received the Ten Commandments is a speculative tradition.

Inscription from Beth Shean in Palestine showing an Egyptian official adoring the names of the 20th Dynasty pharaoh, Ramesses III. Despite a significant Egyptian presence in the region throughout the New Kingdom and later, Egyptian texts make almost no reference to people or events recognizable as those in the earliest books of the Bible.

been widely assumed that the earliest Bible story supported by Egyptian evidence is the plundering of Jerusalem by Shishak, which Champollion confidently identified with the Karnak battle reliefs of Shoshenq I. However, as is argued in this section, even this identification is more problematic than it first appears. It is not until the 9th century BC, when characters from the Bible are first mentioned in Assyrian sources, that we can be sure

The Bible does of course have a genuine historical setting. This has allowed some authors *carte blanche* to reinvent its contents, often on the slenderest of pretexts. Thus Moses' miraculous river of blood might have been a muddy canal (of which there are many in Egypt), and the parting of the Red Sea perhaps entailed no more than fording a tricky marsh (of which there are many on the roads to Palestine). These approaches fillet the Old Testament, and often reduce an incomparable religious epic – in which God reveals his intentions for his chosen people through miracles – to a sequence of natural phenomena – earthquakes, floods and frogs in freak hailstones. Such speculation is rarely founded on an informed understanding of ancient archaeology and texts.

More convincing scholarship accepts that direct evidence for the earliest Bible stories is lacking and so adopts one of two strategies in response, both of which are illustrated in this section. The first is to argue that a wealth of circumstantial evidence demonstrates that the basic historical settings of the Bible stories are authentic, and that people who can be compared with the great figures of the Old Testament undoubtedly did once live. Foreigners did settle in Egypt, and powerful courtiers did govern the country on behalf of Pharaoh. However, most of them have since been lost to history so why be surprised that Joseph's career has not survived in the Egyptian record? Nevertheless, as is argued here for the story of Joseph, there is enough reliable information to connect him to the historical record. Here also we examine the extraordinary claim that Labayu, a little-known troublemaker in ancient Palestine around 1340 BC, was the historical model for Saul, first king of Israel.

The second strategy suggests that there is no evidence for the earliest Bible stories in Egypt because they are great works of literature, not history. What information there is about Egypt is painted in broad brushstrokes: kings are simply 'pharaoh', not named directly; accounts of the geography and government of Egypt reveal no depth of knowledge of the country; and the great events of Egyptian history are not mentioned. Here, for example, we consider Solomon: despite his superficial resemblance to a Bronze Age king, was he actually a myth – who, like King Arthur, embodied a sense of lost nationhood for later generations? If so, no pharaoh ever knew glorious Solomon or his empire, still less offered a daughter's hand in marriage, as the Bible would have it.

Most problematic of all are miracles, such as those central to the story of Moses; for a historian these are properly issues of faith and culture, not of archaeology. In this section we see two authors adopt one or the other strategy in interpreting Moses. On the one hand, it is argued that the Exodus provides a historical spine for Moses' story. On the other hand, Moses is interpreted as a literary creation based on archetypes well known in the Near East. Crystallized in the minds of people expelled from Jerusalem by the king of Babylon, belief in Moses enabled the exiles to see themselves as a nation destined to return to its Promised Land. It is a measure of the complexity of the links between Egypt and the Bible that two opposing cases can be put forward just for the meaning of the name 'Moses'.

Joseph: an Egyptian vizier?

65

And Pharaoh said to Joseph, 'See, I have set you over all the land of Egypt'.
GENESIS 41:41

The 'rags-to-riches' story of Joseph is well known. Having been sold to traders by his jealous brothers, Joseph was taken to Egypt and became the servant of Potiphar. After being falsely accused of molesting Potiphar's wife he was thrown into prison, where he acquired a reputation as a skilful interpreter of dreams. Eventually Joseph was called upon to decipher the dreams of Pharaoh himself. When he correctly predicted a famine and suggested a policy to avert starvation, he was elevated to high office.

Did Joseph become vizier?

Joseph's exact status in the Egyptian government is unclear. The words attributed to Pharaoh in Genesis (41:40–41) have led many scholars to assume that Joseph became vizier (*tjaty*): 'You shall be over my house … only with regard to the throne will I be greater than you … I have set you over all the land of Egypt.'

Others object that these verses do not give Joseph the titles and responsibilities that normally belong with the office of vizier. Alternatives include 'Overseer of the Granaries' and 'Great Steward of the Lord of the Two Lands'. One suggestion is that Joseph combined both these posts, becoming in effect Egypt's Minister for Agriculture with the additional duty of administering the king's private estates.

Granite statue of a Middle Kingdom vizier, 12th Dynasty, from the temple of Karnak. He wears the typical costume of his rank: a long robe knotted at the chest and a wig and long beard.

Searching for Joseph

Whatever his exact office, Joseph's prestigious rank might suggest that, if the story were historical, it would be easy to identify him with a known official. But things are not so simple. As we see with the story of Moses (p. 277), the date of the Exodus is hard to pin down, and this uncertainty affects the dating of Joseph – with the further problem that we do not know how much time elapsed between Joseph and the Exodus. Was it 430 years (as Exodus 12:40 states), or only half that period (as the Greek version of the Old Testament suggests), or less than four generations (as in Genesis 15:16 and Exodus 6:16–20)? The uncertainty surrounding Joseph's date has allowed scholars to search for him in many different periods of Egyptian history. He has been identified with Montuhotep, the powerful vizier of the Middle Kingdom pharaoh Senwosret I around the end of the 20th century BC, and with Yanhamu, an official of Akhenaten of the mid-14th century BC in the New Kingdom. In fact there is no evidence to support either theory, and other candidates have been equally unconvincing.

Even if Joseph's status was as high as that of vizier (and this

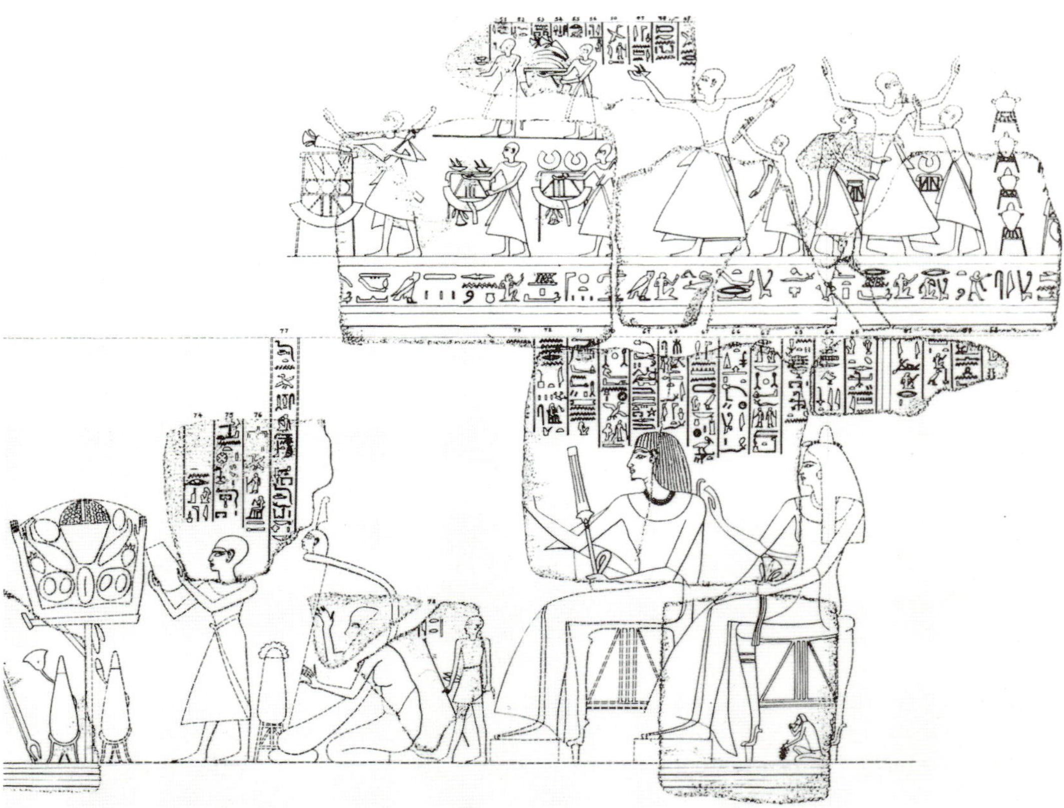

The investiture of Vizier Paser. 'Removing his signet ring from his hand, Pharaoh put it on Joseph's hand; he arrayed him in garments of fine linen, and put a gold chain around his neck.' Joseph's ceremonial elevation is paralleled in many investiture scenes from the New Kingdom, such as this, from the Theban tomb of the Vizier Paser.

Aper-el, vizier of Akhenaten, depicted in a relief in his tomb at Saqqara. His name, as are those of all his family, is Semitic.

cannot be ruled out), we would not necessarily know of him from Egyptian texts. The Vizier Aper-el, who served under Amenhotep III and Akhenaten, was completely unknown until the discovery of his tomb at Saqqara in the 1980s. Compared with Saqqara, where excavations have been going on for over a hundred years, the Delta region in which Joseph was most probably active is still under-explored.

In spite of all the uncertainties, we can confidently say that the story of Joseph does fit convincingly into an Egyptian context. During the Middle Kingdom period many Semites (speakers of West Semitic) were entering Egypt by various routes. Some arrived as prisoners of war, some were sent as tribute by Semitic chieftains and some seem to have been traded, like Joseph. The Egyptians called them 'Asiatics'. They appear in texts in the service of temples and private households. As happened to Joseph, many 'Asiatic' slaves were given Egyptian names and married Egyptians.

What's in a name?

According to Genesis 41:45, Joseph's Egyptian name was Zaphenath-paneah. There has been much speculation as to the Egyptian original behind the Hebrew spelling. The second part of the name probably represents Ipiankh or Paiankh – an Egyptian name common in the Middle Kingdom. But the first part has caused more difficulty. The most promising suggestion is that by Kenneth Kitchen, who thinks that in the transfer from Egyptian to Hebrew the consonants *ph* and *th* were reversed – a common occurrence when words pass from one language to another. This would allow the first part of the name to have been the Egyptian *djatenaf*, which means 'who is called'. This phrase is often used in the Brooklyn Papyrus (from the 18th century BC) to introduce the Egyptian names given to 'Asiatics'; e.g. 'the Asiatic Aamu *djatenaf* Werni'. Joseph would therefore have been known in full as *Yosep djatenaf Ipiankh*, 'Joseph who is called Ipiankh'.

But could a Semite like Joseph have risen to high office in Egypt? Certainly. An example from the Middle Kingdom is the great Chancellor Hur, and the New Kingdom provides many more. These include the Vizier Aper-el mentioned above; he and his family all have Semitic names. Hatshepsut also had a Semitic vizier, and in the 12th century BC a Syrian called Bay became 'Great Chancellor of the entire land'. We may never identify Joseph in an Egyptian text, or even narrow down the time when he lived, but there is no reason to doubt the basic veracity of his story.

Joseph as vizier in Egypt, filling his brothers' sacks with grain. Relief from the ivory throne of Maximian, 6th century AD, Archbishop's Palace, Ravenna.

Faience tiles depicting Libyan, Nubian and Semitic captives, from Medinet Habu.

66

Was Moses at the court of Akhenaten?

Moses stands amidst the flourishing splendour of the sacred story of the Israelites, so much so that his historical form can hardly be recognized any more behind this splendour.
H. DONNER, 1984

Since antiquity, many writers have tried to associate Moses with Akhenaten (p. 122), the king of Egypt who, in the second half of the 14th century BC, championed the worship of a single god, the Aten, in an apparent instance of monotheism. No connection is actually stated in the Old Testament, and no direct evidence of Moses has ever been found in Egypt. However, strict monotheism is first demanded of the Israelites in connection with Moses and the Israelite Exodus from Egypt (p. 277). On the other hand, monotheism plays no significant role in the Book of Exodus, which is assumed to be the earliest version of Moses' story.

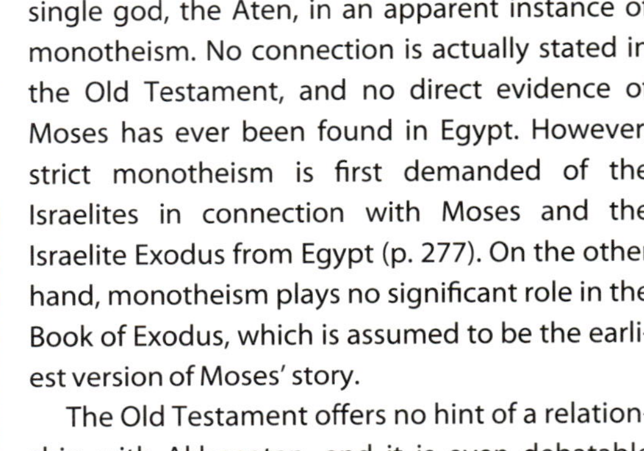

The Old Testament offers no hint of a relationship with Akhenaten, and it is even debatable whether its authors could have known about him at all. Traces of Akhenaten and his belief in the sun god were largely eliminated from the official tradition in Egypt after his death. They only returned to the light of day with the arrival of Greek rulers in Egypt (from the 4th century BC), not least because of the anti-Jewish polemic prevalent in those times.

A link between Akhenaten and Moses can be found in the writings of the Egyptian priest Manetho (*c.* 300 BC), who claimed that the founder of monotheism – whom he called Osarsiph – assumed the name Moses, and led his followers out of Egypt in Akhenaten's reign. Presumably Manetho intended that the Egyptians should be absolved of the false doctrine of monotheism. However, the spectre of Akhenaten was also transformed into Moses by writers such as Lysimachus, Tacitus and Strabo. In modern times, the beliefs of Akhenaten have once again been highlighted – especially through Sigmund Freud's influential study of Moses and monotheism.

If Moses was not certainly at the court of Akhenaten, is there any historical link between him and Egypt at all? The books from Exodus to Deuteronomy tell Moses' life-story. Between his birth in Egypt (Exodus 2) and death in Moab (Deuteronomy 34), Moses plays many different roles: one privileged to speak with God, one who pleads on behalf of his community, leader of the Israelites, miracle-worker, prophet, lawmaker and lawgiver, and priest.

Presumably many of these functions were only attributed to him in the course of tradition, but the key theme in the story of Moses is clear and crucial (Exodus 2:1–10). Moses is the link between the Hebrews and Egypt. He is born a Hebrew but raised by an unnamed pharaoh's daughter. As a young man he kills an Egyptian for tormenting Hebrew slaves (2:11ff.), and flees to Midian. Even his name may be derived from the Egyptian language, as discussed below.

One way of interpreting the biblical Exodus from Egypt and settlement in Canaan is to set it against the known historical context of the kingdom of Israel after the fall of Samaria to the Assyrians in 721 BC. More specifically, the Exodus story could have been modelled on the peoples of Samaria forcibly deported by their Assyrian conquerors, and so reflect the circumstances, experiences and hopes of the deportees. Above all, they were in need of a leader who would deliver them – one like Moses. The deportees were in a foreign country, which would not preclude a degree of assimilation: accordingly the story of Moses' childhood has many features in common with the Mesopotamian legend of King Sargon, who, as an infant, was said to have been abandoned on the river in a bitumen-smeared basket. Nevertheless, while the contemporary situation of the biblical authors in the 8th–7th centuries may explain the adoption of the Sargon legend and the exodus, are the Egyptian setting and the name of Moses evidence of the memory of an older, actual connection with Egypt?

The name Moses and the story of his birth

Various known Egyptians have been proposed as the historical original of Moses, but the sheer number of these proposals in itself provokes scepticism: most recently Bay (E. A. Knauf), Amenmesse (R. Krauss) or Ramessesemperre (M. Görg) have been favoured, but none is compelling. In fact, the name of the child is best explained by the story of his birth through the use of a pun: '... and he became a son for her [the Egyptian princess]. And she called his name Moses [*Mosheh* in Hebrew]: and she said, Because I have pulled [*mashâ*] him out of the water.' (Exodus 2:10).

Left *A relief depicting Sargon II of Assyria (722–705 BC), from Dur-Sharrukin (Khorsabad). The king is shown in his role as a priest presenting offerings to the gods.*

Opposite *Akhenaten before the radiant Aten. The controversial pharaoh insisted that only the sun god, shown in the form of the radiant heavenly disk, or Aten, was suitable for worship.*

'And she called his name Moses: and she said, Because I have pulled him out of the water.' Moses rescued by the Egyptian princess, in a painting by Nicolas Poussin, 1638.

Nothing further is said about his childhood. Because of the pun *mashâ*-Mosheh, we should consider Moses to be in fact a *Hebrew* name, created specifically for the story of his birth, or even for the mythical story of the birth of Israelites.

If the legend of Sargon is regarded as a direct parallel, it is interesting to note that the name Sargon is also recognizable as an invented literary name, meaning 'the king is established'. For Exodus, our author may also have used the Hebrew *mashâ* to create in his hero's name an echo of the Egyptian word *mesi* ('give birth' or 'child'), which also fits well with the story.

Was the Mesopotamian legend subversively adapted and mixed with Egyptian elements by the Hebrew author? If so, whether or not the mythic-historical figure of Moses that we now have – created in the 7th century BC – may also recall an earlier Egyptian historical figure ultimately becomes moot. As far as the traditional figure of Moses goes, the Levant proves to be a cultural melting-pot with influences coming as much from Mesopotamia and Midian as from Egypt, and within which the various traditions are inseparable.

A wooden statuette of a Semitic prisoner, from Egypt, 18th or 19th Dynasty.

Tradition and reality

Moses is as historically valid as the founding father of Egyptian history – King Menes (p. 33). To the modern critical reader of the Bible, Moses seems to oscillate between tradition and reality, and more secure historical knowledge is probably not possible at present. On the other hand, the tradition of the originator of a people generated, in ancient Israel, an extraordinary sense of history – and so he became a historical fact.

In this sense we may wonder whether he is not historically more 'real' than the likes of Achilles, Agamemnon or Hector. Nevertheless, if one were to seek a genuinely historical founder of Hebrew monotheism influenced by a foreign culture, one would certainly not find him at the court of Akhenaten.

The Israelite Exodus: myth or reality?

67

But the Lord has taken you, and brought you forth ...
out of Egypt, to be a people of his own possession ...
DEUTERONOMY 4:20

Attempts to locate the Exodus in Egyptian history have produced no agreed results, and today it is fashionable to doubt the truth of the whole biblical story. This tells of the oppression of the Israelites as slaves in Egypt, their flight from the country led by Moses, and their journey through the wilderness to settle eventually in the Promised Land. But such complete scepticism is undeserved. It ignores the extent to which the Exodus account rings true within an Egyptian setting.

The problem of dates

Attempts to date the Exodus face a dilemma produced by the Bible itself, for it gives us two conflicting clues as to when it might have taken place. In 1 Kings 6:1 we have an apparently clear statement that the Exodus occurred 480 years before the founding of Jerusalem's temple by King Solomon. In round figures, this points to a date of about 1450 BC. However, Exodus 1:11 gives us the information that Pharaoh put the enslaved Hebrews to work on two 'store-cities', named Pithom and Raamses.

The location of Pithom is debated, but Raamses is agreed to be a Hebrew rendering of the Egyptian royal name Ramesses, and as a place

The northern pair of four colossal statues of Ramesses II which front his temple at Abu Simbel, in the far south of Egypt. Ramesses II has been identified by some as the Pharaoh of the Exodus because the enslaved Hebrews were said in the Bible to have been put to work on the store-city of 'Raamses', identified as the site of Piramesse, the Delta capital built by Ramesses II.

name it is the equivalent of the Egyptian Piramesse, 'Estate/Domain of Ramesses'. This was the name of an extensive Delta capital built by Ramesses II, so if the Hebrews worked on this city they obviously cannot have left Egypt before the 13th century BC.

Various solutions have been proposed. Perhaps there was more than one exodus of Hebrew slaves from Egypt; perhaps the figure of 480 years given in 1 Kings is symbolic, or derived from adding together shorter periods that actually overlapped (such as those contained in the Book of Judges); or perhaps the name Raamses was a later updating of the original name, and the Hebrews in fact worked on one of the earlier cities which flourished in the general area of the Delta.

For biblical scholars the issue is further complicated by the question of how subsequent events (Joshua's conquest of Canaanite cities) might fit into the archaeological history of Palestine – but that is beyond the scope of the discussion here.

An inscription from the reign of Merenptah, successor to Ramesses II, indicates that we should not place the Exodus much later than the middle of the 13th century BC. In the final lines of this inscription, carved on a stela set

Merenptah's stela contains what is probably the first reference to Israel outside the Bible. The relevant lines read:

'Plundered is Canaan with every evil:
Carried off is Ashkelon,
Seized upon is Gezer, Yanoam is made non-existent; Israel is desolate,
And has no seed. Kharu is become a widow for Egypt.'

As Ashkelon, Gezer and Yanoam were all city-states in Canaan, and Kharu was a general term for part of Syria-Palestine, the context of the reference to Israel shows clearly that the clash took place in that region.

up to commemorate Merenptah's victory over the Libyans in his Year 5 (1209/08 BC), the pharaoh boasts of his victories over various peoples and places in Syria-Palestine. He claims (with the exaggeration common in Egyptian royal inscriptions): 'Israel is desolate, and has no seed'. The word 'seed' here may refer to the destruction of grain crops, but it is more likely that it means 'offspring'.

Clearly, Merenptah's troops had clashed with some part of Israel and had scored a victory. The context shows us there were Israelites in the land of Canaan by the end of the 13th century BC, but it does not help us to date their arrival. The majority view places the Exodus in the 13th century BC, but a date in the 15th century cannot be ruled out.

Statue of the pharaoh Merenptah, successor of Ramesses II, who boasted on his stela of the people and places he had conquered in Syria-Palestine, including Israel.

The man with half a name

The figure of Moses towers over the story of the Exodus. Born in Egypt of enslaved Hebrew parents, saved from Pharaoh's genocidal policy when his mother placed him adrift on the Nile in a basket, found by a daughter of Pharaoh and brought up at the royal court, he grew up to become his people's deliverer, leader and lawgiver (p. 274).

Left *Pylon and statuary at Tanis, taken from the abandoned capital of Piramesse. Ramesside in origin, these pieces were reused at Tanis by kings of the 21st Dynasty, misleading early Egyptologists into thinking this was the site of Piramesse.*

One widely accepted interpretation is that behind the name Moses (*Mosheh* in Hebrew) is the Egyptian word *mesi*, meaning 'give birth'. This verb was regularly added to the name of an Egyptian god, producing names such as Ptah*mose*, Ra*mose* and the familiar Thut*mose*. In this interpretation, the name Moses looks like an Egyptian name from which the divine element has been dropped. But in that case what are we to make of the explanation given in Exodus 2:10, where Pharaoh's daughter gives Moses his name, saying: 'Because I drew him out of the water'?

It seems to be one of many cases in the Old Testament where the 'explanation' for a personal name is actually a word-play by the writer. This is almost certainly so here, for the word-play works only in Hebrew, while the speaker is supposedly an Egyptian princess. In fact the word-play seems to have a double point. The name Moses can also be related to the Hebrew verb 'to draw out' (*mashâ*), but in a form that means 'he draws out' rather than 'he is drawn out'. The word-play is thus designed to point forward to Moses' role as leader of the Exodus, as well as reflecting the circumstances of his adoption.

Moses' origins may have been unusual, but there is nothing surprising about his upbringing at the Egyptian royal court. As noted elsewhere (p. 273), Semites are found in court positions at many periods of Egyptian history. During the New Kingdom the sons of foreign vassals were sometimes taken to Egypt to be trained in the service of Pharaoh; Moses differs in that he belonged to a foreign population living within Egypt, but as a foreigner raised in Pharaoh's service he was far from unique.

Hebrews in Egypt?

According to the Bible, Moses belonged to a large group of Semitic settlers whose ancestors had arrived in Egypt from the land of Canaan. Archae-

A wall-painting from the tomb of Rekhmire, Thebes, mid-15th century BC, showing Semites and other foreign labourers at work, including brick-making.

ological evidence shows that groups of people from Canaan (as indicated by the styles of their pottery and weapons) were settling in parts of the Eastern Delta from around the middle of Egypt's 12th Dynasty (*c.* 1970–1795 BC). One place where evidence for this has been unearthed is Tell el-Dab'a (p. 166), in the Delta, and the excavator of the site, Manfred Bietak, has concluded that the incomers were of mixed origin, including pastoral nomads like the Hebrews described in Genesis 47:1-11.

This is not to say that we can actually identify Israel's ancestors in Egypt, but the evidence does give a plausible background to the story of their settlement there. In the 17th century BC the site of Tell el-Dab'a was developed as the Hyksos capital Avaris (p. 162), and in the 13th century BC – intriguingly – it was absorbed by the sprawling city of Piramesse, which had its centre a short distance to the north. By the time of Moses the Israelites had been pressed into slavery. Several of the details of their brick-making activities, as recorded in Exodus 5, can be paralleled from Egyptian New Kingdom texts and tomb paintings, such as that from the tomb of Rekhmire at Thebes.

Impossible numbers?

It should come as no surprise that there is no Egyptian account of the Exodus (whenever it may have occurred). The Egyptians were not in the habit of recording humiliations and losses. The route chosen by the escaping Israelites, from Piramesse to Tjeku (biblical Succoth: Exodus 12:37) and eastwards, was exactly the same as that used by two escaping slaves in the late 13th century BC, as reported in Papyrus Anastasi V. However, the number of Israelites involved in the Exodus as recorded in the Bible is often mentioned as proof that the event was probably fictitious, or at least exaggerated.

Based on the number of men alone, which is given as 600,000 at the time of the Exodus (Exodus 12:37 and following), a figure of about two million people is commonly estimated. Such a large number of people is quite unrealistic for the time and would have outnumbered the entire population of Canaan by at least 20:1– the Israelite conquest of the land would therefore have been straightforward.

In fact it has been pointed out several times over the last century that the Hebrew word *'elef*, conventionally translated as 'thousand', can mean other things as well, such as 'family', 'tribal unit' or even 'leader'. Applying the range of possibilities to various passages in the books of Exodus and Numbers, biblical scholars have come up with more realistic estimates for the total of individuals involved in the migration. The most recent study suggests a figure of about 20,000 for the whole group. When compared with the numbers of prisoners claimed by New Kingdom pharaohs in their campaigns, this is completely plausible.

Above *The miraculous parting of the Red Sea, from a medieval manuscript, the Rylands Haggadah.*

Was Labayu King Saul?

O daughters of Israel, weep for Saul, who clothed you in scarlet and finery, who adorned your garments with ornaments of gold.
II Samuel 1:24

According to the Books of Samuel, Saul was the first king of ancient Israel. Despite his humility and undoubted abilities, Saul was abandoned by his own god, Yahweh, and eventually perished in battle, along with three of his sons, on the slopes of Mount Gilboa. Afterwards another son, Ishbaal, was murdered, and the throne of Israel passed to David.

A letter to Pharaoh from the Amarna archive. Sent by Biridiya, king of Megiddo, the letter reports that Labayu has been killed by his enemies, in defiance of Pharaoh's clear instructions that he should be taken alive.

Saul's tragedy reads straightforwardly as great literature. According to the Bible, having a king over Israel meant rejecting the rule of Yahweh and his prophets, and so the first king was literally and inevitably god-forsaken. Even the name Saul, which ironically means 'asked for', reflects the desire of his people to have a king against the will of Yahweh. As a result Saul is rejected by his god, his people, a son and a daughter, each of whom comes to love David instead. David then founds a ruling dynasty, which includes the glorious Solomon and leads ultimately to Jesus Christ.

More specifically, the story of Saul allowed the biblical authors to move their narrative away from tales of wandering tribes and towards the political complexity of the 6th century BC, when the Books of Samuel were actually written. Therefore many historians regard Saul's story as fiction, and doubt that there could ever be authentic evidence of his existence outside the Bible.

How surprising, therefore, when a group of researchers in the 1980s – Bernard Newgrosh, David Rohl and Peter van der Veen – claimed that a well-known archive from Egypt included correspondence between Saul and no lesser figures than the Egyptian kings Amenhotep III and Akhenaten.

The bandit, Labayu

The archive of clay tablets, discovered in 1887 in an office beside the palace of Amarna (ancient Akhetaten), includes 350 or more letters between the king of Egypt and other rulers across the Levant and the Near East. They date from the end of the reign of Amenhotep III, through the reign of Akhenaten and possibly into the reign of Tutankhamun – some 20 to 30 years up to around 1335 BC. The majority were written between the Egyptian palace and the chiefs of cities in an area corresponding roughly to modern Palestine, Israel and Lebanon. These men present themselves as inferiors to Pharaoh, but they also represent a network of contacts by which the Egyptian palace was able to monitor its interests in the region. Above all, this meant the safe passage of trading ships and caravans.

Among these chiefs was Labayu, who ruled an indeterminate area in the hills of Palestine. Other chiefs in the region clearly regarded him as a bandit who threatened the trade centres of the lowlands and coastal plains, especially in the crucial area of Megiddo. This in itself would have excited the interest of the Egyptians, so Labayu was obliged to write letters protesting his loyalty:

I have obeyed the orders of the king, my lord and my sun, and I am, of course, guarding Megiddo, the city of the king, my lord, day and night.

Indeed, Labayu presents himself as the victim of his enemies' aggression:

Moreover, when even an ant is struck, does it not fight back and sting the hand of the man who struck it?

It is this Labayu whom Rohl and his collaborators propose was the historical face of Saul. The difference in their names is unimportant because 'Saul' was presumably invented by the authors of Samuel. And there are intriguing similarities between the careers of Labayu and Saul.

Most intriguing is the death of Labayu, who was killed by the people of Gina. This is probably modern Jenin, near Megiddo and also near Mount Gilboa, where Saul died. Letters in the aftermath indicate that his death was plotted by rival chiefs, including some in towns occupied in the Samuel narratives by Saul's enemies, the Philistines. These letters also include names which can be compared to those of key figures in the death of Saul, including his son Ishbaal, a general Joab, enemy chiefs called Achish and Hadadezer, and, most daringly, David himself.

There are also broader similarities in the two narratives. Jerusalem is under attack in the Labayu correspondence, and, in Samuel, David captures Jerusalem once he becomes king. Saul characterizes David as an *'ibri*, meaning an outlaw or mercenary typical of the political landscape of his story. This term bears close comparison with *'abiru* used often in the Amarna letters, also to

The fortress of Megiddo, also known as biblical Armageddon. Megiddo dominated trade routes lying between the sea and the Jezreel Valley, which linked the Levant to Egypt and Mesopotamia. Inevitably, it was a political hotspot for many centuries.

mean an outlaw or bandit. However, given the volatile politics of the Palestinian hills, such outlaws were present for many centuries.

Likewise, coincidences between the careers of Labayu and Saul are not necessarily surprising because it was typical in ancient times for kings in the hill-country to clash with their neighbours. More specifically, neither Israel nor Judah is actually mentioned in Labayu's letters, nor indeed in any other sources of this time. Even Saul's principal enemies, the Philistines and Amalekites, are conspicuous by their absence in the archive.

Problems of chronology

This raises the crucial stumbling block – chronology. The Bible records that Saul lived a few generations before the first kings of Israel and Judah known in the historical record – Ahab and Jehu of the 9th century BC, and possibly even Rehoboam of the 10th century. As a result, Saul's death is usually dated to around 1000 BC by those who believe he is an actual historical figure. To account for the discrepancy between this date and the date of the Amarna archive (*c.* 1335 BC)

Above *Javelin-head from el-Khadr, Palestine. Some historians speculate that it belonged to Saul's bodyguards, but others doubt that there could ever be such tangible evidence for his reign, which is otherwise known only from the Bible.*

Right *'Office of Correspondence of Pharaoh' beside the Great Palace of Amarna. The archive of letters discovered here in 1887 is the most important single source of information about relations between Africa and the Near East in the New Kingdom.*

Mount Gilboa, where, according to the Books of Samuel, Saul fell on his own sword when faced with defeat at the hands of the Philistines and Amalekites.

Rohl and his collaborators have suggested that the dates of Amenhotep III and Akhenaten should be lowered to coincide with Saul. To remove three centuries, however, would mean rewriting not just Egyptian history but the history of the whole Near East in ways that most scholars are not prepared to accept.

On the other hand, the alternative would be equally controversial: to increase the date of Saul to that of the Amarna archive would force us to abandon the Books of Samuel as any kind of reliable guide to history. If Saul really did live, but 500 years before Ahab and Jehu, then the biblical golden age of David and Solomon would be far removed in time from the known history of ancient Israel. Undoubtedly, therefore, the Amarna letters and the Books of Samuel lead in different directions, and it would need more to reconcile them than a handful of similarities, however striking, between a bandit-chief from history and the forsaken king of the Bible.

Medieval illustration of the Second Book of Kings, showing the death, lamentation and burial of Saul.

Who was Solomon's father-in-law?

He had seven hundred wives of royal birth and three hundred concubines, and his wives led him astray.
I KINGS 11:3

According to the books of Kings and Chronicles, the reign of Solomon was a golden age:

> The people of Judah and Israel were as numerous as the sand on the seashore; they ate, they drank and they were happy. And Solomon ruled over all the kingdoms from the River to the land of the Philistines, as far as the border of Egypt.

The territorial claim of the Israelites stretched from Lebanon to Sinai, and was bordered by the Mediterranean Sea on one side and the River Jordan on the other. According to the Bible, those indigenous peoples whom the Israelite settlers could not destroy were enslaved and set to work rebuilding Solomon's main cities, including Hazor and Megiddo, as well as a royal palace and a temple for his god, Yahweh, in Jerusalem. Thus glorious Solomon became a king of kings, celebrated in the international community for his wealth and wisdom. Even his name is derived evocatively from the Hebrew word for 'peace'.

As befitted his imperial status, he filled his harim with the sisters and daughters of other great kings, including even the king of Egypt. His dowry from Pharaoh was a city, Gezer. However, his wives were to be his downfall because he soon adopted their religious customs and so Yahweh ultimately rejected him. Nevertheless, for the authors of the Bible the story of Solomon was a powerful evocation of nationhood. It presupposed an era when the disparate peoples of Israel and Judah formed a powerful united nation, which was far from being the case when Chronicles and Kings were first written in the 6th century BC. It was also a cautionary tale about how the greatest of men can be led astray by power, overindulgence and the attentions of women.

Solomon overseeing the construction of the temple in Jerusalem. According to the biblical tradition, Solomon's magnificence was manifested in the unsurpassed architecture of his kingdom.

Solomon in history

The central mystery of Solomon's story is that so little of it is supported by archaeology or by texts other than the Bible. For example, according to the Bible his successors as rulers of Israel and Judah – Jeroboam and Rehoboam respectively – were involved with 'King Shishak of Egypt'. In turn, 'Shishak' is usually identified as the pharaoh Shoshenq I (p. 289). The Bible also places Solomon a few generations before Ahab and Jehu, who were undoubtedly kings of Israel in the 9th century BC. Therefore, Solomon should have been king in the 10th century BC. However, as the historian James Pritchard – for one – noted, in the 10th century BC 'the so-called cities of Megiddo, Gezer and Hazor, and Jerusalem itself, were in reality more like villages'.

It is also noteworthy that Chronicles and Kings refer only to the unnamed 'Pharaoh the king of Egypt' and 'pharaoh's daughter', which may suggest that they were invoked by the writers as stock characters rather than as known historical figures. Who was the father of Solomon's Egyptian queen? The Bible certainly does not tell us. It does, however, claim that a sister of Pharaoh's wife, Tahpenes, became a wife in the royal house of Edom at this time, and her name does seem credibly Egyptian, though we cannot identify her with any known queen or princess.

The Bible also indicates that Solomon built a complex of temples and palaces for each one of his wives, as well as for 'Chemosh, the detestable god of Moab, and for Molech, the detestable god of the Ammonites'. No trace of such a complex has emerged so far, and no compelling evidence of Solomon in Jerusalem at this time has emerged.

More pointedly, no known text from any nation between the 13th century BC and the reign of Ahab (*c.* 873–853 BC) mentions Solomon himself, nor any significant fact relating to him, nor to Israel nor Judah. It thus remains an inescapable fact that the glorious kingdom of Solomon has left no trace in the written history of the great nations with whom he is said to have traded.

Haram al-Sharif, the religious heart of the city of Jerusalem, traditionally founded by Solomon. Its origins are now disputed by scholars.

Below *Ivory plaque from Megiddo, depicting a king in front of his court. This scene shows unambiguous Egyptian influence on the artists of Palestine during the New Kingdom.*

The gates of Hazor, one of many cities ascribed to Solomon in the Bible. However, no trace of his alleged building activity has ever been discovered.

Right *Reconstructed stela of Mesha, king of Moab around 840 BC, which mentions events during the reigns of Omri and Ahab in Israel. This is the earliest undisputed record of events also mentioned in the Bible, many centuries after the New Kingdom in Egypt.*

Solomon in the New Kingdom?

One solution to this mystery, which has occasionally been proposed, is that Solomon was not a king of the 10th century BC, but lived in an earlier era. For example, Tahpenes' children, according to the Bible, were brought up in the royal palace in Egypt alongside Pharaoh's children, which is consistent with the practice of the Egyptian court during the 18th Dynasty. Likewise, a key topic in the 18th Dynasty archive of letters from Amarna is dynastic marriage, by which great kings traded their own sisters and daughters in exchange for peace between 'brothers'. This does seem to sound like the Solomonic era described in the Bible. Moreover, a stela of King Merenptah in the 19th Dynasty (p. 278) includes the only known reference to Israel in an ancient Egyptian text, although it is so peremptory ('Israel is laid waste, and has no seed') that it does not reveal whether Israel at that time was even a kingdom, still less who its king might have been. So could Solomon possibly have been the son-in-law of Merenptah, or of another New Kingdom pharaoh?

David Rohl has recently suggested that discoveries of Egyptian artifacts – including a funerary stela and a statuette – on a hill which might have overlooked Solomon's Jerusalem could belong to his Egyptian wife. Quite possibly they are fragments of an Egyptian tomb of the 18th Dynasty, which is certainly a unique and unexpected discovery. However, the fragments are entirely anonymous.

The texts and archaeology of the 14th–13th century BC do evoke a confident and wealthy Palestine. Nevertheless, they do not mention Solomon, king of Israel and Judah. So who was the father of Solomon's Egyptian queen? Most likely, he must remain anonymously 'Pharaoh the king of Egypt' because there is little in the surviving record to confirm any historical reality behind Solomon's story, and even the Bible itself says so very little. We could speculate that an Egyptian pharaoh, unnamed in the Bible and anywhere else, once offered his daughter in marriage to an impoverished 10th-century king of Israel – but for the time being such a king is unknown to archaeology and ancient history.

Who was 'King Shishak of Egypt'?

70

In the fifth year of King Rehoboam, King Shishak of Egypt came up against Jerusalem ...
I KINGS 14:25

The Bible relates that on the death of Solomon the kingdom forged by his father David fell apart. The northern tribes rebelled and became a separate kingdom, Israel, ruled by Jeroboam I. The southern kingdom of Judah, with its capital at Jerusalem, continued under the rule of Solomon's son Rehoboam. Diminished and weakened, Judah barely had time to recover from the rebellion before it suffered another blow. 'In the fifth year of King Rehoboam, King Shishak of Egypt came up against Jerusalem; he took away the treasures of the house of the Lord and the treasures of the king's house; he took everything' (1 Kings 14:25–26). Who was this Egyptian king who looted Judah's capital?

Prisoners of Shoshenq I from his campaign relief in the temple of Karnak.

Champollion at Karnak

In the 1820s, not long after his breakthrough in deciphering Egyptian hieroglyphs, Jean-François Champollion teamed up with the Italian Ippolito Rosellini to record Egypt's great monuments. In the course of this project Champollion examined a triumphal relief next to the Bubastite Gate at Karnak. The gate and its adjoining wall were parts of a large open forecourt planned by the pharaoh Shoshenq I, founder of the Libyan 22nd Dynasty, around the middle of the 10th century BC. The court was to have been an addition to the great Temple of Amun-Re, giving it an impressive new frontage facing the Nile. Shoshenq died before the project could be completed, but in his triumphal relief he has left us a valuable if puzzling historical record.

The relief portrays the god Amun-Re and the city of Thebes shown as a goddess leading long lines of captives for presentation to Shoshenq. Amun-Re and his companion face to the observer's right, where the pharaoh himself stands in typical smiting pose over his cowering enemies. Each of the captives being led to the king is represented by the head and shoulders of a human figure on top of an oval ring containing a place name. Champollion concluded that the captives were 'the leaders of more than thirty vanquished nations', and he read the 29th name-ring in the sequence as '*Ioudahamalek*', which he took to be the biblical Judah followed by 'the kingdom' in Hebrew. Consequently he translated that name-ring as 'the kingdom of Judah'. Connecting this with the events in 1 Kings 14, Champollion felt that the identity of the biblical Shishak and the pharaoh Shoshenq was 'confirmed in the most satisfactory manner'.

In the late 19th century the biblical scholar Julius Wellhausen suggested that Shoshenq's list was of no historical value, the pharaoh having merely copied strings of names from the inscriptions of his predecessors. Suspicion lingered into the 20th century, but the theory has now been discarded. This fragment of a huge stela bearing Shoshenq I's cartouches was found at Megiddo, proving that his troops reached that far.

Not nations but towns

Champollion's interpretation of the inscription was widely accepted in the years that followed. Some scholars even claimed that the head surmounting name-ring 29 provided us with a portrait of Solomon's son Rehoboam himself. However, as Egyptology developed and standards of translation improved, Champollion's view was challenged. The great scholar Heinrich Brugsch made a new and detailed study of the names, proposing fresh identifications which, in many cases, have stood the test of time. Brugsch's important contribution was to recognize that the names were chiefly those of towns rather than nations.

Further doubt was cast on Champollion's reading of number 29 when Brugsch identified names both before and after it as belonging to Israel as well as Judah. He also felt that Champollion's translation 'kingdom of Judah' was impossible grammatically. The first person to propose the translation of name-ring 29 which is accepted today was W. Max Müller in 1888. He suggested '*Yad-hamelek*' – literally 'Hand of the King', though in biblical usage it could also mean 'Monument of the King'. From its place in the list it would seem to have been a town on the coastal plain of the kingdom of Israel.

These revised understandings of Shoshenq's list did nothing to weaken the conviction that he was the Bible's 'King Shishak of Egypt', however. For although the 'kingdom of Judah' had been dropped from the new translations, it was clear that the bulk of the list consisted of towns belonging to both Judah and Israel. In short, it was evidence that Shoshenq had conducted a significant campaign into Palestine. Furthermore, as both Egyptian and biblical chronology were developed and refined, Shoshenq's place as a contemporary of Rehoboam in the 10th century BC seemed to be confirmed beyond reasonable doubt. So, for the majority of Egyptologists and biblical historians, Shoshenq I was the biblical Shishak.

Our understanding of Shoshenq's triumphal relief has continued to improve, thanks to the labours of many Egyptologists and biblical scholars. From the many names that have been identified with places known from the Bible, the extent of Shoshenq's campaign can now be reconstructed with some confidence.

Shoshenq's exact line of march is still a matter of debate. In this interpretation, put forward by Kenneth Kitchen, the army followed the coast road as far as Gaza where it divided: the main force, led by Shoshenq himself, moved northwest to Aijalon and then into the central hills via the Beth-Horon pass; meanwhile a task-force headed south and east, taking towns of southern Judah and the Negeb. The main force moved north from Gibeon to Tirzah, from where a second task-force was dispatched east of the Jordan. The main force continued north as far as Megiddo, where the Transjordan contingent probably rejoined it. A foray northward from Megiddo may be attested by the fourth row of the relief shown on p. 292, but few names are legible. The army eventually turned south from Megiddo, crossing the Carmel ridge at the pass of Aruna and returning to Egypt along the coastal plain.

The devil in the detail

Shoshenq's relief scene is generally thought to throw valuable extra light on an obscure episode in biblical history. However, in examining the details of Shoshenq's campaign a few scholars have found difficulties with the idea that he was the biblical Shishak. The towns listed by Shoshenq suggest that his objective was not the heartland of Judah but Israel in the north and the Negeb in the south. The only Judean towns in the list are ones that lie on the fringes of these two areas. The Bible on the other hand does not mention an attack on Israel, Judah alone being Shishak's target.

Supporters of the conventional view suggest that the Bible ignores Shoshenq's extensive campaign into Israel because the Jerusalem-based writers of 1–2 Kings were not very interested in the history of the northern kingdom. This simply does not hold water. In the parts of 1–2 Kings relating the parallel histories of Israel and Judah (1 Kings 12:25 to 2 Kings 16:20), Israel receives 650 verses of text while Judah receives only 155.

Furthermore, an invasion of Israel by Shishak would be at odds with other details given in the biblical account. In the time of Solomon, Jeroboam, the future king of Israel, was already perceived as a political rival: 'Solomon sought therefore to kill Jeroboam; but Jeroboam promptly fled to Egypt, to King Shishak of Egypt, and remained in Egypt until the death of Solomon' (1 Kings 11:40). So Shishak and Jeroboam were allies, not enemies.

Why no Jerusalem?

The biggest mystery for the conventional view is the absence of Jerusalem from Shoshenq's list. Various explanations have been offered, the most obvious being that Jerusalem once featured in a part of the list that is now damaged. However, none of the gaps seem to be in the right places for this explanation to work.

Another explanation is that Jerusalem was omitted because it was not destroyed – it escaped violent conquest because Shoshenq was bought off by Rehoboam. But there is no reason to think that only destroyed towns would have been mentioned. Rehoboam's hefty payment was an acknowledgement of Jerusalem's vassal status (2 Chronicles 12:7–9), and as a subjugated city Jerusalem should have been listed by Shoshenq if he were its conqueror.

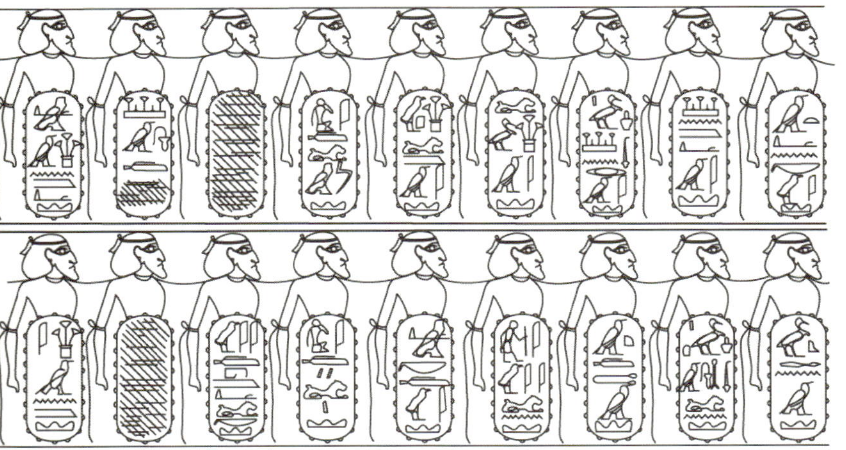

Questions of chronology

But if Shoshenq was not the biblical Shishak, who was? Here we venture on to controversial ground. Opponents of the Shoshenq-Shishak equation favour a drastically revised chronology for ancient Egypt, one that would lower currently accepted dates for the New Kingdom period by some two and a half centuries. In their view Shishak could be Ramesses III, or – with an even more drastic reduction of dates – Ramesses II. Both these pharaohs were sometimes known by a shortened form of their name, Sessi or Sysa, and it is suggested that this gave rise to the biblical name Shishak.

Exponents of this view are not simply trying to find a new candidate for the biblical Shishak, however. They are also attempting to solve a whole range of historical and archaeological anomalies, many of which lie far beyond the borders of Egypt but which they believe are the result of faulty Egyptian dates.

We must leave aside the vigorous debate over whether Egyptian history can in fact be telescoped in the way these theories require and return to our original question: was the Shishak mentioned in the Bible the same person as Shoshenq I of Egypt, or not? Weighty objections have been raised to the derivation of Shishak from Sysa. By contrast, the conventional view has no difficulty deriving the Hebrew spelling of Shishak from the Egyptian name Shoshenq (the lost 'n' is no problem, since it was a nasal sound which was not always written).

So, while the political situations found in the Bible and the Shoshenq inscription do not match, the names Shoshenq and Shishak match very well. The debate goes on; the issues are far-reaching and complex, and not likely to be resolved in the near future.

Above and left *Like children's pull-along toys, rows of captive towns (detail left) are led to Shoshenq by Amun-Re and the city of Thebes shown as a goddess. The top five rows, led by Amun-Re, belong mainly to Israel and the northern limit of Judah. The next five rows are towns in the extreme south of Judah and the Negeb. An eleventh row once extended along the base of the scene but is now almost entirely destroyed.*

Further reading

The Earliest Egyptians

1 Where did the Egyptians come from?

Hoffman, M. A., *Egypt Before the Pharaohs* (New York 1979/London, 1984)
Midant-Reynes, B. (tr. I. Shaw), *The Prehistory of Egypt. From the First Egyptians to the First Pharaohs* (Oxford, 2000)
Wilkinson, T. A. H., *Genesis of the Pharaohs* (London & New York, 2003)

2 Did the Egyptians invent writing?

Bard, K. A., 'Origins of Egyptian writing', in Friedman,R. and Adams, B. (eds), *The Followers of Horus: Studies Dedicated to Michael Allen Hoffman* (Oxford, 1992), 297–306
Dreyer, G., *Umm el-Qaab I: das prädynastische Königsgrab U-j und seine frühen Schriftzeugnisse* (Mainz am Rhein, 1998)
Postgate, N., Tao Wang & Wilkinson, T., 'The evidence for early writing: utilitarian or ceremonial?', *Antiquity* 69 (1995), 459–80
Ray, J. D., 'The emergence of writing in Egypt', *World Archaeology* 17 (1986), 307–16
van den Brink, E. C. M., (1992) 'Corpus and numerical evaluation of the "Thinite" potmarks', in Friedman, R. and Adams, B. (eds), *The Followers of Horus: Studies Dedicated to Michael Allen Hoffman* (Oxford, 1992), 265–96

3 Who were the first kings of Egypt?

Baines, J., 'Origins of Egyptian kingship', in O'Connor, D. & Silverman, D. (eds), *Ancient Egyptian Kingship* (Leiden & New York, 1995), 95–156
Dreyer, G., 'A hundred years at Abydos', *Egyptian Archaeology* 3 (1993), 10–12
Wilkinson, T. A. H., *Early Dynastic Egypt* (London & New York, 1999)
Wilkinson, T. A. H., *Royal Annals of Ancient Egypt* (London & New York, 2000)
Wilkinson, T. A. H., 'Political unification: towards a reconstruction', *Mitteilungen des Deutschen Archäologischen Instituts, Abteilung Kairo* 56 (2000), 377–95
Wilkinson, T. A. H., 'What a king is this: Narmer and the concept of the ruler', *Journal of Egyptian Archaeology* 86 (2000), 23–32
Williams, B. B., 'Forebears of Menes in Nubia: myth or reality?', *Journal of Near Eastern Studies* 46 (1987), 15–26

4 King Menes: myth or reality?

Emery, W. B., *Archaic Egypt* (Harmondsworth, 1961), 32–37
Gardiner, A. H., *Egypt of the Pharaohs* (Oxford, 1961)
Wilkinson, T. A. H. *Early Dynastic Egypt* (London & New York, 1999), 66–68

5 Human sacrifice in the royal tombs

Hoffman, M. A., *Egypt Before the Pharaohs* (New York, 1979/London, 1984), 275–79
Rice, M., *Egypt's Making* (London, 1990)
Wilkinson, T. A. H., *Early Dynastic Egypt* (London & New York, 1999), 227, 265–67

6 The royal boat burials at Abydos

O'Connor, D., 'Boat graves and pyramid origins' *Expedition* 33.3 (1991), 5–17
O'Connor, D. & Adams, M., 'Moored in the desert' *Archaeology* (2001), 44–45
Ward, C., *Sacred and Secular: Ancient Egyptian Ships and Boats* (Boston, 2000)

Pyramids & Tombs

7 Origins of the pyramids

Dreyer, G., 'Zur Rekonstruction der Oberbauten der Königsgräber der 1 Dynastie in Abydos', *Mitteilungen des Deutschen Archäologischen Instituts Abteilung Kairo,* Band 47 (1991), 93–97
Lehner, M., *The Complete Pyramids* (London & New York, 1997)
O'Connor, D., 'Pyramid origins: a new theory' in Ehrenberg, E. (ed.), *Leaving No Stones Unturned* (Winona Lake, 2002), 169–82

8 What is a pyramid for?

Davies, V. & Friedman, R., *Egypt* (London & New York, 1998)
Edwards, I. E. S., *The Pyramids of Egypt* (Harmondsworth, 4th ed., 1993)
Lehner, M., *The Complete Pyramids* (London & New York, 1997)
Shaw, I. (ed.), *The Oxford History of Ancient Egypt* (Oxford & New York, 2000)
Verner, M., *The Pyramids. Their Archaeology and History* (London, 2002)

9 Were the pyramids built by slaves?

Arnold, D., *Building in Egypt. Pharaonic Stone Masonry* (New York & Oxford, 1991)
Hawass, Z., 'The workmen´s community at Giza' in Bietak, M. (ed.), *Haus und Palast im alten Ägypten* (Vienna, 1996), 53–67
Hawass, Z. & Lehner, M., 'Builders of the pyramids', *Archaeology* 50 (1997), 31–38
Pfirsch, L., 'Les batisseurs des pyramides de Saqqara' in Berger, C. (ed.), *Saqqara,* Les Dossiers d'Archéologie, 146–47 (Dijon, 1990), 32–35
Stadelmann, R., 'La ville de pyramide à l´Ancien Empire', *Revue d'Égyptologie* 33 (1981), 67–77

10 The multiple pyramids of Snofru

Dreyer, G. & Kaiser, W., 'Zu den kleinen Stufenpyramiden Ober- und Mittelägyptens', *Mitteilungen des Deutschen Archäologischen Instituts, Abteilung Kairo* 36 (1980), 43–59
Edwards, I. E. S., 'The pyramid of Seila and its place in the succession of Snofru's pyramids', in Goring, E., Reeves, N. & Ruffle, J. (eds), *Chief of Seers: Egyptian Studies in Memory of Cyril Aldred* (London & New York, 1997), 88–93
Gunn, B., 'Concerning King Snefru', *Journal of Egyptian Archaeology* 12 (1926), 250–52
Harpur, Y., *The Tombs of Nefermaat and Rahotep at Maidum: Discovery, Destruction and Reconstruction* (Oxford, 2001)
Maragioglio, V. & Rinaldi, C., *L'architettura delle Piramidi Menfite* III (Rapallo, 1964)

11 The Great Pyramid

Bauval, R., *Secret Chamber. The Quest for the Hall of Records* (London, 1999)
Lehner, M., *The Egyptian Heritage* (Virginia Beach, 1974)
Lehner, M., *The Complete Pyramids* (London & New York, 1997)
Verner, M., *The Pyramids. Their Archaeology and History* (London, 2002)

12 Riddles of the Great Sphinx

Allen, J. & Gauri, K. L., 'The ARCE Sphinx Project: a preliminary report', *Newsletter of the American Research Center in Egypt*, 112 (1980), 3–33
Edwards, I. E. S., *The Pyramids of Egypt* (Harmondsworth, 4th ed., 1993)
Hawass, Z. & Lehner, M., 'The Sphinx: who built it and why?', *Archaeology* 47 (1994), 30–47
Lehner, M., 'A contextual approach to the Giza pyramids', *Archiv für Orientsforschung* 31 (1985), 136–58
Lehner, M., 'Reconstructing the Sphinx', *Cambridge Archaeological Journal*, 2.1 (1992), 3–26
O'Connor, D., 'The interpretation of the Old Kingdom pyramid complex', in Guksch, H. and Polz, D. (eds), *Stationen: Beiträge zur Kulturgeschichte Ägyptens; Rainer Stadelman gewidmet* (1998), 135–44

13 Are the pyramids aligned with the stars?

Bauval, R. & Gilbert, A., *The Orion Mystery* (Oxford & New York, 1994)
Edwards, I. E. S., *The Pyramids of Egypt* (Harmondsworth, 4th ed., 1993)
Lehner, M., *The Complete Pyramids* (London & New York, 1997)
Shaw, I. (ed.), *The Oxford History of Ancient Egypt* (Oxford, 2000)
Verner, M., *The Pyramids: Their Archaeology and History* (London, 2002)

14 The anonymous Qurneh burial

Eremin, K., Goring, E., Manley, W. P. & Cartwright, C., 'A 17th-Dynasty Egyptian Queen in Edinburgh?', *KMT*, 11/3 (2000), 32–40

Eremin, K., Manley, W. P., Shortland, A. & Wilkinson, C., 'The facial reconstruction of an ancient Egyptian queen', *Journal of Audiovisual Media in Medicine*, 25/4 (2002), 155–59

Petrie, W. M. F., *Qurneh* (London, 1909)

Sheridan, A., *Heaven and Hell, and Other Worlds of the Dead* (Edinburgh, 2000)

15 Abydos: the last royal pyramid?

Ayrton, E., Currelly, C. & Weigall, A., *Abydos Part III* (London, 1903)

Harvey, S. J., 'Monuments of Ahmose at Abydos', *Egyptian Archaeology* 3 (1995), 3–5

Harvey, S. J., *The Cults of King Ahmose at Abydos* (Ann Arbor, 1998)

Harvey, S. J., 'Abydos, South: early 18th Dynasty monuments' in Bard, K. (ed.), *Encyclopedia of the Archaeology of Ancient Egypt* (London, 1999), 107–09

Lehner, M., *The Complete Pyramids* (London & New York, 1997)

Randall-MacIver, D. & Mace, A. C., *El Amrah and Abydos 1899–1900* (London, 1902)

16 The lost tomb of Amenhotep I

Carter, H., 'Report on the Tomb of Zeser-ka-Ra Amen-hetep I, discovered by the Earl of Carnarvon in 1914', *Journal of Egyptian Archaeology* 3 (1916), 147–54

Dodson, A. M., *After the Pyramids: the Valley of the Kings and Beyond* (London, 2000)

Polz, D., 'Bericht über die 4. und 5. Grabungskampagne in der Nekropole von Dra' Abu el-Naga/Theben-West', *Mitteilungen des Deutschen Archäologisches Instituts, Abteilung Kairo* 51 (1995), 207–25

Polz, D., 'Excavations in Dra Abu el-Naga', *Egyptian Archaeology* 7 (1995), 6–8

Polz, D., 'The location of the tomb of Amenhotep I: a reconsideration', in Wilkinson, R. H. (ed.), *Valley of the Sun Kings* (Tucson, 1995), 8–21

Reeves, C. N., *Valley of the Kings: the Decline of a Royal Necropolis* (London, 1990)

Rose, J., *Tomb KV39 in the Valley of the Kings: A Double Archaeological Enigma* (Bristol, 2000)

Schmitz, F.-J., *Amenophis I. Versuch einer Darstellung der Regierungzeit eines ägyptischen Herrschers der frühen 18. Dynastie* (Hildesheim, 1978)

Thomas, E., *The Royal Necropoleis of Thebes* (Princeton, 1966)

17 Where is the body of Akhenaten?

Aldred, C., *Akhenaten, King of Egypt* (London & New York, 1988)

Hornung, E., *Akhenaten and the Religion of Light* (Ithaca, 1999)

Montserrat, D., *Akhenaten. History, Fantasy and Ancient Egypt* (London & New York, 2000)

Redford, D., *Akhenaten, the Heretic King* (Princeton, 1984)

Reeves, N., *Akhenaten: Egypt's False Prophet* (London & New York, 2001)

18 The mausoleum of the sons of Ramesses II

Dodson, A. M. & Hilton, D. L., *The Royal Families of Ancient Egypt: A Genealogical Sourcebook of the Pharaohs* (London & New York, forthcoming)

Kitchen, K. A., *Pharaoh Triumphant: The Life and Times of Ramesses II, King of Egypt* (Warminster, 1982)

Weeks, K. R, *The Lost Tomb: The Greatest Discovery in the Valley of the Kings since Tutankhamun* (London & New York, 1998)

Weeks, K. R. (ed.), *KV 5: A Preliminary Report on the Excavation of the Tomb of the Sons of Rameses II in the Valley of the Kings* (Cairo, 2000)

19 Who robbed the Valley of the Kings?

Capart, J., Gardiner, A. H. & van de Walle, B., 'New light on the Ramesside tomb-robberies', *Journal of Egyptian Archaeology* 22 (1936), 169–93

Coutts, H. (ed.), *Gold of the Pharaohs* (Edinburgh, 1988)

Maspero, G., *Les momies royales de Déir el-Baharî* (Cairo, 1889)

Peet, T. E., *The Great Tomb-Robberies of the Twentieth Egyptian Dynasty* (Oxford, 1930)

Reeves, C. N., *Valley of the Kings. The Decline of a Royal Necropolis* (London & New York, 1990)

Reeves, C. N. & Wilkinson, R. H., *The Complete Valley of the Kings* (London & New York, 1996)

Romer, J., *Valley of the Kings* (London & New York, 1981)

20 The missing tombs of Tanis

Aston, D. A., 'Takeloth II – a king of the "Theban Twenty-third dynasty"?', *Journal of Egyptian Archaeology* 75 (1989), 139–53

Brunton, G., 'Some notes on the burial of Shashanq Heqa-kheper-Re', *Annales du Service des Antiquités d'Égypte* 39 (1939), 541–47

Derry, D. A., 'Note on the remains of Shashanq', *Annales du Service des Antiquités d'Égypte* 39 (1939), 549–51

Dodson. A. M., *After the Pyramids: the Valley of the Kings and Beyond* (London, 2000)

Dodson, A. M., 'A new King Shoshenq confirmed?', *Göttinger Miszellen* 137 (1993), 53–58

Montet, P., *La nécropole royale de Tanis*, 3 vols (Paris, 1947–60)

Rohl, D., *A Test of Time: The Bible – from Myth to History* (London & New York, 1995)

21 Are there more royal tombs in Egypt?

Arnold, D., 'Amenemhat I and the early Twelfth Dynasty at Thebes', *Metropolitan Museum Journal* 26 (1991), 5–48

Berlandini, J., 'La pyramide ruinée de Sakkara-nord et le roi Ikaouhor-Menkaouhor', *Revue d'Égyptologie* 31 (1979), 3–28

Dodson, A. M., *After the Pyramids* (London, 2000)

Malek, J., 'King Merykare and his pyramid', in Berger, C., Clerc, G. & Grimal, N. (eds), *Hommages à Jean Leclant* (Cairo), 203–14

Polz, D., 'The location of the tomb of Amenhotep I: a reconsideration', in Wilkinson, R. H. (ed.), *Valley of the Sun Kings* (Tucson, 1995), 8–21

Winlock, H. E., 'The tombs of the kings of the Seventeenth Dynasty at Thebes', *Journal of Egyptian Archaeology* 10 (1924), 217–77

Pharaohs & Queens

22 Did the pharaohs marry their sisters?

Hölbl, G., *A History of the Ptolemaic Empire* (London, 2001)

Robins, G., 'A critical examination of the theory that the right to the throne of ancient Egypt passed through the female line in the 18th Dynasty' *Göttinger Miszellen* 62 (1983), 67–77

Robins, G., *Women in Ancient Egypt* (London & Cambridge, MA, 1993)

Troy, L., *Patterns of Queenship in Ancient Egyptian Myth and History* (Uppsala, 1986)

23 The assassination of kings

Clayton, P., *Chronicle of the Pharaohs* (London & New York, 1994)

Grimal, N. (tr. I. Shaw), *A History of Ancient Egypt* (Oxford, 1992)

Parkinson, R., *The Tale of Sinuhe and Other Ancient Egyptian Poems 1940–1640 BC* (Oxford & New York, 1997)

Redford, S., *The Harem Conspiracy* (Dekalb, 2002)

Waddell, W. G., *Manetho* (Cambridge, MA & London, 1940)

24 The first woman to rule Egypt

Callender, G., 'Materials for the reign of Sebekneferu', in Eyre, C. J. (ed.), *Proceedings of the Seventh International Congress of Egyptologists* (Leuven, 1998), 227–36

Dodson, A. M. & Hilton, D. L., *The Royal Families of Ancient Egypt: A Genealogical Sourcebook of the Pharaohs* (London & New York, forthcoming)

Newberry, P. E., 'Queen Nitocris of the Sixth Dynasty', *Journal of Egyptian Archaeology* 29 (1943), 51–54

Robins, G., 'A critical examination of the theory that the right to the throne of ancient Egypt passed through the female line in the 18th Dynasty', *Göttinger Miszellen* 62 (1983), 67–77

Ryholt, K. S. B., *The Political Situation in Egypt During the Second Intermediate Period, c. 1800–1550 BC* (Copenhagen, 1997)

Ryholt, K. S. B., 'The late Old Kingdom in the Turin King List and the identity of Nitokris', *Zeitschrift für ägyptische Sprache und Altertumskunde* 127 (2000), 87–100

Verner, M., *Abusir III. The Pyramid Complex of Khentkaous* (Prague, 1995)

25 Senenmut: a partner for Hatshepsut?

Dorman, P., *The Monuments of Senenmut: Problems in Historical Methodolology* (London & New York 1988)

Dorman, P., *The Tombs of Senenmut: The Architecture and Decoration of Tombs 71 and 353* (New York, 1991)

Meyer, C., *Senenmut: eine prosopographische Untersuchung* (Hamburg, 1982)

26 What became of Hatshepsut?

Ratie, S., *La Reine Hatchepsout; sources et problèmes* (Leiden, 1979)

Ray, J., *Reflections of Osiris: Lives from Ancient Egypt* (London, 2001)

Redford, D., *History and Chronology of the Eighteenth Dynasty: Seven Studies* (Toronto, 1967)

Tyldesley, J., *Hatchepsut: The Female Pharaoh* (Harmondsworth, 1996)

27 The enigma of Akhenaten

Aldred, C., *Akhenaten, King of Egypt* (London & New York, 2nd ed., 1988)

Arnold, D., et al., *The Royal Women of Amarna* (New York, 1996)

Freed, R., et al., *Pharaohs of the Sun* (Boston & London, 1999)

Freud, S., *Moses and Monotheism* (London, 1939)

Hornung, E., *Akhenaten and the Religion of Light* (Ithaca, 1997)

Montserrat, D., *Akhenaten: History, Fantasy and Ancient Egypt* (London & New York, 2000)

Murnane, W. J., *Texts from the Amarna Period in Egypt* (Atlanta, 1995)

Reeves, N., *Akhenaten: Egypt's False Prophet* (London & New York, 2001)

28 Why did Nefertiti disappear?

Aldred, C., *Akhenaten, King of Egypt* (London & New York, 2nd ed., 1988)

Allen, J. P., 'Nefertiti and Smenkh-ka-re', *Göttinger Miszellen* 141 (1994), 7–17

Dodson, A., 'Kings' Valley Tomb 55 and the fates of the Amarna kings', *Amarna Letters* 3 (1994), 92–103

Gabolde, M., *D'Akhenaton à Toutânkhamon* (Lyon, 1998)

Reeves, N., 'New light on Kiya from texts in the British Museum', *Journal of Egyptian Archaeology* 74 (1988), 91–101

Reeves, N., *Akhenaten: Egypt's False Prophet* (London & New York, 2001)

Sampson, J., 'Nefertiti's regality', *Journal of Egyptian Archaeology* 63 (1977) 88–97

Tawfik, S., 'Aton Studies 3', *Mitteilungen des Deutsches Archäologisches Insituts Abteiling Kairo* 31 (1975), 159–68

29 The Tutankhamun conspiracy

Brier, B., *The Murder of Tutankhamun* (New York & London, 1998)

el-Mahdi, C., *Tutankhamen: the Life and Death of a Boy-king* (London, 1999)

Reeves, N., *The Complete Tutankhamun* (London & New York, 1990)

30 The 'Elder Lady'

Harris, J. E. & Wente, E. F., *An X-ray Atlas of the Royal Mummies* (Chicago, 1980)

James, S. E., 'Who is the mummy Elder Lady?' *KMT* 12:2 (2001)

Smith, G. E., *The Royal Mummies* (Cairo,1912; repr. London, 2000)

31 Smendes: the alternative king?

Kitchen, K. A., *The Third Intermediate Period in Egypt (1100–650 BC)* (Warminster, 3rd ed., 1986)

Lichtheim, M., *Ancient Egyptian Literature*, II: *The New Kingdom* (Berkeley, Los Angeles & London, 1976), 224–30

Taylor, J. H., 'Nodjmet, Payankh and Herihor: the end of the New Kingdom reconsidered', in Eyre, C. J. (ed.), *Proceedings of the Seventh International Congress of Egyptologists* (Leuven, 1998), 1143–55

32 The Nubian 'Dark Age'

James, P., *Centuries of Darkness* (London, 1991/New Brunswick, 1993)

Morkot, R. G., *The Black Pharaohs, Egypt's Nubian Rulers* (London, 2000)

33 Khababash, the guerrilla king

Spalinger, A., 'The reign of Chabbash: an interpretation.' *Zeitschrift für Ägyptische Sprache* 105 (1978) 142–54

34 The fatal attraction of Cleopatra

Ashton, S.-A., 'Identifying the Egyptian-style Ptolemaic queens', in Walker, S. & Higgs, P. (eds), *Cleopatra of Egypt: from History to Myth* (London, 2001) 148–71

Bianchi, R. (ed.), *Cleopatra's Egypt: The Age of the Ptolemies* (New York, 1988)

Hughes-Hallett, L., *Cleopatra: History, Dreams and Distortions* (London, 1990)

Plutarch, *Life of Antony*, ed. and tr. C. B. R. Pelling (Cambridge, MA, 1988)

Volkmann, H., *Cleopatra; A Study in Politics and Propaganda* (London, 1958)

Walker, S. & Higgs, P. (eds), *Cleopatra of Egypt: from History to Myth* (London, 2001)

Wyke, M. & Montserrat, D., 'Glamour Girls: Cleomania in Mass Culture' in Miles, M. M. (ed.), *Cleopatra: A Sphinx Revealed* (Baltimore, MD)

People & Places

35 Where was the kingdom of Yam?

O'Connor, D., 'The locations of Yam and Kush and their historical implications', *Journal of the American Research Center in Egypt*, 23 (1986), 26–50

O'Connor, D., 'The location of Irem', *Journal of Egyptian Archaeology* 73 (1987), 99–136

O'Connor, D., 'Early states along the Nubian Nile' in Davies, W. V. (ed.), *Egypt and Africa: Nubia from Prehistory to Islam* (London, 1991), 145–65

36 Sinuhe: literary hero or real-life deserter?

Baines, J. R., 'Interpreting Sinuhe', *Journal of Egyptian Archaeology* 68 (1982), 31–44

Kitchen, K. A., 'Sinuhe: scholarly method versus trendy fashion', *The Bulletin of the Australian Centre for Egyptology* 7 (1996), 55–63

Lichtheim, M., *Ancient Egyptian Literature*, I: *The Old and Middle Kingdoms* (Berkeley, Los Angeles & London, 1973)

Parkinson, R. B., *The Tale of Sinuhe and Other Ancient Egyptian Poems 1940–1640 BC* (Oxford & New York, 1997), 21–53

Parkinson, R. B., 'Sinuhe', in Redford, D. B. (ed.), *The Oxford Encyclopedia of Ancient Egypt* (Oxford, 2001), Vol. III, 292

Parkinson, R. B., *Voices from Ancient Egypt: An Anthology of Middle Kingdom Writings* (London & Norman, 1991)

37 Who were the Hyksos?

Bietak, M., *Avaris, the Capital of the Hyksos. Recent Excavations at Tell el-Dab'a* (London, 1996)

Davies, W. V. & Schofield, L. (eds), *Egypt, the Aegean and the Levant. Interconnections in the Second Millennium BC* (London, 1995)

Dever, W. G., 'Relations between Syria-Palestine and Egypt in the "Hyksos" period' in Tubb, J. N. (ed.), *Palestine in the Bronze and Iron Ages: Papers in Honour of Olga Tufnell* (London, 1985), 69–87

Dever, W. G. 1990 '"Hyksos," Egyptian destructions, and the end of the Palestinian Middle Bronze Age', *Levant* 22 (1990), 75–81

Oren, E. D. (ed.), *The Hyksos: New Historical and Archaeological Perspectives* (Philadelphia, 1997)

Redford, D. B., 'The Hyksos in history and tradition' *Orientalia* 39 (1997), 1–52

38 The Minoan paintings of Avaris

Bietak, M., 'Die Wandmalereien aus Tell el-Dab'a/'Ezbet Helmi, Erste Eindrücke', *Egypt and the Levant* IV (1994), 44–58

Bietak, M., *Avaris, the Capital of the Hyksos. Recent Excavations at Tell el-Dab'a* (London, 1996)

Bietak, M., 'Une citadelle royale à Avaris de la première moitié de la XVIIIe dynastie et liens avec le monde minoen' in *L'acrobate au taureau: Les découvertes de Tell el-Dab'a et l'archéologie de la Méditerranée orientale.* Actes du colloque organisé au musée du Louvre par le Service culturel le 3 décembre 1994 (Paris, 1999), 29–81

Bietak, M., 'Rich Beyond the Dreams of Avaris: Tell el-Dab'a and the Aegean

World – A Guide for the Perplexed: A Response to Eric H. Cline', *Annual of the British School at Athens* 95 (1998), 185–205
Bietak, M., Dorner, J. & Jánosi, J., 'Ausgrabungen in dem Palastbezirk von Avaris, Vorbericht Tell el-Dab'a/'Ezbet Helmi 1993–2000', *Egypt and the Levant* XI (2001) 27–129
Bietak, M. & Marinatos, N., 'The Minoan wall paintings from Avaris', *Egypt and the Levant* V (1995) 49–62
Bietak, M., Marinatos, N. & Palyvou, C., 'The Maze Tableau from Tell el-Dab'a' in Sherratt, S. (ed.), *Proceedings of the First International Symposium: The Wall Paintings of Thera*, 2 vols. (Athens, 2000), 77–88
Bietak, M., Marinatos, N. & Palyvou, C., *Taureador Scenes in Avaris and Knossos*, Untersuchungen der Zweigstelle Kairo des Österreichischen Archäologischen Instituts, Vienna (forthcoming)
Marinatos, N., 'The Tell el-Dab'a Paintings: A Study in Pictorial Tradition', *Egypt and the Levant* VIII (1998), 83–99
Niemeier, B. & Niemeier, W.-D., 'Minoan Frescoes in the Eastern Mediterranean', *Aegaeum* 18 (1996), 69–98
Niemeier, B. & Niemeier, W.-D., 'Aegean Frescoes in Syria-Palestine: Alalakh and Tel Kabri' in Sherratt, S. (ed.), *Proceedings of the First International Symposium: The Wall Paintings of Thera*, 2 vols (Athens, 2000), 763–802

39 Was Alashiya Cyprus?
Knapp, A. B., *Sources for the History of Cyprus II. Near Eastern and Aegean Texts from the Third to the First Millennium BC*, Greece and Cyprus Research Centre (1996)
Merrillees, R. S., 'Alashiya Revisited', *Cahiers de la Revue Biblique* 22 (Paris, 1987)
Moran, W. L., *The Amarna Letters* (Baltimore & London, 1992)
Steel, L., *Cyprus Before History* (London, in press)

40 Punt and God's Land
Kitchen, K., 'Punt and how to get there', *Orientalia* 40 (1971), 184–207
Kitchen, K., 'The land of Punt' in Shaw, T. et al. (eds), *The Archaeology of Africa: Food, Metals and Towns* (London, 1993)

41 The 'Sea Peoples': raiders or refugees?
Dothan, T., *The Philistines and their Material Culture* (Jerusalem, 1982)
Drews, R., *The End of the Bronze Age. Changes in Warfare and the Catastrophe ca. 1200 BC* (Princeton, 1993)
Gitin, S., Mazar, A. & Stern, E. (eds), *Mediterranean People in Transition: Thirteenth to Early Tenth Centuries BCE* (Jerusalem, 1998)
Oren, E. D. (ed.), *The Sea Peoples and their World: A Reassessment* (Philadelphia, 2000)
Pritchard, J., 'Medinet Habu inscriptions, reign of Ramesses III', in *Ancient Near Eastern Texts* (New Jersey, 1969), 262–63
Redford, D. B., *Egypt, Canaan and Israel in Ancient Times* (New Jersey, 1992)
Sandars, N. K., *The Sea Peoples: Warriors of the Ancient Mediterranean* (London & New York, rev. ed., 1985)
Ward, W. A. & Joukowsky M. S. (eds), *The Crisis Years: The Twelfth Century BC* (Dubuque, 1992)

42 The Report of Wenamun: fact or fable?
Goedicke, H., *The Report of Wenamun* (Baltimore, 1975)
Golenischeff, V., 'Papyrus hiératique de la collection W. Golénischeff, contenant du voyage de l'égyptien Ounu-Amon en Phénicie', *Recueil de travaux relatifs à la philologie et à l'archéologie égyptiennes et assyriennes* 21 (1899), 74–102
Lichtheim, M., *Ancient Egyptian Literature*, II: *The New Kingdom*, (Berkeley, Los Angeles & London, 1976)

Ancient Wisdom & Belief

43 The mysterious gods of Egypt
Hornung, E., *Conceptions of God in Ancient Egypt: The One and the Many* (London & Ithaca, 1983)
Morenz, S., *Egyptian Religion* (London & Ithaca, 1973)
Quirke, S., *Ancient Egyptian Religion* (London, 1992)
Shafer, B. (ed.), *Religion in Ancient Egypt* (London & Ithaca, 1991)
Wilkinson, R. W., *The Complete Gods and Goddesses of Ancient Egypt* (London & New York, 2003)

44 Was the king really a god?
Frankfort, H., *Kingship and the Gods. A Study of Ancient Near Eastern Religion as the Integration of Society and Nature* (Chicago, 1948, repr. 1978)
Hornung, E., *Geschichte als Fest. Zwei Vorträge zum Geschichtsbild der frühen Menschheit* (Darmstadt, 1966)
O'Connor, D. & Silverman, D. P. (eds), *Ancient Egyptian Kingship*. Probleme der Ägyptologie 9 (Leiden, 1995)
Posener, G., *De la Divinité du Pharaon*. Cahiers de la Société Asiatique (Paris, 1960)
Quirke, S. J., *Ancient Egyptian Religion* (London, 1992)

45 Mummification and the passion of Osiris
Griffiths, J. G., *The Origins of Osiris and his Cult* (Leiden, 1980)
Harris, J. E. & Wente, E. F., *An X-Ray Atlas of the Royal Mummies* (Chicago, 1980)
Ikram, S. & Dodson, A. M., *The Mummy in Ancient Egypt. Equipping the Dead for Eternity* (London & New York, 1998)
Quirke, S. J., *Ancient Egyptian Religion* (London, 1992)
Taylor, J. H., *Death and the Afterlife in Ancient Egypt* (London, 2001)
Troy, L., 'Creating a God: the Mummification Process', *Bulletin of the Australian Centre for Egyptology* 4 (1993), 55–81

46 Why write letters to the dead?
Gardiner, A. H. & Sethe, K., *Egyptian Letters to the Dead, Mainly from the Old and Middle Kingdoms* (London, 1928)
Parkinson, R. B., *Voices from Ancient Egypt: An Anthology of Middle Kingdom Writings* (London & Norman, 1991), 142–45
Wente, E. F., *Letters from Ancient Egypt*. Society of Biblical Literature Writings from the Ancient World Series, 1 (Atlanta, 1990), 210–20
Wente, E. F., 'Correspondence', in Redford, D. B. (ed.), *The Oxford Encyclopedia of Ancient Egypt* (Oxford, 2001), vol. I, 311–15

47 The power of magic
Andrews, C., *Amulets of Ancient Egypt* (London & Austin, 1994)
Borghouts, J. F., *Ancient Egyptian Magical Texts*. Religious Texts Translation Series NISABA, 9 (Leiden, 1978)
Étienne, M., *Heka. Magie et envoûtement dans l'Égypte ancienne* (Paris, 2000)
Nunn, J. *Ancient Egyptian Medicine* (London & Norman, 1996)
Pinch, G., *Magic in Ancient Egypt* (London & Austin, 1994)
Ritner, R. K., *The Mechanics of Ancient Egyptian Magical Practice*. Studies in Ancient Oriental Civilizations, 54 (Chicago, 1993)
Ritner, R. K., 'Magic', in Redford, D. B. (ed.), *The Oxford Encyclopedia of Ancient Egypt* (Oxford, 2001), vol. II, 321–36

48 Why use hieroglyphic writing?
Allen, J. P., *Middle Egyptian. An Introduction to the Language and Culture of Hieroglyphs* (Cambridge & New York, 2000)
Collier, M. A. & Manley, W. P., *How to Read Egyptian Hieroglyphs. A Step-By-Step Guide to Teach Yourself* (London, rev. ed., 2003)
Davies, W. V., *Egyptian Hieroglyphs* (London & Berkeley, 1987)
Parkinson, R. B., *Voices from Ancient Egypt. An Anthology of Middle Kingdom Writings* (London & Norman, 1991)

49 The origins of Egyptian literature
Assmann, J. & Blumenthal, E. (eds), 'Literatur und Politik im pharaonischen und ptolemäischen Ägypten', *Bibliothèque d'Égyptologie* 127 (1999)
Gnirs, A. (ed.), 'Reading The Eloquent Peasant', *Lingua Aegyptiaca* 8 (2000)
Loprieno, A. (ed.), *Ancient Egyptian Literature. History and Forms* (Leiden, 1996)
Morenz, L. D., 'Beiträge zur ägyptischen Schriftlichkeitskultur des Mittleren

Reiches und der Zweiten Zwischenzeit' *ÄAT* 29 (Wiesbaden, 1996)

Parkinson, R. B., *Voices from Ancient Egypt: An Anthology of Middle Kingdom Writings* (London & Norman, 1991)

Parkinson, R. B., *The Tale of Sinuhe and Other Ancient Egyptian Poems 1940–1640 BC* (Oxford & New York, 1997)

50 Hidden symbols of sex in Egyptian art

Derchain, P., 'Symbols and metaphors in literature and representations of private life', *Royal Anthropological Institute Newsletter* 15 (1976), 6–10

Manniche, L., *Sexual Life in Ancient Egypt* (London & New York, 1987)

O'Connor, D., 'Eros in Egypt', *Archaeology Odyssey* 45 (2001), 43–51

Historical Mysteries

51 What did the Egyptians know of their history?

Gardiner, A. H., *The Royal Canon of Turin* (Oxford, 1959)

O'Mara, P., *The Palermo Stone*. 2 vols (La Canada, CA, 1979–80)

Redford, D. B., *Pharaonic King-lists, Annals, and Day-books* (Mississauga, 1986)

Waddell, W. G., *Manetho* (Cambridge, MA & London, 1940)

52 The end of the great pyramid age

Bell, B., 'The dark ages in ancient history, 1: The first dark age in Egypt' *American Journal of Archaeology* 75 (1971), 1–26

Kanawati, N., *The Egyptian Administration in the Old Kingdom: Evidence on its Economic Decline* (Warminster, 1977)

Müller-Wollermann, R., *Krisenfaktoren im ägyptischen Staat des ausgehenden Alten Reichs* (Tübingen, 1986)

Seidlmayer, S., 'The First Intermediate Period' in Shaw, I. (ed.), *The Oxford History of Ancient Egypt* (Oxford, 2000), 118–47

Vercoutter, J., *Le fin de l'Ancien Empire: un nouvel examen*. Atti di VI Congresso di Egittologia II (Turin, 1993), 557–62

53 The First Intermediate Period – a dark age?

Herzog, R. & Koselleck, R., *Epochenschwellen und Epochenbewußtsein*. Poetik und Hermeneutik XII (Munich, 1987)

Lichtheim, M., *Ancient Egyptian Literature*, I: *The Old and Middle Kingdoms* (Berkeley, Los Angeles & London, 1973)

Morenz, L., 'Geschichte als Literatur – Reflexe der Ersten Zwischenzeit in den Mahnworten' in Assmann, J. & Blumenthal, E. (eds), *Literatur und Politik im pharaonischen und ptolemäischen Ägypten* (Cairo, 1999), 111–38

Morenz, L., 'Geschichte(n) der Zeit der Regionen (Erste Zwischenzeit) im Spiegel der Gebelein-Region, Eine fragmentarische dichte Beschreibung'. Thesis, University of Tübingen, 2001 (forthcoming in the Probleme der Ägyptologie, Leiden)

Seidlmayer, S., *Gräberfelder aus dem Übergang vom Alten zum Mittleren Reich*, SAGA 1 (Heidelberg, 1990)

Seidlmayer, S., 'The First Intermediate Period' in Shaw, I. (ed.), *The Oxford History of Ancient Egypt* (Oxford, 2000) 118–147

54 The end of the second pyramid age

Bell, B., 'Climate and the history of Egypt: the Middle Kingdom', *American Journal of Archaeology* 79 (1975), 223–69

Hayes, W. C., 'Notes on the government of Egypt in the late Middle Kingdom', *Journal of Near Eastern Studies* 12 (1953), 31–39

Kemp. B. J., 'Old Kingdom, Middle Kingdom and Second Intermediate Period,' in Trigger, B. G. (ed.), *Ancient Egypt: A Social History* (Cambridge, 1985), 71–182

Quirke, S., *The Administration of Egypt in the Late Middle Kingdom* (New Malden, 1990)

55 Did the Egyptians go to sea?

Landström, B., *Ships of the Pharaohs: 4000 years of Egyptian Shipbuilding* (London, 1970)

Vinson, S., *Egyptian Boats and Ships* (Princes Risborough, 1994)

56 Did Egypt rule Palestine?

Ahlström, G. W., *The History of Ancient Palestine from the Palaeolithic Period to Alexander's Conquest*, JSOT 146 (Sheffield 1993)

Görg, M., *Die Beziehungen zwischen dem alten Israel und Ägypten* (Darmstadt, 1997)

Hasel, M., *Domination and Resistance. Egyptian Military Activity in the Southern Levant, c. 1300-1185 BC* (Leiden, 1998)

Higginbotham, C. R., *Egyptianization and Elite-Emulation in Ramesside Palestine. Governance and Accommodation on the Imperial Periphery*. Culture and History of the Ancient Near East 2 (Leiden, 2000)

Morenz, L. D. & Bosshard-Nepustil, E., *Herrscherpräsentation und Kulturkontakte: Ägypten – Levante – Mesopotamien. Acht Fallstudien* (Leipzig, 2002)

Redford, D. B., *Egypt, Canaan and Israel in Ancient Times* (Princeton, 1992)

57 Who won the Battle of Qadesh?

Gardiner, A. H., *The Kadesh Inscriptions of Ramesses II* (Oxford, 1960)

Goedicke, H., *Perspectives on the Battle of Kadesh* (Baltimore, 1985)

Kitchen, K. A., *Pharaoh Triumphant* (Warminster, 1982)

Manley, W. P., *The Penguin Historical Atlas of Ancient Egypt* (London, 1996)

Murnane, W. J., *The Road to Kadesh. A Historical Interpretation of the Battle Reliefs of King Sety I at Karnak*. Studies in Ancient Oriental Civilization 42 (Chicago, 1985/1990)

Ockinga, B., 'On the interpretation of the Kadesh record', *Chronique d'Égypte* 62 (1987), 38–48

58 What became of Egypt's Golden Empire?

Drews, R., *The End of the Bronze Age. Changes in Warfare and the Catastrophe ca. 1200 BC* (Princeton, 1993)

Kitchen, K. A., *The Third Intermediate Period in Egypt (1100-650 BC)* (Warminster, 3rd ed., 1997)

Manley, W. P., *The Penguin Historical Atlas of Ancient Egypt* (London, 1996)

Morkot, R. G., *The Black Pharaohs. Egypt's Nubian Rulers* (London, 2000)

Redford, D. B., *Egypt, Canaan and Israel in Ancient Times* (Princeton, 1992)

59 The missing Apis bull burials

Dodson, A., 'Bull cults', in Ikram, S. (ed.), *Divine Creatures: Animal Mummies in Ancient Egypt* (Cairo, forthcoming)

Dodson, A., 'The canopic equipment from the Serapeum of Memphis', in Leahy, A. & Tait, W. J. (eds), *Studies on Ancient Egypt in Honour of H. S. Smith* (London, 1999), 59–75

Dodson, A., 'The Eighteenth-Century discovery of the Serapeum', *KMT*, 11:3 (2000), 48–53

Ibrahim, M. & Rohl, D., 'Apis and the Serapeum', *Journal of the Ancient Chronology Forum* 2 (1988), 6–26

Malinine M., Posener, G. & Vercoutter, J., *Catalogue des stèles du Sérapéum de Memphis*, I (Paris, 1968)

Mariette, A., *Le Sérapeum de Memphis decouvert et décrit par Aug. Mariette* (Paris, 1857)

Mariette, A., *Le Sérapeum de Memphis par Auguste Mariette-Pacha; publié d'après le manuscrit d'auteur par G. Maspero*, I (Paris, 1882)

60 Did Necho send a fleet around Africa?

Carpenter, R., *Beyond the Pillars of Hercules: The Classical World Seen through the Eyes of its Discoverers* (London, 1966)

Cary, M., *The Ancient Explorers* (Harmondsworth, 1963)

Harden, D. B., 'The Phoenicians on the West Coast of Africa', *Antiquity* 22 (1948), 141ff.

Lacroix, W. G. F., *Africa in Antiquity. A Linguistic and Toponymic Analysis of Ptolemy's Map of Africa* (Saarbrücken, 1998)

Lloyd, A. B., 'Necho and the Red Sea: some considerations', *Journal of Egyptian Archaeology* 63 (1977), 142–55, especially 148–55

Taylor, E. G. R., *The Haven-Finding Art: A History of Navigation from Odysseus to Captain Cook* (New York, 1957)

61 How did the Egyptians work granite?

Arnold, D., *Building in Egypt: Pharaonic Stone Masonry* (New York & Oxford, 1991)

Aston, B. G., Harrell, J. & Shaw, I., 'Stone' in Nicholson, P. T. & Shaw, I. (eds), *Ancient Egyptian Materials and Technology* (Cambridge & New York, 2000)

Clarke, S. & Engelbach, R., *Ancient Egyptian Masonry* (London, 1930)

Engelbach, R., *The Problem of the Obelisks: from a Study of the Unfinished Obelisk at Aswan* (New York, 1923)

Isler, M., 'The technique of monolithic carving', *Mitteilungen des Deutschen Archäologischen Institut, Abteilung Kairo*, 48 (1992), 45–55

Stocks, D., 'Making stone vessels in ancient Mesopotamia and Egypt', *Antiquity* 67 (1993), 596–603

Stocks, D., 'Stone sarcophagus manufacture in ancient Egypt', *Antiquity* 73 (1999), 918–22

62 Did the Egyptians invent glass?

Beck, H. C., 'Glass before 1500 BC', *Ancient Egypt* (June 1934), 7–21

Lilyquist, C. & Brill, R. H., *Studies in Early Egyptian Glass* (New York, 1993)

Moorey, P. R. S., *Ancient Mesopotamian Materials and Industries* (Oxford, 1994)

Nicholson, P. T., *Egyptian Faience and Glass* (Aylesbury, 1993)

Nicholson, P. T. & Henderson, J., 'Glass' in Nicholson, P. T. & Shaw, I. (eds), *Ancient Egyptian Materials and Technology* (Cambridge & New York, 2000), 195–224

Oppenheim, L., 'Towards a history of glass in the ancient Near East' *Journal of the American Oriental Society* 93 (1973), 259–66

Oppenheim, A. L., Brill, R. H., Barag, D. & von Saldern, A. (eds), *Glass and Glassmaking in Ancient Mesopotamia* (Corning, 1970)

Rehren, T. & Pusch, E., 'New Kingdom glass melting crucibles from Qantir-Piramesses, Nile Delta', *Journal of Egyptian Archaeology* 83 (1997), 127–41

Shortland, A., Nicholson, P. T. & Jackson, C., 'Glass and faience and Amarna: different methods of both supply for production, and subsequent distribution' in Shortland, A. J. (ed.), *The Social Context of Technological Change* (Oxford, 2001), 147–60

63 Why was there no Egyptian Iron Age?

Haarer, P., 'Problematising the transition from bronze to iron' in Shortland, A. J. (ed.), *The Social Context of Technological Change* (Oxford, 2001), 255–73

Lucas, A. *Ancient Egyptian Materials and Industries*, 4th ed., rev. J. R. Harris (London, 1962), 235–43

Moorey, P. R. S., *Ancient Mesopotamian Materials and Industries* (Oxford, 1994) 278–92

Ogden, J. 'Metal', in Nicholson, P. T. & Shaw, I. (eds), *Ancient Egyptian Materials and Technology* (Cambridge & New York, 2000), 148–76

Snodgrass, A., 'Iron and early metallurgy in the Mediterranean' in Wertime, T. & Muhly, D., *The Coming of the Age of Iron* (New Haven, 1980), 335–74

64 What did Herodotus see in Egypt?

Herodotus, *The Histories* (Oxford, 1998)

Lateiner, D., *The Historical Method of Herodotus* (Toronto, 1989)

Lloyd, A. B., 'Herodotus on Egyptian buildings. A test case' in Powell, A. (ed.), *The Greek World* (London & New York, 1995)

Lloyd, A. B., *Herodotus Book II. Commentary*. Études preliminaires aux religions orientales dans l'empire romain, 43. 3 vols (Leiden, 1975–93)

Munson, R. V., *Telling Wonders. Ethnographic and Political Discourse in the Work of Herodotus* (Ann Arbor, 2001)

Thomas, R., *Herodotus in Context. Ethnography, Science and the Art of Persuasion* (Cambridge, 2000)

Egypt & the Bible

65 Joseph: an Egyptian vizier?

Currid, J. D., *Ancient Egypt and the Old Testament* (Grand Rapids, 1997)

Hoffmeier, J. K., *Israel in Egypt: The Evidence for the Authenticity of the Exodus Tradition* (New York & Oxford, 1997)

Kitchen, K. A., 'Joseph', in Douglas, J. D. et al. (eds), *New Bible Dictionary* (Leicester & Wheaton, 2nd ed., 1982), 617–20

66 Was Moses at the court of Akhenaten?

Assmann, J., *Moses the Egyptian. The Memory of Egypt in Western Monotheism* (Cambridge, MA, 1997)

Freud, S., *Moses and Monotheism* (London, 1939)

Kratz, R. G., *Die Komposition der erzählenden bücher des Alten Testaments*. UTB 2157 (Göttingen, 2000)

Krauss, R., *Das Moses-Rätsel* (Stuttgart, 2001)

Otto, E. (ed.), *Mose. Ägypten und das Alte Testament*. SBS 189 (Stuttgart, 2000)

Seters, J. van, *The Life of Moses. The Yahwist as Historian in Exodus-Numbers* (Louisville, 1994)

67 The Israelite Exodus: myth or reality?

Bimson, J. J., *Redating the Exodus and Conquest* (Sheffield, 2nd ed., 1981)

Currid, J. D., *Ancient Egypt and the Old Testament* (Grand Rapids, 1997)

Hoffmeier, J. K., *Israel in Egypt: The Evidence for the Authenticity of the Exodus Tradition* (New York & Oxford, 1997)

Kitchen, K. A., 'Egyptians and Hebrews, from Ra'amses to Jericho', in Ahituv, S. & Oren, E. D. (eds), *The Origin of Early Israel – Current Debate* (Beersheba & London, 1998), 65–131

68 Was Labayu King Saul?

Moran, W. L., *The Amarna Letters* (Baltimore & London, 1992)

Redford, D. B., *Egypt, Canaan and Israel in Ancient Times* (Princeton, 1992)

Rohl, D. M., *A Test of Time. The Bible from Myth to History* (London, 1995)

69 Who was Solomon's father-in-law?

Redford, D. B., *Egypt, Canaan and Israel in Ancient Times* (Princeton, 1992)

Rohl, D. M., *A Test of Time. The Bible from Myth to History* (London, 1995)

Thompson, T. L., *Early History of the Israelite People: From the Written and Archaeological Sources* (Leiden, 1992)

Whitelam, K. W., *The Invention of Ancient Israel* (London & New York, 1996)

70 Who was 'King Shishak of Egypt'?

Currid, J. D., *Ancient Egypt and the Old Testament* (Grand Rapids, 1997)

James, P., *Centuries of Darkness: A Challenge to the Conventional Chronology of Old World Archaeology* (London, 1991/New Brunswick, 1993)

Kitchen, K. A., *The Third Intermediate Period in Egypt (1100–650 BC)* (Warminster, 3rd ed., 1997)

Sources of Quotations

1 W. B. Emery, *Archaic Egypt* (Harmondsworth, 1961), p. 40; 2 W. B. Emery, *Archaic Egypt* (Harmondsworth, 1961), p. 192; 3 B. Midant-Reynes, *The Prehistory of Egypt* (Oxford, 2000), p. 247; 4 Herodotus, *Histories*, II. 99; 5 Michael Hoffman, *Egypt before the Pharaohs* (London, 1984), p. 276; 7 Piazzi Smyth, *The Great Pyramid. Its Secrets and Mysteries Revealed* (London, 1864); 8 R. O. Faulkner, *The Ancient Egyptian Pyramid Texts* (Oxford, 1969); 9 Herodotus, *Histories*, II. 124; 11 J. L. Borges, *El Aleph* (1949), trans. J. R. Pérez-Accino; 13 R. O. Faulkner, *The Ancient Egyptian Pyramid Texts* (Oxford, 1969); 14 W. M. F. Petrie, *Seventy Years in Archaeology* (London, 1932); 18 E. W. Lane, 1827, in Thompson, J. (ed.), *Description of Egypt* (Cairo, 2000), p. 375; 20 D. A. Derry, 'Note on the remains of Shashanq', *Annales du Service des Antiquités d'Égypte* 39 (1939); 21 T. M. Davis, *The Tombs of Harmhabi and Touatânkhamanou* (London, 1912); 27 Margaret Murray, *The Splendour that was Egypt* (London, 1949); 28 C. Aldred, *Akhenaten, Pharaoh of Egypt* (London, 1968); 30 G. Elliot Smith, *The Royal Mummies* (London, 1912); 32 T. Kendall *Kush: Lost Kingdom of the Nile* (Massachussetts, 1982), p.9; 38 Saki, *Chronicles of Clovis* (London, 1911); 46 M. Heidegger, *On theWay to Language* (New York, 1959); 47 R. Burton, *Anatomy of Melancholy*, 1621; 50 E. Friedl, 'Sex the Invisible', in *American Anthropologist* 96 (1994), p. 833; 54 A. H. Gardiner, *Egypt of the Pharohs* (Oxford, 1961), p.155; 60 Herodotus, *Histories*, IV. 42; 61 Strabo, Geography, XVIi:1,3; 62 W. M. F. Petrie, *Tell el-Amarna* (London, 1894), p.25; 63 J. Ogden in P.T. Nicholson and I. Shaw (eds), *Ancient Egyptian Materials and Technology* (Cambridge, 2000), p.148; 64 Herodotus, *Histories*, II. 123

Sources of illustrations

a: above; b: below; c: centre; l: left; r: right.

The following abbreviations are used to identify sources : BPK – © Bildarchiv Preussischer Kulturbesitz, Berlin, 2002; BM – © The Trustees of the British Museum; PC – Peter Clayton; DAI – Deutsche Archäologische Institut, Cairo; AD – Aidan Dodson; JF – Joann Fletcher; HG – Photo Heidi Grassley, © Thames & Hudson Ltd, London; JL – Jürgen Liepe; NMS – © Trustees of the National Museums of Scotland; ZR – Zev Radovan, Jerusalem; JR – John G. Ross; WS – William Schenck; KS – Kate Spence; DT – Drazen Tomic

1 The Art Archive/Egyptian Museum, Cairo/Dagli Orti; 2–3 Getty Images; 4 JR; 5l HG; 5r The Art Archive/Egyptian Museum, Cairo/Dagli Orti; 6l AKG London/Erich Lessing; 6r The Art Archive/Dagli Orti; 7l © Lesley and Roy Adkins; 7r JL; 10–11 JR; 12 The Art Archive/Musée du Louvre, Paris/Dagli Orti; 13a Werner Forman Archive/Dr Eugen Strouhal; 13b © Manfred Bietak, The Austrian Archaeological Institute in Cairo; 14 BPK. Photo Margarete Büsing; 15 JR; 16a JL; 16b AKG London/Erich Lessing; 17 DT; 18–19 WS; 20 © Petrie Museum of Egyptian Archaeology, University College, London; 21 WS; 22a BM and Professor F. Wendorf 22b BM; 23a Toby Wilkinson; 23b BM and Professor F. Wendorf; 24 JL; 25 DAI; 26a W. M. F. Petrie, *The Royal Tombs of the Earliest Dynasties*, Pt 2, 1901; 26b W. M. F. Petrie, *The Royal Tombs of the First Dynasty*, Pt 1, 1900; 27a AD; 27b BM; 29 JL; 30 Werner Forman Archive/Ashmolean Museum, Oxford; 31a ML Design; 31b W. M. F. Petrie, *The Royal Tombs of the First Dynasty*, Pt 1, 1900; 31r KS; 32a Toby Wilkinson; 32b DAI; 33a W. M. F. Petrie, *The Royal Tombs of the Earliest Dynasties*, Pt 2, 1901; 33b JR; 34a KS; 34b JL; 35l W. M. F. Petrie, *The Royal Tombs of the Earliest Dynasties*, 1901; 35r KS; 36a DAI; 36b BM; 37a, c W. M. F. Petrie, *The Royal Tombs of the First Dynasty*, Pt 1, 1900; 37b DAI; 38 ML Design, after David O'Connor; 39a ML Design, after David O'Connor; 39b David O'Connor; 40l ML Design, after David O'Connor; 40a David O'Connor; 40–41 The Art Archive/ Solar Barque Museum, Giza/Dagli Orti; 41 David O'Connor; 42–43 Andrea Jemolo; 44 Photo by Francis Dzikowski, © Theban Mapping Project; 45 JR; 46, 47a ML Design, after David O'Connor; 47b David O'Connor; 48a AKG London/Gilles Mermet; 48b DT; 49 HG; 50a JR; 50–51 Philip Winton; 51a KS; 52a KS; 52b, 52–53 DT after Philip Winton; 53 KS; 54 AKG London; 55a J.-R. Pérez-Accino; 55b NOVA/WGBH; 56a Brita LaVe; 56b Mark Lehner; 57 Egyptian Museum, Cairo; 58 HG; 58–59 AKG London/François Guenet; 59b HG; 60 AD; 61 © Archivio Whitestar/Giulio Veggi; 62a JR; 62b Frank Teichmann; 63a HG; 63b Richard Burgess; 64 Piazzi Smyth, *Our Inheritance in the Great Pyramid*, 1874; 65 JL; 66 Egyptian Museum, Cairo; 67 JR; 68a Mark Lehner; 68b HG; 69 ML Design; 70 JR; 71 KS; 72al DT after I. E. S. Edwards; 72ar DT after KS; 72b DT after R. Bauval, *The Orion Mystery* (Oxford & New York, 1994), fig. 15; 73a JR; 73c DT; 73r Celestial Image Co./Science Photo Library; 74l, r © Petrie Museum of Egyptian Archaeology, University College, London; 75l, r, 76a, b NMS; 77 David O'Connor; 78a ML Design; 78b ML Design from a drawing by Stephen Harvey; 79l From W. M. F. Petrie *Abydos*, Part I, 1885; 79c WS; 79b JL; 80 AD; 81a ML Design, after Aidan Dodson; 81b AD; 82a AD; 82b Photo by Francis Dzikowski, © Theban Mapping Project; 83 AD; 84 N. de Garis Davies, *The Tomb of Queen Tiyi*, 1910; 85a JR; 85b JF; 86a&b N. de Garis Davies, *The Tomb of Queen Tiyi*, 1910; 87ar © BPK. Photo Margarete Büsing; 87bl Metropolitan Museum of Art, Gift of Theodore M. Davis, 1907; 87br G. B. Johnson; 88 HG; 89 © Theban Mapping Project; 90a watercolour by Susan Weeks, © Theban Mapping Project; 90b, 91 Photo by Francis Dzikowski, © Theban Mapping Project; 92 From G. Elliot Smith, *The Royal Mummies*, 1901; 93l BM; 93r JL; 94a Photo by Francis Dzikowski, © Theban Mapping Project; 94c, b JR; 95 AD; 96 ML Design; 97a JR; 97b PC; 98, 99a, b, 100a, b AD; 101a WS; 101b Sally Nicholls; 102–03 © Araldo De Luca/Archivio White Star; 104 BM; 105 PC; 106l, &r JR; 107 HG; 108 PC; 109 JF; 110a The Art Archive/Dagli Orti; 110b Michael Duigan; 111, 112a, b, 113 AD; 114 JR; 115 Egyptian Museum, Cairo; 116a JF; 116b © Howard Carter (courtesy Theban Mapping Project); 117 Nigel Strudwick; 118 KS; 119 JL; 120a, b KS; 121l ML Design, after Philip Winton; 121br HG; 122 NMS; 123a Ny Carlsberg Glyptotek, Copenhagen; 123b BPK; 124 © CNRS/CFEETK. Fonds Chevrier; 125 Egyptian Museum, Cairo; 126a W. M. F. Petrie, *Tell El Amarna*, 1894; 126b Dominic Montserrat; 127 JL; 128 Museum of Fine Arts, Boston; 129 JR; 130a W. M. F. Petrie, *Tell El Amarna*, 1894; 130b JL; 131l Egyptian Museum, Cairo; 131r © Justin Kerr; 132 *Antiquity, 46*, 1972; 133 Kodansha Ltd, Tokyo; 134a JR; 134b Paul T. Nicholson; 135 JL; 136l, r JL; 137 G. Elliot Smith, *The Royal Mummies*, 1901; 138a JL; 138b G. Elliot Smith, *The Royal Mummies*, 1901; 139 JL; 140 Private Collection, photo AD; 141a D. L. Hilton; 141b WS; 142a JL; 142b Museum of Fine Arts, Boston; 143 © Jacke Phillips; 144a, b Museum of Fine Arts, Boston; 145, 146 PC; 147a, b AD; 148l Dominic Montserrat; 148b BPK; 149 The State Hermitage Museum, St Petersburg; 150a HG; 150b BPK; 151 The Art Archive/Musée des Augustins, Toulouse/Dagli Orti; 152–53 JL; 154 Werner Forman Archive/Eugen Strouhal; 155a ML Design; 155b JF; 156 JL; 157 Werner Forman Archive; 158 Musée du Louvre, Paris; 159 JL; 160l, r Ashmolean Museum, Oxford; 161 P. Newberry, *Beni Hasan*, 1893; 162 JR; 163a PC; 163b BM; 164a J-F. Champollion, *Monuments de l'Egypte et de la Nubie*, 1835–45; 164b PC; 165a G. Elliot Smith, *The Royal Mummies*, 1901; 165bl, r PC; 166 © Manfred Bietak, Austrian Archaeological Institute, Cairo. J. Dorner & T. Herbich; 167a © Manfred Bietak, Austrian Archaeological Institute, Cairo. Reconstruction M. Bietak, N. Marinatos, C. Palyvou; 168a © Manfred Bietak, Austrian Archaeological Institute, Cairo; 168b © Manfred Bietak, Austrian Archaeological Institute, Cairo. Reconstruction N.Marinatos & C. Palyvou; 168–69 HG; 169b © Manfred Bietak, Austrian Archaeological Institute, Cairo; 170 BM; 171a Department of Antiquities, Cyprus; 171b Egyptian Museum, Cairo; 172a Department of Antiquities, Cyprus; 172bl BM; 172br Cyprus Museum, Nicosia; 173 JL; 174a DT; 174b JL; 175a HG; 175b AKG London/Erich Lessing; 176–77 © Lesley and Roy Adkins; 177 HG; 178a Courtesy of the Oriental Institute, University of Chicago; 178–79 J.-F. Champollion, *Monuments de L'Egypte et de la Nubie*, 1835–45; 179a Courtesy of the Oriental Institute, University of Chicago; 180a BM; 180b Cyprus Museum, Nicosia; 181a Pushkin Museum, Moscow; 181b J.-R. Pérez-Accino; 182 ML Design; 183a The Art Archive/Archaeological Museum, Beirut/Dagli Orti; 183 BPK; 184–85 The Art Archive/Egyptian Museum, Cairo/Dagli Orti; 186 JL; 187, 188a, b, 189, 190al, ar, b, 191 Steven Snape; 192 Photo © RMN – Ch. Larrieu; 193 JL; 194l JL; 194ar Milan Zemina; 194br, 195 JL; 196bl The Kobal Collection; 196br AD; 197l G. Elliot Smith, *The Royal Mummies*, 1901; 197r After E. Naville, *Das Ägyptischer Totenbuch der XVIII. bis XX. Dynastie*, 1886; 198 The Art Archive/Egyptian Museum, Cairo/Dagli Orti; 199 Roemer-und Pelizaeus Museum, Hildesheim; 200l AD; 200r NMS; 201bl JF; 201br PC; 202bl BPK; 202br A. H. Gardiner and K. Sethe, *Egyptian Letters to the Dead*, 1928; 203 National Museums and Galleries on Merseyside; 204 Photo © RMN – Franck Raux; 205 Photo © RMN – Chuzeville; 206a NMS; 206b JL; 207 BM; 208 NMS; 209 BM; 210a Egyptian Museum, Cairo; 210b NMS; 211 J. E. Quibell, *Excavations at Saqqara 1907–8*, 1909; 212 BPK; 213 P. Newberry, *Beni Hasan*, 1893; 214bl Museo Egizio, Turin; 214br Brooklyn Museum; 215, 216a HG; 216b, 217 Egyptian Museum, Cairo; 218–19 WS; 220 JR; 221 Bill Manley; 222a JR; 222b BM; 223a AD; 223b JR; 224 Brooklyn Museum; 225a Rijksmuseum van Oudheden, Leiden; 225b HG; 226 BPK. Photo Margarete Büsing; 227a University of Liverpool Mo'alla Expedition; 227b JR; 228, 229 JL; 230a, b Ludwig Morenz; 231 University of Liverpool Mo'alla Expedition; 232 WS; 233l BM; 233r JL; 234 BM; 235l Sally Nicholls; 235r Musée du Louvre, Paris; 236 AD; 237 AKG London/Erich Lessing; 238 HG; 239, 240 ZR; 241a HG; 241b, 242 ZR; 243 The Art Archive/Dagli Orti; 244a Hirmer Fotoarchiv; 244b DT; 244–45 WS; 246a PC; 246b BPK; 247 HG; 248a BPK; 248b AD; 249 PC; 250 WS; 251 Photo © RMN – B.Hatala; 252 WS; 253a AD; 253b JL; 254 Werner Forman Archive; 255 The University Museum, University of Pennsylvania; 256 Sally Nicholls; 257 © Lesley and Roy Adkins; 258a AD; 258c ML Design, after D. Arnold, *Building in Egypt,* 1990; 258b N. de Garis Davies, *The Tomb of Rekh-mi-Re*, 1943; 259l Ashmolean Museum, Oxford; 259r BM; 260 Dr Caroline M. Jackson, © Egyptian Exploration Society; 261a JR; 261b BM; 262 BPK; 263a PC; 263b After watercolours by Winifred M. Brunton from A. H. Gardiner, *JEA 27*, 1941; 264 –65 *Description de L'Égypte*, 1822; 265 The Art Archive/Archaeological Museum, Naples/Dagli Orti; 266 J.-R. Pérez-Accino; 267 HG; 268–69 Mark Millington; 270 ZR; 271 JL; 272a After S. Schott, *Wall Scenes from the Mortuary Chapel of the Mayor Paser at Medinet Habu*, 1957; 272b © Hypogées. Photo Alain Zivie/MAFB; 273a The Art Archive/Archbishop's Palace, Ravenna/Dagli Orti; 273b, l–r JL; 274 AKG London/Erich Lessing; 275 Musée du Louvre, Paris; 276a The Art Archive/Musée du Louvre, Paris/Dagli Orti; 276b ZR; 277 HG; 278 JR; 279a JL; 279b WS; 280 AKG London/Erich Lessing; 281 John Rylands University Library; 282 PC; 283, 284l ZR; 284b PC; 284–85 ZR; 285b, 286 The Art Archive/Bodleian Library, Oxford; 287a, b, 288a, b ZR; 289 AKG London/Erich Lessing; 290 Oriental Institute, University of Chicago; 292a AKG London/Erich Lessing; 292b DT

Index

Page numbers in *italic* refer to illustrations